Law School for Everyone

PUBLISHED BY:

THE GREAT COURSES

Corporate Headquarters
4840 Westfields Boulevard, Suite 500
Chantilly, Virginia 20151-2299
Phone: 1-800-832-2412
Fax: 703-378-3819
www.thegreatcourses.com

Copyright © The Teaching Company, 2017

Table of Contents

Litigation and Legal Practice

Criminal Law and Procedure

Supplementary Material

DISCLAIMER:

The legal information provided in these lectures is for informational purposes only and not for the purpose of providing legal advice. These lectures may not reflect the most current legal developments in any particular applicable jurisdictions and cannot substitute for the advice of a licensed professional with specialized knowledge who can apply it to the particular circumstances of your situation. Use of and access to these lectures do not create an attorney-client relationship with The Teaching Company or its lecturers, and neither The Teaching Company nor the lecturer is responsible for your use of this educational material or its consequences. You should contact an attorney to obtain advice with respect to any particular legal issue or problem. The opinions and positions provided in these lectures reflect the opinions and positions of the relevant lecturer and do not necessarily reflect the opinions or positions of The Teaching Company or its affiliates. Pursuant to IRS Circular 230, any tax advice provided in these lectures may not be used to avoid tax penalties or to promote, market, or recommend any matter therein.

The Teaching Company expressly DISCLAIMS LIABILITY for any DIRECT, INDIRECT, INCIDENTAL, SPECIAL, OR CONSEQUENTIAL DAMAGES OR LOST PROFITS that result directly or indirectly from the use of these lectures. In states that do not allow some or all of the above limitations of liability, liability shall be limited to the greatest extent allowed by law.

Litigation and Legal Practice

Molly Bishop Shadel, J.D.

Molly Bishop Shadel, J.D.

Professor of Law
University of Virginia
School of Law

Molly Bishop Shadel is a Professor of Law at the University of Virginia School of Law, where she teaches negotiations and advocacy classes and is a senior fellow at the Center for National Security Law. She graduated magna cum laude from Harvard University with an A.B. in English and American Literature and Language. Professor Shadel earned her J.D. from Columbia University, where she served as a note editor for the *Columbia Law Review* and was a Harlan Fiske Stone scholar. After graduation, she clerked for Judge Eugene H. Nickerson of the U.S. District Court for the Eastern District of New York. Professor Shadel then spent four years as a litigation associate with the firm Covington & Burling. In 2002, she joined the U.S. Department of Justice's Office of Intelligence Policy and Review, where she represented the United States on terrorism-related matters before the Foreign Intelligence Surveillance Court. Professor Shadel taught oral advocacy classes at the University of Virginia for a year as a lecturer before joining the faculty in 2005. She also served as the law school's director of public service from 2005 to 2007.

Professor Shadel is the author of *Finding Your Voice in Law School: Mastering Classroom Cold Calls, Job Interviews, and Other Verbal Challenges* and coauthor (with Robert N. Sayler) of *Tongue-Tied America: Reviving the Art of Verbal Persuasion*. She is conducting an empirical study of law school teaching practices and how those methods affect student experiences and outcomes. Professor Shadel is also a planning faculty member of the Leadership in Academic Matters program, a biannual, semester-long leadership course for University of Virginia professors and administrators. ∎

Litigation and Legal Practice

I n this series of 12 lectures, you will explore the important roles that litigation and the adversarial system play in American law. The course begins with an examination of the American legal system generally, including the significance of law and lawyers in our history and society. You will then consider what it means to think like a lawyer, learning about matters of precedent, textual analysis, inductive and deductive logic, logical fallacies, and the use of analogy. You will also examine the practical and ethical issues of the attorney-client relationship, learning why a lawyer might want to represent a seemingly guilty person, for example, and what a lawyer should do if a client asks her to break the law. As the course continues, you will learn about pretrial preparation, jury selection, opening statements, direct examination, cross-examination, and closing arguments. You will consider how media coverage and social media can impact what happens in the courtroom. You will learn about evidence—what types of evidence might be introduced at trial, how to handle common objections, and how to address the problems caused by false confessions, mistaken eyewitness identification, and flawed expert testimony. As you approach the end of the course, you will begin to examine the appeals process, including the various procedures, standards of review, and approaches to effective advocacy that distinguish appellate courts from trial courts. Finally, the course concludes with an exploration of the United States Supreme Court—its history, its function, and the unique challenges and opportunities that it presents for lawyers, clients, and the American people as a whole. ▪

LITIGATION AND THE AMERICAN LEGAL SYSTEM

L itigation holds a special role in the American legal system, and learning about it offers a valuable orientation to the study of law generally. In this lecture, you will explore why we adopted the particular legal system we have in this country, how that system works, and why law is taught in America the way it is.

LAW IN AMERICAN SOCIETY

✴ America is a nation of laws. From the very beginning, America has grappled with the question of how much power the government should have over the people, and the rules under which people interact with one another. When America broke away from England in 1776, it famously rejected the notion that a king gets to make those rules. Instead, the power of the government and of lawmaking belongs to the people.

✴ When our country was founded, the Founding Fathers were, in essence, breaking the law. By rebelling against the British monarchy, they were, in the eyes of England, committing treason. To make the case that breaking away from England was the right thing to do, the Founding Fathers wrote the Declaration of Independence in 1776, proclaiming that "governments are instituted among men, deriving their just powers from the consent of the governed."

★ The notion that the people are in charge was an extraordinary idea at the time our country was founded. Given the number of authoritarian governments that continue to exist in other parts of the world, it's still remarkable today.

★ After gaining independence, the Founding Fathers began replacing the legal system they were rejecting with a new one. In 1787, they drafted the U.S. Constitution, which limited the power of the federal government and established a system in which the people could undo everything if they wanted to.

★ America has continued to be a nation where people question the laws, challenge them, change them, and rely on them. Our nation is composed of people who quite often do not agree with one another. Every election cycle, we take some people out of power and put new people in charge. Regular citizens are able to be involved with the law, to influence the shape of the law, simply by voting or raising a claim in court.

★ Because of the importance of law to the functioning for our country, lawyers have long played a prominent role in American society. More than half of the 45 U.S. Presidents have been lawyers. So are many members of Congress, most judges, and many prominent leaders in business and banking.

★ You will certainly see lawyers at work if you go to a courtroom. But lawyers are also often the people who lead large corporations or help them do business or merge with one another. Lawyers also frequently run our various administrative agencies, which govern things like taxes, the environment, the Internet, elections, and the financial markets.

STRUCTURAL DISTINCTIONS

✶ The American legal system is a common law system, and is derived from English legal tradition. Some countries, like France, Italy, and others in continental Europe, have a civil law system. In a civil law system, written-down rules—often called codes—are the primary basis of the law. Judges in these systems interpret the code and make sure it is followed, but their decisions have no lasting authority.

✶ In our common law system, by contrast, written-down laws—we call them statutes—and judicial decisions are both important sources of law. What a judge says about the law can be every bit as important as a statute, and sometimes more so. Yet our judges are also bound by statutes and by the decisions of other judges who have come before them.

✶ A common law system checks the power of the legislature, which creates a statute, because a judge gets to interpret it. It also limits a judge's power, however, because he has to follow the rulings of previous judges. He can't just make up an outcome according to his own personal desires.

✶ America's legal system is also an adversarial system. In an adversarial system, parties make their best arguments before a judge or jury, and from the conflict between them, the judge or jury determines the truth of what happened. This is different from the inquisitorial system used in some civil law countries. In an inquisitorial system, the judge acts as an investigator in a case, questioning witnesses and suspects.

LEVELS OF REVIEW

✶ Trial courts are the courts where cases start. At trial, both sides present evidence to demonstrate what happened in the dispute that brought them to court. There is a judge who decides what evidence can be considered and whether the procedural rules are being followed. A trial can be decided either by a judge or a jury, depending on the type of case.

* Many jurisdictions have trial-level courts that hear a wide variety of cases. These courts are sometimes called general district courts. Some jurisdictions also have specialized trial courts. For example, a court system might have a specialized traffic court, a divorce court, or a court for juveniles.

* Legal cases are divided into two broad categories: civil and criminal. Civil cases involve disputes between private parties. The person who brings a civil lawsuit is called the plaintiff, and the person who is sued is called the defendant.

* In a criminal case, a person is accused of breaking a criminal law. In criminal cases, the person against whom the suit is brought is still called the defendant, but the person bringing the suit is a prosecutor representing either the state or federal government.

* If a party believes that something has been wrongly decided at trial, he or she may be able to appeal that issue to an appellate court. The issue has to be preserved for appeal, however, which usually means that the attorney has to flag the perceived problem during the trial by objecting and indicating the nature of the error. In addition, the appeal typically has to be filed within a certain time period.

* In an appellate court, there are no witnesses and no jury, and the parties do not present evidence. Instead, lawyers argue legal issues to group of judges, often referred to as a panel. Appellate courts do not rehear all the facts of a case; instead, they focus on the specific question of law being appealed to determine whether that question was decided correctly.

* If the trial court has made an error, the appellate court may overrule the trial court's decision and issue a written opinion about it. If a party disagrees with an appellate court decision, it may appeal to the ultimate judicial tribunal of a court system, which is often referred to as the jurisdiction's supreme court. That court may overrule or affirm the appellate court's decision and issue a written opinion of its own.

FEDERALISM AND PREEMPTION

* America has both federal and state laws, and the two are not always consistent with one another. What might be legal in one state might not be legal in another, and state laws and federal laws also clash on occasion. Because we have a dual system of laws, we also have a dual system of courts—federal and state.

* This system again has its roots in the American Revolution. The framers of our Constitution wanted to limit the power of our federal government. So our Constitution gives certain powers to the federal government, but leaves other powers to the states, and it does not require the states to have laws identical to one another.

✷ Federal courts are courts of limited jurisdiction, which means they can only hear certain kinds of cases. They can hear cases that raise a federal question, which means the plaintiff or prosecutor has alleged a violation of the U.S. Constitution, a federal law, or a treaty. They can also hear cases involving disputes between parties from different states.

✷ In addition to state and federal statutes, and the case law written by judges, laws also comes from constitutions (both federal and state), from treaties, and from regulations. Regulations are rules made by an agency at either the state or federal level pursuant to a statute.

✷ The U.S. Constitution preempts any laws established by other authorities that are inconsistent with the Constitution itself. After the U.S. Constitution come the laws of the United States—federal laws, federal common law, and federal regulations—plus federal treaties. State constitutions, state statutes and court decisions, and state regulations come under that, followed by regional and local ordinances.

Suggested Reading

⬧ Constitution of the United States.

⬧ De Tocqueville, *Democracy in America.*

Questions to Consider

↗ Does the judicial system occupy the place you think it should in the balance of powers? If not, why not?

↗ What is your reaction to our adversarial system? Do you think this is the best way to get to the truth of a dispute?

LITIGATION AND THE AMERICAN LEGAL SYSTEM

I magine a courtroom in Florida in 1961. The setting is formal. Close to the entrance are rows of seats for the public and the media. In front of the public seating is a wooden railing, and behind that, two long tables. At one table sits a prosecutor and his team. Lawyers. They know what they're doing. They've got legal training, all the power of the government behind them, and they're ready to try this case.

At the other table, sits a defendant, all alone. His name is Clarence Earl Gideon. He is a poor ex-con who has only an 8th grade education. He left home and went out on his own in middle school. He's accused of breaking into the Bay Harbor Poolroom in Panama City and stealing $5 in change, $50 from the jukebox, and some drinks. Mr. Gideon claims he's innocent. He can't afford a lawyer, so he asks the court to appoint one for him. And here's what the judge says:

"Mr. Gideon, I am sorry, but I cannot appoint Counsel to represent you in this case. Under the laws of the State of Florida, the only time the Court can appoint counsel to represent a Defendant is when that person is charged with a capital offense. I am sorry, but I will have to deny your request to appoint Counsel…"

So, with the odds stacked heavily against him, Mr. Gideon does the best he can to represent himself.

The situation I'm describing to you is the basis for an important Supreme Court decision from 1963 known as *Gideon v. Wainwright*. We're going to examine it in this lecture the way law students would, but it will also serve as a touchstone as we consider the American legal system and the special role that litigation holds in it. We'll explore why we adopted the particular legal system we have in this country, how that system works, and why law is taught in America the way it is. Now, let me confess right now that litigation isn't a typical subject for a first year law student to study—it's the stuff of upper-level courses. But learning about it offers a valuable orientation to the study of law generally, and I think you'll see the great value of acquiring legal skills, even if you have no plans to become a lawyer yourself.

Let's start our discussion with the role of law in American society. It's fair to say that law and the idea of America are inexorably intertwined. America is a nation of laws. From the very beginning, the American experiment has grappled with the question of how much power the government should have over the people, and the rules under which people interact with one another. When America broke away from England in 1776, it famously rejected the notion that a king gets to make those rules. Instead, the power of the government and of lawmaking belongs to the people. Although that idea is, of course, much more complicated than it sounds. Our Declaration of Independence proclaims, "governments are instituted among men, deriving their just powers from the consent of the governed." The notion that the people are in charge was an extraordinary idea at the time our country was founded. And when you consider the number of authoritarian governments that continue to exist in other parts of the world today, it's still remarkable.

Think of this, though: When our country was founded, the founding fathers were, in essence, breaking the law. They were rebelling against the British monarchy, which means they were committing treason, in the eyes of England. How did they justify their actions? What made them different from a rioting mob? What gave them the right, in their eyes, to seize power? To make the case that breaking away from England was the right thing to do, the founders wrote the Declaration of Independence in 1776, explaining, "When in the Course of human events, it becomes necessary for one people to dissolve the political bands which have connected them with another, and to assume among the powers of the earth, the separate and equal station to which the Laws of Nature and of Nature's God entitle them, a decent respect to the opinions of mankind requires that they should declare the causes which impel them to the separation."

They didn't just rebel, they explained why they were rebelling. They then replaced the legal system they were rejecting with a new one, starting with the U.S. Constitution, signed in 1787. And in that document, they limited the power of government, creating a system in which the people could undo everything if they wanted to. That's how the founding fathers made the idea of America legitimate. They created a legal framework and they wrote it down. They did what lawyers do. And we've continued to be a nation where people question the laws, challenge them, change them, and rely on them. Our nation is composed of people who quite often do not agree with each other. Every election cycle, we take some people out of power and put new people in charge. We rewrite the rules.

But with the exception of our bloody Civil War, we haven't done it by means of armed conflict. We've mostly done it peacefully, by using our legal framework. That's really empowering. Regular citizens are able to be involved with the law, to influence the shape of the law, simply by voting or by raising a claim in court.

Because of the importance of law to the functioning for our country, lawyers have long played a prominent role in American society. Alexis de Tocqueville famously observed in 1835: "When one visits Americans and when one studies their laws, one sees that the authority they have given to lawyers and the influence that they have allowed them to have in the government form the most powerful barrier today against the lapses of democracy." That influence continues. More than half of the 45 U.S. Presidents have been lawyers. So are many members of Congress, most judges, and many prominent leaders in business and banking. Lawyers are involved in making laws, seeing that they are enforced, testing the parameters of laws, changing laws, and creating the business deals and other contracts that keep our society functioning. You will certainly see lawyers at work if you go to a courtroom—when you think "lawyer," you may think Perry Mason or Atticus Finch. But lawyers are also often the people who lead large corporations or help them do business or merge with one another. Lawyers often run our various administrative agencies that govern things like taxes, the environment, the Internet, elections, and the financial markets. If you read in the news about a complicated issue that will impact a lot of people, or involve a lot of money, there is probably a lawyer involved.

Many lawyers have influence and power, but it's a kind of power that's open to anyone willing and able to go to law school and pass a bar exam. You don't have to be born into that power, like a king. That's a pretty American idea, the self-made man or woman, and also a very democratic one. If you keep in mind the guiding principle of the United States—that the power belongs to the people, not to a king—you can understand why we ended up with the legal system that we have. There are democratic principles woven throughout it.

And so you can also see why the judge in the *Gideon* case sounded so uneasy about not being able to appoint Mr. Gideon a lawyer, because the power imbalance felt really unfair. The judge even apologized to Mr. Gideon for not being able to do it. The Supreme Court, in its review of the *Gideon* case, described the problem like this: "[I]n our adversary system of criminal justice, any person haled into court, who is too poor to hire a lawyer, cannot be assured a fair trial unless counsel is provided for him. This seems to us to be an obvious truth." In other words, without effective assistance of counsel, a defendant is unlikely to be a match for the power of the government that is prosecuting him.

So why couldn't that Florida judge just appoint Mr. Gideon a lawyer if he wanted to? Here's why. The American legal system is a common law system, and is derived from English legal tradition. Some countries, like France, Italy, and others in continental Europe, have a civil law system. In a civil law system, written-down rules, called codes, are the primary basis of the law. Judges in these systems interpret the code and make sure it is followed, but their decisions have no lasting authority; they are not bound by earlier decisions of other judges, nor are other judges bound by theirs. In our common law system, by contrast, written-down laws—we call them statutes—and judicial decisions are both important sources of law. What a judge says about the law can be every bit as important as a statute, and sometimes more so. Yet our judges are also bound by statutes, and by the decisions of other judges who have come before them. A common law system checks the power of the legislature, which creates the statute, because a judge gets to interpret it. It also limits the power of the judge deciding a case, because he has to follow the rulings of previous judges. He can't just make up an outcome according to his own personal desires. The common law legal system is one of the ways we limit the power of the government over the people in America. The law as established by judicial opinions is called case law. And case law really shapes the whole way we teach law in the United States.

Until around 1870, American law schools were pretty informal. Law students attended lectures—if they chose to—and self-reported their accomplishments rather than being graded by a professor. After a year or two, they were awarded a diploma. There were no academic prerequisites for being admitted to law school, no required courses, and no exams. It was probably less stressful than law school today, but the system also did not ensure that graduates had actually learned anything about the law. In 1870, Christopher Columbus Langdell became dean of Harvard Law School. The next year, he published a book called *A Selection of Cases on the Law of Contracts*, in which he described law as "a science." The best way to master that science, he said, was "by studying the cases in which it is embodied." Notice that Langdell didn't propose that people learn the law by studying the Constitution, although there are certainly plenty of cases involving Constitutional law to be studied. He didn't propose that people study statutes, either. He proposed the study of judicial opinions, and appellate opinions at that. That gives you some idea of the significance of litigation and judicial opinions in the American legal system.

In his classes, Dean Langdell began methodically questioning his students about the cases in his casebook, seeking to provoke active, critical thinking in order to reconstruct the underlying doctrines. This particular technique of reasoning and arguing is now known as "thinking like a lawyer." Langdell's mode of teaching is similar to one used by Socrates in ancient Greece, so it is known as the Socratic method. Soon, law schools all over the country were using Langdell's method. It's not the only way law school professors teach, but most professors in the first year use it to this day. It allows a single professor to teach large groups of students while providing those students with some opportunity to practice their verbal skills—a cost-effective model for a law school. And *Gideon v. Wainwright* is one of the cases law students are likely to be asked about during their first year.

Back to Mr. Gideon's story—here's how the common law system affected it. Because of the nature of our system, the state court judge presiding over the *Gideon* trial was limited by what other judges had said about the law. And at the time of the Gideon trial, there existed an old case called *Betts v. Brady*, which held that, even though the Sixth Amendment of the Constitution guarantees a right to counsel in all criminal prosecutions, that right didn't necessarily extend to prosecutions in state court. Florida's system at that time only guaranteed a lawyer for cases involving the death penalty—which stealing $55 certainly would not. So the judge's hands were tied.

But that put Clarence Gideon in a terrible bind, because America's is an adversarial system. In an adversarial system, parties make their best arguments before a judge or jury, and from the conflict between them, the judge or jury determines the truth of what happened. The idea is that we're more likely to figure out the right answer if we hear the best arguments from both sides, and that in certain cases, we want a jury, representing the regular citizenry, to hold the ultimate power of deciding what that truth is.

This is different from the inquisitorial system used in some civil law countries. In an inquisitorial system, the judge acts as an investigator in a case, questioning witnesses and interrogating suspects. In an adversarial system, the judge serves as an impartial referee, ensuring that the rules are followed. The parties retain the power of deciding what evidence to present, which arguments to make, and whether to settle the dispute out of court altogether. The jury, representing the public, renders a verdict. The jury is typically composed of everyday people, but they ultimately hold a lot of power in the courtroom. There are parallels here to America's view of government; we believe that democracy, which involves hashing out opinions in the marketplace of ideas, will ultimately lead to the best way to govern. Similarly, we believe that having both sides to a conflict present their best arguments to a judge or jury will lead to a just outcome in court.

But imagine navigating that adversarial system without the assistance of a lawyer, as Mr. Gideon had to do. The Supreme Court, reviewing his case, wrote, "Gideon conducted his defense about as well as could be expected from a layman. He made an opening statement to the jury, cross-examined the State's witnesses, presented witnesses in his own defense, declined to testify…and made a short argument 'emphasizing his innocence to the charge contained in the Information filed in this case.'" Nevertheless, the Court noted, "The jury returned a verdict of guilty and petitioner was sentenced to serve five years in the state prison."

But that's not the end of the story. Mr. Gideon appealed his case. And this is another important aspect of our court system. To make sure that we get it right, we have layers of judicial review. Let me take you through them. Trial courts are the courts where cases start—we've been talking about a trial court so far in our Gideon discussion. At trial, both sides present evidence to demonstrate what happened in the dispute that brought them to court. They bring in witnesses and exhibits, such pictures, documents, a murder weapon. There is a judge who decides what evidence can be considered and whether the procedural rules are being followed. A trial can be decided either by a judge or a jury, depending on the type of case.

Many jurisdictions have trial level courts that hear a wide variety of cases. These courts are sometimes called general district courts. Some places have created specialized kinds of trial courts. For example, the District of Columbia has a landlord-tenant court, where the judges hear only disputes between renters and their landlords. There is a benefit to this because the judges become very familiar with D.C. landlord-tenant law and are more able to apply it properly. A court system might have a specialized traffic court, or a divorce court, or a court for juveniles.

As you may know, legal cases are divided into two broad categories: civil and criminal. Civil cases involve disputes between private parties. An example might be a lawsuit by a person who bought a car against the seller of the car, when it turns out the car is a lemon. The person who brings a civil lawsuit is called the plaintiff. The person who is sued is the defendant. In a criminal case, a person is accused of breaking a criminal law. So if the person who bought that defective car decided to settle the dispute by burning down the car dealership, that person could be accused of committing arson, which is a crime. In that case, the person against whom the suit is brought is still called the defendant, but because a criminal law has apparently been violated, the person bringing the suit is a prosecutor and represents the state or federal government, depending on whose law was broken.

If a party believes that something has been wrongly decided at trial, he or she may be able to appeal that issue to an appellate court. The issue has to be preserved for appeal, however, which usually means that the attorney has to flag the perceived problem during the trial by saying "Objection!" and indicating the nature of the error. And the appeal has to be filed within a certain time, usually 30 days after a case has been decided or a final judgment on the issue has been ordered.

Remarkably, Mr. Gideon was able to do all this properly. He appealed his conviction to the Florida Supreme Court. In an appellate court, there are no witnesses and the parties do not present evidence. There is also no jury. Instead, lawyers argue legal issues to a panel or group of judges. Appellate courts do not rehear all the facts of a case; instead, they focus on the specific question of law that's being appealed to determine whether it was decided correctly. So the focus of a hearing before an appellate court is much narrower than an entire trial would be. If the trial court has made an error, the appellate court may overrule the trial court's decision and issue a written opinion about it. If a party disagrees with an appellate court decision, it may appeal to the ultimate judicial tribunal of a court system, typically known as a supreme court. That court may overrule or affirm the appellate court's decision and issue a written opinion about that. These are the cases that law students study—reported decisions by a court of appeals or a supreme court. Typically, the written opinions worth studying in law school are the ones where a court has made a new interpretation of the law. Those decisions are actually pretty rare in everyday life, but they are what we focus on in law school because they are the most difficult, and the most interesting.

To further complicate things, America has both federal and state laws, and they are not always consistent with one another. What might be legal in one state might not be legal in another, and state laws and federal laws also clash on occasion. Since we have a dual system of laws, we also have a dual system of courts: federal and state.

This system again has its roots in the American Revolution. The framers of our Constitution wanted to limit the power of our federal government. They recognized that we needed unity for purposes of strength, "in Order to form a more perfect union," but worried about the dangers of a strong central government because of their experiences with the British monarchy. The framers also came from different states. They felt loyal to their states, and knew that different states had different priorities and values. They wanted to permit room for the states to make their own laws to preserve those different points of view. So our Constitution gives certain powers to the federal government but leaves other powers to the states, and does not require the states to have laws identical to one another.

Federal courts are courts of limited jurisdiction, which means they can only hear certain kinds of cases. They can hear cases that raise a federal question, which means the plaintiff or prosecutor has alleged a violation of the U.S. Constitution, a federal law, or a treaty. They can also hear cases involving disputes between parties from different states. So if you have a lawsuit about freedom of speech, for example, you could go to a federal court because the suit involves an alleged violation of the Constitution. If you have a lawsuit in which a person from Alabama has bought a defective car from a person from Mississippi, you can go to federal court because the dispute involves parties from different states. But if you have a dispute about someone in Alabama buying a defective car from someone else in Alabama, you're going to be in state court. About 90% of all the cases heard in America are in state court.

Both the federal court system and the state court system have trial courts, courts of appeals, and a supreme court or other court of last resort. The names of state courts vary from state to state, and can sometimes be confusing. For example, in New York, the trial level court is called the New York Supreme Court; the appellate court is called the Appellate Division; and the supreme or the highest court is called the New York Court of Appeals. Federal courts, not surprisingly, employ the same names throughout the country: the trial court is called a federal district court; the appellate-level court is a U.S. Court of Appeals; and the court of last resort is, of course, the U.S. Supreme Court.

In addition to state and federal statutes and the case law written by judges, law also comes from constitutions—both federal and state—from treaties, and from regulations. Regulations, as you might be aware, are rules made by an agency at either the state or federal level pursuant to a statute. Sometimes laws conflict with one another. Perhaps a state legislature enacts a law that declares, "No one is allowed to talk about the color blue." That would be in conflict with the U.S.

Constitution, which prohibits the making of any law abridging the freedom of speech. Which trumps, the state law or the Constitution?

The Constitution trumps. But why? To answer that question, you need to know the hierarchy of sources of law. The U.S. Constitution is at the top of the legal heap. It sets up the whole system of law in America. What it says, goes. The Constitution itself says so, in Article VI, Section 2: "This Constitution, and the Laws of the United States which shall be made in Pursuance thereof; and all Treaties made, or which shall be made, under the Authority of the United States, shall be the supreme Law of the Land; and the Judges in every State shall be bound thereby, any Thing in the Constitution or Laws of any State to the Contrary notwithstanding." So from that, you can see that after the U.S. Constitution, what comes next in importance are the laws of the United States, which means federal laws, what judges have said about those laws, and federal regulations pursuant to those laws, plus federal treaties. State constitutions, state statutes and court decisions, and state regulations come under that. Regional and local ordinances would come after that. So if a state tries to pass a law that violates the U.S. Constitution, that law is invalid. That's why you can talk about the color blue, even if your state says you can't.

Sometimes, a case can begin in state court but be resolved in federal court. And that's what happened in Clarence Gideon's situation. His case began in a Florida trial court. He then appealed to the Florida Supreme Court, which denied his appeal. So Mr. Gideon petitioned the U.S. Supreme Court, handwriting his plea on lined paper that he got from the prison. And the Supreme Court found that his claim had merit. It held that the Sixth Amendment of the Constitution, which guarantees the right to counsel in a criminal case, applies even in state court proceedings like Mr. Gideon's. So that's an example of the Constitution— the highest law of the land—trumping what Florida state law said, and the Supreme Court—a federal court—overturning the judgement of a state court.

Gideon v. Wainwright also shows how important a lawyer can be. Here's how the Supreme Court explained it: "That government hires lawyers to prosecute and defendants who have the money hire lawyers to defend are the strongest indications of the widespread belief that lawyers in criminal courts are necessities, not luxuries. The right of one charged with crime to counsel may not be deemed fundamental and essential to fair trials in some countries, but it is in ours. From the very beginning, our state and national constitutions and laws have laid great emphasis on procedural and substantive safeguards designed to assure fair trials before impartial tribunals in which every defendant stands equal before the law. This noble ideal cannot be realized if the poor man charged with crime has to face his accusers without a lawyer to assist him."

The Supreme Court's decision in *Gideon v. Wainwright* expanded the right to counsel to all cases in which defendants are accused of felonies—that is, serious crimes. It continues to protect the rights of defendants to this day. That's one important reason why first year law students still study it. They might be asked in class to explain why the case was decided in the way it was, what the ramifications of the case are, what might happen if some fact of the case were changed, how the logic of the Justices' decision worked, how the case is similar to or different from other cases that the class is studying, and so forth. By thinking through these questions about *Gideon* and other cases, law students begin to understand not only what judges have said about the law, but why they made the decisions that they made. They acquire the knowledge to help people obtain the equal justice that *Gideon* promised.

I hope you can now see why legal training is valuable well beyond the courtroom and the other places lawyers work. If you can think like a lawyer, you have gained valuable insight into how things get done in this country. And if you can think like a courtroom lawyer, then you are able to apply that knowledge quickly and use it to articulate your positions aloud. That's a valuable skillset for anyone to have, particularly in a representative democracy such as ours.

Let me leave you with one last piece of the Gideon story. After the Supreme Court sent his case back to Florida, Mr. Gideon was tried again for the theft of the $55 and the drinks—but this time he had a lawyer on his side. And that lawyer made mincemeat of the prosecution's only witness. Mr. Gideon was acquitted after the jury deliberated for only an hour. Now that's effective assistance of counsel!

THINKING LIKE A LAWYER

This lecture addresses a concept that is at the very heart of American legal education: the idea of thinking like a lawyer. Thinking like a lawyer means mastering the ability to think actively and critically about legal doctrine. Once you learn how to do that, you'll not only understand the law better; you will also have a better understanding of how to make an argument, even in a nonlegal context.

THE POWER OF PRECEDENT

⋆ You may have noticed that when you argue with family members—your spouse or your kids, say—they are rarely persuaded that they must do something because "that's the way we've always done it." But when you are a lawyer making an argument to a judge, you will find that if you're advocating a position that no other judge has ever adopted, you are probably going to lose. "That's the way we've always done it" is a pretty powerful legal argument. This is the notion of precedent.

⋆ Precedent means following the decisions that have been handed down in the past. In a common law system like the one we have in America, what judges say about a statute is every bit as important as the statute itself—the opinion a judge writes about the statute becomes part of the law, too. Because of this, other judges deciding a case have to look at both the statute at issue and what other judges have said about that statute. If the issue has been decided in the past by the court hearing your case or by a higher court in that same jurisdiction, then the matter is settled.

* Law is fundamentally conservative so that people trying to follow the law will know what to expect. If the law could change at the mere whim of a judge, then society would be so unsettled that people would not know how to behave. Law is also conservative to protect people from being treated unfairly by judges who don't like them. Requiring a judge to follow precedent makes it more likely that the law will be applied consistently, not according to the whims and prejudices of individual judges.

* Another reason the law is conservative is purely practical: If judges were asked to decide every legal issue from the beginning in every single case, the workload would be overwhelming. This may sound terribly unfair to the parties, but it would be unfair for everyone if the courts got so bogged down that you couldn't get a hearing for years and years because judges were deciding things anew every time.

* When a lawyer is reading a judicial opinion, he or she will keep an eye out for a discussion of precedent. This will usually involve the judge citing older cases and comparing them to the decision at hand. The judge will try to explain why the two cases are similar—which means that the precedent binds the case at hand and dictates its outcome—or why they aren't.

* Importantly, precedent means that the case has been decided in the past either by a judge in the same court or by a higher court in the same jurisdiction. If a case was decided by a court in a different jurisdiction—in the state next door, for example—that court's opinion might be informative, but it wouldn't be precedential. Lawyers sometimes talk about this as being persuasive authority, but not binding authority.

* Of primary importance in any case is what the court decided in the dispute at hand, and why. This is known as the holding of the case. By contrast, anything the court said that isn't essential to actually resolving the matter at hand is called dicta. The holding of the case is what judges will follow in subsequent cases, and is binding. The dicta, while informative, is not binding.

* If you can find binding authority to support your argument, you are on firmer ground than if you would be if you were relying on dicta, or on a secondary source—an academic article written by a law professor, for example, which no judge is required to follow. If you must rely on persuasive authority, you will need to be able to articulate why the authority is credible. The more credible the authority, the more convincing your argument will be.

TEXTUAL INTERPRETATION

* Legal analysis can seem peculiar in the way it emphasizes the exact words of a statute, constitutional provision, or case. A lawyer must always pay close attention to the text of the legal rule or the precedent governing his case. When you make a legal argument, it is not sufficient to paraphrase the language. Very often, the best legal argument will be the one that parses the words the most carefully.

* Along the same lines, the judicial system is devoted to adhering strictly to the text of rules. You can see this, for example, in the application of a filing deadline at a courthouse. It hardly ever matters what the purpose of the rule was, or if you have a good reason why you didn't meet a particular filing deadline. The filing deadline is generally what's known as a bright-line rule: the requirements are clearly stated and inflexible. A bright-line rule is something you see quite a lot in various laws and legal opinions.

* Sometimes, however, the text of a rule is less clear. There are many examples—most notably those involving interpretation of the U.S. Constitution—in which a text could be interpreted literally, but isn't. Often, one side might rely on the plain meaning of the words in the

text, while the other might look at the purpose of the provision, or how it fits into other parts of the law. As a lawyer, you might argue based on the letter of the law, or you might argue the intention behind the law. Either way, you can't ignore the text.

LOGICAL REASONING

⭑ Lawyers often rely on analogy to make a point. That is, they point out how a case is similar in some way to some other case, and argue that the two cases should therefore be decided in the same way.

* To use analogy well, you start by laying out the facts of your case and the facts of the case you want to compare it to. Then you compare the facts of the cases. Emphasize the similarities that are relevant, and throw away the ones that are not relevant. If the cases are similar in central ways, then they should result in similar outcomes. Of course, you need to be ready for the likelihood that opposing counsel will challenge your analogy, arguing that the facts that you called irrelevant actually make the case that you're citing inapplicable to the one at hand.

* Many legal arguments are based on deductive logic. Reasoning deductively, you can figure out the right outcome if you identify the correct legal proposition and apply it to the facts at hand. Aristotle explained this concept as a syllogism, in which a major premise and a minor premise point the way to a conclusion (if A and B are true, then C must be true).

* When reading a case, you should try to identify the major premise (the rule of law governing the case), the minor premise (the facts particular to your case), and the conclusion (the application of the law to the facts). You must also be sure that the major premise is true. If it isn't, then your conclusion will be flawed.

* Some legal arguments are based on inductive logic. Reasoning inductively means using a number of specific observations to draw a broad generalization. This can be a useful sort of argument when it's difficult to prove something.

* If you make an argument based on inductive reasoning, you probably shouldn't rely only on personal experiences; instead, you would be wiser to draw upon a large number of examples from which to generalize. You would also want to think about how your sample might be criticized. If, for example, your sample is not representative of the population at large, your argument might be considered less credible.

Suggested Reading

- Hart, *The Concept of Law.*

- Schauer, *Thinking Like a Lawyer*

- Sullivan, *Educating Lawyers.*

Questions to Consider

↗ Law schools emphasize teaching students to "think like a lawyer." Is this different from the way you are accustomed to thinking about things, and if so, how?

↗ One aspect of "thinking like a lawyer" involves putting aside your own personal reaction to a case, and instead to focus on issues like precedent. What are the pros and cons of that idea?

THINKING LIKE A LAWYER

L et me tell you the story of young Harvey Hynes. Harvey was a 16-year old boy who went swimming with his pals in the Harlem river during the summer of 1916. That river must have been much cleaner then than it is now, because the neighborhood kids swam there regularly. Someone had even nailed a plank onto a bulkhead adjacent to the river, and the boys used it as a diving board. That bulkhead and the land on which it was built belonged to the New York Central Railroad. But the diving board extended over the river, which didn't belong to the railroad, it was a public waterway. The train at that location operated by means of high tension electrical wires, which were strung along poles and held up by crossarms.

On this fateful day, one of those crossarms with electrical wires attached broke off the pole just as Harvey Hines stood on the plank, ready to dive. The wires hit him and flung him from the diving board, and the fall killed him. The boy's mother, Florence Hynes, believed that the railroad was responsible for her son's death. The railroad owned those electrical wires, it didn't maintain them properly, and as a result, these dangerous wires fell on her boy and killed him. The railroad's response was that it didn't owe anything to Mrs. Hynes, because her boy had trespassed on its land to reach that diving board. The railroad said that it didn't have an obligation to maintain its poles and crossarms to protect trespassers on its own land, because trespassers weren't supposed to be there anyway. Mrs. Hynes refused to accept the railroad's claim that it bore no responsibility to prevent this accident. Instead, she chose, like so many Americans before and since, to litigate—and in doing so, she helped shape the law. Today, *Hynes v. New York Central Railroad* remains an influential opinion that most law students encounter in law school. But to make sense of it, you need to understand how to "think like a lawyer." Once you learn how to do that, you'll not only understand the law better, you will also have a better understanding of how to make an argument even in a non-legal context.

Thinking like a lawyer means mastering the ability to think actively and critically about legal doctrine. In law school, we teach this by asking students to read judicial opinions like *Hynes v. New York Central Railroad*, and then to talk with us about those cases. We ask questions like, "Why did the judge decide the case this way? How does this case fit with other, similar opinions that came before it? Would the case have turned out differently if particular facts were different? How would this opinion be applied to another hypothetical fact pattern? What's the best argument against this decision?" And so forth. To answer those questions, law students learn to read cases looking for particular things. One of those things is precedent, so let's start there.

Legal analysis is a special way of thinking. You may have noticed that when you argue with a family member—your spouse or your kids, say—they are not persuaded that they must do something because "that's the way we've always done it." But when you are a lawyer making an argument to a judge, you will find that if you're advocating a position that no other judge has ever adopted, you are probably going to lose. "That's the way we've always done it" is a pretty powerful legal argument. This gets into the notion of precedent.

Precedent means following the decisions that have been handed down in the past. Remember that America's is a common-law legal system. As we've discussed, this means that what judges say about a statute is every bit as important as the statute itself; the opinion a judge writes about the statute becomes part of the law, too. Because of this, other judges deciding a case have to look both at the statute at issue, and at what other judges have said about that statute. If the issue has been decided in the past by the court hearing your case or by a higher court in that same jurisdiction, then the matter is settled, even if the result in your case seems preposterous. This principle is known as stare decisis, which is a Latin phrase that means "to stand by things decided." You have to follow past precedent, even if you are a judge and don't like the result that will occur.

To some people, that seems awfully rigid. Why would we create such a system? Law is fundamentally conservative so that people trying to follow the law will know what to expect. If the law could change at the mere whim of a judge, then society would be so unsettled that people would not know how to behave. Law is also conservative to protect people from being treated unfairly by judges who don't like them. Requiring a judge to follow precedent makes it more likely that the law will be applied consistently, not according to the whims and prejudices of individual judges. That's essential to a system governed according to the rule of law, which is a hallmark of a free and fair society.

In addition, the law is conservative for purely practical reasons. If judges were asked to decide every legal issue in every single case from the beginning every single time, the workload would be overwhelming. Supreme Court Justice

Louis Brandeis explained it like this: "In most matters it is more important that [the question] be settled than that it be settled right." This may sound terribly unfair to the parties, but it would also be unfair for everyone if the courts got so bogged down that you couldn't get a hearing for years and years because judges were deciding things anew every time. So when a lawyer is reading a case, he or she will keep an eye out for a discussion of precedent. This will usually involve the judge citing older cases and comparing them to the decision at hand. The judge will try to explain why the two cases are similar, which means that the precedent binds the case at hand and dictates its outcome, or why they aren't.

Note that precedent means that the case has been decided in the past either by a judge in the same court, which is called horizontal precedent, or by a higher court in that same jurisdiction, which is called vertical precedent. We talked previously about how we have various court systems—state courts, federal courts, and so forth. If a case was decided by a court in a different jurisdiction, in the state next door, for example, that court's opinion might be informative, but it wouldn't be precedential. The court deciding your case would be free to reject it. Lawyers sometimes talk about this as being persuasive authority, but not binding authority.

Of primary importance in any case, naturally, is what the court decided in the dispute at hand and why. This is known as the holding of the case. Anything else the court said that isn't essential to actually resolving the matter at hand is called dicta. The holding of the case is what judges will follow in subsequent cases, and is binding. The dicta, while informative, is not binding. For example, the holding of a case might say that the defendant broke the law by driving a car through a public park. The judge might also have spent some time in that decision musing over whether the outcome might have been different had the defendant driven a scooter through the park. But if the actual case did not involve a scooter, this musing would be classed as dicta and wouldn't be binding. A court deciding a scooter case wouldn't have to follow it.

If you can find binding authority to support your argument, you are on firmer ground than if you were to point to dicta, or to a secondary source like an academic article written by a law professor, which no judge is ever required to follow. If you want to rely on non-binding persuasive authority, then you will need to be able to articulate why the authority is credible. The more credible the authority, the more convincing your argument will be. Here's another thing that is central to the notion of "thinking like a lawyer:" Textual analysis.

Legal analysis can also seem peculiar in the way it emphasizes the exact words of a statute, constitutional provision, or case. A lawyer must always pay close attention to the text of the legal rule or the precedent governing his case. When you make a legal argument, it is not sufficient to paraphrase the language. Very often, the best legal argument will be the one that parses the words the most carefully.

Along the same lines, the judicial system is devoted to adhering strictly to the text of rules. You can see this, for example, in the application of a filing deadline at a courthouse. The rule may say that a brief must be filed by 6 p.m. on a particular day. The original motivation for this rule might be to keep the employees in the clerk's office from having to work past seven, or to make sure that the brief is on the judge's desk in a timely fashion. Whatever the case, you may arrive at the courthouse at 6:05 p.m. and attempt to file your brief you will be turned away. You might argue that there's very little difference between 6 and 6:05, that there was a good reason you were late because you were rescuing a child from a burning house, that the clerk won't have to work late because you would be happy to walk the brief up to the judge's chambers yourself, but your arguments are not going to succeed. The rule is clear: 6 P.M. It doesn't matter what the purpose of the rule was, or if you have a good reason why the rule shouldn't apply to you. Clerk's offices are very good at enforcing the rules, and rightfully so. They don't want to be in the business of deciding who has to follow the rules and who should get an exception—that wouldn't be fair. A clerk's office rule is generally what's known as a bright-line rule: the requirements are clearly stated and inflexible. A bright-line rule is something you see quite a lot in various laws and legal opinions.

What happens when the text of a rule is less clear? Take, for example the text of the Second Amendment of the U.S. Constitution. The Second Amendment says, "A well-regulated Militia, being necessary to the security of a free State, the right of the people to keep and bear Arms, shall not be infringed." The text, read literally, seems to draw a connection between the necessity of having a well-regulated militia and the right to bear arms. It could be interpreted as saying that people have the right to bear arms if they are going to be part of a militia. But we now understand the Second Amendment to mean that Americans have the right to bear arms regardless of whether they are serving in a militia. The Supreme Court said so in *District of Columbia v. Heller*. So the Second Amendment is an example of a text that could be interpreted literally, but isn't.

A typical Socratic dialogue in law school might involve a professor asking one student to take one position about the meaning of the text, and another student to take the opposite position. One student then might rely on the plain meaning of the words, while the other might look at the purpose of the provision or how it fits into other parts of the law. So as a lawyer, you might argue based on the letter of the law, or you might argue the intention behind the law. Either way, you can't ignore the text.

Another concept that is central to "thinking like a lawyer" is understanding the use of analogy. Lawyers often rely on analogy to make a point. That is, they point out how a case is similar in some way to some other case, and argue that the two cases should therefore be decided in the same way. Note that analogy isn't always the same thing as precedent. If you can draw an analogy with a case in the same jurisdiction, you may be able to establish that the case is binding, but you can also analogize your case to similar ones that don't exactly control it—cases in a different jurisdiction, for example. To use analogy well, you start by laying out the facts of your case and the facts of the case you want to compare it to. For example, your case might involve a farmer who is being sued for the damage that his cow caused to his neighbor's field. And the case you are comparing it to might involve a zookeeper who was held liable because his lion ate a tourist. Then you compare the facts of the cases. Emphasize the similarities that are relevant. For example, both cases involve animals that are negligently housed, and throw away the ones that are not relevant. For example, does it matter that one victim was a field and the other was a person? If the cases are similar in central ways, then the cases should result in similar outcomes. Of course, you need to be ready for the likelihood that opposing counsel will challenge your analogy, arguing that the facts that you called irrelevant actually make the case that you are citing inapplicable to the one at hand.

Let's turn to the topic of logic and legal arguments. Many legal arguments are based on the sort of deductive logic that Aristotle spelled out long ago. You can figure out the right outcome if you identify the correct legal proposition and apply it to the facts at hand. Aristotle explained this in the form of a syllogism, in which a major premise and a minor premise point the way to a conclusion. So if A is true and B are true, then C must be true. Here's his famous example: All men are mortal beings, that's your major premise. Socrates is a man is the minor premise. Therefore, Socrates is a mortal being. That's the conclusion. So if you apply this to a modern-day legal example: Anyone who takes an item from a store without paying for it has committed larceny—that's your major premise, your rule of law. John took a necklace from a store without paying for it—that's the minor premise, the facts of your case. Now you're going to apply the law to those facts and you're going to come up with therefore, John has committed larceny. That's the conclusion.

You also have to pay particular attention to making sure that your major premise is true. If it isn't, then your conclusion will be flawed. Look at the larceny example again. Common law defines larceny as a taking, not "from the person," with the intent to permanently deprive the owner of the item. Let's imagine that the store in question was on fire, and John was one of the firefighters who grabbed some valuable items in an effort to save them. In that case, it seems wrong to say that he committed larceny. The erroneous conclusion that John has committed larceny arises from a misstatement of the major premise—that is, a misstatement of the law of larceny. A better analysis of the case would be: Anyone who takes an item from a store without paying for it intending to permanently deprive the owner of it has committed larceny. John took a necklace from a store without paying for it but intended to return it to the owner. Therefore, John has not committed larceny.

So that's deductive reasoning.

Aristotle also wrote about the power of inductive reasoning. Inductive reasoning means you use a bunch of specific observations to draw a broad generalization. This can be a useful sort of argument when it's difficult to prove something. For example, a lawyer might need to argue that a certain kind of medicine does not harm women. It's hard to prove a negative, but if you can show that lots of women took the medicine and weren't harmed, your claim might be credible. Your argument will be more compelling the greater the number of known, observed facts you have, and the more reliable they are. If you try to argue that medicine doesn't harm women because your sister took that medicine and wasn't harmed, that's clearly not going to be as persuasive as an argument based on hundreds of women taking the medicine.

So if you make an argument based on inductive reasoning, you probably shouldn't rely only on personal experiences; instead, you would be wiser to draw upon a large-enough number of examples from which to generalize. You would also want to think about how your sample could be criticized. For example, if I drew a sample from people at the university where I teach, that might not be representative of the population at large—it might include mostly college-aged people. This is how a lawyer might attack the testimony of an expert witness as well. If the sample upon which he bases his opinion is flawed, then his opinion won't be credible.

Let's apply these ideas we've been exploring to *Hynes v. New York Central Railroad Co.* The opinion in the case was handed down in 1921 by the New York Court of Appeals, which is the highest state court in New York, and was written by Benjamin Cardozo, a famous judge. He was a state court judge at the time he wrote this opinion, but he eventually became a U.S. Supreme Court justice, the second Jewish person to serve on the Supreme Court. Justice Cardozo was known for his belief that the law should meet the needs of real people in the real world. He wanted judges to pay attention to public policy when deciding cases.

You can hear Justice Cardozo's concern for people and public policy in his approach to the *Hynes* case. He starts his opinion recounting the facts from the point of view of "Harvey Hynes, a lad of sixteen" and the "boys" with whom he went swimming. When he describes the diving board, he emphasizes that "for more than five years, swimmers had used it as a diving board without protest or obstruction," and "for seven and a half feet the springboard was beyond the line of the defendant's property, and above the public waterway." Cardozo goes on to tell the story vividly: "On this day Hynes and his companions climbed on top of the bulkhead intending to leap into the water. One of them made the plunge in safety. Hynes followed to the front of the springboard, and stood poised for his dive. At that moment a crossarm with electric wires fell from the defendant's pole. The wires struck the diver, flung him from the shattered board, and plunged him to his death below."

One can imagine that the railroad might have stated the facts differently. It might have preferred the judge to say something about how this is a case about "The New York Central railroad, which operated its trains by high tension wires, strung on poles and crossarms." And it might want to the judge to point out that railroads are dangerous, and that danger is obvious. "Despite the obvious danger, or perhaps attracted to it, teenage hooligans liked to trespass on railroad land. On this particular day, a teenager named Harvey Hynes and some other teens came uninvited onto railroad property and were leaping from the shore into the water. Through no willfulness on the part of the railroad, Hynes was killed in an accident when an electrical wire fell on him. If he had not been on the property, where he was not permitted to be, he would not have been injured." Clearly, how one views the facts of a tragic incident can govern whom one holds responsible for it. A law student might be asked to recite the facts in the light most favorable to the railroad or to Harvey Hynes' estate, laying the foundations for a case either about trespass and delinquency and an obvious danger, or about a "lad of sixteen" out for a swim.

According to Judge Cardozo's opinion, the lower court which found for the railroad and the judgment of which Cardozo is reviewing, started with the premise that the railroad didn't owe a duty of care to a trespasser. That means it didn't have to regulate its conduct on its private land to protect people who entered that land uninvited. The issue for the lower court, according to Cardozo, was whether, and here I'm quoting, "Hynes at the end of the springboard above the public waters was a trespasser on the defendant's land." So, the rule in that analysis: landowners don't owe a duty to trespassers. Application of this rule to this case: Hynes was a trespasser because he entered the land without permission, therefore—conclusion—the railroad did not owe a duty of care to Hynes. You can think of the lower court's logic in terms of one of Aristotle's syllogisms. Major premise: no duty of care owed to trespassers. Minor premise: Hynes is a trespasser. Conclusion: no duty of care owed to Hynes.

Justice Cardozo thought the lower court got both the major and minor premises wrong. He said that this wasn't a case about trespassing at all. This was a case about the duty of care that the railroad owes to the public in a public space when the railroad's equipment moves into that space. According to Cardozo, the diving board extended out 7 ½ feet from the railroad's property into the river, which is a public waterway. Because Harvey Hynes was on the diving board, in the air over the river, he wasn't on the railroad's land at the moment of the accident, he was in a public space. Cardozo writes, "Bathers in the Harlem river on the day of this disaster were in the enjoyment of a public highway, entitled to reasonable protection against destruction by the defendant's wires." So the logic of this opinion goes like this—Major premise: the railroad owes a duty of "care and vigilance in the storage of destructive forces" (the electrical wires) to the public using a public space; Minor premise: Hynes was a member of the public using a public space (the river); Conclusion: the railroad owed a duty of care to Hynes.

Here's an interesting thought, though: Hynes seems to have trespassed on the railroad's land to reach that diving board. So if those electrical wires had fallen on Hynes as he approached the diving board, when he was squarely on the defendants' land and trespassing, would the railroad have owed him a duty of care? Probably not, because then he wouldn't have been in a public space. But since he was on the diving board, and the diving board extended above the water, the railroad is on the hook. In Cardozo's analysis, the way that Hynes got to the diving board doesn't factor in at all. Cardozo writes,

"Landowners are not bound to regulate their conduct in contemplation of the presence of trespassers intruding upon private structures. Landowners are bound to regulate their conduct in contemplation of the presence of travelers upon the adjacent public ways."

Notice that the first sentence, "Landowners are not bound to regulate their conduct in contemplation of the presence of trespassers intruding upon private structures," is not the holding of the case. It sounds like a clear pronouncement of law, but it is dicta because, in Judge Cardozo's analysis, this case wasn't about a trespasser intruding on a private structure. Cardozo says this is a case about a boy using a public waterway. So even though that first sentence sounds like a ruling by a court, and even though it might be persuasive because Cardozo said it and he is famous, it's not the holding of the case. It's not going to bind other courts in this jurisdiction. You could find a different case to stand for that proposition, but not this one.

That second sentence is the holding of the case: "Landowners are bound to regulate their conduct in contemplation of the presence of travelers upon the adjacent public ways." So if you are a lawyer bringing a suit in this jurisdiction—New York—and you are suing a landlord who is doing something that affects public spaces—flooding a road, perhaps, or throwing things into a river—then this case helps you. The judge deciding your case will have to take as his starting point the law as handed down by Judge Cardozo, that landowners can't do things to hurt the public on public property. That's the part of the case that will serve as precedent for cases that follow.

Now, if you are representing the landowner, you could try to narrow that holding. You could argue that *Hynes* is specifically about dangers to the public involving electrical wires, and therefore doesn't apply to your case, which involves none. That would be a fair argument—the court would have to think about whether electrical wires and flooding a road are the same thing in that they can both potentially harm the public, or if they're different because electrical wires are inherently dangerous. That's the sort of thing a law school professor is likely to ask about in class.

It's also interesting to see how Judge Cardozo uses analogy in this case, because it gives you a window into how lawyers argue. At one point in the opinion, Cardozo imagines this scenario: "Two boys walking in the country or swimming in a river stop to rest for a moment along the side of the road or the margin of the stream. One of them throws himself beneath the overhanging branches of a tree. The other perches himself on a bough a foot or so above the ground. Both are killed by falling wires. The defendant would have us say that there is a remedy for the representatives of one, and none for the representatives of the other. We may be permitted to distrust the logic that leads to such conclusions." His point is that this outcome would be absurd, the location of the two boys is essentially the same under the tree or up in the tree, so the remedies shouldn't be different. Similarly, *Hynes'* remedy should not turn on whether he was on the diving board or in the air above the diving board or in the water below it. The lower court's ruling implies that Hynes' estate could recover if he was under or over the diving board, therefore in public space, but not if he was on it since it's attached to the railroad's land. Cardozo thinks this makes no sense. He writes, "Hynes would have gone to his death if he had been below the springboard or beside it. The wires were not stayed by the presence of the plank. They followed the boy in his fall, and overwhelmed him in the waters."

The *Hynes* case gives you a sense of how litigation shapes the law. Through this particular dispute, the shape of the law for everyone changes. The railroad is now more likely to make sure its electrical lines and crossbeams are in good repair, but that change in behavior will not be limited to the railroad. After this decision, all landowners adjacent to public waterways in this jurisdiction would have to take care that their activities don't cross into those waterways and hurt the public. And yet, notice how Justice Cardozo carved out a space to find a fair outcome in this case without completely upending the established right of property holders to make use of their land as they please without a duty toward any and all trespassers. He's refining the law, but he's also seeking to uphold it.

As you continue thinking about the law, consider what we've talked about in this discussion of thinking like a lawyer. It will help you make sense of what you are reading and give you a framework for thinking about why the cases come out the way they do.

REPRESENTING YOUR CLIENT

N̲o matter whom they are representing, lawyers have dual responsibilities: to their clients, and to the integrity of justice system. This lecture explores the important relationship between attorney and client, including the ethical rules that guide lawyers when their dual responsibilities come into conflict with one another.

THE IMPORTANCE OF REPRESENTATION

☆ The structure of the American legal system requires that we have lawyers willing to represent any defendant zealously within the bounds of the law, no matter what that defendant may have done. Many people accept that idea in principle, but still can't stomach the thought of representing a killer, a swindler, a rapist, a child molester. Such representation is critical, however—and not only for the client.

☆ America's is an adversarial legal system. That means we resolve legal disputes by assigning a lawyer to each side, and leaving it to the lawyers to ask the right questions, present the proper evidence, and raise appropriate objections. Judges make sure that lawyers, jurors, and witnesses are playing their proper roles, but the lawyers are the ones who shape the substance of a trial.

☆ The advantage of a system like this is that the parties have greater incentive than anybody else to gather and present the evidence that supports their respective views of the case. If it were up to the judge to develop the factual record, he might not do as thorough a job of it as the parties themselves would do. Also, a judge asked to gather the evidence might develop a bias in favor of or against a party before the trial starts. Our system produces a more complete factual record, and helps the judge remain impartial.

✯ Our system is governed by complex rules, and litigants have to make many decisions that have long-lasting consequences. A defendant without a lawyer finds himself at a serious disadvantage. He may not even know where to start to gather evidence. And even someone who is not innocent may have had his rights violated—evidence may have been obtained illegally, or a confession may have been coerced.

✯ To make sure that our system is fair and just, we need good defense lawyers to test prosecutions and make sure that evidence against a defendant was obtained lawfully. We want those lawyers to do the best job possible, because we believe that, through the clash of two effective advocates, juries will best be able to determine the truth. If a defendant doesn't have a lawyer, it's more likely that the system will malfunction.

PROFESSIONAL CONDUCT

✯ What if a lawyer thinks that his client is guilty? Should that make a difference in how the lawyer represents him? The answer is a resounding no. It's not up to the lawyer to decide whether the client is guilty or innocent—that determination is left to the jury. Otherwise, the lawyer would be subsuming the role of the jury without giving his client the benefit of a fair trial, which is just the sort of tyranny the Constitution forbids. Moreover, the lawyer would also be violating his ethical obligations to his client.

✱ Most states have adopted some form of the American Bar Association's Model Rules of Professional Conduct. Rule 1.3 requires a lawyer to "act with reasonable diligence and promptness in representing a client." The comment to this rule explains:

> A lawyer should pursue a matter on behalf of a client despite opposition, obstruction or personal inconvenience to the lawyer, and take whatever lawful and ethical measures are required to vindicate a client's cause or endeavor. A lawyer must also act with commitment and dedication to the interests of the client and with zeal in advocacy upon the client's behalf.

✱ When is it okay for a lawyer to make a decision—for example, about how to respond to an unexpected question from the press concerning trial strategy—without first consulting with his client? To answer this question, we turn again to the Model Rules of Professional Conduct. Rule 1.2 governs the allocation of authority between client and lawyer. The rule says, in part:

> [A] lawyer shall abide by a client's decisions concerning the objectives of representation and ... shall consult with the client as to the means by which they are to be pursued. A lawyer may take such action on behalf of the client as is impliedly authorized to carry out the representation ... . In a criminal case, the lawyer shall abide by the client's decision, after consultation with the lawyer, as to a plea to be entered, whether to waive jury trial and whether the client will testify.

* This means that a criminal defendant gets to decide whether to enter a plea of guilty or not guilty, whether to waive his right to a jury trial, and whether or not to testify. But his lawyer has the authority to take the on-the-ground actions necessary to carry out the representation of his client.

* Lawyers on TV and in the movies are often depicted as attack dogs, and sometimes that's what a client wants. What should a lawyer do if a client says, "Be as aggressive as possible in every situation when representing me?"

* Under Model Rule 1.3, the lawyer is required to represent his client "diligently." The lawyer must "act with commitment and dedication to the interests of the client and with zeal in advocacy upon the client's behalf." But that doesn't mean he has to be unreasonable. It doesn't require him to yell, or to refuse reasonable scheduling requests made by opposing counsel, or to demean other people.

* In fact, acting as an attack dog all the time is not a smart strategy. Judges detest lawyers who squabble over petty things, or who file motion after motion to make opposing counsel's life miserable. Over time, you will lose your good reputation if you are unreasonable.

* A lawyer is not just the representative of his client. He is also an officer of the court—that is, a representative of the legal system as a whole. The Preamble to the Model Rules of Professional Responsibility makes this clear:

> A lawyer should use the law's procedures only for legitimate purposes and not to harass or intimidate others. A lawyer should demonstrate respect for the legal system and for those who serve it, including judges, other lawyers and public officials. While it is a lawyer's duty, when necessary, to challenge the rectitude of official action, it is also a lawyer's duty to uphold legal process.

CLIENT CONFIDENTIALITY

✳ Another important aspect of the attorney-client relationship is the confidentiality of certain communications between the attorney and the client. Under Model Rule of Professional Conduct 1.6, a lawyer is prohibited from revealing "information relating to the representation of a client unless the client gives informed consent, the disclosure is impliedly authorized in order to carry out the representation," or the disclosure is otherwise permitted by the rules.

✳ It is difficult to imagine how any lawyer could properly advise a client if the client were not free to speak candidly. The attorney-client privilege protects the client, who benefits from the lawyer's advice. It also protects the lawyer, who relies on information from his client to do his job properly. And it protects society, which has an interest in the fair administration of justice that, in our adversarial system, depends on the giving and receiving of competent and informed legal advice.

✳ Are there any circumstances in which a lawyer could disclose things his client said, even if his client didn't want him to? Rule 1.6(b) addresses this question. It says that a lawyer can reveal information in circumstances like the following:

- To prevent reasonably certain death or substantial bodily harm;

- To keep the client from committing a crime or fraud that is "reasonably certain" to cause substantial injury to someone else's property or financial interests and in furtherance of which the client used the lawyer's services, or to rectify it if the client's already committed the crime or fraud; or

- To obtain legal advice from another attorney in order to make sure he is properly complying with the rules, or to help him in a dispute with the client about the representation.

★ So what if you were a defense lawyer, and your client confessed that he did it—he committed the crime of which he was accused? Could you reveal that information? Under Rule 1.6, probably not. An attorney has an obligation to keep a client's secrets. If the client said, "I murdered the victim," that's a secret, and it doesn't fall among the things in Rule 1.6(b) that a lawyer can disclose.

★ What if the client tells the attorney, "I murdered the victim," then decides to testify at his own trial, and on the stand says, "I did not murder the victim"? The attorney knows that his client's testimony is false, but also knows that the confession is protected by attorney-client privilege. What should the attorney do? If a lawyer's client, or a witness called by a lawyer, testifies falsely, the Model Rules of Professional Conduct require that the lawyer "take reasonable remedial measures" to correct the perjury—including, if necessary, telling the court about it.

✳ Ethical dilemmas like these also arise in civil lawsuits, where lawyers are also bound by the same rules governing professional conduct. Attorneys in civil suits might find themselves struggling with similar issues—how to manage interpersonal disputes, which strategic calls are theirs to make, and what to do if they discover that a client is using their services to perpetrate fraud.

Suggested Reading

⬦ Cohen, *The State of Lawyer Knowledge*.

⬦ Harr, *A Civil Action*.

⬦ Model Rules of Professional Conduct Rules 1.3, 1.2, 1.6.

Questions to Consider

↗ If you were a lawyer, are there certain defendants you simply would not represent? Why or why not?

↗ Would you always want your lawyer to be as aggressive as possible for you? Are there any downsides to aggression?

REPRESENTING YOUR CLIENT

M any law students imagining their future careers have probably pictured themselves as Atticus Finch in *To Kill a Mockingbird*, a noble crusader fighting to protect an innocent man who is struggling against an unjust system. As we've seen, the role of the lawyer is particularly important in litigation, because the system by which cases are tried is quite complicated. Even the smartest person is likely to have a hard time navigating his way through a trial without a lawyer to help him. He's not going to know whether he was indicted properly, or what the rules of evidence are, or what he's allowed to do or not do in court. But does every defendant really deserve a lawyer? And what does the law require that a lawyer do for a client in the litigation process?

To explore the relationship between lawyer and client, let's consider the case of the *State of Florida v. George Zimmerman*. This case captured the imagination of Americans in 2013, and it was the initial impetus for the movement for civil rights known as Black Lives Matter. The case involved the death of young Trayvon Martin in Sanford, Florida at the hands of George Zimmerman. Here's a disclaimer: I don't have any inside information about George Zimmerman's actual relationship with his lawyers. But some of the things that happened during the case offer insights into the choices and pressures faced by lawyers who represent clients in criminal trials. They also help explain why trials sometimes don't turn out the way the public thinks they should.

To understand the choices confronting Zimmerman's lawyers, you need to be familiar with the events leading up to the case. On the night that Trayvon Martin died, George Zimmerman was living in a gated community in Florida that had experienced burglaries, thefts, and dozens of attempted break-ins. The residents had organized a neighborhood watch program and Zimmerman was the coordinator. On February 26, 2012, Zimmerman was out "on patrol." He wasn't a cop, but he was acting like one, on the lookout for bad behavior. He was in his car when we observed a black teenager wearing a hooded sweatshirt or a "hoodie," and he deemed the teenager to be suspicious. He called the non-emergency police number to report what he was seeing. The dispatcher told Zimmerman to wait in his car for the police to arrive. Zimmerman didn't listen to that instruction. Instead, he left his car, confronted the boy, and ultimately shot and killed him.

That boy was Trayvon Martin, was a 17-year-old high school student who was visiting his father, who lived in the community. He was out after dark because he'd gone to the 7–11 on a snack run, to buy candy and juice. The police arrived at the scene, determined that Zimmerman acted in self-defense, and did not arrest him. The prosecutor also declined to prosecute him. This was because of Florida's self-defense law, which permits the use of deadly force in self-defense. Zimmerman had a bloody nose—it turned out to be broken—and injuries on the back of his head. Plus, an eye-witness said that he saw Martin on top of Zimmerman as the two fought just prior to the shooting. The cops and the prosecutor concluded that Zimmerman was defending himself and so could use lethal force.

But that wasn't the end of the story. Civil rights leaders championed the case, and demonstrators, many of them wearing hoodies, marched in Sanford, Miami, and elsewhere to demand action. The narrative: Zimmerman racially profiled Martin because he was black and was wearing a hoodie, he hunted Martin down, and he killed him. This story made headlines across the country. Even then-President Barack Obama weighed in a month after the shooting, expressing sympathy for Mr. Martin's family and urging a thorough investigation. "If I had a son," Mr. Obama said, "he'd look like Trayvon." Pressure to prosecute George Zimmerman continued to mount. On March 22, 2012, Police Chief Bill Lee, Jr. announced that he would temporarily resign as head of the Sanford police because of criticism over his handling of the Trayvon Martin shooting. Governor Rick Scott of Florida appointed a special prosecutor to bring charges against George Zimmerman. Six weeks after the shooting, Mr. Zimmerman was charged with second-degree murder for the death of Trayvon Martin. That's when Mr. Zimmerman hired Mark O'Mara to be his lawyer.

Things were looking pretty grim for Mr. Zimmerman. Much of the public was sure he was guilty, and he was being accused of something pretty awful—the murder of a boy, motivated by racial animus. Which brings us back to the question, does every defendant deserve a lawyer? And why would a lawyer agree to represent someone like Mr. Zimmerman, one of the most hated men in America at the time? Why would you want to be the lawyer for a "bad guy?"

The answer to all three questions is that we have to have lawyers willing to represent any defendant zealously within the bounds of the law, no matter what that defendant may have done, because that's what our system demands. Many people accept that idea in principle, but still can't stomach the thought of representing a killer or a rapist or a child molester. But remember that America's is an adversarial legal system. That means we resolve legal disputes by assigning a lawyer to each side, and leaving it to the lawyers to ask the right questions, present the proper evidence, and raise appropriate objections. Judges make sure that lawyers, the jurors, and the witnesses are playing their proper roles, but the lawyers are the ones who shape the substance of a trial.

The advantage of a system like this is that the parties have greater incentive than anybody else to gather and present the evidence that supports their respective views of the case. George Zimmerman is going to care more about making sure his side of the story is told properly than anyone else is. If it were up to the judge to develop the factual record, he might not do as thorough a job of it as the parties themselves would do. Also, a judge asked to gather the evidence might develop a bias in favor of or against a party before the trial starts. Our system produces a more complete factual record and helps the judge remain impartial.

But our system is governed by complex rules, and litigants have to make many decisions that have long-lasting consequences. A defendant without a lawyer finds himself at a serious disadvantage. He may not even know where to start to gather evidence. And even someone who is not innocent may have had his rights violated; evidence may have been obtained illegally, or a confession may have been coerced. To make sure that our system is fair and just, we need good defense lawyers to test prosecutions and to make sure that evidence against a defendant was obtained lawfully. We want those lawyers to do the best job possible because we believe that, through the clash of two effective advocates, juries will best be able to winnow out the truth. If a defendant doesn't have a lawyer, it's more likely that the system will malfunction.

Is our system really necessary? There are, after all, plenty of places in the world where there are no lawyers or juries or trials. But that situation can sometimes produce terrible results. For example, a person in such a society might be accused of a heinous crime, and the public—basing its opinions on rumors or erroneous reporting, perhaps—might decide this person is guilty and dispatch justice on its own. The danger, of course, is that the public might have it wrong. An innocent person could be imprisoned or killed for something he didn't do. That's an outcome that our system is designed to try to prevent. As jurist William Blackstone famously remarked in his *Commentaries on the Laws of England* in the 1760s, "It is better that ten guilty persons escape than that one innocent suffer." This is a foundational belief of the American legal system. It is why our law presumes that all people are innocent until proven guilty. We reject mob justice in America, although it has certainly occurred at terrible moments in our history. One of the fundamental objectives of our Constitution is to "establish Justice and insure domestic Tranquility." Trials are a peaceful mechanism for making this happen.

Why not leave justice to the police? Shouldn't we just have a system where the police can decide if someone is guilty? After all, they've seen the evidence firsthand. Again, our society has chosen otherwise, and this goes all the way back to our nation's founding. The U.S. Constitution, Article III, Section 2, guarantees that "The Trial of all Crimes, except in Cases of Impeachment, shall be by Jury." Similarly, the Sixth Amendment states, "In all criminal prosecutions, the accused shall enjoy the right to a speedy and public trial, by an impartial jury." The right to a jury trial is a protection against tyranny, or oppressive power exerted by the government. If we left the determination of guilt up to the police, we would be vesting a great deal of power in a single government actor. Jury trials are a vital part of our system of checks and balances that deliberately limits the power of any particular government body. Police and prosecutors play important roles in bringing charges against a defendant, but the people in the form of a jury, are given the power to make the final determination of the defendant's guilt or innocence.

Well, what if a lawyer thinks that his or her own client is guilty? Should that make a difference in how the lawyer represents him? The answer is a resounding no. It's not up to the lawyer to decide whether the client is guilty or innocent. That determination is up to the jury. If a lawyer were to decide that a client was guilty and therefore did a less thorough job of representing him, there would be two problems. First, the lawyer would be subsuming the role of the jury without giving the client the benefit of a fair trial, which is just the sort of tyranny the Constitution forbids. Second, the lawyer would be violating his or her duty to the client.

Most states have adopted some form of the American Bar Association's Model Rules of Professional Conduct. Rule 1.3 requires a lawyer to "…act with reasonable diligence and promptness in representing a client." The comment to this rule explains: "A lawyer should pursue a matter on behalf of a client despite opposition, obstruction or personal inconvenience to the lawyer, and take whatever lawful and ethical measures are required to vindicate a client's cause or endeavor. A lawyer must also act with commitment and dedication to the interests of the client and with zeal in advocacy upon the client's behalf." That means it doesn't matter if you don't like your client, or think he may have done what he's accused of doing. If you are his lawyer, you have to represent him diligently.

When Mark O'Mara agreed to represent George Zimmerman, he demonstrated his devotion to all of these ideas in spite of widespread hostility towards his new client. O'Mara acknowledged the strong feelings surrounding Trayvon Martin's death at his first press conference after taking the Zimmerman case, but he asked the public to trust the legal process. He said, "So there's a lot of issues, and there's a lot of emotions that we need to calm this down. It needs to be tried in a courtroom, which is the only place it's supposed to be tried...Let the system work—it really, truly...it works."

When reporters asked O'Mara why he had taken on the Zimmerman case, he simply replied, "That's what I do." O'Mara was soon joined by Don West, who left his job as a federal public defender to join the defense team. O'Mara and West were very quickly forced by events to choose how they were going to approach their representation of George Zimmerman. Their decisions raise to important questions: What are the bounds of a lawyer's responsibility in representing a client? And is every lawyer obligated to be as aggressive as possible at all times in furthering a client's interests?

At the same press conference just after he became Zimmerman's lawyer, O'Mara was asked about a statement that had been made by Trayvon Martin's mother, Sybrina, during a television interview. Here is the question posed to O'Mara:

The Reporter said, "What do you make of Sybrina's comments today on the Today Show today, where she said she believes this was an accident...the encounter between Mr. Zimmerman and Trayvon was [an] accident?"

Mr. O'Mara replied, "I look forward to having a conversation with her to see exactly what her feelings are on it. Obviously it was a horrible intersection of two young men's lives and it ended in tragedy. We have to figure out how it happened, why it happened, and who might be responsible for it."

And the reporter pressed. "Really? You won't be using those words against her in the future?"

Mr. O'Mara, you could see displeasure on his face, he said, "This is—they went through a horrible tragedy. They lost their son. We're not gonna be talking about using words against the mother of a deceased child. We're not doing that."

Was is okay for O'Mara to say this? Sybrina Fulton had apparently suggested that the encounter between George Zimmerman and her son was an accident. That seems at odds with the idea that Zimmerman was guilty of murder. Yet Mark O'Mara seems to have promised not to use Sybrina Fulton's words against her at George Zimmerman's trial. Should he have done that? What if George Zimmerman wanted him to use Sybrina's statement?

Let's start with the question of why O'Mara might make the decision not to use Ms. Fulton's words against her as a matter of strategy. Ms. Fulton was the mother of Trayvon Martin. She ultimately was called as a witness for the prosecution at trial to testify that she could hear her son screaming on the 911 call to police during the shooting. She clearly was going to be a sympathetic figure. A defense lawyer needs to be careful cross-examining an innocent witness who has suffered a grievous loss. If the jurors believe that the lawyer is too rough on such a witness, they may dislike the lawyer, and that may damage his client's case.

O'Mara limited his cross-examination to raising the suggestion that Ms. Fulton might have hoped to hear her son calling for the police on the tape, because it would suggest that Trayvon wasn't to blame for his own death. He noted, though, that if instead the voice on the tape was that of George Zimmerman, that could be evidence that Trayvon Martin was attacking him. It made sense for O'Mara to limit his cross to this point. If instead he had tried to get Ms. Fulton to repeat on the stand her belief that the encounter was an accident, he probably wouldn't have succeeded, and he would have looked like a bully. Again, a tactic like that is risky and likely to backfire.

But was it okay for Mark O'Mara to make the decision on his own to declare Ms. Fulton's statement off-limits during the press conference, without first consulting with his client about it? To answer this question, we turn again to the Model Rules of Professional Conduct, which Florida, the jurisdiction in this case, has adopted. Rule 1.2 governs the allocation of authority between client and lawyer. The Rule says, in part: "[A] lawyer shall abide by a client's decisions concerning the objectives of representation and…shall consult with the client as to the means by which they are to be pursued. A lawyer may take such action on behalf of the client as is impliedly authorized to carry out the representation…In a criminal case, the lawyer shall abide by the client's decision, after consultation with the lawyer, as to a plea to be entered, whether to waive jury trial and whether the client will testify." So this means that George Zimmerman gets to decide, after consulting with his lawyer, whether to enter a plea of guilty or not guilty, whether to waive his right to a jury trial, and whether or not to testify. But Mr. O'Mara has the authority to take the "on the ground" actions necessary to carry out the representation of his client.

One of Mark O'Mara's strengths throughout his representation of George Zimmerman was his even-keeled nature. He was tough, diligent, but not vicious. He stayed calm throughout the process, imparting a sense of dignity to the defense. But lawyers on TV or in the movies are often depicted as attack-dogs, and sometimes that's what a client wants. So what should a lawyer do if a client says, "Be as aggressive as possible in every situation when representing me?"

Under Model Rule 1.3, the lawyer is required to represent his client "diligently." The lawyer must "act with commitment and dedication to the interests of the client and with zeal in advocacy upon the client's behalf." But that doesn't mean he has to be unreasonable. It doesn't require him to yell, or to refuse reasonable scheduling requests made by opposing counsel, or to demean other people. The comment to this rule says, "A lawyer is not bound, however, to press for every advantage that might be realized for a client...The lawyer's duty to act with reasonable diligence does not require the use of offensive tactics or preclude the treating of all persons involved in the legal process with courtesy and respect."

In fact, acting as an attack-dog all the time is not a smart strategy. Judges detest lawyers who squabble over petty things such as when to schedule depositions or who file motion after motion to make opposing counsel's life miserable. Over time, you will lose your good reputation if you are unreasonable. It is wise for an attorney to remember that he is not just a representative of a client, he is also an officer of the court; that is, a representative of the legal system as a whole. The Preamble to the Model Rules of Professional Responsibility makes this clear. It says,"A lawyer should use the law's procedures only for legitimate purposes and not to harass or intimidate others. A lawyer should demonstrate respect for the legal system and for those who serve it, including judges, other lawyers and public officials. While it is a lawyer's duty, when necessary, to challenge the rectitude of official action, it is also a lawyer's duty to uphold legal process."

Mark O'Mara didn't act like an attack dog, either in court or with the media, but he did zealously defend his client's interests. For example, he was selective in answering the questions reporters posed about what that George Zimmerman had told him. This raises another important aspect of the relationship between attorney and client: What's confidential and what's not? Under Model Rule of Professional Conduct 1.6, a lawyer is prohibited from revealing "information relating to the representation of a client unless the client gives informed consent, the disclosure is impliedly authorized in order to carry out the representation, or the disclosure is permitted in another part of the rule." This is the well-known attorney-client privilege. It's fundamental to the attorney-client relationship, and to the proper functioning of our legal system.

The Supreme Court, in the 1981 case of *Upjohn Co. v. United States*, described the attorney-client privilege as "the oldest of the privileges for confidential communications known to the common law," existing "to encourage full and frank communication between attorneys and their clients and thereby promote broader public interests in the observance of law and the administration of justice. The privilege recognizes that sound legal advice or advocacy serves public ends and that such advice or advocacy depends upon the lawyers being fully informed by the client."

It is difficult to imagine how any lawyer could properly advise a client if the client were not free to speak candidly. The attorney-client privilege protects the client, who benefits from the advice, and it also protects the lawyer, who relies on receiving information from his client to do his or her job properly. And it protects society, which has an interest in the fair administration of justice that, in our adversarial system, depends on the giving and receiving of competent and informed legal advice. The attorney-client privilege allowed George Zimmerman to tell Mark O'Mara everything about what happened the night that Trayvon Martin died, without worrying that Mr. O'Mara would reveal what he said. It was up to Mr. Zimmerman to decide whether to give Mr. O'Mara permission to repeat the information. The client, Mr. Zimmerman, was the holder of the privilege, so he, not his attorney, got to decide when to disclose privileged information.

Are there any circumstances in which Mr. O'Mara could disclose things Mr. Zimmerman said, even if Mr. Zimmerman didn't want him to? Rule 1.6(b) covers this. It says a lawyer can reveal information in circumstances like these: To prevent reasonably certain death or substantial bodily harm; to keep the client from committing a crime or fraud that is "reasonably certain" to cause substantial injury to someone else's property or financial interests and in furtherance of which the client used the lawyer's services, or to rectify it if the client's already committed the crime or fraud; or to obtain legal advice from another attorney in order to make sure he is properly complying with the rules, or to help him in a dispute with the client about the representation.

So what if you are a defense lawyer, and your client confesses to you that he did it—he committed the crime of which he was accused. Could you reveal that information? Under Rule 1.6, probably not. An attorney has an obligation to keep a client's secrets. If the client said, "I murdered the victim," that's a secret, and it doesn't fall among the things in Rule 1.6(b) that a lawyer can disclose, then you have to keep that secret. Now, if the client said, "I murdered the victim, and tomorrow I plan to murder his brother," then the lawyer could disclose the plan to murder the brother under Rule 1.6(b)(1), because it would "prevent reasonably certain death or substantial bodily harm." But he still couldn't reveal the confession of the initial murder, which happened in the past—that confession is still privileged.

What if the client tells the attorney, "I murdered the victim," then decides to testify at his own trial, and on the stand says, "I did not murder the victim?"

The attorney knows this is a lie, but also knows the confession is protected by attorney-client privilege. What should the attorney do?

This scenario is tricky because it's not just about Rule 1.6. Under Rule 1.6, the attorney can't reveal privileged information. But the attorney is also governed by Rule 1.2(d), which says that a lawyer may not "assist a client in conduct that the lawyer knows is criminal or fraudulent." Also, an attorney is an officer of the court. And Rule 3.3 requires "candor toward the tribunal," providing: "A lawyer shall not knowingly...make a false statement of fact or law to a tribunal or fail to correct a false statement of material fact or law previously made to the tribunal by the lawyer...or...offer evidence that the lawyer knows to be false." So if a lawyer's client, or a witness called by a lawyer, testifies falsely, the rule requires that the lawyer "take reasonable remedial measures" to correct the perjury, including, if necessary, telling the court about it.

So let's imagine you are a lawyer, and your client tells you he committed the crime of which he stands accused. Then he tells you he wants to take the stand and lie about it. What should you do? First, make sure the lie really is a lie. The Rule "does not permit a lawyer to refuse to offer the testimony of such a client where the lawyer reasonably believes but does not know that the testimony will be false. Unless the lawyer knows the testimony will be false, the lawyer must honor the client's decision to testify." If you reasonably believe the testimony is false, but you don't know for sure that it's false, then you can't preclude the client from saying it. Admittedly, this is a gray area that can cause a lawyer sleepless nights.

But let's imagine that you know for sure that the client is going to lie, because the client told you so. Under the rule, you first are supposed to try to persuade your client not to perjure himself. You would want to tell him about the penalties for perjury, and also warn him that as an officer of the court, you can't suborn perjury, meaning that you can't knowingly present his lie as evidence before the court. If that doesn't work, you can try to avoid the sticky situation by asking the court for permission to withdraw from the representation. You might have to do that if you think you can't competently represent the client anymore while still upholding your duty of candor to the court. Rule 1.16 requires a lawyer to withdraw from the representation of a client if, among other things, "the representation will result in violation of the rules of professional conduct or other law," which suborning perjury would. It also permits a lawyer to withdraw from representing a client if "the client persists in a course of action involving the lawyer's services that the lawyer reasonably believes is criminal or fraudulent; ...the client has used the lawyer's services to perpetrate a crime or fraud; ...[or]

the client insists upon taking action that the lawyer considers repugnant or with which the lawyer has a fundamental disagreement."

Withdrawing can be tricky because the lawyer can't tell the judge why he wants to withdraw—he still can't reveal the privileged information. The lawyer can say something like, "Professional considerations require termination of the representation," but not more than that. The judge may order a more frank disclosure, in which case the lawyer could disclose information to the judge under 1.6(b)(6) which says you can disclose things "to comply with...a court order". It would then be up to the judge to decide what to do about the perjury.

But sometimes a court won't let a lawyer withdraw midway through a trial; in that situation, the attorney will have to proceed with the representation, and confront the problem head on. Bear in mind that, if you disclose a client's false testimony, it can destroy your relationship with the client and possibly lead to the client being prosecuted for perjury and losing the criminal case against him. But a lawyer is not permitted to deceive the court. It is vital to the truth-finding process of the adversarial system that lawyers act upon the duty to disclose perjury.

So is a lawyer's job simply to win for his client? As this discussion indicates, that's not the complete picture. The job of an attorney is bigger than that. For example, a prosecutor is charged with "doing justice." He can decide whether or not to bring a charge against a defendant and can call witnesses, introduce evidence, and advocate vigorously, to make those charges stick. But he is also required to disclose evidence favorable to the defense. His job is not simply to win convictions; it is also play his role within the system to unearth the truth.

Similarly, a defense lawyer must advocate within the limits of the law for his client. But he must also serve as an officer of the court, scrupulously upholding the law and his own obligations under the Rules of Professional Conduct. And these obligations don't only hold true in the world of a criminal case, although that's what we've been focused on here—and we'll explore the Zimmerman case further in the future as we examine other aspects of trial practice. Lawyers in a civil lawsuit, which means a dispute between private parties, are bound by the same Rules of Professional Conduct that we've been discussing. They might find themselves struggling with similar issues—how to manage interpersonal disputes, which strategic calls are theirs to make, and what to do if they discover that a client is using their services to perpetrate fraud.

No matter whom they are representing under what circumstances, lawyers have dual responsibilities: to their clients, and to the integrity of the system of justice itself.

TRIAL STRATEGY BEHIND THE SCENES

I n some cases, trials are won or lost because of the lawyering that takes place outside the view of the jury. In this lecture, we will talk about the things that lawyers do before trial, how a jury is selected, and the importance of jury instructions.

BEFORE THE TRIAL

★ A smart lawyer will use the period before trial to gather evidence and plan for the trial. If you represent the plaintiff in a civil case—the party who brings the lawsuit—you would be wise to gather evidence well before you officially file the case. This informal process of gathering facts might include interviewing your client and other witnesses, reading documents and reports related to the dispute, and perhaps consulting with experts who can advise you about your case or testify in court on particular questions of fact.

★ A defense lawyer, however, often doesn't have the opportunity to gather information before a case is filed. After the case is filed, defense lawyers gather information using formal discovery methods. They may also file a number of important pretrial motions.

★ Discovery is the process by which parties gather facts once a lawsuit has been filed. The scope of discovery—the breadth of the things you can ask for—is determined by the rules of the particular jurisdiction you're in. Typically, the applicable rule will say that parties may obtain anything relevant to a party's claims or defenses.

* Discovery results in fairer trials, because it enables lawyers to better defend their clients. Discovery can also encourage settlement. For example, if the state shows during discovery that it has a lot of evidence against a criminal defendant, that defendant might decide to plead guilty—possibly in exchange for a lighter sentence—rather than go through a trial he is most likely going to lose.

* In civil cases, discovery rules generally permit the filing of interrogatories, which are another important discovery tool. Interrogatories are written questions that lawyers use to learn facts about the case, identify possible witnesses, and learn the location of useful documents or other relevant items. Interrogatories must be answered in writing. Answers are given under oath and subject to the penalty of perjury.

* Discovery also includes obtaining documents that might be helpful to the case. In a civil case, most jurisdictions permit the filing of a document request, which is a request to a party in the case to produce identified documents and electronically stored information. The documents have to be described with reasonable particularity, however, which means that a document request can't be a fishing expedition.

* Another important part of discovery is the taking of depositions. A deposition is a question-and-answer session with a potential witness or, in a civil case, with the plaintiff or defendant. A deposition is taken under oath, which means the person being questioned must answer truthfully or be subject to the penalty of perjury. A court reporter transcribes the proceedings, which are sometimes also videotaped.

* Depositions allow attorneys to gather more information about a case. The scope of what you can ask during a deposition is very broad: you can ask anything that might be useful to the case, including questions you couldn't ask at trial because they might be prohibited by the rules of evidence. Opposing counsel appears at the deposition to voice objections for the record, but can rarely prevent the witness from answering the question.

✴ A deposition is a useful way to test out potential witnesses—you can see how people are likely to appear on the stand. And deposition testimony can be used at trial to impeach a witness. If a witness says one thing at a deposition, and then says another at trial, you can read or play the deposition for the jury to show that the witness has contradicted himself.

✴ The pretrial period is also a time for lawyers to file motions about how the case will proceed. These motions may involve discovery disputes, objections to the jurisdiction of the court, objections about evidence or interpretations of the law, and even objections to the judge who will preside over the case.

✴ It's common for a criminal defendant to get to go home for the period before his trial. He can't do this, however, unless he first pays bail or a posts a bond—a financial sum set by the judge to ensure that the defendant will appear at subsequent trial proceedings. The amount is chosen based on considerations like the type of crime at issue and the financial resources of the defendant.

JURY CONSIDERATIONS

✻ The right to a trial by jury is guaranteed by the Sixth Amendment of the Constitution. Although it's often described as an individual right, it's also a right of the people: it makes the citizenry, and not their rulers or the police, the deciders of who did what to whom. Parties can waive the right to a jury trial, and often do, but the right remains important.

✻ The process of jury selection involves lawyers from both sides asking potential jurors questions to ascertain whether they would be appropriate jurors for the case at hand. The questions generally are designed to tease out whether a potential juror has a bias, a connection to the parties or the lawyers, or previous knowledge of the case that would render him unfit to serve.

✻ Potential jurors may be excused from service if the service would cause undue hardship—for example, if the person has a medical issues, or is the sole caretaker of a disabled family member.

✻ After questioning the potential jurors, the attorneys can eliminate people from the pool. They might do this by challenging for cause, which allows the attorneys to eliminate potential jurors who are legally unsuitable to serve. Lawyers also get a limited number of peremptory challenges, which allow them to strike a certain number of jurors for any reason. Peremptory challenges cannot be used in a discriminatory way, however.

✻ The instructions that the jury is given about the law are tremendously important to the outcome of the trial. The lawyers work with the judge to determine what the jury should and should not be instructed to consider. This can be determined before the trial begins, if the trial will be a short one. In a longer trial, these issues are often hashed out later, in a hearing outside of the presence of the jury.

PUBLICITY AND SOCIAL MEDIA

✲ In highly publicized cases, public opinion, media coverage, and social media commentary can all influence the course of the trial. Finding a jury can be particularly tricky in these circumstances. So many people have heard of the events, and formed opinions about the participants, that it can be difficult to find people who are impartial.

✲ Highly publicized trials often have a cultural significance that extends beyond the outcome of the case. This larger cultural significance is as much a product of the traditional and social media that surround the trials as it is of the trials themselves. To adequately represent a client in today's media-saturated landscape, an attorney cannot ignore the media's influence.

Suggested Reading

♦ Mauet, *Pretrial*.

Questions to Consider

➚ Why do some trials capture the public imagination? Were those disputes resolved in trial, or have they continued to live on?

➚ How might an attorney consider media coverage or social media when designing the strategy of her case?

TRIAL STRATEGY BEHIND THE SCENES

Sometimes, trials are won or lost because of the lawyering that takes place outside of the view of the jury. In this lecture, we will talk about the things that lawyers do before trial, how a jury is selected, and the importance of jury instructions. To illustrate, we'll revisit the case of George Zimmerman, who shot and killed Trayvon Martin in Sanford, Florida in 2012. And we'll also consider how media coverage and social media can impact what happens in the courtroom and beyond. Let's start by talking about what happens before a trial starts.

A smart lawyer will use the period before trial to gather evidence and plan for the trial. If you represent the plaintiff in a case—the party who brings the lawsuit—then you would be wise to gather evidence well before you officially file the case. The informal process of gathering facts can include interviewing your client and other witnesses, reading documents and reports related to the dispute, and perhaps consulting with experts who can advise you about your case or testify in court on particular questions of fact. Your search for evidence should be organized around the things that you need to prove to win your case. For example, if your case involves a car accident, you might research what you need to show in your jurisdiction to prove that the defendant—the other driver—was negligent. Maybe that would require you to show that the defendant was travelling above the speed limit. You might talk to your client to ask what he experienced, including whether there were any other witnesses to the accident who might be able to say how fast the defendant was driving. If there were, you would reach out to them, and so forth. People are often willing to provide information even though the case hasn't yet been filed, and this can give you a head start on figuring out what kind of case you want to bring. Maybe you will learn in your investigation that the defendant was actually an unlicensed teenager who was driving the family car unsupervised to run an errand for her mother. So you might decide to bring a lawsuit against both the teen for driving negligently and the parent for negligent supervision. Your investigation may change both the people you decide to sue and your theory of what the case is about.

A defense lawyer, doesn't have the opportunity to gather information before a case is filed. That was the situation confronting George Zimmerman's lawyer, Mark O'Mara, when Zimmerman hired him. As you'll recall, Zimmerman's fateful encounter with Trayvon Martin on the night of February 26, 2012 began when Mr. Zimmerman spotted Martin and decided that he was behaving suspiciously. Trayvon Martin, a 17-year-old boy, was actually returning home after a snack run to the local 7–11, but Zimmerman pursued him and eventually shot him dead. After weeks of public outrage, the state charged Zimmerman with second-degree murder on April 11, 2012. On that same day, Zimmerman hired Mark O'Mara to represent him.

So it was between April 2012 and June 2013, when the trial began, that Zimmerman's lawyers laid the groundwork for Zimmerman's defense. They did this by using formal discovery methods to gather information, and by filing some important pretrial motions. Discovery, as you may know, means the process by which parties gather facts once a lawsuit has been filed. The scope of discovery—the breadth of the things you can ask for—is going to be determined by the rules of the particular jurisdiction you're in, but usually the applicable rule will say that parties may obtain discovery about anything relevant to a party's claim or defense.

In Florida, where the *Zimmerman* case was tried, the defendant gets to choose whether or not to participate in discovery. Mr. Zimmerman's attorneys decided they would like to be able to obtain information through discovery, and filed the required notice saying so. This triggered an obligation by the prosecutor to disclose a bunch of information to the defense: Things like witness lists; copies of witness statements; any written or oral statements made by the defendant in the possession of the state, including statements to the police; any papers or objects that were obtained from or belong to the defendant; information about whether the state has information from a confidential informant; and information obtained from electronic surveillance, so for example, things obtained by wiretapping of the defendant's phone); reports by experts related to the case; and any exhibits the state plans to use in the hearing or at trial. That list, that disclosure obligation, is pretty typical for a criminal case in most jurisdictions. The information, however, comes at a price. In exchange, a defendant in Florida must provide the prosecution with a list of witnesses he expects to call at trial or a hearing; witness statements; reports by experts related to the case; and any exhibits the defense plans to use in a hearing or at trial. Neither side is required to disclose work product, which means things like legal research, lawyers' notes about their theory of the case, and so forth.

As you may have noticed, the disclosure obligation on the prosecution is greater than the obligation on the defense. The point is that prosecutors can't spring surprise evidence on a defendant like you may have seen in a TV show. The government, in the form of the police and the prosecutors, has a lot of power, and we want to be sure that an accused person isn't convicted simply because the state holds all the cards. Disclosure leads to trials that are fairer because it enables lawyers to better defend their clients. Disclosure can also encourage settlement; if the state has a lot of evidence against a defendant and shows that in discovery, that defendant might decide to plead guilty, possibly in exchange for a lighter sentence rather than go through a trial he is certain to lose.

In civil cases, discovery rules generally permit the filing of interrogatories, which are another important discovery tool. Interrogatories are written questions that lawyers use to learn facts about the case and to identify possible witnesses or the location of useful documents or other relevant items. They must be answered in writing, under oath and subject to the penalty of perjury. Interrogatories are less common in criminal cases, because a defendant is protected by the Fifth Amendment of the Constitution from being "compelled in any criminal case to be a witness against himself." So that's an important limit on the power of the state.

Discovery also includes obtaining documents that might be helpful to the case. In a civil case, most jurisdictions permit the filing of a document request, which is a request to a party in the case to produce identified documents and electronically stored information. The documents have to be described with reasonable particularity; so that means a document request can't be a fishing expedition. You can't ask for "all documents related to this case," for example; you have to be more specific than that—perhaps "all documents related to the meeting of the General Motors Board of Directors on January 10, 2006, including but not limited to notes, memoranda, e-mails, letters, minutes"—you get the idea. You want to be careful to think through what documents to ask for. If your requests are too broad, you could find yourself scolded by the judge for ignoring that rule requiring particularity in your description, or alternatively, drowning in a sea of papers. The party producing the documents can't just dump the documents on the party requesting them, they have to be produced in some organized way, such as labelled to correspond with the particular request that elicited them.

Florida's criminal discovery rules required the parties in the Zimmerman case to exchange some documents at the initial stages of discovery, such as witness statements and expert reports. But the attorneys for the defense soon realized that they also wanted documents that were in the hands of third parties. To obtain those, they asked the court to issue a subpoena. A subpoena is a writ compelling someone to testify or produce evidence. For example, George Zimmerman's legal team filed subpoenas for Trayvon Martin's school records, his Twitter and Facebook posts, and his cellphone records. These documents helped them identify potentially useful witnesses and events that could help them with a self-defense claim.

Still another important part of discovery is the taking of depositions. A deposition is a question and answer session with a potential witness or, in a civil case, with the plaintiff or defendant. The defendant in a criminal case isn't likely to be deposed because, again, under the Fifth Amendment, the state can't force him to testify, but it's common for other witnesses to be deposed in a criminal case. A deposition is taken under oath, which means the person being questioned must answer truthfully or be subject to the penalties of perjury. A court reporter transcribes the proceedings, and they're also sometimes videotaped.

A deposition lets the attorney gather more information about the case. The scope of what you can ask during a deposition is very broad—you can ask anything that might be useful to the case, including questions you couldn't ask at trial because they might be prohibited by rules of evidence like hearsay. Opposing counsel appears at the deposition to voice objections for the record, but rarely can he prevent the witness from answering the question. A deposition is a useful way to test out potential witnesses—you can see how people are likely to appear on the stand. And deposition testimony can be used at trial to impeach a witness. If a witness says one thing at a deposition, and then says another at trial, you can read or play the deposition for the jury to show that the witness has contradicted himself. Mark O'Mara took many depositions in the George Zimmerman case, at one point telling the news media that he planned to depose 50 to 75 people.

The pretrial period is also a time for lawyers to file motions about how the case will proceed. These motions could involve discovery disputes, objections to the jurisdiction of the court, objections about evidence or interpretations of the law, or even objections to the judge who will preside over the case.

For example, in the George Zimmerman trial, the judge initially assigned to handle the case disclosed a possible conflict of interest—her husband's law firm had declined to represent Zimmerman, and the lawyer who led the firm was going to serve as CNN's legal commentator about the case. Mark O'Mara filed a motion requesting that the judge recuse herself, which she did. She was replaced by Judge Kenneth Lester, the second judge on the case. But he also ended up being recused. How that happened will give you some sense of the complexities and human emotions that can complicate the pre-trial period.

Here's what happened. On April 8, 2012, before hiring Mark O'Mara, George Zimmerman launched a website for himself, TheRealGeorgeZimmerman.com. The purpose of the site was to raise money for his legal fees, and included a "donate" button linked to a PayPal account. The site raised more than $200,000. Three days after establishing the site, Zimmerman hired O'Mara. Zimmerman then turned himself in and was booked into the Seminole County Jail. It's common for a defendant to get to go home for the period before his trial, but as you probably know, he can't do that unless he first pays bail or a bond—a financial sum set by the judge to ensure that the defendant will appear at subsequent trial proceedings. The amount is chosen based on considerations like the type of crime at issue and how much money the defendant has. Assuming the defendant shows up for all his court dates throughout the trial, the money is returned afterward, although some will be deducted to pay court fees if the defendant is convicted.

Well, because of that PayPal account, George Zimmerman had over $200,000. Mark O'Mara wasn't aware of the PayPal account when he appeared for George Zimmerman's bond hearing on April 20, 2012. George Zimmerman's wife testified that she and her husband had very little money. So Judge Lester set Zimmerman's bond for $150,000, and on April 23, George Zimmerman paid that money and went home. After that, Mark O'Mara learned about the website and the $200,000. O'Mara instructed his client to shut down the site so the lawyers could take control of George Zimmerman's online presence. On April 27th, O'Mara also reported the existence of the site to the court. As an officer of the court, O'Mara had an ethical obligation to correct any misstatement to the court that he had made to the court, and that fell within that obligation.

Mr. Zimmerman's actions offended the judge. On June 1st, the judge revoked George Zimmerman's bond and encouraged the state to file perjury charges against Mr. Zimmerman's wife. The judge chastised Zimmerman, saying he had "flouted" and "tried to manipulate" the system. During the hearing, the judge commented positively about Mr. O'Mara, though, explicitly stating the "misrepresentations" were "not by your fault whatsoever, Mr. O'Mara. You were completely candid and honest with the Court, as you've always been." On July 6th, a new bond was set for Mr. Zimmerman, but this time for a much higher amount: $1 million. A week later, Mark O'Mara filed a motion to disqualify the judge and asking him to recuse himself, citing what he called "gratuitous, disparaging" language in the new bail order.

That must have been a tricky call for Mr. O'Mara. On the one hand, he knew that he himself enjoyed a positive reputation in the eyes of the judge, based on those favorable comments by the judge during the hearing. So filing a motion to disqualify the judge could anger him and sour his opinion of O'Mara, who was likely to appear before Judge Lester again in some future case. On the other hand, it was Mr. O'Mara's job to make sure that the judge overseeing Mr. Zimmerman's trial was impartial, and he must have decided that Judge Lester's negative opinion of Mr. Zimmerman would prejudice him against the defendant. The judge denied the recusal motion, so O'Mara filed a motion for an appeal. The District Court of Appeal granted that motion on August 29, 2012, and Judge Debra Nelson replaced Judge Lester on the case. So it was Judge Nelson who presided over the trial. It is difficult to say whether the change in judge was consequential to the outcome of the trial, but it may have helped Mr. Zimmerman to get away from a judge who thought ill of him.

Once the judge question was settled, the next important players were introduced into the George Zimmerman story—the jury. The right to a trial by jury is guaranteed by the Sixth Amendment of the Constitution. Although it's often described as an individual right, it's also a right of the people: it makes the citizenry, and not their rulers or police, the deciders in a trial of who did what to whom. Parties can waive the right to a jury trial, and often do, but the right remains important.

Jury selection is also called *voir dire*, a phrase derived from Old French that means "to speak the truth." As you will know if you've ever served on a jury, the process involves lawyers from both sides asking potential jurors questions to ascertain whether they would be appropriate jurors for the case at hand. The questions generally are designed to tease out whether a potential juror has a bias, a connection to the parties or the lawyers, or previous knowledge of the case that would render him unfit to serve. Potential jurors may also be excused from service if the service would cause undue hardship. For example, if the person is the sole caretaker of a disabled family member or has a medical issue.

After questioning the potential jurors, the attorneys can eliminate people from the pool. They might do this through "challenging for cause," which means eliminating a potential juror who is legally unsuitable. This might mean the person isn't a U.S. citizen, or doesn't have the mental or physical capacity to sit through and understand the trial, or has a bias that won't let him apply the law impartially. You get an unlimited number of challenges for cause. Lawyers also get a limited number of peremptory challenges, which means you can strike a certain number of jurors for any reason, but you can't use these strikes in a discriminatory way. Lawyers in Florida can't strike jurors solely on the basis of race, gender, religion, or ethnicity.

Five hundred residents of Seminole County, Florida were randomly selected in the George Zimmerman case as potential jurors, and that group was winnowed down to select six jurors—the standard size for a Florida jury—as well as four alternates. It proved difficult to find jurors who hadn't heard about the case. The potential jurors were asked questions about their exposure to it, and most admitted that they were aware of it. For example, one potential juror said that one of the few times he'd watched the news was to see himself after he was interviewed by a TV reporter about Trayvon Martin.

As you can imagine, lawyers take care during jury selection to make sure that the jury is composed of people who will give their client's case fair consideration. The jury that was ultimately chosen in the George Zimmerman trial was made up of six women, none of them black. There's no evidence at all that the lawyers did anything impermissible in choosing this jury, but the gender and racial imbalance in the jury did receive extensive public comment. The jurors remained anonymous throughout the George Zimmerman trial, and were sequestered, as is sometimes required in high-profile cases. They were kept together for 22 nights at a hotel to prevent outside influence. They lived away from their families, and their television, internet use, reading materials, mail, and phone calls were screened to make sure they weren't exposed to anything that could affect the trial.

Not only is the composition of the jury tremendously important to the outcome of a trial, so are the instructions that the jury is given about the law. The lawyers work with the judge to determine what the jury should and should not be instructed to consider. This can be determined before the trial begins if the trial will be a short one, but in a case like George Zimmerman's, this may be hashed out in a hearing outside of the presence of the jury during or toward the end of the period when the case is being tried.

George Zimmerman was accused of second degree murder. As the court stated, it is the "unlawful killing of Trayvon Martin by an act imminently dangerous to another and demonstrating a depraved mind without regard for human life." In the alternative, he was accused of manslaughter—that is, the non-negligent killing of Trayvon Martin. However, the judge also instructed the jury that Zimmerman could not be found guilty of either second degree murder or manslaughter if the killing was either "justifiable or excusable homicide."

If George Zimmerman acted in self-defense, then his use of deadly force was justifiable under Florida law. The judge explained, "A person is justified in using deadly force if he reasonably believes that such force is necessary to prevent imminent death or great bodily harm to himself." Florida also has adopted a "Stand Your Ground" law, which is a law promoted by the National Rifle Association that now exists in about two dozen states. Stand Your Ground allows people to use deadly force in particular situations when they believe their lives are at risk. Stand Your Ground in Florida can also trigger a special hearing, which the defense ended up waiving in this case. The "Stand Your Ground" instruction the judge gave the jury was as follows: "If George Zimmerman was not engaged in an unlawful activity and was attacked in any place where he had a right to be, he had no duty to retreat and had the right to stand his ground and meet force with force, including deadly force, if he reasonably believed that it was necessary to do so to prevent death or great bodily harm to himself or another or to prevent the commission of a forcible felony."

But what if George Zimmerman started the fight? Worse, what if he did so for a despicable reason—racial animus?

Florida law contains an initial aggressor exception to the self-defense protection. If you are the person who started the fight, then you can't claim self-defense. But the jury received no instruction about the initial aggressor exception. This was because the defense argued persuasively to the judge that the exception should not apply and the instruction should not be included. They based their argument on a 2001 decision from the Florida Court of Appeals called *Gibbs v. State*, which held that a defendant loses the right to self-defense as an initial aggressor only if he provokes the victim's use of force through either force or "threat of force." The defense argued to the judge that there was no evidence that Mr. Zimmerman physically initiated the confrontation, and that following someone on foot or by car cannot be considered provocation under the law. Here's what defense attorney Don West said, "Well, let me point out, as a matter of law, following someone on foot or by car is not against the law...That cannot be considered provocation under the law…Force means physical force or the threat of physical force…It would be error, and frankly, promoting miscarriage of justice, if the state were allowed to argue that to the jury."

This is an example of the power of precedent. The court in *Gibbs v. State* interpreted the phrase "threat of force" in the initial aggressor statute, and what the *Gibbs* court said became part of the law. It meant that the judge in the Trayvon Martin case was bound to follow it. If the *Gibbs v. State* opinion did not exist, the judge in the Trayvon Martin case might have decided that a "threat of force" could include following someone on foot or by car. But the precedent did exist, and so the jury was not permitted to consider whether George Zimmerman was the initial aggressor. As we will see, the jury instructions in the Zimmerman trial proved to be crucial for the outcome of the case.

As the drama of the Zimmerman trial unfolded in the courtroom, an intense and often bitter national debate about it was underway outside. Let's take a few moments to consider what happened as a way of exploring how public opinion, media coverage, and social media commentary can influence the course of a trial.

There can be no doubt that public opinion shaped the George Zimmerman trial from the beginning. The police did not arrest George Zimmerman on the night Trayvon Martin died, and the state at first declined to prosecute because they believed Zimmerman's statement that he had acted in self-defense. But after the public became outraged about the events, the police chief ultimately lost his job, the prosecutor stepped aside, and a special prosecutor was brought in specifically to bring George Zimmerman to trial. The pressure to prosecute came from the public—from Trayvon Martin's family, who told their story in press conferences and over social media; from civil and religious leaders, who held protests and galvanized supporters; and from thousands of average citizens, who gathered in rallies to agitate for justice. It seems unlikely that the governor would have appointed a special prosecutor or formed a task force to review Florida self-defense law without this public pressure.

Public opinion was a concern for Zimmerman's lawyer, Mark O'Mara, from the beginning of his representation as well. During his first press conference, O'Mara spoke of the need to tamp down the heated emotions surrounding the case because he feared that this would impede the proper functioning of justice. And as we've seen, it was tricky to find a jury for this case. So many people had heard of the events and had formed opinions about George Zimmerman, that it was difficult to find people who were impartial.

George Zimmerman's use of social media also proved problematic for his case at first. We've talked about how set up a website for himself to raise money for his legal fees. That in itself wasn't the problem, but the fact that he didn't disclose it affected the judge's view of him and created extra work for his legal team. Interestingly, Mark O'Mara then decided to set up his own website for Zimmerman, called GZLegalcase.com. He also used Facebook and Twitter in an effort to humanize his client. This was a pretty unusual step, but resulted in his being able to raise additional funds to pay for Zimmerman's legal representation. O'Mara also hired a digital media manager to oversee these efforts, and used interns to monitor what people were saying about the case online. Mr. O'Mara said, "You have to know what people are saying. It could contain some nugget of truth."

The prosecution is often not allowed to say much of anything about a case, and the prosecutor in the Zimmerman case asked the court for a gag order to shut down O'Mara's website, arguing that it could influence potential jurors. But O'Mara argued that the state had already benefitted from media coverage about the case, and that his website was necessary to combat this influence. "What we have done is deal with a case that when it got to my doorstep is already in the throes of an enormous, overriding, tidal wave of misinformation." The court sided with O'Mara.

There is no evidence that the media coverage, social media, or Mark O'Mara's website directly influenced the jury's eventual decision. Indeed, the jury was sequestered to prevent exactly this kind of influence. But a website that can help a defendant defray the cost of litigation can play a significant role in the outcome of a trial. Moreover, trials can have a cultural significance that extends beyond the outcome of the case, and that may be of concern to a client, whether because it affects his reputation, or because he has views on broader social issues that are involved in his case. The Zimmerman case has come to stand for many things: an example of the consequences of the "Stand Your Ground" law, evidence to some that guns are too widespread in America, the genesis of the Black Lives Matter movement. The larger cultural significance of the case is as much a product of the traditional and social media that surrounded it as of the trial itself. To adequately represent a client in today's media-saturated landscape, an attorney cannot ignore the media's influence.

OPENING STATEMENTS: THE MOMENT OF PRIMACY

The opening statement by an attorney in a trial is a crucial opportunity. It represents the attorney's first chance to connect with the jurors and create a lasting impression in their minds of what the case is really about. Preparing an effective opening statement takes careful thought, however, and there are strict limits on what the attorney can say.

THE BASICS

* An attorney's opening statement should be constructed around her theory of the case—that is, what the case is really about, and why her client should prevail.

* The opening statement is a bit like a table of contents: It orients the jurors to the nature of the dispute, who the witnesses are that they're going to see, and what each side is trying to prove. The lawyers then fill in the actual story of the case during the trial, using witness testimony and other pieces of evidence.

* Imagine what a trial would be like if there were no opening statements. A lawyer could begin by calling a witness, who might be able to testify about a fact or two, but the jury would have no idea why the testimony was significant or how it fit into the big picture of the case.

* If the only purpose of an opening statement were orientation, a simple sequence of events and a list of witnesses would be enough. But that's not enough. An opening statement must also grab jurors' attention.

* The first few lines of an opening statement come at an important moment psychologically: the moment of primacy. The moment of primacy is the one time you can be sure that the jury is listening attentively, so you should start with the things that you want them to remember most.

ESTABLISHING ETHOS

* Jurors are usually a little nervous at the outset of a trial, wondering what is going to happen, and feeling the weight of their roles in the process. They're looking for guidance. They're trying to find out whom they can believe—who the "good guys" are. As a lawyer, you want to be one of those good guys. Your first impression must be a good one.

* The opening statement is an exercise in persuasion, and the character of the speaker counts. Aristotle, the father of classical rhetoric, referred to this concept as ethos—persuasion based on the character of the speaker.

* Tone is central to establishing ethos. In the heat of battle, a trial lawyers may be tempted to adopt an aggressive, sarcastic tone. This is a mistake, particularly during the opening statement, when the jurors don't yet know the lawyer. A tone of conviction and credibility is more likely to gain trust than an overheated one.

* At the same time, you don't want to go too far in the other direction—you don't want to be a bully, but you also don't want to seem like a pushover. If you are apologetic, or excessively polite, or if you mumble, hesitate, fumble with visual aids, and use passive body language, the jury will believe you lack confidence in your case and yourself. A wise lawyer will practice his opening statement, including how he will interact with any visual aids he might use, so that he can project self-assurance.

* Another key to establishing ethos is not to exaggerate. It's too easy to disprove an inflated claim, especially one that's offered in an overheated way. You can be sure that opposing counsel will point out the discrepancy. If the jury realizes that you were misleading them about evidence, your credibility will suffer, and so will your client's.

* It is a good practice to identify any facts that are bad for your case. If you know that opposing counsel is aware of them and is likely to mention them, you can lessen their impact by mentioning them first. You should spend most of your time in your opening statement emphasizing the good facts that help you. If you do, mentioning a bad fact as part of the story rather than leaving it out altogether will actually help you stay credible.

PERSUADING WITH PATHOS

* To be persuasive, you must figure out how to get the jury emotionally invested in your client and your case. This is Aristotle's second element of persuasion, a concept he referred to as pathos—engaging the emotions of your audience effectively.

* As a lawyer, you need to figure out how to explain your client's view of events through a believable and compelling story that jurors can identify with. In other words, it's not enough just to present your theory of the case—you need to get the jurors to relate to your client's point of view.

＊ Let's say, for example, that you represent a company that is suing another one for violating a contract that the two companies previously signed. Many lawyers might present their theory of the case by saying something like, "This is a case about a breach of contract." That's an accurate statement, and it is pithy, so it's a good first step. But there are no human beings in that version, and you can't tell who did what to whom. It also contains jargon. Some people don't know what "breach of contract" means, nor do they care.

＊ It's better to look for some people to put into the story. You might instead say something like, "This is a case about Laurie Kind, who owns a small craft store in town, and about the fire insurance company that broke its promise to her and let her down when she needed it most." Now your theory of the case has some heart to it, the jurors know who did what to whom, and you even have a theme—broken promises— that you can use to drive your theory home.

BUILDING WITH LOGOS

✴ The impressions that one makes in the first moments of an opening statement are vital, and connecting with the jury emotionally is essential. But of course, an effective opening statement and an effective case depend, at the most basic level, on logic. If a case makes no sense, a jury is unlikely to buy it. Aristotle referred to this concept as logos—persuasion based on sound logic.

✴ Logos is especially important in an opening statement, because, strange as it may seem, you aren't allowed to argue in an opening statement. You can offer the jury a preview of the facts you expect to bring out in the course of the trial, and of the witnesses who will testify, but you aren't permitted to tell the jury what you think the facts mean, or to suggest any conclusion or inference from them.

✴ It is difficult, but not impossible, to make a persuasive opening statement without arguing. The best lawyers do it by lining up the facts so that their meaning is obvious. The jury can then see the theory of the case for themselves. This takes practice, however. Even experienced lawyers struggle with it.

✴ Good logos requires structure. If the structure is clear—if you've thought about what you really want to convey—it's more likely that the audience will absorb what you hope to communicate. In an opening statement, the structure is largely driven by the theory of the case. That might mean that the parties in the case start with completely different parts of the story.

✴ Let's say, for example, that you are a prosecuting attorney in a criminal case. Your story might start with events leading up to the crime that show the defendant's motive. Or it might start with the crime itself, to grab the jury's attention. If you are the defense lawyer, your theory of the case may be that the police lab made a mistake in processing the evidence. In that instance, you might start with a description of the police lab and what happens there.

✷ Good logos also demands that you pay attention to what you want to include in your opening statement and what you want to leave out. One thing you should leave out is any evidence that the jury doesn't really need to consider yet. Likewise, you should omit anything that you can't actually introduce into evidence. The opening statement is supposed to be an overview of the facts that you're going to prove. If you know you won't be able to bring something into evidence—perhaps because you don't have a witness, or because of a pretrial ruling by the judge—you can't talk about it.

✷ Another tricky logos issue in opening statements is the danger of opening up evidence for the other side. If you've carefully filed a pretrial motion in which you successfully persuaded the judge to prohibit some type of evidence, you could undo all that good work if you end up mentioning that evidence yourself. That will give opposing counsel the right to present it in order to rebut your claim.

Suggested Reading

⟡ Mauet, *Trial Techniques and Trials.*

Questions to Consider

↗ How is an opening statement similar to any persuasive speech, and how does it differ?

↗ Aristotle wrote that persuasion requires credibility, emotional engagement, and logic (ethos, pathos, and logos, respectively). Do you agree? Which element do you think is the most important?

OPENING STATEMENTS: THE MOMENT OF PRIMACY

The opening statement by an attorney in a trial is a crucial opportunity. It represents his or her first chance to connect with the jurors and create a lasting impression in their minds of what the case is really about. But preparing an effective opening statement takes careful thought, and there are strict limits on what the attorney can say. To get a sense of what works and what doesn't in an opening statement, let's return to the case of the *State of Florida v. George Zimmerman*. This is the case we've looked at previously, in which Zimmerman shot and killed young Trayvon Martin, a 17-year-old boy in Sanford, Florida, in 2012. As you'll recall, the case captured the public imagination and ultimately became the impetus for the Black Lives Matter movement.

The prosecution in the George Zimmerman case was trying to prove that Zimmerman was guilty of second degree murder, or, failing that, manslaughter. The Florida statute governing murder defines second degree murder as follows: "The unlawful killing of a human being, when perpetrated by any act imminently dangerous to another and evincing a depraved mind regardless of human life, although without any premeditated design to effect the death of any particular individual." In the jury instructions at the end of the trial, the judge explained that a killing demonstrates a depraved mind it if it "done from ill will, hatred, spite or an evil intent."

So keep that in mind—the prosecution is trying to show ill will, hatred, spite or an evil intent on Zimmerman's part. In this lecture, actors will read the words the lawyers spoke in court. So here's how John Guy, the prosecutor, begins, making reference to Zimmerman as he speaks:

"Good morning. 'Fucking punks. These assholes; they always get away.' Those were the words in that grown man's mouth as he followed in the dark a 17-year-old boy who he didn't know. And excuse my language, but those were his words, not mine. 'Fucking punks. These assholes; they always get away.' Those were the words in that man's chest when he got out of his car, armed with a fully loaded semi-automatic pistol and two flashlights, to follow on foot Trayvon Benjamin Martin, who was walking home from a 7–11, armed with 23 ounces of Arizona brand fruit juice and a small bag of Skittles candies. 'Fucking punks. These assholes; they always get away.' Those were the words in that defendant's head, just moments before he pressed that pistol into Trayvon Martin's chest and pulled the trigger. And then, as the smoke and the smell of that fatal gunshot rose into a rainy Sunday, Sanford night, Trayvon Martin, 21 days removed from his 16th year was face down in wet grass, laboring through his final breaths on this earth, and that defendant, at that same time, was upright, walking around, preparing, preparing to tell law enforcement why he had just profiled, followed, and murdered an unarmed teenager."

Now that is a vivid opening statement! The prosecutor paints a picture with his words—the rainy Sunday night, the wet grass, the smell of the gunshot, the contrast between a boy with candy and fruit juice lying face-down, contrasted with the "grown man," "upright, walking around, preparing," "profiling" and "murdering." The expletives that Mr. Guy quotes seem to convey anger and hostility on Zimmerman's part. It's all disturbing information, and it's the foundation of what the prosecution ultimately will argue at the end of the case—that from Zimmerman's actions and words, the jury can conclude that he was motivated by ill will, hatred, spite, or an evil intent. Mr. Guy creates that impression because it supports what he's going to have to prove to win the case. At the heart of an attorney's choices in constructing an opening statement is his or her theory of the case—that is, what the case is really about, and why his or her client should prevail. In a sense, the opening statement is a bit like a table of contents, it orients the jurors to the nature of the dispute, who the witnesses are that they are going to see, and what each side is trying to prove. And then the lawyers fill in the actual story of the case during the trial through witness testimony and other pieces of evidence.

You can imagine what a trial would be like if we didn't have opening statements. A lawyer could begin by calling a witness, who might be able to testify about a fact or two, but the jury would have no idea why the testimony was significant or how it fit into the big picture of the case. For example, in the *Zimmerman* case, the first witness the prosecution called was a boy who was playing video games with Trayvon Martin the night he died—the same boy for whom Trayvon bought the Skittles. Without the benefit of the prosecution's opening statement, the jurors might have scratched their heads over that witness, thinking "Why are we listening to this 7th grader? Did he have something to do with the shooting?" But because Mr. Guy mentioned the boy in another part of his opening statement, the jurors knew exactly who he was when he took the witness stand, and when he mentioned the Skittles, that moment popped.

If orientation were all that an opening statement is about, though, a simple sequence of events and a list of witnesses would be enough. Consider how you reacted to Mr. Guy's opening statement. I bet it really grabbed your attention. It was clearly designed to make the jurors sit up in their seats. You want to do that with the first paragraph of an opening statement, or really with the first paragraph of any effective speech. That first moment is an important one psychologically. It's called the moment of primacy. It's the one time when you can be sure that the jury is listening attentively. As the trial goes on, the jurors are going to get tired. Attentions will wander, and the jurors may tune out what the lawyers say. But not during the very first moment of the trial. You know for sure they're paying attention then, so you want to start with the things that you want them to remember most. So often, though, a lawyer will feel nervous when the trial is starting. It's tempting to try to comfort yourself by easing your way into the opening statement with some pleasantries, or some other unnecessary wind-up. This is a mistake—you are wasting the impact of the moment of primacy.

Let me show you what I'm talking about with another famous case: the trial of O.J. Simpson. In case you missed the massive news coverage that the case garnered, O.J. Simpson was a star football player who was accused of murdering his ex-wife, Nicole Brown Simpson, and her friend, a waiter named Ronald Goldman. O.J.'s fame would have attracted great media attention by itself, but O.J. was African American and the two murder victims were white, so the case ignited a public debate on race and justice in the United States. Listen to how the prosecution began its opening statement in O.J.'s highly charged criminal trial:

"Your Honor, Judge Ito, Mr. Cochran and Mr. Shapiro and Dean Uelmen, and to my colleagues seated here today in front of you and to the real parties in interest in this case, the Brown family, the Goldman family, and the Simpson family and to you, ladies and gentlemen of the jury, good morning. I think it's fair to say that I have the toughest job in town today except for the job that you have. Your job may just be a little bit tougher. But your job, and like my job, both have a central focus, a single objective, and that objective is justice obviously. It's going to be a long trial and I want you to know how much we appreciate your being on the panel. We appreciate the personal sacrifices you're making by being sequestered. We understand that can be difficult."

Are you on the edge of your seat? Seven sentences into its opening statement, the prosecution still hasn't said a thing about its theory of the case. The jury could be excused for being bored already. Not all material that grabs the jury's attention is good material, however. Let's go back to Mr. Guy's opening in the trial of George Zimmerman. His use of Mr. Zimmerman's profanities also grabbed your attention I bet, but it was a risky choice. Mr. Guy made the point that those were the words of Mr. Zimmerman, not his. Fair enough. But he repeated the profanity several times, and to some ears that can seem like too much—too heavy-handed, or maybe just too unpleasant. The risk is that the jurors will decide they don't like Mr. Guy, because he is banging them over the head with that repeated profanity.

Keep in mind that jurors are usually a little nervous at the outset of a trial, wondering what is going to happen, and feeling the weight of their roles in this process. They are looking for guidance on what's about to happen and whom they can believe, who the "good guys" are. As a lawyer presenting a case, you want to be one of those good guys. You want your first impression on the jury to be a good one. Why? Because the opening statement is an exercise in persuasion, and the character of the speaker counts. Aristotle, who is the father of classical rhetoric, wrote about how important that positive impression can be. In a book called *The Rhetoric*, he said, "Persuasion is achieved by the speaker's personal character. We believe good men more fully and more readily than others. There are three things which inspire confidence in the orator's own character: Good sense, good moral character, and good will."

Aristotle's concept of persuasion based on the character of the speaker is known as ethos. Tone is central to achieving good ethos. In the heat of the battle of a trial, lawyers sometimes will adopt an aggressive, sarcastic tone. This is a mistake, particularly during the opening statement. Again, the jury doesn't know you yet. You have to earn their trust, and a tone of conviction and credibility is more likely to gain trust than an overheated one. At the same time, you also don't want to go too far in the other direction. While you don't want to be a bully, you also don't want to seem like a pushover. If you are apologetic or excessively polite or if you mumble, hesitate, fumble with visual aids, and use passive body language, the jury will believe you lack confidence in your case and yourself. A wise lawyer will practice his opening statement, including how he will interact with any visual aids he might use, so that he can project self-assurance. And by the way, those tips are actually useful to any public speaker, not just lawyers.

Another key to establishing ethos: you cannot exaggerate. It can be tempting during the opening statement to puff a little, to stretch facts or leave out bad facts entirely. But that, too, is a mistake. It's too easy to disprove an inflated claim, especially one that's offered in an overheated way. If you say that your client is an exemplary person, for example, but the other side's attorneys have witnesses who will testify that the guy cheated on his wife, dodged his creditors, and abused his pets, then you can be sure that opposing counsel will point out the discrepancy. If the jury realizes you were misleading them about evidence, your credibility will suffer, and so will your client's.

In fact, Mr. Guy's use of profanity in his opening statement turned out to be an exaggeration. Mr. Zimmerman didn't say exactly what Mr. Guy said he said— Mr. Guy was quoting two separate parts of George Zimmerman's conversation with a 911 dispatcher. At one point Mr. Zimmerman talks about punks; at another, he complains about them getting away. Moreover, his tone on the tape is more frightened than aggressive. So, of course, Mr. Zimmerman's lawyers played that tape for the jury and made the point that the prosecutor exaggerated about them in his opening. That became an ethos problem for the prosecutor.

It is a good practice to identify any facts that are bad for your case. If you know that opposing counsel is aware of them and is likely to mention them, you can draw the sting or lessen their impact by mentioning them first. Make sure you spend most of your time in your opening statement emphasizing the good facts that help you. If you do, mentioning a bad fact as part of the story rather than leaving it out altogether will actually help you stay credible. That's much better than omitting the bad fact and giving opposing counsel the opportunity to say, "Here's what that lawyer didn't tell you."

In spite of the issue with profanity, Mr. Guy's opening statement was really quite good. It was so good, in fact, that it seems to have caused Mr. Zimmerman's lawyers to feel like they needed to do something to break the spell the prosecutor had cast. And so Don West, one of the defendant's attorneys, opened in very strange way—with a knock-knock joke. See what you think of this excerpt from his moment of primacy:

"I think the evidence will show that this is a sad case, that there are no monsters here. Sometimes you have to laugh to keep from crying. So let me, at considerable risk, let me say, I'd like to tell you a little joke. I know how that may sound a bit weird, in this context under these circumstances. But I think you're the perfect audience for it. As long as you don't—if you don't like it or you don't think it's funny or inappropriate, that you don't hold it against Mr. Zimmerman. You can hold it against me if you want, but not Mr. Zimmerman. I have your assurance you won't. Here's how it goes:

Knock knock.
Who's there?
George Zimmerman.
George Zimmerman who?
All right, good, you're on the jury.

Whatever your reaction to West's joke, the jury's response was dead silence. What was he trying to do? He was trying to get the jury to like him by getting them to laugh at a joke—it's an attempt to use a positive emotion to connect. But it badly misfired. Nobody laughed. The joke wasn't appropriate—after all, a murder is no laughing matter—and in fact, the joke was at the expense of the jury. It implied that the only qualification to be on that jury was to be so clueless that you didn't know who George Zimmerman was. A good rule of thumb: If you find yourself preemptively apologizing for a joke, or worrying aloud that it could be used against your client, it's probably not a good idea.

That impulse to connect with the jury by engaging them is a good one, though, even though West's execution was clumsy. To be persuasive, you must figure out how to get the jury emotionally invested in your client and your case. This is Aristotle's second rule of persuasion. He said, not only do you have to exhibit ethos, or credibility, you also need to use pathos—that is, you need to engage the emotions of your audience effectively. As a lawyer, you need to figure out how to explain your client's view of events through a believable and compelling story that jurors can identify with. In other words, you don't only need to present your theory of the case, you need to get the jurors to relate to your client's point of view.

Let's say you represent a company that is suing another one for violating a contract that the two companies previously signed. Many lawyers might present their theory of the case by saying something like, "This is a case about a breach of contract." That's an accurate statement, and it's pithy, so it's a good first step. But there are no human beings in that version, and you can't tell who did what to whom. It also contains jargon. Some people don't know what "breach of contract" means, nor do they care. Some people don't care about breaches, or contracts, and very often they don't care about companies. People tend to care most about other people.

So it's better to look for some people to put into the story. Let's imagine that one of the companies is a craft shop owned by a woman named Laurie Kind.

The other is a fire insurance company that sold Ms. Kind a policy; the company agreed to compensate Ms. Kind for damages in the event of a fire. There's been a fire, and now the insurance company refuses to pay. You are representing the craft store, and you want to tell a story that includes people and makes clear who did what. So now your theory of the case is, "This is a case about Laurie Kind, who owns a small craft store in town, and about the fire insurance company that broke its promise to her and let her down when she needed it most." Now you have a theory of the case with a heart to it, and you even have a theme that you could use to drive that theory home: broken promises. Much better.

The prosecutors in O.J. Simpson's criminal trial had two terrific themes that they wove through everything they did in the case. The first seems to have been taken straight from Shakespeare's *Othello*. Here's what prosecutor Marcia Clark said about O.J. in her opening statement: "He killed for a reason almost as old as mankind itself. He killed her out of jealousy. He killed her because he couldn't have her. And if he couldn't have her, he didn't want anybody else to have her. He killed her to control her." That's a great theme. People make movies with themes like that. The prosecution's second theme? This is a case about a man who is so rich and famous that he thinks the rules of normal human behavior don't apply to him. That's the idea of hubris in Greek tragedy. If the great Greek playwrights wrote about it, it's probably a good theme.

But Johnnie Cochran, who represented O.J., had an even better theme. He chose one that the jury could accept even if it wasn't sure whether O.J. was guilty of murder. Cochran's theme: This is a case of, and I'll quote him here, "A "rush to judgment, an obsession to win at any cost and by any means necessary." So Cochran argues that this is a case about a racist cop, a cop named Mark Fuhrman, who hates O.J. so much because of the color of his skin that he has no problem planting evidence, tainting evidence, to get O.J. thrown into jail. He introduced this theme in his opening statement, and its real power became clear during the most memorable moment in the trial, when the prosecution made O.J. try on the bloody glove that had been used in the commission of the crime, and it didn't fit. The implication was that the glove couldn't have been O.J.'s, and must have been planted on his property to make him look guilty. That gave Cochran the perfect refrain to use in his closing argument to drive home his theme: "If it doesn't fit, you must acquit." Great theme.

The impressions that one makes in the first moments of an opening statement are vital, and connecting with the jury emotionally is essential, but of course, an effective opening statement and an effective case depend, at the most basic level, on logic. If a case makes no sense, a jury is unlikely to buy it. Aristotle identified logos, or sound logic, as the third key element of verbal persuasion. It's especially important in an opening statement, because, strange as it may seem, you are not allowed to argue during an opening statement. That's right, you are simply supposed to offer the jury a preview of the facts you expect to bring out in the course of the trial, and of the witnesses who will testify. You are not permitted to tell the jury what you think the facts mean, or to suggest any conclusion or inference from them. That's not considered appropriate until you have presented your evidence. And yet, as I said earlier, an opening statement is an exercise in persuasion. So how does a lawyer persuade without arguing?

The best lawyers line up the facts so that their meaning is obvious, and the jury can see their theory of the case for themselves. I use opening statements as logic exercises in the classes that I teach at the University of Virginia School of Law. If a student can line up evidence so that the conclusion is clear, without reaching for the crutch of impermissible connective explanations, then you know she really understands the logic of the case. It takes practice, though. The prohibition against arguing in an opening statement is a peculiar constraining rule because we draw conclusions from things in normal conversation all the time. It's perfectly natural in everyday life to comment on facts by saying things like, "That's not fair," or "That doesn't make sense," or "I don't believe that." But even hinting that the opposing counsel's case lacks credibility is forbidden in an opening statement. Even experienced lawyers struggle with it.

For example, we've talked about how prosecutor Marcia Clark argued in her opening statement that O.J. killed Nicole Brown Simpson to control her. In that statement, she was drawing a conclusion about the evidence, so it was technically impermissible argument. Opposing counsel didn't make an objection at that moment so the judge didn't stop it, but he did a few sentences later, when Ms. Clark continued. She said, "You are going to have to be ever vigilant in acting as the judges in this case. Each one of you is a judge. Each one of you is a trier of fact. You have to examine all the evidence very carefully and ask yourselves, 'Is this reasonable? Is this logical? Does this make sense? Would I look at this evidence the same way?'...We must all be equal in the eyes of the law and we cannot use a sliding scale to judge guilt or innocence based on a defendant or a victim's popularity."

Again, this is impermissible argument—the attorney is talking about how to make sense of and weigh the evidence, not laying out what the evidence will show. And so Johnnie Cochran interrupted with an objection. The judge responded, "Sounds like argument to me...Counsel, this has all been argument for the last five minutes." By the way, Johnnie Cochran's opening statement also contained impermissible argument that drew an admonition from the judge—both sides had trouble avoiding argument.

So what does it sound like when a lawyer lines up facts to point toward the conclusion he wants the jury to reach, without employing argument? Here's a good example from another part of the prosecution's opening statement in the O.J. trial that starts to build the case against O.J. It refers to a witness named Brian "Kato" Kaelin, who was living in a guest house on O.J. Simpson's property on the night of the murders. The prosecution said, "And so, the evidence will prove that Kato last saw the defendant on the night of June the 12th at 9:35 at the latest. He did not see the defendant again until after 11:00. In between those two times, at 10:15, a dog is heard barking that the evidence will show was Nicole's dog, which fixes the time at which the murder occurred. At 10:45, Kato heard thumps on his wall and shortly after 11:00, he saw the defendant. An hour and 10 minutes, during which the murders occurred, in which the defendant's whereabouts are unaccounted for."

Do you see how the facts here tell a story and point to the guilt of the defendant? But each fact recited by the prosecutor was going to be testified to by a witness. That's a good test for whether something is impermissible argument. Do you have a witness you're going to put on the stand to testify to this fact? If so, then it's usually okay. If instead you're telling the jury what the facts mean, that's probably argument. A good lawyer will draw these conclusions in her closing argument, which we'll discuss in the future—but they are not allowed in an opening statement.

If it's not obvious, a good prosecutor needs to organize the facts in her opening statement carefully. Good logos, or logic, requires structure. If the structure is clear—if you've thought about what you really want to convey—then it's more likely the audience will absorb what you hope to communicate. In an opening statement, the structure is largely driven by the theory of the case. That might mean that the parties in the case start with completely different parts of the story. For example, if you are the prosecution in a criminal case, your story might start with the events leading up to the crime that show the defendant's motive, or perhaps you start with the crime itself because that's going to be attention-grabbing. If you are the defense lawyer, your theory of the case may be that the police lab made a mistake in processing the evidence. So you might start with a description of the police lab and what happens there. The lawyer will be guided by the story he wants to tell—that is what you're emphasizing in your opening statement. Good logos also demands that you pay attention to what you want to include and what you want to leave out. You want to leave out things the jury doesn't need to really dig into yet. For example, in the George Zimmerman case, the jurors ultimately heard detailed testimony about how to interpret gunshot wounds. But they didn't need that level of detail in the opening statement—they just needed to know that an expert would be coming to explain it to them at some point.

One category of information that you want to be careful to omit from your opening statement is anything that you can't actually introduce into evidence. The opening statement is supposed to be an overview of the facts you are going to prove. If you know you won't be able to bring something into evidence, perhaps because you don't have a witness or because of a pretrial ruling by the judge, then you can't talk about it. Johnnie Cochran ran into this problem in his opening statement in the O.J. Simpson case by referring to two people who had not been placed on the court's witness list. Cochran believed that the witnesses had been placed on the witness list, but they hadn't, nor had their witness statements been turned over to the prosecution. So it was impermissible for Cochran to talk about what they might have said, and he was scolded by the judge for this.

Another tricky logos issue for a lawyer in an opening statement: You have to be careful not to open up evidence for the other side. If you have carefully filed a pretrial motion in which you successfully persuaded the judge to prohibit some line of evidence, you could undo all that good work if you end up mentioning that evidence yourself. That will give opposing counsel the right to present it in order to rebut your claim.

So, as you can see, the opening statement is a really critical part of the trial. It's a moment of primacy, where you want to take advantage of the fact that they jury is really paying attention, and where you want to make a good impression. You want to persuade by showing good character, emotional engagement, and making your logic clear. But it's also a tricky exercise because of its limitations. You have to be careful not to argue, not to wander into subjects that you won't actually be able to introduce into evidence, and not to make a mistake that allows opposing counsel to delve into topics that otherwise would be off the table. One can look at an opening statement as a terrific laboratory for studying persuasive rhetoric. At its best, an opening statement is clear, engaging, memorable, and leaves the jury eager to hear the testimony to come.

Lecture 6

DIRECT EXAMINATION: QUESTIONING YOUR WITNESSES

After opening statements, the prosecution and the defense (or the plaintiff and the defense, in a civil trial) take turns presenting evidence to the jury. One way to present evidence is through direct examination, which involves calling witnesses to the stand to testify about the facts of the case. After each witness testifies, opposing counsel is given the opportunity to question—or cross-examine—the witness, typically to poke holes in the witness's testimony.

TELLING YOUR STORY

✭ Imagine yourself as a lawyer conducting direct examinations. Your first challenge is to figure out whom you want to put on the witness stand. That means starting with your theory of the case. What do you have to prove? What version of facts must the jury believe in order for your side to prevail, and who can best testify to those facts?

✭ To address these questions, it can help to create a chart showing your theory of the case, your proof to support that theory, and how each witness will shore up or reinforce that theory. This exercise will help you see what big-picture point you need to make with each witness. It's a good idea to make a list of the testimony you absolutely must elicit from each witness, and bring that list with you to the lectern during questioning so you don't forget anything.

* Keep in mind that you don't have to call every single person who has a connection to the case. A lawyer may spend a significant amount of time before trial taking depositions—questioning witnesses under oath, with the exchange transcribed by a court reporter. Depositions are an opportunity to learn what a witness knows and what really happened. They also show you how the witness will appear to the jury. As common sense would suggest, you want to choose witnesses who are reliable and credible, and avoid people who are disreputable.

* Once you've decided which witnesses you are going to call to prove your case, you need to figure out the order in which to put them on the stand. The order in which witnesses are called is an important part of presenting a credible story to the jury. For example, you might begin with a witness who can provide a broad context for the jury, follow with witnesses who can fill in details in an order that makes sense, and end with a particularly strong witness.

* You're not allowed to tell the jury why you called a witness—that could bias the jurors toward or against what the witness says. But the reasons for the witness's testimony will come out if you ask the witness the right questions. If you start and end with particularly strong witnesses, that can help make your case memorable and convincing.

✯ Once you've determined the order in which your witnesses will appear, you need to think about what to ask them. Usually you start the examination with questions that tell the jury why the witness is testifying—his relation to the case, why he's credible. Then you move straight to questions about the main points you need the witness to make.

✯ You want each witness to make a few, well-chosen points rather than hundreds of them, because it's easier for the jury to follow if you are selective about what you ask. It can be helpful to think of these points as separate chapters. You need to use clear transition sentences to signal to the jury when you are shifting from one chapter to the next.

✯ By organizing your questions into a logical sequence, you can help each witness tell her story and make it memorable. In addition to helping the jury make sense of the testimony, this kind of structure will help the witness feel more comfortable on the stand.

✭ An effective direct examination must do more than simply plod through the evidence, however. It should relate a vivid story for the jury, one that they're going to care about and believe in. That's why it's important that the witness do most of the talking. If the lawyer is having to prompt the witness too much about what happened, the examination will be dull and tedious, and the jury might tune out. Or even worse, the jury might not believe the witness is telling the truth.

MAKING IT COUNT

✭ During direct examination, your witness is the star. The lawyer plays a supporting role—gently feeding the witness short, nonleading questions that will help her tell her story.

✭ A nonleading question is one that's open-ended—one that lets the witness answer in her own words. In contrast, a leading question is one that suggests its own answer, such as, "You went to work, didn't you?" In direct examination you are not permitted to ask leading questions. Until they become experts in direct examination, most lawyers write their questions in advance to make sure they aren't leading.

✭ A direct examination should sound like a conversation that the jury gets to hear. The lawyer is essentially the voice of the jury, asking the questions that the jurors would want to know answers to. So the lawyer needs to ask questions in an order that makes sense. That doesn't mean you need to stick to the questions you've prepared no matter what, though. If a witness says something interesting, follow up on it. Don't just move on to the next question on your list.

✭ Be careful not to let the witness stray from the case that you're trying to make. Sometimes witnesses attach significance to things that are simply beside the point. If the witness begins to discuss things that have nothing to do with the case, the wise lawyer will circumvent the topic through careful questioning.

★ Some witnesses are nervous and blurt out their stories so quickly that the jury can't absorb them. You can help slow down the pace by asking the witness about events in increments, or by circling back to ask follow-up questions. By doing so, you will ensure that jury can focus on the details, and you will be able to emphasize the things you want to emphasize.

★ If you have a witness whose testimony you need but who doesn't want to be there in the first place, or who is sympathetic to the other side, the judge will usually allow you to ask leading questions on direct examination. You can also ask leading questions if the witness is a child, or has mental disabilities, or is someone for whom language is an issue.

PREPARING YOUR WITNESSES

★ It's important to be able to think on your feet during direct examination, but a successful direct examination isn't just about what happens in court. You have to prepare the witness. You have to think strategically about what you'll be asking, and you have to give the witness a chance to practice so he or she will feel comfortable and be credible.

★ Witnesses aren't required to meet with you in advance of the trial if they don't want to. A cooperative witness probably will want to, but other witnesses may not. In such cases, the best you can do is to subpoena them and then give a lot of thought to what you will ask them at trial.

★ To prepare a witness for trial, you should first review all the relevant reports, interrogatories, witness statements, and interview notes, and decide what testimony you want from the witness. You should write out your questions and the anticipated answers, but don't give those answers to the witness. You aren't allowed to coach the witness—it would be unethical to tell the witness what to say, and it would also make the witness less credible.

★ Instead, practice with the witness. Ask her your questions, listen to her answers, and adjust what you are asking based on what she says. Make sure you're eliciting clear information. If you're going to use an exhibit

or a visual aid with the witness, show it to her and get her comfortable with it. Work with the witness to help her appear open, positive, clear, and respectful to the court and to opposing counsel. Pay attention to her physical appearance, eye contact, and language to help her be more credible. And emphasize the importance of telling the truth.

★ When working with a witness, you must remember that conversations with witnesses who aren't your clients aren't privileged. This means that your conversations with non-client witnesses are fair game on cross-examination. You have to be thoughtful about what you say and don't say.

★ Sometimes a witness will become so terrified on the stand that she cannot remember something she used to know. As a lawyer, you want to reassure your witness in advance that it's okay if that happens. In that situation, the rules of court permit you to refresh the witness's recollection. You can use anything that might jog the witness's memory—a transcript of a deposition that she gave about the events in question, for example, or notes she made about the case.

★ The preparation session should also include preparing your witness to be cross-examined. Witnesses who are nervous about cross-examination will be less effective during your direct examination. So let witnesses know about the habits of opposing counsel, and remind them that whatever happens, they shouldn't argue or get angry.

★ The unexpected can always happen when a witness takes the stand. But if you've lined up credible witnesses who can present your theory of the case clearly, prepared them well, and know exactly what you want to ask them, you have put your client and yourself in the best possible position as you head to trial.

Suggested Reading

◊ Shadel, *Finding Your Voice in Law School.*

Questions to Consider

↗ Do you see an application for direct examination techniques in your own life? If so, how might they be helpful?

↗ How can you use questions to get a witness to tell a story? Consider practicing this by asking direct-examination questions to a friend.

DIRECT EXAMINATION: QUESTIONING YOUR WITNESSES

After opening statements, the plaintiff in a civil trial or the prosecution in a criminal trial tries to prove its case by calling witnesses to tell its side of the story. As you'll know if you watch TV crime dramas, this process is called direct examination. After each witness testifies, the counsel for the defense will cross-examine him or her—that is, question the witness to try to poke holes in his or her testimony. Once the prosecution or plaintiff has made its case, then the defense has its turn—it conducts direct examinations of witnesses that are favorable to its case or that rebut testimony elicited by the prosecution, and the prosecution can cross-examine those witnesses.

I'm going to focus in this lecture on how a direct examination works, and ask you to imagine yourself as the lawyer conducting one. Your first challenge is to figure out whom you want to put on the witness stand. That means starting with your theory of the case. What do you have to prove? What version of facts must the jury believe in order for your side to prevail, and who can best testify to those facts?

An example will help convey the choices involved here. We've previously discussed the *State of Florida v. George Zimmerman*, the trial of the man who killed Trayvon Martin, a teenager in Florida. The prosecution in the George Zimmerman case was trying to prove that Zimmerman was guilty of second degree murder. As you'll recall, that means the prosecutors had to prove that George Zimmerman killed Trayvon Martin while having "a depraved mind without regard for human life," which the judge defined as showing "ill will, hatred, spite or an evil intent." So the prosecutors called some witnesses to make that point. For example, they called a police officer who could talk about George Zimmerman's 911 call about Trayvon Martin, in which Zimmerman used profanity that could be evidence of ill will and spite. They also put someone from the Sheriff's communications office on the stand. That person could talk about the five police dispatch calls Zimmerman made in the six months leading up to the shooting. The point of that testimony was to show that Zimmerman was growing increasingly frustrated with break-ins in his neighborhood, clouding his judgment the night he encountered Trayvon Martin. These and other witnesses called by the prosecutors supported their theory of the case: That George Zimmerman was a man who racially profiled and murdered Trayvon Martin, a boy making his way home after buying juice and candy from a 7–11.

As you consider how to approach your direct examinations, it can help to create a chart showing your theory of the case, your proof to support that theory, and how each witness will shore up or reinforce that theory. That exercise helps you see what big-picture point you will need to make with each witness. It's a good idea to make a list of the testimony you absolutely must elicit from each witness, and bring that list with you up to the lectern during questioning so you don't forget anything. Bear in mind that you don't have to call every single person who has a connection to the case. As we've discussed, a lawyer may spend a significant time before trial taking depositions of witnesses, questioning them under oath, with the exchange transcribed by a court reporter. Depositions are an opportunity to learn what a witness knows and what really happened, and they also show you how the witness will appear to the jury. As common sense would suggest, you want to choose witnesses who are reliable and credible; you'll want to avoid people who are disreputable, because you want the jury to believe them, and who come across as jerks, because that could make the jury discount their testimony.

Once you've decided which witnesses you are going to call to prove your case, you need to figure out the order in which to put them on the stand so that they present a credible story to the jury. You might start with a witness who can provide a broad context for the jury, then follow with witnesses who can fill in details in an order that makes sense, perhaps chronologically, and then end with a strong witness such as a scientific expert. You're not allowed to tell the jury why you called a witness—that could bias the jurors toward or against what the witness says—but the reasons will come out when you ask the witness the right questions. If you start and end with particularly strong witnesses, that can help make your case memorable and convincing.

Applying this to the George Zimmerman case, the first witness that the prosecution called was a boy named Chad Joseph. Chad was a seventh grader who was playing video games with Trayvon Martin the night Trayvon died. He asked Trayvon to buy him some Skittles, but did not go with Trayvon to the nearby 7–11 because he wanted to keep playing his PlayStation game. The next witness was the clerk from the 7–11, who sold Trayvon Skittles and fruit juice, and who said that Trayvon wasn't acting suspiciously. It makes sense that the prosecution would want to start with witnesses like these. They painted a picture of Trayvon as a kid whose only concern on the night of his death was playing games and buying juice and candy. They helped the jury start to think of Trayvon Martin as an innocent boy who was no threat to anyone, which would make it easier for the prosecution to persuade the jury that George Zimmerman's actions in killing him were particularly "depraved," as required by the second degree murder statute.

Once you've determined the order in which your witnesses will appear, you then need to think about what to ask them. Usually you start the examination with questions that tell the jury why the witness is testifying—his relation to the case, why he's credible. Then you move straight to questions about the main points you need the witness to make. You want each witness to make a few well-chosen points rather than hundreds of them, because it's easier for the jury to follow if you are selective about what you ask. It can be helpful to think of these points as separate chapters. You need to use clear transition sentences to signal to the jury when you are shifting from one chapter to the next. By putting those chapters into a logical sequence, you can help the witness tell her story and make it memorable.

For example, let's revisit an imaginary case that we've considered before, in which you are representing a craft shop owned by a woman named Laurie Kind. You've helped Ms. Kind sue a fire insurance company that sold her a policy under which the company agreed to compensate her for damages in the event of a fire. There's been a fire, and now the company refuses to pay. You're going to put one of the employees of the store, Jenna Park, on the stand. You might start with questions that establish Ms. Park's connection to the case, showing that she's an employee of the craft store, that she knows the owner well, and that she was the person who locked the store up on the night of the fire so she can describe the condition of the premises that night. Then you get her to tell her story, but with a structure. You could organize Ms. Park's testimony chronologically, starting with what happened before the fire, establishing what a responsible person Laurie Kind is and how she took care with her business, and then you could move to what happened during the fire, establishing that nothing suspicious transpired. You could conclude with what happened after the fire, establishing that no one's been able to find work, so all the employees are much worse off because of the fire. In addition to helping the jury make sense of the testimony, this kind of structure can also help the witness feel more comfortable on the stand.

It's important that an effective direct examination do more than simply plod through the evidence, though. It should relate a vivid story for the jury, one that they're going to care about and believe in. That's why it's important that the witness do most of the talking. The witness was there, the lawyer wasn't. If the lawyer is having to prompt the witness too much about what happened, the examination will be dull and tedious, and the jury might tune out. Or even worse, the jury might not believe the witness is telling the truth. After all, if the witness is recounting her story truthfully, why would she need a lawyer to help her remember it? During direct examination, your witness is the star. You are playing a supporting role—gently feeding the witness the short, non-leading questions that will help her tell her story.

What is a non-leading question? It's a question that's open-ended, that lets the witness answer in her own words. In contrast, a leading question is one that suggests its own answer such as, "You went to work, didn't you?" In direct examination you are not permitted to ask leading questions. Getting the form of the question right may take practice because in everyday life we ask leading questions all the time. Until they become experts in direct examination, most lawyers write their questions in advance to make sure they aren't leading. If you start each question with "who," "what," "where," "when," "how" or "explain," your question is probably okay.

Here's an excerpt of a direct examination from the criminal trial of O.J. Simpson, who was accused of murdering his ex-wife, Nicole and a waiter, Ronald Goldman. The words here will be read by actors here and in excerpts later in this lecture. The witness was a former police officer named Ron Shipp, who was a friend of O.J.'s but was called by the prosecution to testify about the history of domestic violence in O.J.'s marriage. The prosecutor is Christopher Darden.

MR. DARDEN: Mr. Shipp, are you acquainted with the defendant in this case?

MR. SHIPP: Yes, I am.

MR. DARDEN: How long have you known him?

MR. SHIPP: Approximately 26 years.

MR. DARDEN: And do you recall the circumstances in which you first met him?

MR. SHIPP: Yes, I do.

MR. DARDEN: What were those circumstances?

MR. SHIPP: Um, when I was about 16-years old my brother Mike played against O.J. in high school up in San Francisco, and he had come down to Los Angeles right after O.J. had won the Heisman Trophy, and myself, Mike, and my brother Skip went over to O.J.'s house and congratulated him and this is when I was 16-years old.

MR. DARDEN: And did you and the defendant develop a friendship after that meeting?

MR. SHIPP: Um, not—we weren't very close at that time. I had run into him from time to time, and, um, every time I would see him he would ask me how was Mike doing, but we weren't really that close at that time.

MR. DARDEN: Okay. Well, as the years went on, did you develop a close relationship?

MR. SHIPP: I would say approximately from about 1978 on.

Notice how the prosecutor's questions are not leading, they are open-ended, allowing the witness to do most of the talking. You get a sense of who Mr. Shipp is, and that makes him more credible. Now listen as Darden zeroes in on the nature of Shipp's relationship with O.J. and his ex-wife.

MR. DARDEN: ...and did you consider Nicole Brown a friend?

MR. SHIPP: Yes, I did.

MR. DARDEN: As you did the defendant?

MR. SHIPP: Yes, I did.

MR. DARDEN: Do you and the defendant remain friends today?

MR. SHIPP: I still love the guy, but, um, I don't know. I mean, this is a weird situation I'm sitting here in.

MR. DARDEN: You say you still love him?

MR. SHIPP: Sure.

Shipp may express his affection awkwardly, but he sounds genuine. Again, we believe him because Darden allows him to answer freely. In contrast, let's look at what happens when a lawyer does most of the talking on direct examination. Here's that first witness from the George Zimmerman case, the boy, Chad

Joseph, for whom Trayvon Martin was buying Skittles. Here's how his direct examination starts:

MR. GUY: How old are you?

MR. JOSEPH: Fifteen.

MR. GUY: Are you in school?

MR. JOSEPH: Yes.

MR. GUY: What grade were you in this past school year?

MR. JOSEPH: Eighth.

MR. GUY: In February of last year, 2012, did you live here in Sanford?

MR. JOSEPH: Yes.

MR. GUY: What neighborhood did you live in?

MR. JOSEPH: Retreat at Twin Lakes.

MR. GUY: And what was your street address?

MR. JOSEPH: 2631 Retreat View Circle.

MR. GUY: Who did you live with in February 2012?

MR. JOSEPH: My mom.

MR. GUY: And what is your mother's name?

MR. JOSEPH: Brandi Gaines.

MR. GUY: Did anyone else live with you and your mother back in February 2012?

MR. JOSEPH: No.

MR. GUY: Were you in school in February 2012?

MR. JOSEPH: Yes.

MR. GUY: Where did you go to school?

MR. JOSEPH: Sanford Middle.

MR. GUY: And what grade were you in then?

MR. JOSEPH: Seventh.

MR. GUY: Did you know a person by the name of Trayvon Martin?

MR. JOSEPH: Yes.

Notice how the lawyer is doing most of the talking? That may be for good reason; the witness is a seventh grader, and some children that age can be difficult to draw out. But with Chad saying hardly anything, the testimony is pretty tedious, and worse, it's not very persuasive. A direct examination should sound like a conversation that the jury gets to hear. The lawyer is essentially the voice of the jury, asking the questions that the jurors would want to know answers to. So the lawyer needs to ask questions in an order that makes sense. That doesn't mean you need to stick to the questions you've prepared no matter what, though. If a witness says something interesting: "I was scared!" then follow up with "Why were you scared?" rather than the next question on your list like, "Where did you go to school?".

But you also don't want to let the witness stray from the case that you're trying to make. Sometimes witnesses attach significance to things that are simply beside the point. For example, in our hypothetical case about a craft store that burned down, perhaps the employee, Jenna Park, really hated the uniform she was required to wear and can't resist talking about it. Since it has nothing to do with the case, the wise lawyer will circumvent the whole topic through careful questioning.

Some witnesses are nervous and blurt out their stories so quickly that the jury can't absorb them. You can help slow down the pace by asking the witness about events in increments or by circling back to ask follow-up questions. For example, imagine you ask Jenna Park about the night of the fire and she says, "I locked up and went home. That's it." But you need to show that Laurie required the employees to follow a methodical system for closing up for the day, including making sure the coffee pot was turned off to prevent a fire. To slow Jenna down to elicit more details, you could ask her single-fact questions, like this:

What time did the store close the day of the fire? [6 p.m.]

Who was there at closing time? [Just me.]

Tell us about what you do to lock up for the day. How do you know what to do? [Laurie makes us use this checklist.]

What's first on your checklist? [Well, first I lock the door so no one else comes in.]

Then what do you do? [Then I put out the "Closed" sign.]

What comes next? [Then I have to do kitchen inspection.]

What does kitchen inspection mean? [Well, I turn off the coffee pot, wash any dishes we used, take out the trash, that sort of thing.]

Why do you turn off the coffee pot? [So there's no fire.]

Did you turn off the coffee pot the night of the fire? [Yes.]

See how this slowed time down? By asking Jenna to go through the steps of closing up, you can get the jury to focus on the details, and emphasize the things you want to emphasize.

What do you do if you have a witness whose testimony you need, but who doesn't want to be there in the first place, perhaps, or who is sympathetic to the other side? Under Federal Rule of Evidence 611(c), you may ask leading questions of such a witness. You usually have to start with non-leading questions to establish that the witness is hostile, but once it is clear that you aren't getting anywhere, you can ask the judge to permit an examination of the witness through leading questions. You can also ask leading questions if the witness is a child, or has mental disabilities, or is someone for whom language is an issue—essentially any time leading is "necessary to develop the witness's testimony."

It's important to be able to think on your feet during direct examination, but a successful direct examination isn't just about what happens that day in court. You have to prepare the witness. You have to think strategically about what you'll be asking, and you have to give the witness a chance to practice so he or she will feel comfortable and be credible. Now, witnesses aren't required to meet with you in advance of the trial if they don't want to. A cooperative witness probably will want to, but other witnesses may not, so the best you can do is to subpoena them and then give a lot of thought to what you will ask them at trial. If a witness will meet with you to prepare, here's what you do.

First, you review all the relevant reports, interrogatories, witness statements, and interview notes, and decide what testimony you want from the witness. You write out your questions and the anticipated answers—but you don't give those answers to the witness. You can't coach the witness, it would be unethical to tell the witness what to say, and it will make the witness less credible anyway. The witness is going to be more believable if she is telling her story in her own words. And there's another downside to handing your notes to a witness, Under Federal Rule of Evidence 612, if a witness before trial uses any writing to refresh her memory for the purpose of testifying, the court can order that writing to be turned over to opposing counsel, and that would include your questions and answers. So you want to be careful about that.

Instead, practice with the witness. Ask her your questions, listen to her answers, and adjust what you are asking based on what she says, so that you elicit clear information. If you are going to use an exhibit or a visual aid with the witness, you show her that prop and get her comfortable with it. The smart lawyer will work with the witness to help her appear open, positive, clear, and respectful to the court and to opposing counsel. You want to pay attention to her physical appearance, eye contact, and language to help her be more credible. And you must emphasize the importance of telling the truth.

In working with a witness, a lawyer must remember that conversations with witnesses who aren't the lawyer's clients are privileged. If the witness is your client, then opposing counsel can't ask what you've said to each other—that's protected by attorney-client privilege. But if the witness isn't your client, then your conversations with the witness are fair game on cross-examination. So you have to be thoughtful about what you say and don't say. Sometimes a witness will become so terrified on the stand that she cannot remember something she used to know. So, as a lawyer, you want to reassure your witness in advance that it's okay if that happens. In that situation, the rules of court permit you to "refresh the witness' recollection." You can use anything that might jog the witness's memory—a transcript of a deposition that she gave about the events in question, or notes she might have made, for example.

The preparation session should also include preparing your witness to be cross-examined. Witnesses who are nervous about the cross-examination will be less effective during the direct examination. So you let witnesses know about the habits of opposing counsel, and remind them that whatever happens, they shouldn't argue or get angry. If they can stay calm and respectful, they will be more credible. It can also be a good idea to do a practice cross examination of your witnesses and offer them feedback about their answers. We'll be talking about how cross examination works in the future.

The George Zimmerman trial illustrates the importance of witness preparation. The prosecution in that case ultimately was not successful in proving the defendant guilty of second degree murder beyond a reasonable doubt. Part of the difficulty may have been the charge of second-degree murder—it's difficult to prove the "ill will, hatred, spite or...evil intent" that the Florida statute requires. But another part of the difficulty lay with the state's witnesses.

Remember that the police originally did not want to arrest George Zimmerman, and a special prosecutor was brought in to take charge the case. Normally, the star witnesses for the prosecution would include the police officers on the scene the night the victim died. But in this case, Officer Chris Serino of the Sanford police ultimately testified that Mr. Zimmerman seemed to be telling the truth when he said he acted in self-defense, based in part on the injuries he apparently had suffered. That was a tough blow for the prosecution. Other important witnesses for the prosecution should have been the medical examiner, who examined Trayvon Martin's body and could testify about how the boy died, and a friend of Trayvon Martin's, Rachel Jeantel, who was on the phone with Trayvon when George Zimmerman began to follow him. But both of these witnesses seemed ill-prepared. Ms. Jeantel was difficult to hear and understand. She spoke so softly that some members of the jury cupped their hands around their ears in an effort to hear her better. She used slang that made her testimony difficult to follow, and she was visibly irritated during cross-examination, which made her much less credible. These are all things that should have been addressed in preparation.

The testimony of the medical examiner, Shiping Bao, another key witness for the prosecution, was equally damaging. He appeared confused on the stand, repeatedly shuffling through his notes because he could not remember much about the forensic evidence related to the case. Perhaps to excuse his confusion, he took the bizarre position that people can't really remember anything about the past, which eroded his credibility. And he brought notes up to the stand with him that ultimately were subject to disclosure to defense counsel, which was another blow to the prosecution.

In contrast, the testimony of the defense's forensic expert, Dr. Vincent Di Maio, was extremely strong. In his direct examination, Dr. Di Maio explained, in concise and clear language, that the physical evidence showed that Trayvon Martin was on top of George Zimmerman when he was shot. This was a very important point. During the prosecution's opening statement, as you'll recall, the prosecutor claimed that Zimmerman "pressed that pistol into Trayvon Martin's chest and pulled the trigger." The prosecutor painted a vivid picture of young Trayvon face down on the ground, dying, while Zimmerman was upright, walking, preparing to claim self-defense. But if instead Trayvon Martin had Zimmerman pinned to the ground when he was shot, Zimmerman's story that he feared for his life would be a lot more believable, and the injuries that the police said he had suffered to his head and nose would have made more sense.

Keep that in mind as you listen to this segment of Vincent Di Maio's direct examination. He explains how you can tell that Martin was on top of Zimmerman, leaning over him, and that Zimmerman didn't press the pistol into Martin's chest: "The photographs show contact discharge of the weapon against the clothing. In this, I agree 100% with the firearms examiner, that at the time of discharge, the gun was against the clothing; the gas came out, tore the clothing—there's a defect, and there's tears from it, there's deposit of soot all around it. And so, what you know is, is that the muzzle was in contact with the clothing at the time of discharge. And again, this is what the firearms examiner said, and she also did, I believe, some experiments proving that.

"When you look at the wound to the chest, there's a different picture. The wound to the chest was about an inch to the left of the midline, about a half-inch below the level of the nipples, and what you have was a circular, punched-out wound, which was an entrance, but it lay in an area of powder tattooing, measuring 2 inches by 2 inches. Now, powder tattooing are marks on the skin due to powder grain that come out the muzzle of a gun...when the powder grain comes out of the barrel and the barrel is close enough to the body, that grain of powder hits the skin, and produces a mark and a reaction...and these marks are called powder tattoo marks...And this indicates that a grain of powder has hit the skin, and the person was alive at the time. You do not get powder tattoo marks on dead people. And there was a distribution measuring 2 inches by 2 inches and a certain density in these tattoo marks. And this indicated that the gun was not against the skin. It was not a ½ inch away. It was more than an inch. And based upon the concentration of the marks, and the size of the pattern, it is my opinion that the muzzle of the gun in this case was 2–4 inches away from the skin. So the barrel of the gun was against the clothing, but the clothing itself had to be 2–4 inches away from the body at the time Mr. Martin was shot."

Dr. Di Maio explained that the marks on Trayvon Martin's shirt and body were consistent with him sitting on top of George Zimmerman and leaning over him as they fought, as one would do to deliver blows to the person underneath. As he testified, Dr. Di Maio spoke slowly and clearly, and also used a pen and his own shirt to show where the gun would have been in relation to Trayvon Martin's body. He didn't use jargon. He spoke in plain English, with short, straightforward sentences. He was very calm and polished. And after the section of the testimony you just heard, he went through his points again, this time using an exhibit, a picture of the tattoo marks. That gave the jury the opportunity to think about what he was saying a couple of times, so they could really understand it.

Dr. Di Maio's testimony was crucial to Mr. Zimmerman's self-defense case, which ultimately resulted in his exoneration. It illustrates the power of a clear, engaging direct examination. The unexpected can always happen when a witness takes the stand, but if you've lined up credible witnesses who can present your theory of the case clearly, you've prepared them well, and you know exactly what you want to ask them, you have put your client and yourself in the best possible position as you head into a trial.

THE ART OF THE OBJECTION

The task of voicing objections at trial is one of a trial lawyer's most important responsibilities. Making objections correctly requires knowledge of both procedural and evidentiary rules. This lecture explores the rules of evidence, focusing especially on the kinds of evidentiary objections you're most likely to hear during a trial.

THE BASICS

* The Federal Rules of Evidence govern the introduction of evidence—a category that includes both witness testimony and exhibits—in all federal courts. State courts have their own evidentiary rules, but many states have adopted rules that are similar to the Federal Rules of Evidence.

* Lawyers objecting to evidence offered by opposing counsel can do so before or during the trial. You can't wait until after the trial to make an objection, however. The whole point is that you're trying to keep the jury from hearing about the evidence at all. If you wait until the trial is over, the damage has already been done.

* Having your objection overruled by a judge can be as valuable as having it sustained. Under Rule 103 of the Federal Rules of Evidence, a party who makes a timely objection has preserved his right to raise the evidentiary issue on appeal. If the judge overrules your objection, you don't have to keep objecting each time the evidence in question

comes up during the trial. As long as you objected properly the first time, your client's right to appeal the judge's ruling on that issue has been preserved.

★ If you know that opposing counsel wants to introduce particular testimony and you think there's a good reason it shouldn't be allowed, it can be a smart move to file a motion to preclude the testimony before the trial even starts. This gives the judge more time to think about the correct outcome, and it gives you more time to think about and make your best argument.

★ You must always keep your eyes on the evidence introduced during the trial, and be ready to object if necessary. Making objections quickly and properly is a difficult skill to master, because—like so many other courtroom skills—it requires thinking on your feet. It's also important to understand any pretrial rulings the judge has made so that you know when opposing counsel is trying to bring in evidence that would run afoul of those rulings.

RELEVANCE

* Relevance is one of the most common grounds for objection to a particular piece of evidence. In order to be admissible in court, evidence must be relevant to the dispute at hand. Rule 401 of the Federal Rules of Evidence says that evidence is relevant if "it has any tendency to make a fact more or less probable than it would be without the evidence and the fact is of consequence in determining the action."

* Evidence can be relevant but still inadmissible if the evidence violates some other exclusionary rule. Under Rule 403, for example, the court may exclude relevant evidence "if its probative value is substantially outweighed" by a danger that it will prejudice, confuse, or mislead the jury, or waste time.

* A common situation in which this analysis arises is the proposed introduction of evidence about the character of a criminal defendant. Prosecutors may want to introduce evidence that the defendant has done bad things in the past, to show that it's likely that he's behaved badly again this time. When offered for that purpose alone, such evidence is inadmissible under Rule 404(b).

* Evidence of a defendant's prior bad acts might still be admitted, however, if it is offered for other purposes. Rule 404(b) allows evidence of prior bad acts to prove, for example, that a defendant had a motive or a plan, or to show that the defendant had special knowledge that is relevant to the case at hand.

* A lawyer can also introduce evidence of prior bad acts when they relate to the truthfulness of a witness testifying on the stand. Rule 608 provides that "a witness's credibility may be attacked or supported by testimony about the witness's reputation for having a character for truthfulness or untruthfulness." This rule is limited, however. You can question the witness about the bad act, but unless it's a criminal conviction, you can't bring in outside evidence.

HEARSAY

* Hearsay refers to a statement made out of court that is being offered into evidence so that the jury will believe the statement is true. The general rule is that hearsay is inadmissible. However, there are many exemptions and exceptions to the general rule.

* The idea behind the rule against hearsay is that it's better to have a witness come to court to talk to the jury directly, rather than to have someone else say what an absent person said. An in-court witness is testifying under oath, subject to the penalty of perjury, and is therefore considered more likely to tell the truth. In addition, the jury can size up the witness and determine if he seems credible, the lawyer who called the witness can ask questions to flesh out his testimony, and opposing counsel can examine the witness to see if he knows what he's talking about.

* Certain categories of evidence are exempt from the rule, and are therefore not considered hearsay. For example, Rule 801 provides that statements made by an opposing party aren't hearsay. The logic behind this exemption is that the opposing party will have ample opportunity during the trial to correct any misstatements, and that the jury will have plenty of context to evaluate the evidence.

* Rule 801 also says that a statement isn't hearsay if it's offered to prove something other than the truth of the statement. For example, testimony by Mark that he heard John say, "The Eagles won the game!" is not hearsay if it's not being introduced to show that the Eagles did, in fact, win the game, but is instead being introduced for some other purpose (perhaps to show that John mistakenly believed that the Eagles had won when, in fact, they hadn't).

* Another important exemption applies to reports that a witness said something under oath in the past, but has now changed his story and is saying something different on the stand. You can introduce his prior inconsistent statement because the jury should know that he's told two different stories; that makes him less credible.

★ Rule 803 lists a number of exceptions to the rule against hearsay. For example, Rule 803 provides that hearsay is admissible if the statement at issue was made to a doctor for purposes of receiving medical treatment. The reasoning behind this exception is that people have a strong incentive to tell the truth in such situations, and their statements are therefore more likely to be credible.

★ Another exception to the rule against hearsay applies to present sense impressions. "Gosh, it's hot in here!" is an example of a present sense impression. Because such statements are usually made without thinking, they are more likely to be credible. The same reasoning underlies the exception for excited utterances, like "Watch out for that truck!" There are also exceptions pertaining to public records, marriage certificates, and property documents.

EXHIBITS

* Documents or other pieces of physical evidence can often help prove your case. The judge must admit these items into evidence before the jury can look at them. They are labeled as exhibits and typically assigned a letter or number to make it clear in the record which item you are talking about.

* Exhibits can help drive home a witness's testimony by making a point more vividly than testimony alone can. If you're a trial lawyer, it's important for you to understand how to get something admitted into evidence—not only because you may need to introduce exhibits as you present your case, but also so you know when to object if someone else is introducing evidence incorrectly.

* To enter a document into evidence, you must authenticate it—that is, you must establish that the document is what you are claiming it is. Generally, the witness authenticating the exhibit should be someone with knowledge of it. In the case of a report, for example, the authenticating witness might be the author of a report.

* If opposing counsel is attempting to enter a document into evidence, you may object if the proper foundation hasn't been laid—for example, if opposing counsel hasn't asked the appropriate questions to show that the document is what he claims it to be. In some instances, it might not be worth it to object, particularly if the problem is one that can be easily corrected. But that's not always the case. When introducing a report, for example, attempted authentication by someone who didn't write the report (and can't otherwise establish its authenticity) might very well garner an objection.

* Usually it's okay for a lawyer to offer a copy of a document into evidence. However, if there is a question about whether the document has been forged or altered, the court can require that the original document be produced. This is called the best evidence rule, and is contained in Rules 1001–1004.

★ When preparing for trial, a smart lawyer will review her witnesses and exhibits, and consider any objections that might be raised by opposing counsel. Similarly, she will think about the testimony and exhibits that opposing counsel might introduce, and determine if there are reasons she might object.

★ The smart lawyer will also pick her battles. That way, the judge will pay attention to the objections she raises. Judges and jurors won't like objections if they think you're simply trying to slow things down.

Suggested Reading

○ Federal Rules of Evidence 401, 403, 404, 608, 801, 802.

○ Sacks and Spellman, *The Psychological Foundations of Evidence Law.*

Questions to Consider

↗ What do you think of the prohibition against hearsay evidence? Do you think it is a reasonable rule, or do you see a problem with it?

↗ We require attorneys to make objections at trial to preserve errors on appeal. If an error has not been preserved, it cannot be appealed. Do you think this is a good system? Why or why not?

THE ART OF THE OBJECTION

T rials can be intense. The stakes are high. That's certainly true for the litigants, or they wouldn't be in court in the first place. And it's true for the attorneys as well. Your client is counting on you to do everything in your power to represent her interests well, and the eyes of the judge, jury, and everyone in the courtroom are on you. In the face of all that pressure, you have to stay laser-focused on what's happening around you and on what people are saying, because any lapse in attention could be extremely costly. A primary example of this is the task of voicing objections at trial. If there's a problem with either procedure or with the evidence, a lawyer must object right on the spot. And you only get one shot at raising an objection. If you don't do it properly and in a timely fashion, you usually can't go back and fix the problem later.

To make objections correctly, lawyers have to know about the procedural rules, for example, what kind of case can be heard in a particular court, where you're supposed to stand, and so forth, and the rules of evidence. In this lecture, we'll focus on evidence and the kinds of evidentiary objections you're most likely to hear in a trial. Evidence includes both witness testimony, what people say on the stand, and exhibits, documents, the murder weapon, and so forth. The rules of evidence can vary depending on which kind of court you are in, but the Federal Rules of Evidence govern all federal courts and are similar to the rules a lot of state courts use, so we'll take those as our guide. When a lawyer says, "Objection!" he's saying that something that's just happened violates one of those rules of evidence or a procedural rule. You can raise an evidentiary objection before trial or when a problem arises during trial. But you can't wait until after the trial to make an objection, because the whole point is that you're trying to keep the jury from hearing about the evidence at all. If you wait until after the trial is over, the damage has already been done.

It's important to understand that having your objection overruled by the judge can be as valuable as having it sustained. Rule 103 of the Federal Rules of Evidence says that a party who makes a timely objection has preserved the right to claim error in a ruling to admit or exclude evidence and can therefore raise that error on appeal. So your real goal in objecting is to force the judge to rule one way or the other. If the judge overrules you and decides that the evidence is admissible, you don't have to keep repeating your objection to it each time it comes up so long as you did it properly the first time—you've already preserved your claim of error for appeal.

If you know that opposing counsel would like to introduce particular testimony and you think there's a good reason it shouldn't be allowed, it can be a smart move to file a motion to preclude it before the trial even starts, as we've discussed previously. This lets the judge have time to think about the correct outcome, and gives you time to think about and make your best argument. But you're still going to have to keep your eye on the evidence throughout the trial, and be ready to object if necessary. A budding lawyer needs to practice how to make objections quickly and properly. It's quite a difficult skill to master, because, like so many other courtroom skills, it requires thinking on your feet. A lot of lawyers and judges memorize particular buzz words that are likely to be objectionable, which can help you know when to voice an objection. It's also important to really understand any pretrial rulings the judge has made so that you know when opposing counsel is trying to bring in evidence that would run afoul of those rulings.

Here's a look at some of the most common types of evidentiary issues that might call for objections. Let's start with relevance. Evidence has to be relevant to the dispute at hand in order to be admissible in court. Rule 401 of the Federal Rules of Evidence says that "Evidence is relevant if it has any tendency to make a fact more or less probable than it would be without the evidence and the fact is of consequence in determining the action." In general, all relevant evidence is admissible, unless it violates some exclusionary rule. But if a witness starts to testify about something that has no bearing on the issue in the case, then you can object to it by simply saying, "Objection. Relevance."

Sometimes, evidence is relevant but still isn't admissible because it would unfairly prejudice the jury. Under Rule 403, "The court may exclude relevant evidence if its probative value is substantially outweighed" by a danger that it will prejudice, confuse, or mislead the jury, or waste time.

For example, in the trial of O.J. Simpson, who was charged with the murder of his ex-wife, Nicole Brown Simpson and a waiter who was her friend, Ronald Goldman, the prosecution wanted to introduce the testimony of Ron Shipp, a police officer who was also a friend of O.J.'s. O.J. talked to Shipp about Nicole Simpson, saying, "Hey, to be honest, Shipp...I've had some dreams of killing her." The defense argued that this statement was about dreams, fantasy, and not about evidence that O.J. actually killed Nicole, and would prejudice the jury against him. But the prosecution was able to persuade the judge to admit the evidence, arguing that it showed the defendant's mental state and intention around the time of the murder.

To raise this objection, if you were O.J.'s lawyer, you would want to do it before Ron Shipp took the stand, outside of the presence of the jury. If you didn't do that before the testimony started, you would stand up while Shipp was on the stand and say, "Objection, Your Honor. May we approach the bench?" Then you would make your argument quietly. Your objection would be that the testimony is likely to prejudice the jury against your client, so you wouldn't want to say that so the jurors could hear you, or you would be doing that damage yourself.

Here's another common circumstance at trial in which the court must balance the probative versus prejudicial nature of the evidence: A person flees the scene of a crime, which could be seen as evidence that he must be guilty. Courts sometimes will admit evidence of flight as relevant to guilt. Interestingly, that didn't happen in the O.J. Simpson trial, though it could have. You may remember that O.J. Simpson led the police on a bizarre car chase in his friend's white Ford Bronco through the streets of L.A. rather than turn himself in. Thousands of spectators lined the streets to watch, chanting O.J.'s nickname, "Juice! Juice! Juice!" He eventually surrendered at his Brentwood home. The footage of the Bronco chase wasn't shown to the jury at trial, nor were the jurors told that he had potentially incriminating evidence in the car, including a fake beard, a passport, and more than $8,000 in cash. For reasons that are still being debated today, the prosecution chose not to introduce that evidence, but if it had, it could have argued that the evidence showed that O.J. intended to flee. The defense could have countered, however, that O.J.'s actions might have been about fear of prosecution, not admission of guilt, and that the evidence would unfairly prejudice the jury against him.

Here's another issue that often arises regarding potentially prejudicial evidence. How about if you want to show that a defendant is a really bad guy, that he's done bad things in the past, and you think that makes it more likely that he's behaved badly again this time? If you try, opposing counsel is likely to object. Rule 404(b) says, "Evidence of a crime, wrong, or other act is not admissible to prove a person's character in order to show that on a particular occasion the person acted in accordance with the character." In other words, you can't introduce the previous bad act just to show someone's a bad guy. It's too prejudicial. Courts worry that juries will convict an accused because he seems to be an individual with a bad character, rather than because there is proof beyond a reasonable doubt that he actually committed the particular crime for which he is on trial.

So you could imagine a drug dealer who makes methamphetamines in his garage, who's been convicted for making meth in the past, and who is now on trial for tax evasion. Could you introduce his prior meth conviction in his tax evasion case if he's not taking the stand? No. The argument you would be making is that he's a bad guy, a drug dealer, and therefore is likely to have committed this tax evasion crime, too. And that's prohibited by this rule. How about if he decides to take the stand? Could you introduce it to impeach him, to signal to the jury that he can't be believed? Probably not. The judge would weigh whether the conviction is more probative than prejudicial, and in this case, a conviction for cooking meth doesn't have a lot to do with whether the defendant is likely to tell the truth, but sure could prejudice the jury against the defendant. The judge is likely to prohibit reference to it.

But you could introduce past bad acts, according to Rule 404(b), to prove something else, like to prove that a defendant had a motive or a plan, or to show that a defendant had certain knowledge. So this time, let's imagine the defendant is on trial for making meth again, not tax fraud. He has gone to jail for making meth in the past. He's not going to take the stand, so you can't introduce the prior conviction to impeach him. And, as we just learned, you can't introduce it to show that he committed the crime in the past, and therefore is likely to commit it again. But then imagine that during the opening statement, the lawyer for the defense says the defendant doesn't even know how to make meth. You would be able to introduce the defendant's prior conviction to show that he does, in fact, know how to make meth. You would be introducing the conviction to show that the defendant had knowledge, and that's permissible.

Here's another example. In the trial of O.J. Simpson, the prosecution's theory of the case was that O.J. murdered Nicole Brown Simpson and Ronald Goldman out of jealousy, obsession, and a need to dominate Nicole. To prove this, the prosecutors needed to introduce evidence of his violence toward her in the past: disturbing photographs, hospital records, police reports, and a recording of a 911 call. The prosecution argued that the record of domestic violence was evidence of O.J.'s motive, intent, plan, and identity as the killer. The judge ruled the evidence admissible. Why? In many jurisdictions, the law favors the admissibility of evidence of prior bad acts in domestic violence cases. It can show motive and identity, because the current crime may be one of a series of acts committed by the defendant toward the victim. It can also show intent and absence of mistake or accident, if the pattern of behavior between defendant and victim has happened before.

A lawyer can also raise prior bad acts related to truthfulness to impeach a witness when he does take the stand. Rule 608 provides that "A witness's credibility may be attacked or supported by testimony about the witness's reputation for having a character for truthfulness or untruthfulness." But the rule is limited. You can question a witness about prior bad acts "if they are probative of the character for truthfulness or untruthfulness," but you're not allowed to bring in extrinsic evidence of the bad act unless that act is a criminal conviction. So the rule only applies to instances of conduct that pertain to honesty, and if the witness denies that the bad act occurred, you're stuck. You can't bring in extrinsic evidence to show he's lying.

Another really common objection that you will hear at trial is: "Objection! Hearsay!" Hearsay is a statement that was made out of court, which you're repeating in court in the hope that the jury will think it is true. You generally can't introduce hearsay evidence, unless it falls into one of the exceptions listed in the rules of evidence, or unless you can show that you're introducing it for some reason other than simply hoping the jury will believe it.

Why would we have a rule like that? The idea is that it's better to have a witness come to court to talk to the jury directly, rather than to have someone else say what an absent person said. Think about it. If you have a witness in court testifying, that person is speaking under oath, under penalties of perjury, and so is more likely to tell the truth. The jury can size up that person to decide if he seems credible, the lawyer calling that witness can ask questions to really flesh out the testimony, and opposing counsel can ask the person questions to test whether he really knows what he's talking about. Instead of having someone say, "John told me x," we've decided as a matter of evidence that it's more reliable to have John himself show up and testify. That's what Rule 802 says: Hearsay isn't admissible, unless it falls into an exception or isn't hearsay at all. So when a lawyer hears a witness say, "He told me…" or "He said…" those buzzwords are likely to cause the lawyer to consider making a hearsay objection.

Wait, you may be thinking, what about that example we considered earlier, in which Ron Shipp testified that O.J. Simpson said about his ex-wife, "Hey, to be honest, Shipp…I've had some dreams of killing her." Isn't that hearsay? It's an out of court statement—OJ said it in a private conversation with Ron, not in court—and it's being offered for its truth. The prosecution wants it to come in to show that O.J. was dreaming about murdering Nicole. Why? Because it wants to show that was his state of mind around the time of the murder. But this is an example of an out of court statement that the rule classifies as not hearsay at all. And that's because the person making the statement is the defendant.

To figure this out, you need to look at Rule 801. Rule 801 says that statements made by an "opposing party," which means the plaintiff or defendant in the case, aren't hearsay. This is a huge loophole. It permits you to introduce at trial something a party to the case said in the past. The logic behind this is that the whole case is going to be about the opposing parties, so they've got ample opportunity during the trial to correct any misstatements they've made, and the jury will have plenty of context to evaluate how much weight to give their statements. So if a witness is testifying about something that the plaintiff or defendant said out of court, you wouldn't want to jump up to make a hearsay objection. You will be overruled.

Rule 801 also says that it isn't hearsay when you're offering a statement for some reason other than to say that the statement is true. For example, Mark reports hearing John say, "The Eagles won the game!" and you offer Mark's statement not to show that the Eagles, in fact, won, but as evidence that this is what John mistakenly thought at the time. And it isn't hearsay if someone reports hearing a witness say something under oath in the past, but the witness has changed his story and is now saying something different on the stand. You can introduce his prior inconsistent statement because the jury should know that he's told two different stories. That makes him less credible.

Rule 803 lists a whole bunch of other exceptions to the hearsay rule. These are out of court statements offered for the truth of the matter asserted, but there are really good reasons to believe they're credible, so we let them in. One example is a statement to a doctor when you're seeking medical treatment, which presumably is credible because you want to tell your doctor the truth in order to receive the proper medical treatment, and also because if you lie to the doctor, she'll be able to tell. Another is a present sense impression, like, "Gosh, it's hot in here!" which is probably truthful because you say stuff like that without thinking about it. Still another is an "excited utterance," like "Watch out for that truck!" because, once again, people tend to say these things reflexively, so they're probably true. Things like public records, marriage certificates, and property documents also show up in this list.

Sometimes you will hear lawyers make objections to the form of questions or answers. As we've discussed, for example, a lawyer who is conducting a direct examination is not supposed to lead the witness by asking a question that suggests the answer. This violates Rule 611. So would a narrative answer, which is a long, rambling answer that could allow a witness to say something inadmissible without giving opposing counsel a chance to object. So you might hear, "Objection, the question calls for a narrative answer," or "Objection, leading." But a lawyer would want to think about whether to make these objections. It's pretty easy to fix a leading question, the lawyer receiving the objection will just ask the question again in a more open-ended way. And if the lawyer is leading, the testimony is probably going to be pretty dull anyway. And a narrative answer may be really hard to follow, which could be good for you if you don't want the jury to listen to that witness. If you object, you might be helping opposing counsel by reminding him to break up his witness's testimony with punctuating questions.

Other common testimonial objections are that a question is repetitive, that is, it's been asked and answered before, is cumulative, that is, a series of witnesses are saying exactly the same thing and adding nothing new, or calls for an opinion. It's okay for an expert to give an opinion within the area of his expertise, and a lay witness can offer opinions based on the witness's perception if it's helpful to the jury to understand the facts. But if a lay witness is asked for an opinion about something that might require particular expertise, that might be grounds for an objection. Questions that start with, "Isn't is conceivable that…" may be problematic. A question that asks the witness to answer hypothetically or to guess is objectionable as speculative. The trial should be about facts, not speculation.

We've been focusing so far on objections relating to testimonial evidence; now let's focus on objections one might encounter relating to evidence in the form of things. Documents or other pieces of physical evidence very often can help prove your case. The judge must admit them into evidence before the jury can look at them. They are labeled as exhibits and typically assigned a letter or number in order to make it clear in the record which item you are talking about. Exhibits can help drive home a witness's testimony because they make a point more vividly than testimony alone can. Who can forget the blood-soaked gloves from the O.J. Simpson trial? One glove was discovered in O.J.'s house, another outside Nicole Brown Simpson's home, covered in a mixture of the blood of both victims and O.J. But when the prosecution asked O.J. try on the gloves in front of the jury, they didn't fit. And as Johnnie Cochran argued, "If it doesn't fit, you must acquit."

It's important for a lawyer to understand how to get something admitted into evidence, both so that you can use it as an exhibit as you present your case, and also so that you know when to object if someone else is introducing evidence incorrectly. Let's imagine that you want to enter a report by a fire investigator into evidence in a case about whether the owner of the property can recover under a fire insurance policy. To enter a document into evidence, you must authenticate it; that is, establish that the document is what you are claiming it is. Generally, the witness authenticating the exhibit should be someone with knowledge of it, such as the fire inspector who wrote the report. So here's what this process might sound like:

You approach opposing counsel and give him a copy of the document, and then say: "Let the record reflect I am showing opposing counsel a document previously marked for identification as Plaintiff's Exhibit 1."

Then you ask the judge, "May I approach the witness?" You always ask the judge for permission like this when you are going to give a witness something. You then give the witness a copy of the document, and give the judge a copy, too.

You say, "Let the record reflect I am handing the witness a document that has been marked Plaintiff's Exhibit 1 for identification." You say to the witness, "Inspector Ross, do you recognize this document? [He'll say something like, "I do."]

"Can you tell us what it is?" ["It is the fire report about the fire that occurred at Crafty Crafts on January 12, 2012."]

"Who is the author of this report?" [And he'll say, "I am."]

"When did you write this report?" ["Some of it I wrote the night of the fire, January 12, and the rest I wrote the next day."]

"Is this report a statement you made about matters you observed as part of your duties as fire chief?" ["Yes."] The reason you ask this question is to make it clear that this report qualifies for an exception to the hearsay rule because it is a public record under Rule 803(8).

Then you must ask, "Does this appear to be a fair and accurate copy of the report?" ["Yes."]

"Your honor, at this time we tender Plaintiff's Exhibit 1 into evidence."

Once the exhibit has been admitted, you give a copy to each member of the jury so they can see it, and then question the witness about the document so the jury can see why it's important.

If opposing counsel is entering a document into evidence, you could object if the foundation has not been laid properly—if the lawyer hasn't asked the questions to show that the document is what he claims it to be. For the example I just gave you, it might not be worth it to opposing counsel to make an objection if it's easy for you to correct the problem; for example, if you forgot to ask, "does this appear to be a fair and accurate copy of the report" and can cure that problem simply by asking the missing question. Not a lot of sense for him to object if the error is easily fixed and raising the objection might make him look like a jerk. But let's imagine instead that you are trying to introduce a copy of the fire report via the testimony of a witness who isn't the fire inspector, and the copy of the report you are using isn't a certified copy, which would be self-authenticating under Rule 902(4). Then opposing counsel could object to the lack of foundation—that person didn't write the report and can't establish that it is what he claims it to be.

With a documentary exhibit, you should listen carefully to see if there are hearsay objections you could raise. Maybe this fire inspector's report is generally fine, but it includes notes he took of a conversation he had with someone at the scene. You might be able to object to those notes as hearsay on grounds that they aren't just the fire inspector's recollections, but include the out of court statement of someone else that is being offered for the truth of what that person was saying.

Usually it's okay for a lawyer to offer a copy of a document into evidence, but if there is a question about whether it has been forged or altered, you can require that the original document be produced. This is called the "best evidence rule," and is contained in Rules 1001–1004. So the objection would be, "Objection, your honor, on the grounds of the best evidence rule."

Sometimes you will need to enter into evidence a tangible object other than a document, such as something found at the scene of the incident. Suppose you are the attorney for Assure Fire Insurance Company, and you would like to enter into evidence a can of paint thinner, a fire accelerant, that the fire inspector found near Crafty Crafts the day after the store burned down. Simply laying the foundation that the fire inspector found a can of paint thinner will not be enough. Instead, you need to establish that this is the same can that the fire inspector found. So your colloquy might sound like this:

"Can you describe the can of paint thinner you found near the scene?" ["It was a rectangular metal can—a brand called 'PaintAway.'"]

"Would you recognize the can of paint thinner if I showed it to you?" ["Yes, I would."]

Then you approach opposing counsel, "Let the record reflect I am showing opposing counsel what has been previously marked for identification as Defense Exhibit A."

"May I approach the witness?"

Then you bring the paint thinner up. "Let the record reflect I am handing the witness Defense Exhibit A. What is this?" ["It's the can of paint thinner that I found."]

"How can you tell it's the same can?" [He'll say, "It has 'Crafty Crafts' written on the bottom of it in permanent marker—just like the one I found. It's also the same brand—PaintAway. And when I found it, I marked it with that evidence sticker that you see affixed to the bottom and wrote my initials and the date on that sticker. I then locked it in our evidence room. I retrieved the can from the evidence room to bring it to the courtroom today."]

And then you would say, "At this time we tender Defense Exhibit A into evidence."

When preparing for trial, a smart lawyer will look at all her witnesses and exhibits, and think about any objections that could be made about them so she will be ready to persuade the judge that they are admissible. Similarly, she will think about the testimony and exhibits that opposing counsel might introduce, to see if there are reasons she could object. She will also pick her battles. That way, the judge will pay attention to the objections she raises. Note that if you object to mistake that is easy to correct—for example, objecting to the form of a question—then you're not really preserving an error that will help you on appeal and you might end up looking like you're just being difficult. Judges and jurors don't like objections if they think you're simply trying to slow things down. But trial is combat, and you might raise an objection to the form of a question if it will break the flow of opposing counsel's presentation, provided your objection is grounded in the rules of evidence or procedure.

We've covered a number of essential evidentiary objections in this lecture, and it would be nice if they were the only ones a lawyer ever had to raise. But there are some other, deeply troubling types of evidence that sometimes find their way into court, and a good lawyer needs to be able to spot them to prevent significant miscarriages of justice. We'll look at a few of the most dangerous ones next.

PROBLEMATIC EVIDENCE

W hy are innocent people sometimes convicted of crimes they didn't commit? Why is the party at fault in a civil suit not always held liable? In some cases, it's because of problematic evidence. Lawyers must understand the issues associated with problematic evidence so they can take measures to have it excluded. This lecture examines three kinds of problematic evidence: false confessions, mistaken eyewitness identification, and flawed expert testimony.

FALSE CONFESSIONS

✳ If a jury hears that a defendant has confessed to the crime of which he's been accused, jurors may be entirely convinced that the defendant is guilty. After all, why would anyone confess to something he didn't do? That's one of the questions Brandon Garrett set out to answer in his groundbreaking work *Convicting the Innocent.*

✳ DNA testing first became possible in the late 1980s. In 1992, attorneys Peter Neufeld and Barry Scheck founded the Innocence Project, which began using DNA testing to exonerate wrongly convicted people. So far, 349 people have been exonerated, including 20 people who were on death row. In many of those cases, DNA evidence also identified the real culprit.

✳ Garrett studied the first 250 cases in which a convicted defendant was later exonerated by DNA evidence. In the first 40 such cases, the exonerated defendant actually confessed to the crime of which he was later proven innocent. False confessions are particularly problematic in death penalty cases—so much so, in fact, that half of the 20 death penalty cases in which the convicted defendant was later exonerated by DNA evidence involved a false confession.

✳ In 38 of the 40 cases Garrett studied that involved false confessions, detectives claimed that the defendant provided details about the crime that only the perpetrator could know. But those details may well have come from the detectives themselves, either deliberately or inadvertently. They may have been mentioned during interrogation, for example, by detectives pressing the defendant to confess to the crime.

✳ In 14 of the 40 cases Garret studied that involved false confessions, the confessing defendant was mentally retarded. Three more defendants were mentally ill, and an additional 13 were juveniles. That's 30 out of 40 cases where false confessions came from particularly vulnerable defendants—defendants who might have confessed simply because police told them to, for example, or because they didn't understand the gravity of the situation.

* False confessions can also have tragic consequences for people other than those who make them. a false confession might implicate another innocent person, for example, who might then be inclined to provide a false confession of his own to receive leniency in sentencing.

* To avoid obtaining false confessions, police departments in many states are adopting reforms suggested in *Convicting the Innocent*, including videotaping all police interrogations and educating judges about the research on false confessions.

EYEWITNESS IDENTIFICATION

* Imagine a rape case in which the victim is able to positively identify the defendant in court. She is able to point to him and say with certainty that he is the person who committed the crime. She got a good look at his face; in fact, his face was quite close to hers throughout the attack. She is therefore 100 percent positive that the defendant is the man who attacked her—except that he isn't.

* In 190 of the first 250 cases in which a convicted defendant was later exonerated by DNA evidence, eyewitnesses identified the wrong person as the culprit. Sometimes this happens because the police have done something to suggest to the victim who the culprit should be—during a lineup of potential suspects, for example, or while the victim is examining a photo array prepared by police.

* Sometimes the problem is what police fail to say. For example, social science suggests that police who are showing a victim a lineup need to say in advance, "Now, it's possible that the person who did it isn't included in this group; we may not have found the right guy yet." If they don't, research shows that the victim is likely to pick someone from the lineup, even if that person didn't actually commit the crime.

* In other situations, the problem is that the witness's memory is malleable. During a rape, for example, the victim is likely to be terrified, and under stress it can be hard to remember things accurately. But if the victim sees a certain suspect's picture in a photo array prepared by

investigators, then sees it over and over again in the newspaper and on television, the suspect's image may become stuck in her mind. This can lead the victim to identify the suspect as her attacker, even when the suspect is innocent.

★ False eyewitness identification can happen despite the best intentions of those involved. Police are usually just trying to catch the bad guy. Witnesses are usually just trying to help. Nevertheless, lawyers need to know the problems with eyewitness identification in order to properly defend their clients. Police need to know them, too, to make sure they aren't tainting the process.

★ Improving police procedures is essential to reducing false identifications. For example, studies suggest that using a police sketch artist to help a victim make an identification is problematic, because the process of creating the sketch can distort the victim's memory.

★ Another problematic procedure is the showup, where the police show the victim a single suspect—rather than a lineup of several possible suspects—in order to quickly identify the perpetrator. a showup is permissible shortly after a crime occurs, when a possible suspect is found near the scene, because it can help police protect the public. Photo arrays and lineups are less suggestive than showups and therefore preferable when performed correctly.

EXPERT TESTIMONY

★ When a trial involves expert testimony, the expert is often the star witness. Expert witnesses are especially influential in court because unlike regular witnesses, they can offer opinions in their areas of expertise. In order to do so, however, a witness must first be qualified as an expert.

★ The Federal Rules of Evidence provide that a witness may be qualified as an expert based on the witness's "specialized knowledge" concerning the matter at hand. This could be scientific or technical knowledge, but it doesn't have to be. In a case involving a defective lawn mower, for example, the owner of a landscaping company with years of experience operating the type of mower used by the plaintiff might be qualified as an expert and therefore permitted to offer an opinion.

✶ Most state courts have adopted the same standard for expert testimony as the Federal Rules of Evidence. But there are some states, including California, Illinois, and New York, that follow an older rule known as the Frye standard. The Frye standard requires that experts use methods generally accepted in their field. Under the Frye standard, the owner of the landscaping company in the previous example might not be qualified as an expert witness, because it might be difficult to show that his method of evaluating lawn mowers is generally accepted.

✶ In federal courts, the methods used by expert witnesses don't need to be generally accepted. Instead, they must be shown to be reliable. In a 1993 case called *Daubert v. Merrell Dow Pharmaceuticals, Inc.*, the U.S. Supreme Court clarified this idea by holding that the judge overseeing a case is responsible for making sure that expert testimony is reliable. If the judge isn't persuaded that an expert is using a reliable method, the expert won't be qualified, and the jury won't be allowed to hear his opinion.

✶ When evaluating the reliability of a particular expert's method, federal judges generally apply the nonexclusive checklist established by the Supreme Court in the Daubert case. This includes things like whether the expert's technique can be tested for reliability, whether it's been subject to peer review or publication, what the error rate of the technique is, whether there were standards or controls applied, and how the scientific or peer community views the technique.

✶ When you're putting an expert on the stand, you usually begin with questions establishing the expert's credentials: the degrees they hold, their experience, and so forth. In some state courts, you must then formally offer the witness as an expert. You would then ask the expert whether he has an opinion about the issue he's there to discuss, ask him what his opinion is, and then ask him to explain the basis for his opinion.

* When your expert is discussing his area of expertise, his testimony may be very complicated. You'll want to be sure that he explains himself as clearly as possible, using plain language and visual aids if possible. You'll also want to be sure that he doesn't bore, overwhelm, confuse, or patronize the jury.

* At the request of Congress, the National Academy of Science issued a report about the reliability of forensic methods used in court cases. The report concluded, "In a number of forensic science disciplines, forensic science professionals have yet to establish either the validity of their approach or the accuracy of their conclusions." The one notable exception was DNA evidence, which has proved to be both valid and consistently accurate. Other types of seemingly scientific evidence, such as comparison of bite marks, footprints, fingerprints, voices, and hair, have not.

Suggested Reading

◊ Garrett, *Convicting the Innocent*.

Questions to Consider

↗ What safeguards might we enact that could prevent innocent people from confessing to crimes they didn't commit?

↗ What reforms could be enacted to ensure that expert testimony is reliable?

PROBLEMATIC EVIDENCE

Why are innocent people sometimes convicted of crimes they didn't commit? Why are some wrongdoers in civil actions able to get away with bad acts? Sometimes, it's because juries are persuaded by problematic evidence. Lawyers need to understand the problems connected with such evidence so they can take measures during trials to get it excluded from consideration. In this lecture, we're going to talk about three of the most important kinds of problematic evidence: false confessions, mistaken eyewitness identification, and flawed "expert" evidence.

Let's talk first about false confessions. If a jury hears that a defendant has confessed to the crime of which he's been accused, that's pretty powerful stuff. It really sounds like it solves the whole puzzle of what happened. You know who did it because the defendant told you. After all, why would anyone confess to something he or she didn't do? That's one of the questions Brandon Garrett set out to answer in his groundbreaking work, *Convicting the Innocent*. This is a really interesting book, so if you're looking for further reading in this area, I recommend it. In this book, Garrett looked at the first 250 cases of defendants who went to jail but were later exonerated by DNA evidence—people who were convicted of crimes they simply didn't commit.

DNA testing first became possible in the late 1980s, and in 1992, Peter Neufeld and Barry Scheck at Cardozo School of Law founded the Innocence Project, which began using DNA testing to exonerate wrongly convicted people. Because of that work, at this point 349 people have been shown to be innocent of crimes they went to jail for, including 20 people on death row. In a lot of those cases, the DNA evidence also showed who the real culprit was. And in 40 of the first 250 cases, Garrett found, the exoneree actually confessed to the crime when, in fact, he was innocent. False confessions are particularly a problem in death penalty cases. Half of the 20 cases death penalty cases where individuals were later exonerated by DNA evidence involved a false confession.

To understand why this happens, let's look at the case of Brendan Dassey and his uncle, Steven Avery. You may have watched the Netflix documentary, *Making a Murderer*, which was about the two of them. Steven Avery was an Innocence

Project client—he was wrongfully convicted of rape at the age of 22 and served 18 years in prison before being exonerated when DNA evidence proved that a man named Gregory Allen was actually the rapist. Allen went on to sexually assault another woman during the time that Avery was in prison for the rape that Allen committed.

Avery didn't accept his conviction. He sued the county over his wrongful imprisonment, and won. But he was then charged with, and imprisoned once again for, the rape and murder of a different woman named Teresa Halbach. *Making a Murderer* raises questions about that second conviction, arguing that Avery was framed by police who were angry about his wrongful imprisonment suit against them.

How does all this relate to false confessions? That's where Steven Avery's nephew, Brendan Dassey, fits into the story. Dassey was 16 years old at the time Teresa Halbach was murdered. He was questioned by the police about the murder of Teresa Halbach several times without a parent or his lawyer being present. According to the federal court that later reviewed the case, Dassey has a very low IQ, has difficulty understanding some aspects of language, including "understanding and using nonverbal cues, facial expressions, eye contact, body language, tone of voice." Testing also revealed he exhibits extreme social introversion, social alienation, and social avoidance.

When you watch videotapes of the police questioning him, you can feel how young Dassey is. At one point he asks repeatedly if he can go back to school soon—he's worried because he has a project due in ninth period. But he was never allowed to go home. Instead, based on what he said to the police, Dassey, too, was arrested for Halbach's murder. He was deemed to have confessed to the crime, was convicted, and spent the next ten years in prison. In 2016, a federal district court overturned Dassey's conviction, finding that his confession was not voluntary because of his age, intellectual defects, lack of experience in dealing with the police, and the absence of a parent during the questioning. In its opinion, the court described the questioning as follows:

"The investigators knew that Halbach had been shot in the head and repeatedly told Dassey that they knew 'Something else was done…Something with the head.' Dassey first said that Avery 'cut off her hair,' his inflection suggesting more a question than a statement. After more prompting from the investigators, he then said that Avery 'punched her.' Yet more prompting led to Dassey saying that, at Avery's direction, he cut Halbach's throat. Despite more prompting, eventually Dassey stated, 'That's all I can remember.' Having unsuccessfully gotten Dassey to tell them that Halbach had been shot in the head, much less who had shot her, Wiegert finally said, 'All right, I'm just gonna come out and ask you. Who shot her in the head?' 'He did,' Dassey replied. When asked why he did not say so earlier, Dassey said, 'Cuz I couldn't think of it.'

"Thereafter, the details of the shooting emerged, or perhaps evolved, in a similarly protracted fashion. Initially, Dassey told the investigators that Avery shot Halbach twice. Then it was three times. Later, after Fassbender said, 'Remember [we] got a number of shell casings that we found in that garage,' Dassey said that Avery shot Halbach 'about ten' times while she was on the garage floor. Wiegert responded, 'That makes sense. Now we believe you.'"

This is similar to the kind of contaminated confession Brandon Garrett writes about in *Convicting the Innocent*. In 38 of the 40 cases involving false confessions included in Garrett's study, detectives claimed that the defendant provided details about the crime that only the perpetrator could know. But those details may well have come from the investigators themselves. In the questioning of Dassey, you can hear the investigator telling Dassey the answer he's looking for: Avery shot Halbach in the head about 10 times. The investigator keeps pressing, finally offering up the correct answer. When Dassey agrees, then the questioning is over. Clearly, if police communicate details that only the perpetrator could know to the defendant, either deliberately or inadvertently, they might end up with a confession that sounds real only because it's got those same details in it.

Brendan Dassey's confession falls into a category that psychologists describe as coerced-compliant confessions. In these situations, the police exert pressure that's permitted under the law—they're not beating the defendant, or starving him—but they question him for hours, sometimes telling him that if he'll just confess, he'll be able to go home. In some cases, they lie, as the police did with Brendan Dassey, saying they already know what happened and the defendant just has to confirm it. And the defendant ultimately confesses, hoping that if he tells the police what they want to hear, then the questioning will stop.

Dassey's confession also falls into another troubling category. In *Convicting the Innocent*, Brandon Garrett found that 14 of the 40 exonorees who had falsely confessed were mentally retarded, three were mentally ill, and 13 were juveniles. That's 30 out of 40 false confessions coming from particularly vulnerable defendants. Defendants like these may defer to authority figures like the police, and go along with a false confession to please them, or they might falsely confess because they don't understand the gravity of the situation. Brendan Dassey didn't seem to—and his confession is heartbreaking to watch.

False confessions aren't only tragedies for the people who make them. They can spread. A person might falsely confess and then implicate other innocent people, who then also falsely confess in an effort to get leniency in sentencing or other penalties. To avoid obtaining false confessions, police departments in many states are adopting reforms suggested in *Convicting the Innocent*. These include videotaping all police interrogations from start to finish, to make sure that the police haven't suggested evidence to a defendant and to allow the defendant's lawyer to raise the issue if they have. Another helpful reform involves educating judges about the research on false confessions, so that they are able to properly assess whether the confessions are reliable and whether or not they should be shown to a jury.

Another type of evidence that can be very persuasive to a jury is eyewitness identification. Imagine a rape case, in which the victim is able to positively identify the defendant in court as the man who attacked her. She is able to point to him and say with certainty that he is the person who committed the crime. She got a good look at his face; in fact, his face was quite close to hers throughout the attack, so she really saw him and is 100% positive that the defendant is that man. Except that he isn't.

In 76% of the first 250 DNA exoneree cases—that's 190 cases—eyewitnesses identified the wrong person as the culprit. Sometimes this happens because the police have done something to suggest to the victim who the culprit should be. For example, in advance of showing a victim or a witness a lineup of potential culprits, they might show the person a photo array, which is a series of pictures of possible defendants. As they do, they might linger over one of the pictures longer, or it may be the only one in the group that stands out in some way. Perhaps the police have the person dressed in a different color from the others, or they show the victim or witness a series of pictures in which only one of the people shown is the alleged race of the culprit. Or when the victim chooses someone from a lineup or photo array, the investigator might make a comment like, "Yes, I thought so." That can contaminate the identification because it's telling the witness that she got it "right." That might make a witness who felt tentative about an identification now feel certain about it.

Sometimes, the problem is what police fail to say. For example, social science suggests that police who are showing a victim a lineup need to say, in advance, "Now, it's possible that the person who did it isn't included in this group; we may not have found the right guy yet." If they don't, research shows that the victim is likely to pick someone from the lineup, the best of the bunch, even if that person didn't actually commit the crime.

In other situations, the problem is that the witness's memory is malleable. During a rape, the victim is likely to be terrified, and under stress it can be hard to remember things accurately. But then you see a picture in a line-up. Then you see the picture again in the newspaper. And again, and again. So the face in that picture becomes the one stuck in your brain, the one you are certain hurt you, when actually you are remembering seeing that face before because you saw it in the newspaper or the line-up.

Of the first 250 defendants exonerated by DNA who were convicted based on an eyewitness identification, 84% were convicted of rape, and in 93% of those cases, the eyewitness testimony came from the victim, who typically was a total stranger to the defendant. Perhaps stress affected the ability of these victims to identify the perpetrators correctly. Most of these cases also involved white victims identifying black defendants, which also may have led to misidentification problems. Most rape prosecutions involve victims and defendants who are the same race, so it is significant that the ones that resulted in convicting the wrong person based on eyewitness identification involve victims and defendants of different races.

It's important to note that false eyewitness identification can happen out of the best of intentions. The police are just trying to catch the bad guy. Witnesses are just trying to help. But lawyers need to know the problems with eyewitness identification to properly defend clients, and police need to know them, too, to make sure they aren't tainting the process.

Improving police procedures is essential to reducing false identifications. For example, studies suggest that using a police sketch artist to help a victim make an identification is problematic, because the process of creating the sketch can distort the victim's memory. So can a procedure called a "show-up," which is where the police present a single suspect rather than a line-up to a victim, in order to quickly identify the bad guy. Show-ups are permissible shortly after a crime occurs, when a possible suspect is found near the scene, because it can help the police protect the safety of the public. But photo arrays or line-ups are less suggestive than show-ups, so they are preferable procedures, provided they are done correctly. When conducting a photo array or a line-up, a police department can make sure that it's not suggesting an answer to an eyewitness by having the police officer who conducts the line-up be someone who doesn't even know who the suspects are, and telling the witness that. If the officer doesn't know which person is the suspect, he's less likely to try to influence the witness. The witness also needs to be given the option of saying he doesn't see the true culprit in a lineup or photo array. Police departments that pay attention to these problems are less likely to obtain tainted eyewitness identification. And judges can help the process by admitting social science evidence on the fallibility of eyewitness testimony so that a jury is not unduly swayed by the seeming certainty of the witness, who may be getting it wrong.

One kind of witness that can have particular sway over a jury is the expert witness. Yet expert testimony, too, can result in the introduction of flawed evidence into a trial. Very often, when a trial involves an expert witness, that person is the star of the hearing. As we've seen, the testimony of expert witnesses became central in *State of Florida v. George Zimmerman*. Shiping Bao, the medical examiner, let the prosecution down in that case with his muddled testimony, while Vincent Di Maio, testifying for the defense, was able to explain persuasively how gunshot powder tattooing showed that Trayvon Martin was on top of George Zimmerman when he was shot, helping Zimmerman's claim of self-defense.

Why are expert witnesses so influential in court? Because they can offer opinions. Recall that witnesses generally can't offer opinions. A non-expert witness can offer an opinion based on the witness's perception if it's helpful to the jury to understand the facts; for example, did the victim look cold to you? But he can't testify about something that might require particular expertise if he isn't an expert; for example, do you think the victim had hypothermia? But experts are allowed to offer an opinion within the area of their expertise, provided you can get them qualified as an expert.

Federal Rule of Evidence 702 governs the testimony of expert witnesses. It says, "A witness who is qualified as an expert by knowledge, skill, experience, training, or education may testify in the form of an opinion or otherwise if:

(a.) the expert's scientific, technical, or other specialized knowledge will help the trier of fact to understand the evidence or to determine a fact in issue; (b.) the testimony is based on sufficient facts or data; (c.) the testimony is the product of reliable principles and methods; and (d.) the expert has reliably applied the principles and methods to the facts of the case."

Now, under this Rule 702, you can be an expert if you have specialized knowledge. That could be scientific or technical knowledge, but it doesn't have to be. So you could imagine a case involving something like a defective lawn mower. An expert in that case could be a technical designer who knows about lawn mower design, or it could be a guy who runs a lawn mowing company who has years of experience operating the kind of mower in question. Either of those people might have "specialized knowledge that will help the trier of fact… determine a fact in issue." Either could offer an opinion in the case, once he's been qualified as an expert.

That's what Rule 702 says, and its approach is taken by all federal courts and most state courts as well. But there are some states, including California, Illinois, and New York, that follow an older standard called the Frye standard. That name comes from a 1923 DC Circuit case called *Frye v. United States*, which says that experts have to be scientists who follow scientific methods generally accepted in that field. So under that rule, the guy who owns the lawnmower company might not be qualified as an expert witness, because it might be hard to show that his evaluation of a lawn mower is "generally accepted." In federal courts, you don't have to show that the method the expert uses is generally accepted; you just have to show it's reliable.

In a 1993 case called *Daubert v. Merrell Dow Pharmaceuticals, Inc.*, the Supreme Court clarified this idea by holding that a judge overseeing a case has to make sure that expert testimony is reliable. That means the judge is the gatekeeper. If the judge isn't persuaded that an expert is using a reliable method, then the expert won't be qualified as an expert and the jury won't hear his opinion.

Sometimes the court will have a hearing about an expert outside the presence of the jury, called a Daubert hearing. If you think opposing counsel is going to introduce expert testimony that you don't want the jury to hear it, it can be wise to file a motion in limine—that is, a motion to limit or prevent the introduction of evidence—to prevent the witness from testifying. That motion will trigger a Daubert hearing. At the hearing, the judge is likely to apply the non-exclusive checklist the Supreme Court established in Daubert to assess whether the testimony is reliable. The judge will look at things like whether the expert's technique can be tested for reliability, whether it's been subject to peer review or publication, what the error rate of the technique is, whether there were standards or controls applied, and how the scientific or peer community views the technique.

When you're putting an expert on the stand, you usually begin with questions establishing the expert's credentials—the degrees they hold, their experience, and so forth. In some state courts—not federal courts, but state courts—you then have to formally tender or offer the witness as an expert. For example, you might say, "Your honor, we tender Dr. Smith as an expert in pathology and gunshot wounds." You then ask the expert whether he has an opinion about the issue in the case he's there to talk about, ask him what his opinion is, and then ask him to explain the basis for his opinion. That's when he'll be talking about his area of expertise, which may be very complicated. You'll want to be sure he explains it as clearly as possible, with plain language and helpful visual aids. You'll also want to be sure he doesn't bore, overwhelm, confuse or patronize the jury.

Scientific evidence can be tremendously useful at trial. For example, I've mentioned that the book *Convicting the Innocent*, involves 250 cases in which DNA evidence ultimately proved that people were innocent of crimes they had been convicted of committing. That's powerful stuff. It shows that scientific evidence plays an important role in the proper functioning of justice. But in many of those cases, the defendants were originally convicted because of scientific evidence that turned out to be unreliable. Here's a story of a man who was executed for arson based on evidence that ultimately was debunked. You can read a detailed account of this case in an article from the New Yorker called "Trial By Fire," by David Grann.

Cameron Todd Willingham was the father of three young girls—Karmon and Kameron, who were one-year-old twin girls, and two-year-old Amber—all of who died in a horrible fire in their home in Corsicana, Texas. The children's room was warmed by three space heaters. Willingham's attorneys argued that these space heaters were the cause of the fire; the prosecution argued that Willingham set it deliberately. The fire was investigated by Manuel Vasquez, a deputy fire marshal who was one of the state's leading fire investigators. Vasquez had investigated more than 1,200 fires at the time of the Willingham investigation. Once, under oath, Vasquez was asked if he had ever been wrong in a case. His reply: "If I have, sir, I don't know. It's never been pointed out."

Based on burns marks on the floor of the house, which resembled puddles, as well as other evidence, Vasquez testified that it was his opinion that Willingham intentionally set the fire with an accelerant to murder his little girls. Willingham was sentenced to death, and ultimately was executed, although he insisted to the end that he was innocent. He even turned down a plea bargain that could have saved his life; he said that he didn't want to take the agreement because he didn't do it.

In 2004, a few weeks before Willingham was scheduled to be executed, Dr. Gerald Hurst received his case file. Hurst has a Ph.D. in chemistry from Cambridge University, and had made a study of criminal arson investigations. He was shocked to discover that many state and local arson investigators have only a high-school education and are able to be certified simply by taking a 40-hour course in fire investigation. A lot of the training of these investigators comes on the job, based on conventional wisdom passed down by other investigators with similarly meager training. "People investigated fire largely with a flat-earth approach," Hurst said. "It looks like arson—therefore, it's arson. My view is you have to have a scientific basis. Otherwise, it's not different than witch-hunting."

When he looked at the Willingham case file, Dr. Hurst was struck by a statement that Vasquez made on the stand. He said that, of the roughly twelve hundred fires he had investigated, "Most all of them" were arson. Hurst knew that couldn't be right. The Texas State Fire Marshal's Office typically found arson in only 50% of its cases. Vasquez also testified that the fire burned particularly hot, which he said showed that it had been intentionally set with a liquid accelerant. Dr. Hurst knew that this, too, was nonsense—scientific studies show that wood and gasoline-fueled fires burn at the same temperature. What Vasquez was saying was conventional wisdom that's been repeated in arson trials for decades, but it's not supported by scientific evidence. Vasquez also said that the front door had melted, which could only happen in a fire caused by accelerant. Again, not true— wood fires can burn as hot as fires fuled by an accelerant, sometimes reaching temperatures of 2,000°, a good 800–1,000° hotter than the temperature required to melt an aluminum front door. Dr. Hurst also knew that the puddle patterns on the floor that so bothered Vasquez can be the signs of a flashover, which is the point at which a whole room catches fire, and can happen in fires that aren't intentionally set. This had been shown in something called the Lime Street experiment, in which fire investigators recreated a fire, hoping to prove arson. Instead, the fire displayed characteristics previously thought to be indicative of arson, including puddling. This experiment demonstrated how many "scientific" truths underpinning arson investigations were, in fact, junk science.

But Dr. Hurst's report didn't make a difference. The Texas Board of Pardons and Paroles received it, but did not change Willingham's sentence, and he was executed. In 2005, a year after Willingham was put to death, Texas established a state commission to investigate error by forensic scientists, including in Willingham's case. The resulting report concluded that the investigators in the Willingham case had no scientific basis for claiming the fire was arson, denied "rational reasoning" and produce an opinion more "characteristic of mystics or psychics." *The Chicago Tribune* reported in 2009, "Over the past five years, the Willingham case has been reviewed by nine of the nation's top fire scientists—first for the *Tribune*, then for the Innocence Project, and now for the commission. All concluded that the original investigators relied on outdated theories and folklore to justify the determination of arson."

The Innocence Project requested all records from the Texas Board of Pardon and Paroles pertaining to the report. Barry Scheck from the Innocence Project said, "The documents show that they received the report, but neither office has any record of anyone acknowledging it, taking note of its significance, responding to it, or calling any attention to it within the government. The only reasonable conclusion is that the governor's office and the Board of Pardons and Paroles ignored scientific evidence." One member of the board said that the report didn't ring a bell; another said that the board got reports all the time but didn't have the mechanisms by which to evaluate them. This is why Federal Rule 702 and the Daubert opinion are so incredibly important. Judges do have mechanisms by which to evaluate expert reports—Daubert hearings. Judges are increasingly becoming aware of problems with forensic science, and can educate themselves about these problems.

At the request of Congress, the National Academy of Science has issued a report about the reliability of forensic science used in court cases. That report concluded, "In a number of forensic science disciplines, forensic science professionals have yet to establish either the validity of their approach or the accuracy of their conclusions[.]" The one notable exception is DNA evidence. DNA testing has proved to be both valid and consistently accurate. Other types of seemingly scientific evidence, such as comparison of bite marks, footprints, fingerprints, voices, and hair, have not. So don't believe everything you see on TV detective shows. A good lawyer will question such evidence, bringing in independent experts, and good judges will prohibit "expert" testimony based on questionable methods.

CONTROLLING CROSS-EXAMINATION

There's nothing quite like the conflict, test of wills, strategy, and quick thinking involved in cross-examination. In a cross-examination, opposing counsel asks questions to poke holes in the testimony of a witness unfriendly to her client's case. It's a tricky exercise, requiring the cross-examining attorney to prove her point without losing control of the witness, eliciting an answer she doesn't expect, or offending the jury.

SCOPE AND FORM

✶ Rule 611 of the Federal Rules of Evidence lays out two areas of questioning that are permitted on cross-examination in federal courts. It states, "Cross-examination should not go beyond the subject matter of the direct examination and matters affecting the witness's credibility." Some states have rules permitting broader cross-examination, but most states have rules similar to Rule 611.

✶ On cross-examination, you can ask the witness questions on any topic the witness discussed on direct examination. However, you're not supposed to exceed that scope. You can also cross-examine the witness concerning matters affecting the witness's credibility. For example, if the witness was once convicted of perjury—that is, lying under oath— questions about the perjury conviction would certainly be relevant to the witness's credibility and would therefore be allowed.

★ Rule 611 also provides that a court "may allow inquiry into additional matters as if on direct examination." The court might allow this if the issues you want to raise have some bearing on the case, but you will have to question the witness as if you were performing a direct examination—for example, without asking leading questions.

★ With few exceptions, leading questions are only permitted on cross-examination, where they are a powerful tool for keeping a witness in control. Leading questions are those that suggest their own answer ("You opened the door, didn't you?"). A skillful cross-examining attorney can control the witness by asking a series of simple, single-fact, leading questions. This approach leaves little wriggle room for the witness to argue.

COMMON PITFALLS

★ When cross-examining a witness, it's important not to ask one question too many. This is sometimes called avoiding the ultimate question—the question that really drives home the point that you want to get across to the jury. It can be very tempting, especially if you've spent a lot of time building toward a particular conclusion, but it's a mistake; the witness will never agree with you, and she may say something that makes it harder to prove your case.

★ It's much better to limit your cross-examination strictly to questions with which the witness must agree. Save any conclusions you want the jury to draw for your closing argument, when the witness you cross-examined won't be on the stand to disagree with you.

★ Avoiding the ultimate question is actually an example of a broader, more fundamental rule of cross-examination: Never ask a question unless you already know the answer. The witnesses you cross-examine are usually in court to support the other side's case, and you can't afford to gamble on what they might say. So ask safe questions—ones based on something the witness has said in the past.

★ On cross-examination, you should limit yourself to a few, well-chosen points. As with direct examination, the jury is more likely to remember what a witness says if there are only a few points and the points are very clear.

★ It's not a great idea to use cross-examination to make a point that you could make through direct examination of a friendly witness, or through your closing argument. Cross-examination should be used strategically—to show why a witness can't be believed, for example, or to elicit helpful testimony that only this particular witness can provide.

★ Your cross-examination should be structured in a way that helps tell your story—that promotes your theory of the case. If you spend all your time shooting down the witness's direct examination, the jury probably won't remember your points, and you'll have reemphasized the opposing counsel's structure instead of supporting your own.

★ The tone that a lawyer uses during cross-examination is extremely important. If a witness is hostile, or provides an unexpected answer, some cross-examining attorneys instinctively adopt a more aggressive tone, and may stand too close to the witness. This can backfire, however, if the jury perceives the attorney as a bully.

★ When performing a cross-examination, you should generally stay behind the lectern and maintain a tone of calm confidence. A tone that shows even-tempered professionalism and expertise will appeal to a jury more than one that suggests you enjoy humiliating someone. You may occasionally need to get tough with a witness, but be sure to pick your battles carefully.

IMPEACHMENT AND OBJECTIONS

★ Impeachment is the process of calling into question the credibility of a witness. If you're questioning an important eyewitness to an incident, you might do this by showing that the eyewitness was hiding behind a wall when the events occurred and couldn't actually see anything. If the witness has bias, interest, or motive to lie—for example, if he's a friend of the party calling him to testify or is an expert being paid for his time in court—those are also proper grounds for impeachment.

★ You can impeach a witness by showing that he has been convicted of a felony, or of any crime involving dishonesty or false statements, if the conviction happened in the last 10 years. You can also impeach a witness by asking him about prior bad acts that are probative of his truthfulness, but you won't be able to use extrinsic evidence of the prior bad act.

★ The most complex form of impeachment—but often the most damaging for the witness's credibility—uses a prior inconsistent statement by that witness, typically from a police report or a deposition. Because the witness was talking to the police or was under oath when making the prior statement, it's a major blow to his credibility if he contradicts the statement during his testimony at trial.

★ If you can successfully impeach a witness using a prior inconsistent statement, you will have shown that either the witness is lying now, the witness was lying previously when it was unlawful to do so, or the witness has forgotten a critical part of his testimony. In any case, the jury will be much less likely to believe what that witness has to say.

★ You should only attempt to impeach a witness by prior inconsistent statement if you are certain that he has contradicted something he said previously. You must also have the affidavit or deposition to prove that he has changed his story.

* Before reading the prior statement for the jury, you must have nailed the witness down to his contradictory statement. If the witness realizes that he is playing fast and loose with his prior testimony, he often will back down and contradict himself in court, in which case an impeachment with the prior statement will be unnecessary. If the witness maintains his position, however, you can proceed with the impeachment.

* When conducting the impeachment, read the relevant portion of the witness's prior statement to the witness rather than having the witness read it to you, because if given the opportunity, some witnesses will hijack the examination and muddle your impeachment. A wise lawyer will know the impeachment procedure cold so that she can skillfully make clear that the witness has contradicted himself.

* If the witness admits that his story has changed, then there's nothing else that you need to do. Sometimes, however, the witness might not admit the contradiction, or might claim not to remember.

If the issue you're talking about isn't significant, you might be required to let it drop. But if the matter has important independent significance to the case, then you can prove up the impeachment with extrinsic evidence when it's time for you to call your own witnesses.

✶ A lawyer can do a lot of damage to opposing counsel's case through cross-examination. But if it's your witness who is being cross-examined, you can defend him by objecting, when appropriate, to the cross-examining attorney's line of questioning. For example, you might object if a question your witness is asked on cross-examination exceeds the scope of the direct examination, misstates evidence, assumes facts not in evidence, or asks the witness to speculate, or if the question is argumentative, which means that it doesn't actually elicit any new information.

Suggested Reading

⬧ Younger, *The Irving Younger Collection.*

Questions to Consider

↗ One of the lessons of an effective cross-examination is that you must stay in control of your tone. You can ask aggressive questions, but if your tone is also aggressive, that can backfire. Can you think of ways that this lesson could be useful in your own life?

CONTROLLING CROSS-EXAMINATION

During a trial, there's nothing quite like the conflict, the test of wills, the strategy, and the quick thinking involved in cross-examination. These are the moments that courtroom dramas in TV and film play up, and the high point of many a legal thriller. In real life, cross-examinations, even non-dramatic ones, are critical moments that can make or break a case. We've previously discussed direct examination, in which a lawyer typically uses witnesses to present her theory of the case. In a cross-examination, opposing counsel asks questions to poke holes in the testimony of a witness who is unfriendly to her case. It's a tricky exercise. You must pick questions that prove your point without causing you to lose control of the witness, without eliciting answers that you don't expect, and without offending the jury.

So how do you know what to ask? Cross examination is governed by Federal Rule of Evidence 611. That rule lays out two areas of questioning that are permitted on cross examination. It says, "Cross-examination should not go beyond the subject matter of the direct examination and matters affecting the witness's credibility."

So the first area of permissible inquiry on cross-examination: you can ask about any topic discussed by the witness on direct examination. However, you're not supposed to exceed that scope. For example, if a witness appears in a case to testify about her role as an employee at a craft store, you are not supposed to ask her questions on cross about the years she spent travelling with the circus. That's beyond the scope of direct—and probably isn't relevant. Note that this is a Federal Rule of Evidence that we're discussing. Some states have broader rules about cross examination and might not limit cross to the topics raised on direct, but most states have rules similar to the federal rule.

The second area of permissible inquiry set forth in Rule 611: you can ask about "matters affecting the witness's credibility." So if the witness you are crossing travelled with the circus and during that time was convicted of perjury, that perjury conviction is relevant to whether this witness is credible. She lied under oath. So you would be allowed to ask about that.

Rule 611 also permits a possible third area of inquiry on cross, but it's up to the court to decide whether to allow it. The rule says that the court "may allow inquiry into additional matters as if on direct examination." That means that, if you want to delve into the witnesses' circus life and you can't show that it is relevant to her credibility, then you'll have to ask the permission of the court to inquire about it. The court might let you if it has some bearing on the case, but you will have to question the witness "as if on direct examination." That means you wouldn't be allowed to ask leading questions.

With few exceptions, leading questions are only permitted on cross-examination, and they are a powerful tool for keeping a witness in control. A good lawyer will want to use them whenever possible. As we've seen, a leading question suggests its own answer. For example, "You opened the door, didn't you?" "You turned on the light; isn't that right?" You could think of it as essentially a short sentence with "didn't you" tacked onto it. Leading questions enable a skillful lawyer to control the witness on cross-examination by asking a series of simple, single-fact, leading questions. If you do that, you don't leave a lot of wriggle room for the witness to argue with you.

Let's look at a skillful cross examination by the renowned civil and criminal defense attorney Roy Black. This excerpt comes from one of Black's most famous cases, the trial of William Kennedy Smith, nephew of President John F. Kennedy, Senator Robert F. Kennedy, and Senator Ted Kennedy. Smith was accused of raping a woman, Patty Bowman, and hired Roy Black to defend him. In this cross examination, Mr. Black was questioning a friend of Patty Bowman's, a woman named Ann Mercer. Patty Bowman and Ann Mercer met William Kennedy Smith and two of his relatives at a bar in Palm Beach, Florida. The five went back to a house owned by the Kennedys. William Kennedy Smith and Patty Bowman went for a walk on the beach, where she alleges he raped her. According to Ann Mercer, Patty Bowman called Mercer after the rape, and asked Mercer to retrieve her shoes. Mercer then went with Smith to try to find Patty's shoes. So here's how the cross-examination starts. Here, and later in the lecture, we'll be using actors to recreate the dialogue.

Q1: You say you went to the Kennedy home on the early morning hours of March 30th, is that correct?
A1: Yes.

Q2: Your friend says that she was raped, is that right?
A2: Yes.

Q3: What she tells you is that she wants her shoes, is that correct?
A3: Yes.

Q4: Several times she was worried about her shoes.
A4: Yes.

Q5: So you went into the house, is that correct?
A5: Yes.

Q6: Into the house where the rapist is, right?
A6: I guess you could say that, yes.

Q7: It's dark in there.
A7: Yes.

Q8: You go through the kitchen, right?
A8: Yes.

Q9: Into this little hallway?
A9: Yes.

Q10: It's dark in this hallway, isn't it?
A10: Right.

Q11: You meet up with this man who your friend says is a rapist? Isn't that correct?
A11: I was not afraid of him, no. I was not afraid of him.

Q12: No, that's not my question, Miss Mercer. You understand my question? My question is, did you meet this man who your friend says is the alleged rapist?
A12: Yes.

Q13: In this dark hallway, is that right?
A13: Yes.

Q 14: And you ask him to help...you ask the rapist to help you find her shoes, is that correct?
A14: Yes.

In this cross-examination, Black carefully uses single-fact, leading questions. Notice how they let Black control the narrative. The form of Black's questions lets him do most of the talking, and the witness is given no room to elaborate. When Mercer tries to argue with him by saying she wasn't afraid of Smith, Black is able to point back to his question and insist that she answer it—and because the question is carefully crafted, her answer has to be yes. Let's listen to some more of the cross-examination. Now I want you to notice how using leading questions really lets Roy Black slow down time. By breaking down the action in baby steps, he leaves you with the impression that Mercer and Smith were in the dark together for quite a while, casting doubt on whether Smith really was a threat at all.

Q15: And he turns around and goes with you, out of the house, is that right?
A15: Yes.

Q16: Through the dining room to begin with, is that correct?
A16: Yes.

Q17: It's dark in that house, right?
A17: Yes.

Q18: You're walking through the dining room with this man, is that correct?
A18: Yes.

Q19: The man who is allegedly a rapist, right?
A19: Yes.

Q20: You go out the door of the dining room, don't you? Into a little patio area?
A20: Correct.

Q21: With this man who is the alleged rapist, is that right?
A21: That's right.

Q22: You go out past the patio and onto the lawn, is that right?
A22: Right.

Q23: It's dark out, isn't it?
A23: Right.

Q24: With this man who's the alleged rapist?
A24: Yes.

Q25: You go across the lawn with him, is that right?
A25: Yes.

Q26: Towards the beach?
A26: Yes.

Q27: As you go across the lawn you get to a place where there are hedges and a concrete wall, isn't that right?
A27: Yes.

Q28: And you're still with this man who is the alleged rapist, is that right?
A28: Yes.

By using leading questions, Roy Black dictates the pace of this cross-examination. He could have gone through this material very quickly if he'd chosen to. The cross could simply have been: "You and Smith looked for the shoes, didn't you? And that meant you were alone with him for a while, correct? And it was dark, wasn't it?" But if he'd covered the material in only three questions, that wouldn't drive home the point he wants to make quite so vividly: that it doesn't make sense that Mercer would go walking around a dark estate looking for her friend's shoes for a long period of time with this man if she really thought he was a rapist. Black was able to use this cross-examination to argue, without saying so directly, that the reason Mercer didn't behave as if Smith were a rapist was because she knew he hadn't done anything.

Black goes on to use another powerful argument that raises doubts that Mercer really thought Smith was a rapist, something she said to him during the hunt for the shoes. Mercer tries to explain her statement, but notice how Black shuts her down and once again restricts her to yes-or-no answers. The district attorney objects to Black's tactics, but the judge overrules her. Here's how the cross-examination continues:

Q49: Now there's one thing you forgot to tell us in that scenario on direct examination, what you said to this man who's the alleged rapist when you left, you forgot about that didn't you?
A49: I wasn't asked that, sir.

Q50: Didn't you tell him you were sorry?
A50: No, I did not.

Q51: Oh, didn't you tell him Ms. Mercer that you were sorry that you had to meet under these circumstances?
A5 1: Ah, I used those words...

Q52: I didn't ask you why you used them. I said did you say you were sorry you had met him under those circumstances?
A52: I did not mean I was sorry.

Q53: I didn't ask you what you meant.
D.A.: Objection, not being allowed to answer the question.

Judge: Overruled, please answer the question.

Q54: The question is, did you say to this man, "I'm sorry we met under these circumstances?"
A54: Yes, I said that.

Q55: To the man who's supposedly the rapist, is that right?
A55: Yes.

This moment illustrates the importance of something we discussed previously in the context of direct examination: drawing the sting of a bad fact. As you may remember, drawing the sting means raising a fact that reflects poorly on your client and addressing it to reduce its impact, in case opposing counsel chooses to discuss it. In this case, the district attorney made the mistake of failing to draw the sting on Mercer's problematic comment on direct examination. That left Roy Black in the terrific position of being able to unveil this bad fact for the jury. It helps build his point, that it doesn't make sense that Mercer would have apologized to a man whom she thought had raped her friend. It also hands Black a great moment of drama that is likely to make the jurors side with him as a revealer of truth, and dislike both Mercer and the district attorney for hiding a crucial fact from them.

Here's yet another thing Roy Black's cross-examination of Ann Mercer illustrates: The importance of not asking one question too many, also known as the ultimate question. The ultimate question is the point that you really want to drive home to the jury. Here, the ultimate question might be something like, "Isn't it true that you were willing to walk around in the dark with my client, and even apologize to him, because you didn't believe that he'd raped your friend?" It can be very tempting to ask a question like that, especially after you've built up evidence leading to that conclusion, bit by bit, but it's a big mistake to do it. There's no way the witness is going to agree with an ultimate question like that. She's just going to fight with you, and might even say something you didn't anticipate, something like, "I wasn't scared because I know karate" or "I was so traumatized that I apologized just to get out of there safely!" It's much better to lay out the points you want to make, as Roy Black did, with questions to which the witness must agree, and then save the conclusion that you draw from her statements for your closing argument in the case, when the witness won't be on the stand to disagree with you.

The idea of avoiding the ultimate question is actually an example of a broader, fundamental rule of cross-examination: Don't ask a question unless you already know how the witness will answer it. Never forget that the witnesses you cross-examine are usually in court to support opposing counsel's case. You can't afford to gamble on what they might say, so ask safe questions. A safe question is one based on something the witness has said in the past. For example, Ann Mercer had spoken to the police about the events in question, and Roy Black could listen to the recordings of her interview and read the police reports. That meant he knew what she'd said in the past, so he knew she would have to agree to statements like, "You went onto the beach, didn't you?" Those are safe questions. An unsafe question would be one to which you don't know the answer, such as, "What were you thinking when this happened?" Who knows what she might say to that, and whatever it is, it probably isn't going to help your case. In order to perform cross-examination effectively, you have to master every fact in the case, and in particular, every bit of the witness's prior writings and testimony. You want to find statements in these materials that show the witness is biased or could not have seen what she claims to have seen, and also keep an eye out for any place that the witness has changed her story.

Another important rule to follow is to limit yourself to making a few, well-chosen points. We talked about this idea when we discussed direct examination, and there the theory was that the jury is more likely to remember what a witness has said if there are only a few points and they are very clear. The same principle holds for cross-examination. And cross-examination has the added challenge that the witness may not like your side of the case, and may have reasons to want to resist agreeing with you. So it's not a great idea to use cross-examination to make a point that you could make through a friendly witness on direct examination, or through your closing argument. You want to use cross examination strategically, to show why a witness can't be believed or to bring out evidence uniquely within that witness' area of knowledge that can help you, like Ann Mercer's apology to William Kennedy Smith. You also want to think about the structure of your cross examination. The best structure is the one that tells your story, that's based on your theory of the case. If instead you spend your time shooting down various parts of the direct examination that just ended, the jury probably won't remember your points, and you'll have reemphasized opposing counsel's structure—the one that best suited the other side's theory of the case—instead of supporting your own.

As with all parts of the trial, the tone that a lawyer uses during cross-examination is extremely important. Cross-examination can be stressful because the witness may be hostile or give you an unexpected answer, and you may be nervous. Sometimes this causes lawyers and law students to adopt an overly aggressive tone in an effort to control the witness, or to stand too close to a witness in an effort to intimidate him or her. This can backfire if the jury perceives you as a bully. Instead, it's wise for the lawyer to stay behind the lectern, where you need to be anyway so that you can look at your notes, and maintain a tone of calm confidence. Even when you are proving that a witness is lying, a tone that shows even-tempered professionalism and expertise will appeal to a jury more than one that suggests you enjoy humiliating someone. A lawyer may occasionally need to be tough with a witness, but should be careful of reaching for an aggressive tone if it is uncalled for. If he does, he will have any room to bring on the tough stuff when he actually needs it.

What do you do if you are cross-examining a witness, and the witness starts to lie? For example, let's say that Roy Black knew that Ann Mercer had told the police something during their investigation, or maybe had testified a particular way in a deposition, and now is changing her story. In that case, he would need to impeach her. Impeachment is the process of calling into question the credibility of a witness. If you're questioning an important eyewitness to an incident, you might do this by showing that the eyewitness was hiding behind a wall when the events occurred and couldn't actually see anything. If the witness has bias, interest or motive to lie, such as if he's a friend of the party calling him to testify or is an expert being paid for his time in court, those are proper grounds for impeachment. You can impeach a witness by showing that he has been convicted of a felony, or of anything involving dishonesty or false statements, if the conviction happened in the last 10 years; that's provided in Federal Rule 609. You can also impeach a witness with evidence about prior bad acts that are probative for truthfulness, but you can't use extrinsic evidence—that is, evidence that wouldn't otherwise be properly before the court—to prove up the prior bad acts. For example, maybe a witness lied on his resume. You could question him about the lie, but if he insists that it isn't a lie, and if the resume isn't really central to the case, you're not going to be allowed to call in other witnesses to prove that he's lying. You'll just have to take the witness' answer.

The most complex form of impeachment, but often the most damaging for the witness's credibility, uses a prior inconsistent statement by that witness, typically from a police report or a deposition. Since the witness was talking to the police or was under oath when making these prior statements, it's a major blow to his credibility if he contradicts such statements during his trial testimony. Successfully impeaching a witness with a prior inconsistent statements means you have shown that the witness is lying now, has previously lied when it was unlawful to do so, or has forgotten a critical part of his testimony. In any case, a jury is much less likely to believe what that witness has to say.

Obviously, you only want to attempt to impeach a witness by prior inconsistent statement if you are certain that he has contradicted something he said previously and you have the affidavit or deposition to prove that he has changed his story. Before reading the prior statement for the jury, the lawyer must have nailed the witness down to his contradictory statement. Then you repeat his contradictory answer in the next question by asking, "So it's your testimony today that x?" If the witness knows he is playing fast and loose with his prior testimony, he often will back down and contradict himself in court, so an impeachment with the prior statement will be unnecessary. If the witness maintains his position, you can proceed with the impeachment. When conducting the impeachment, you need to make sure you are able to quickly find the line number in the deposition where the witness contradicts his testimony at trial. Read the relevant portion of the statement to the witness rather than having the witness read it to you, because if given the opportunity, some witnesses will hijack your examination and muddle your impeachment. A wise lawyer will know the impeachment procedure cold so that she can skillfully make clear that the witness has contradicted himself.

Here's what a lawyer's questions in the impeachment of a witness using a prior inconsistent statement typically sound like:

- "Mr. Brown, do you remember giving a deposition in this case on July 21st of this year?"
- "That was just a few months after the events in question, wasn't it?"
- "And your attorney and I and a court reporter were all there, correct?"
- "You raised your right hand and you swore that you would tell the truth during that deposition, didn't you?"
- "And after you testified, you had the chance to review that testimony and correct it, didn't you?"
- "And then you signed it at the bottom, didn't you?"
- "I'm going to read a section of your deposition to you, from page X, line Y." Make sure the witness and opposing counsel have a copy so they can read along. And then you read it, and then you say, "Did I read that right?"

Back to the William Kennedy Smith trial. Roy Black impeached Ann Mercer about various inconsistences in her statements: A statement to the police that her friend had been "raped twice," which she later changed to allege a single event; a claim that Senator Ted Kennedy watched the rape, which she later retracted; and a general impeachment of her character through requiring her to admit that she sold her story to the TV show *A Current Affair* for $40,000, which she and her boyfriend used to finance a trip to Mexico. In one of the most bizarre turns of the trial, Black even impeached Mercer for lying about an antique urn she and her friend stole from the Kennedy estate on the night of the alleged rape.

If a witness admits that her story has changed, as Ann Mercer did during cross-examination, then there's nothing else that the lawyer needs to do. But sometimes a witness won't admit the contradiction, or might say, "I don't remember." If the matter that you're talking about isn't significant, then you might be required to let it drop. For example, if Ann Mercer changed her story about the color of the car she was driving that night, which is neither here nor there in the grand scheme of things, the court won't let you waste time by proving her wrong with extrinsic evidence. But if the matter on impeachment is noncollateral, which means it has important independent significance to the case, then you can prove up the impeachment with extrinsic evidence when it's time for you to call your own witnesses. The urn would be an example of this. Roy Black's theory of the case was that the rape was invented so that Mercer and her friends could sell the story and profit from it. Taking an antique urn from the home supported the idea that the two women were out for profit, and therefore he would have been permitted to prove up the impeachment through extrinsic evidence, had Mercer not admitted to it.

As you've probably gathered by now, a lawyer can do a lot of damage to opposing counsel's case through cross examination. But if it's your witness who is being cross examined, you can defend him or her through the use of objections to the other attorney's line of questioning. Here are some common objections:

The question exceeds the scope of the direct examination, which, as we've discussed, would violate Rule 611 of the Federal Rules of Evidence.

The question misstates evidence; this might arise if opposing counsel paraphrases what a witness has said incorrectly.

The question assumes facts not in evidence. This tends to arise during cross when the premise of the question assumes a fact that's in dispute to be true. For example, in a car accident case, the question, "When you were running away, you didn't look back, did you?" might draw this objection if there wasn't any evidence that the witness ran away.

The question is speculative. As on direct examination, any question that asks a witness to guess is improper. A witness can give an estimate about something he saw. For example, the speed of a car or the distance he was from the scene, but he can't speculate about what might have been. So a question like, "That driver was probably distracted, maybe by his phone or his radio, wasn't he?" would be improper if asked of a witness who couldn't see what the driver was doing.

You can't ask a question that is argumentative, which means the question doesn't actually elicit new information; instead, it draws a conclusion and asks the witness to agree with it. Note that this is different from a leading question, which simply states a fact and asks the witness whether he agrees with it. Argumentative questions are forbidden, and so is just plain arguing with the witness. For example, in the William Kennedy Smith trial, the prosecutor conducted a clumsy cross-examination of Smith, the defendant, in which she questioned his story that Patty Bowman wanted to have sex with him. To do this, she asked, "So you're saying that in the time that she met you at Au Bar, which couldn't have been any earlier than 2:00 in the morning, until the time it closed at 3:00, which is about an hour, that she was just overcome by your animal magnetism, and wanted to go home and have sex with you?" Kennedy calmly responded that he didn't know what was in Patty's mind, and the question would be better directed to Patty. The prosecutor continued, "Well, as you're talking about the evening progressing, it wasn't much of an evening, was it Mr. Smith. You got there at 2:00, last call is 3:00, we're talking about an hour here. We're not talking about an evening, are we?" Kennedy's response: "I was amazed at how things turned out." The prosecutor, "Well, we're all amazed that your animal magnetism just captivated this woman on March 30, 1991, and she wanted to go home with you, and she rubbed against you, and she wanted to take you home, and she wanted to go swimming with you, all in an hour, Mr. Smith."

That's an improper cross-examination. She's arguing with the witness. But Roy Black let it continue for a while because the prosecutor was actually being hurt by the examination. William Kennedy Smith sounded calm and reasonable. The prosecutor, by arguing and using sarcasm, sounded like a bully, and it made her less credible.

So those are objections a lawyer can raise when his witness is being cross-examined. Sometimes in a cross-examination, the lawyer conducting the examination will be the one to raise an objection. For example, in the cross-examination of Ann Mercer that we discussed, when Roy Black asked, "You met up with this man who your friend says is a rapist, isn't that correct?" and Mercer responded, "I was not afraid of him," Black could have objected to that answer as unresponsive, because it was not an answer to the question he asked. Generally, though, it's better on cross to see if you can solve the problem of the unresponsive answer yourself by simply repeating your question, rather than

Litigation and Legal Practice

asking the judge to intervene. That's what Black did. He said, "No, that's not my question, Miss Mercer. You understand my question? My question is, did you meet this man who your friend says is the alleged rapist?" Mercer replied, "Yes."

Black's handling of Mercer at that moment is a good model for how to deal with a problem witness on cross-examination. He maintained control over her testimony primarily by asking leading, single-fact questions. In the moments when she resisted the questions, like the "I was not afraid of him" moment, he was unperturbed. He didn't fight with the witness, but instead calmly insisted on an answer to his question. And he didn't ask the judge for help unless it was absolutely essential. In the end, proceeding methodically and with no great fanfare, he thoroughly destroyed Ann Mercer's credibility. That is an effective cross-examination.

CLOSING ARGUMENTS: DRIVING YOUR THEORY HOME

After both sides in a trial have had the opportunity to make their cases, it's time for closing arguments. Closing arguments allow each side's lawyers to connect all the dots for the jury. This lecture examines how the elements of persuasion can be used to craft an effective closing argument. It also explains why critical missteps in a closing argument can undermine both an attorney's credibility and his client's case.

WHAT TO DO

✴ In a closing argument, a lawyer should make full use of Aristotle's three elements of persuasion—ethos, pathos, and logos. First, it's important for a for a lawyer to remain credible. This is Aristotle's concept of ethos—the idea that a speaker persuades partly through his own good character.

✴ Even though the lawyer is not a party to the dispute, the relationship between the lawyer and the jury is important. The case of a lawyer's client will be stronger if the jury trusts and believes the lawyer, and if it feels a human connection with him.

✴ It's also important to use the closing argument to connect the jury to your client. This is Aristotle's concept of pathos—if the jury feels sympathy for your client, they're more likely to be persuaded by your arguments on his behalf.

★ To get a jury on your client's side, you'll want to be thoughtful about what you call your client. Sometimes you'll hear lawyers talk about "the plaintiff" or "the defendant," or even "my client," all of which can keep you from thinking of this person as a person.

★ A good technique in a closing argument is to remind the jury of their important role and tell them the action they should take. Another smart move is to organize the evidence to make it easy for the jury to digest and remember.

★ Sometimes in a closing argument, lawyers will attack one another. This is a mistake. It's called an ad hominem attack, and it's a logical fallacy; you can't defeat the logic of an argument by attacking the person who made it. What's more, juries won't like it.

★ The two primary tasks in a closing argument are to flesh out your own theory of the case, and to respond to the other side's strongest points. This is where logos—sound logic—plays a key role. It's time to make explicit the conclusions that you hinted at during your opening statement and to answer the ultimate questions you refrained from asking on cross-examination.

★ A great way to drive home your theory of the case is to make it unforgettable by using a visual aid. This could be a demonstrative aid—a chart, for example, or a series of slides—or perhaps an exhibit that's been entered into evidence at trial.

★ In a closing argument, you want to remind the jury of what they learned from the various witnesses, highlighting testimony that's particularly helpful to you. In doing so, try to explain complicated ideas as simply as possible. Sometimes using an analogy or a metaphor can help make a complex idea more accessible.

★ In addition to explaining your theory of the case, you also need to use your closing argument to respond to the other side's strongest points. You shouldn't avoid the parts of the trial that may damage your side. Confront them head on.

★ One very effective approach is to argue that even if everything the other side says is true, your client should still win, and give reasons why. Rather than jeopardizing your credibility with the jury by misrepresenting what the other side is arguing, address the arguments honestly.

WHAT NOT TO DO

✱ We've discussed what you should do in a closing argument. Now let's talk about what not to do. First, you can't misstate the facts. You can argue about what facts mean, and draw reasonable inferences from evidence. But if a witness said one thing, you can't pretend that he said the exact opposite thing. The jury won't buy it, and the rules governing attorney conduct prohibit it.

✱ You can't comment on missing evidence if the evidence was excluded by a pretrial ruling, or if a party didn't have the burden of producing the evidence. In general, you can't talk in your closing argument about any evidence that wasn't actually admitted at trial, whether it was excluded by a pretrial ruling or not.

✱ It's not acceptable for a lawyer to state a personal opinion. A good rule of thumb for a lawyer is to cut out all references to himself and his thoughts altogether. For example, it wouldn't be appropriate for a lawyer to say things like, "I believe this witness and you should, too," or "I promise you that my client is a good man," or "This is the worst miscarriage of justice I've ever seen." The lawyer is not a witness in the trial and should not be testifying.

* While you do want to connect with the jury on an emotional level, you can't ask the jury to base its verdict on anything other than the evidence and the law. An argument that appeals to prejudice or fear would be improper.

* In a civil trial, the jury is typically responsible not only for rendering a verdict, but for awarding damages if they are appropriate. The golden rule for lawyers arguing about damages is not to ask the jury to imagine what it would be like to be the victim and to award damages accordingly.

* If a civil case doesn't involve punitive damages, it would be improper to argue that the jury should return a verdict that would punish the defendant. The idea is that the law defines the proper amount for damages, and that's what the jury should be using to determine what damages to award. The award shouldn't be based on the jury's gut feelings.

* It is impermissible to encourage the jury not to follow the law, or to think about the consequences of a particular verdict when determining whether or not to render that verdict. A lawyer also may not misstate the law. It's okay to refer to what that law is so that the jury understands what they're supposed to do, but it must be correct.

WHAT HAPPENS NEXT

✳ Jury instructions are given by the judge toward the end of a trial. They typically come after the lawyer's closing arguments, though some jurisdictions flip this and have the jury instructions come before closings. Jury instructions tell the jury what the law says and what they need to determine.

✳ In many jurisdictions, a lot of the language in jury instructions is drawn from pattern jury instructions. These are published by the court system of a particular jurisdiction, and contain approved language for explaining the different pieces of the law. The lawyers in a case submit their requests for particular instructions to the judge, and the judge rules on which instructions to include.

✳ When the jury deliberates, it is given a verdict form that it uses to report the verdict. That form tracks the judge's instructions. Sometimes, a lawyer will use this form as a visual aid in closing argument, showing the jury which box the lawyer hopes the jury will check.

Suggested Reading

♧ Sayler and Shadel. *Tongue-Tied America.*

Questions to Consider

➚ What role do you think emotion should play in a closing argument? How far should a lawyer go to bring emotion into a closing argument?

Lecture 10 Transcript

CLOSING ARGUMENTS: DRIVING YOUR THEORY HOME

After both sides in a trial have had the opportunity to make their cases, we reach closing argument. This is your chance, as a lawyer, to connect all the dots for the jury, to explain how everything they've seen and heard adds up in your favor. Closing argument often proves to be the most enjoyable part of a trial for a lawyer, because now, free from the constraints that apply earlier in a trial, you can argue the heck out of your case.

Let me show you what I mean. Here's an excerpt of Johnnie Cochran's closing argument on behalf of football legend O.J. Simpson in his criminal trial. As you'll recall, O.J. was accused of murdering his ex-wife, Nicole Brown Simpson, and her friend, Ronald Goldman. Here, Cochran makes a vivid argument about Mark Furhman, a police officer who investigated the crime and may have planted evidence at the crime scene, and the power that they, the jury, have to right this wrong. An actor will read the following excerpt and later excerpts in this lecture:

"Why did they all try to cover up for this man Fuhrman? Why would this man, who is not only Los Angeles's worst nightmare, but America's worst nightmare, why would they all try to turn their heads and try to cover for him?

Why would you do that if you're sworn to uphold the law? There is something about corruption. There's something about a rotten apple that will ultimately infect the entire barrel. Because if the others don't have the courage that we've asked you to have in this case. People sit sadly by. We live in a society where many people are apathetic. They don't want to get involved. And that's why all of us, to a person, in this courtroom have thanked you from the bottom of our hearts. Because you know what? You haven't been apathetic. You're the ones who made a commitment. A commitment toward justice."

You can see from this excerpt why this case made Cochran famous. That's some inspiring oratory. O.J.'s lawyers, Johnnie Cochran, Alan Dershowitz, Barry Scheck, Robert Shapiro, Robert Kardashian, and F. Lee Bailey, became known as the "Dream Team" because of their skillful lawyering in this trial. So let's examine Cochran's closing argument from this trial to see how it's done.

In a closing argument, a lawyer should make full use of Aristotle's three principles of verbal persuasion: ethos, pathos, and logos. We've talked previously about how important it is throughout a trial for a lawyer to remain credible. This is Aristotle's concept of ethos—the idea that a speaker persuades partly through his own good character. Even though the lawyer is not a party to the dispute, the relationship between the lawyer and the jury is important. The case of a lawyer's client will be stronger if the jury trusts and believes the lawyer, and if it feels a human connection with him. Here's how Johnnie Cochran started his closing argument. You can see him paying attention to his relationship with the jury from the very beginning:

"The Defendant, Mr. Orenthal James Simpson, is now afforded an opportunity to argue the case, if you will, but I'm not going to argue with you, ladies and gentlemen. What I'm going to do is to try and discuss the reasonable inferences which I feel can be drawn from this evidence. At the outset, let me join with the others in thanking you for the service that you've rendered. You are truly a marvelous jury, the longest serving jury in Los Angeles County, perhaps the most patient and healthy jury we've ever seen. I hope that your health and your good health continues. We met approximately one year and one day ago on September 26, 1994. I guess we've been together longer than some relationships as it were."

These aren't mere pleasantries, and Cochran isn't hemming and hawing. He's trying to enhance his rapport with the jury at the conclusion of a long trial, so that the arguments he's about to make have more persuasive power.

Another important task in the closing argument is to connect the jury to your client. This is Aristotle's concept of pathos—if the jury feels sympathy for your client, they're more likely to be persuaded by your arguments on his behalf. To get a jury on your client's side, you'll want to be thoughtful about what you call your client. Sometimes you'll hear lawyers talk about "the plaintiff" or "the defendant," or even "my client," all of which can keep you from thinking of this person as a person. In the O.J. case, the prosecution called O.J. "the defendant," which had the effect of erasing his fame, and making him sound a little more sinister. So Johnnie Cochran addressed this head-on in his closing argument:

"Now, in this case, you're aware that we represent Mr. Orenthal James Simpson. The Prosecution never calls him Mr. Orenthal James Simpson. They call him Defendant. I want to tell you right at the outset that Orenthal James Simpson, like all defendants, is presumed to be innocent. He's entitled to the same dignity and respect as all the rest of us. As he sits over there now, he's cloaked in a presumption of innocence. You will determine the facts of whether or not he's set free to walk out those doors or whether he spends the rest of his life in prison. But he's Orenthal James Simpson. He's not just the Defendant, and we on the Defense are proud, consider it a privilege to have been part of representing him in this exercise and this journey towards justice, make no mistake about it."

So the lawyer is a character in this story, O.J. is a character in this story, and then Johnnie Cochran turns the jurors themselves into characters in the story. He makes them the heroes. That's a great technique in a closing argument, to remind the jury of their important role and tell them the action they should take. Listen to how Cochran called on the jury to take action, offering them a place in history:

"You are empowered to do justice. You are empowered to ensure that this great system of ours works. Listen for a moment, will you, please. One of my favorite people in history is the great Frederick Douglas. He said shortly after the slaves were freed, quote, 'In a composite nation like ours as before the law, there should be no rich, no poor, no high, no low, no white, no black, but common country, common citizenship, equal rights and a common destiny.' This marvelous statement was made more than 100 years ago. It's an ideal worth striving for and one that we still strive for. We haven't reached this goal yet, but certainly in this great country of ours, we're trying. With a jury such as this, we hope we can do that in this particular case."

Now, sometimes in a closing argument, lawyers will attack one another. This is a mistake. It's called an ad hominem attack, which means that you are attacking the person rather than his position, and it's a logical fallacy; you can't defeat the logic of an argument by attacking the person who made it. Ad hominem attacks also don't work. Juries don't like them. Johnnie Cochran took the opposite approach, which made him more credible:

"I'd like to comment and to compliment Miss Clark and Mr. Darden on what I thought were fine arguments yesterday. I don't agree with much of what they said, but I listened intently, as I hope you'll do with me. And together, hopefully these discussions are going to be helpful to you in trying to arrive at a decision in this case."

See how reasonable he sounds? That makes him more persuasive. But the two primary tasks in a closing argument are to flesh out your own theory of the case, and to respond to the other side's strongest points. This is where logos—Aristotle's notion of the power of logic in verbal persuasion—comes into play. Let's focus first on how Johnnie Cochran made his case.

As we discussed with regard to opening statements, a good lawyer will develop a theory of the case. This means a central theme, a persuasive story that the jury can believe about what happened. Now, this was a criminal trial, which means that the prosecution had the burden of showing that O.J. Simpson was guilty of murder. Johnnie Cochran wasn't required to prove that O.J. was innocent. Instead, his task was to show that the prosecution hadn't met its burden, that there was reasonable doubt about whether O.J. was guilty. Here's how Johnnie Cochran explained reasonable doubt:

"It is not a mere possible doubt and we know that because everything relating to human affairs is open to some possible or imaginary doubt. It is that state of the case where after the entire comparison and consideration of all the evidence leaves the minds of the jurors in that condition that they cannot say they feel an abiding conviction of the truth of the charge. That is reasonable doubt."

Under Cochran's theory of the case, a racist cop named Mark Fuhrman planted evidence, including blood-spattered socks, to get O.J. arrested. In a devastating cross-examination, the defense had been able to show that Fuhrman freely used offensive racial epithets when talking about black people, and that he was alone with the evidence at various times. They were also able to show that some of the evidence seemed odd: that blood was sticky when it should have dried, or that it wasn't there and then suddenly it was, or that, in the case of the bloody gloves used in the commission of the crime, it didn't support the prosecution's case—the gloves were too small to fit on O.J.'s hands. So Cochran developed two refrains in his closing argument to drive this theory home: "If it doesn't fit, you must acquit," and "If these messengers have lied to you, you can't trust their message." Those are terrific, memorable themes, and he wove them throughout his closing argument.

Cochran also made another smart move: He organized the evidence to make it easy for the jury to digest and remember. In one particularly memorable moment, he showed the jury a list, 15 questions that raised reasonable doubt about the prosecution's case. He even handed the list over to the prosecutors, suggesting that they deal with these "troublesome questions." His questions included the following:

1. Some blood was found on a sock almost two months after the crime scene was first searched. Experts for the defense opined that the sock had not actually been worn, and the defense also pointed out that 1.5 milliliters of O.J.'s blood that had been in police custody had gone missing. Why did it take them two

months to find blood on the sock? Presumably, because it wasn't there until someone planted it.

2. Why did that blood go missing? Presumably, so Mark Fuhrman could put it on that sock.

3. Why did the police at first try to cover up the fact that the blood had gone missing? Cochran's theory: Because they wanted to cover up Fuhrman's bad actions.

4. Why was the bloody glove found by Mark Fuhrman still moist when if allegedly had been dropped seven hours earlier? Experts testified that blood dries quickly. Again, presumably because Mark Fuhrman put the blood on the glove

5. Why wasn't there any other blood or fiber in the area where Mark Fuhrman said he found the bloody glove? Cochran's answer: Because the glove was planted.

6. "If Mr. Simpson had just killed Mr. Goldman in a bloody battle involving more than two dozen knife wounds where Mr. Goldman remained standing and struggling for several minutes," why wasn't there blood in O.J.'s bedroom, where he was believed to have gone after the attack, and only 7/10ths of one drop of blood in O.J.'s Ford Bronco, the vehicle he drove while being pursued by the police?

7. And why didn't that glove fit?

That's a really effective way to argue this case. Through his list, Cochran distilled all the evidence that the defense had presented and put it into a form that the jury could easily remember. If even one of his questions stuck with the jury, that could be enough to constitute reasonable doubt.

Cochran went on to answer the questions for the jury explicitly. His response was that each issue that he raised pointed to Fuhrman messing with the evidence. In our discussion of opening statements, we talked about how at that stage of the trial you can't argue; you can't make explicit what you think evidence means. We also talked about how on cross examination you don't want to ask the ultimate questions, the ones that could let a hostile witness argue with you about your conclusions. In closing argument, it's time to make explicit the conclusions that you hinted at during your opening statement and to answer the ultimate questions you refrained from asking on cross-examination. That's exactly what Cochran was doing with his list.

Another great way to drive your theory of the case home is to make it unforgettable with a visual aid. This could either be a demonstrative aid—a chart, for example, or a series of slides, which is what Johnnie Cochran used as he discussed his 15 questions before the jury—or perhaps an exhibit that's been entered into evidence at trial, or a prop. Here's a great moment where Cochran uses a prop, a knit cap, to make a point. He refers at the outset to prosecutor Marcia Clark:

"And so she (Ms. Clark) talks about O.J. being very, very recognizable. She talks about O.J. Simpson getting dressed up to go commit these murders. Just before we break for our break, I was thinking—I was thinking last night about this case and their theory and how it didn't make any sense and how it didn't fit and how something is wrong. It occurred to me how they were going to come here, stand up here and tell you how O.J. Simpson was going to disguise himself. He was going to put on a knit cap and some dark clothes, and he was going to get in his white Bronco, this recognizable person, and go over and kill his wife. That's what they want you to believe. That's how silly their argument is. And I said to myself, maybe I can demonstrate this graphically. Let me show you something. This is a knit cap. Let me put this knit cap on (Indicating). You have seen me for a year. If I put this knit cap on, who am I? I'm still Johnnie Cochran with a knit cap. And if you looked at O.J. Simpson over there--and he has a rather large head--O.J. Simpson in a knit cap from two blocks away is still O.J. Simpson. It's no disguise. It's no disguise. It makes no sense. It doesn't fit. If it doesn't fit, you must acquit."

Using the prop makes the point vivid. The jury isn't likely to forget it. And you can hear that refrain again, driving the theme home.

In a closing argument, you also want to remind the jury of what they learned from the various witnesses, highlighting testimony that's particularly helpful to you. Cochran did this very effectively when he talked about the police officer Mark Fuhrman, the villain in his story. He reminded the jury of the testimony of Kathleen Bell, who gave the following damning testimony about Fuhrman. Describing a conversation that she said she had with Fuhrman, Bell recalled: "He said that if, when he sees a black man with a white woman driving in a car, he pulls them over. I said, `What if they didn't do anything?' He said he'd find something." Cochran also re-played some audiotape that he had introduced into evidence earlier in the trial, a recording of an interview Fuhrman gave to a screenwriter in which he used offensive racial epithets. This was a chilling exhibit, and it was effective for Cochran to play the recording a second time for the jury. After playing the offensive recording, Cochran told the jury, "This is how he sees this world. That is this man's cynical view of the world. This is this man who is out there protecting and serving. That is Mark Fuhrman."

It can be very helpful in a closing argument to explain complicated ideas as simply as possible. That can make the logic clear. Sometimes using an analogy or a metaphor can help make a complex idea more accessible to a jury. Here's a famous analogy Cochran used to explain why the prosecution's approach in the case was backwards:

"And so in this scenario…the Prosecution had a puzzle, and it was interesting how they did this puzzle…if you ever have gone to the store and bought a puzzle, when you buy a puzzle, on the outside of the box of the puzzle there is a picture, so you know what the puzzle looks like when it is finished. Well, in this case the Prosecution took a photograph or picture of O.J. Simpson first, then they took the pieces apart. If they really wanted to talk about reasonable doubt, you don't jump to conclusions at the beginning. You don't rush to judgment and then be concerned about an obsession to win. What you do is you take the pieces and put them together and then you come to the conclusion. They have got it all backward."

Notice how well Cochran's puzzle analogy works with his refrain that "If it doesn't fit, you must acquit."

So you need to use your closing argument to explain your theory of the case, but you also need to use it to respond to the other side's strongest points. You shouldn't avoid the parts of the trial that may damage your side, confront them head-on. One very effective approach is to argue that even if everything the other side says is true, your client should still win, and give reasons why. You could say that the other side's case boils down to one or two key points, and refute them. Rather than jeopardizing your credibility with the jury by misrepresenting what the other side is arguing, address the arguments honestly. Think of the doubts you would have if you were in the jurors' shoes, and respond to those. For example, some of the best evidence for the prosecution was O.J. Simpson's history of domestic violence against Nicole Brown Simpson. Cochran dealt with this evidence directly. He admitted that there had been violence in the past, but attempted to draw the sting from these bad facts. In this excerpt, he challenges the arguments made by prosecutor Christopher Darden:

"Let me say that no, none, not one little bit of domestic violence is tolerable between a man and a woman. O.J. Simpson is not proud of that 1989 incident. He is not proud of it. But you know what? He paid his debt to that and it went to court. He went through that program. And the one good thing, and no matter how long Darden talked, from 1989 to now there was never any physical violence between O.J. Simpson and Nicole Brown Simpson."

Cochran not only responds to Darden's points here, he creates sympathy for his client while also enhancing his ethos with the jury.

So we've talked about what you should do on closing argument. Let's look at some of the things you shouldn't do. First, you can't misstate the facts. You can argue about what facts mean, and draw reasonable inferences from evidence. But if a witness said one thing, you can't pretend that he said the exact opposite thing. The jury won't buy it, and the rules governing attorney conduct prohibit it. You also can't comment on missing evidence if the evidence was excluded by a pretrial ruling, or if a party didn't have the burden of producing the evidence. For example, in the O.J. trial, it would have been improper for the prosecution to comment that the defense didn't provide any evidence about who actually committed the crime if O.J. didn't do it. The defense doesn't bear the burden of proving O.J. innocent, so a comment like that would have resulted in a mistrial.

The rules also prohibit a lawyer at trial from alluding to "any matter that the lawyer does not reasonably believe is relevant, or that will not be supported by admissible evidence[.]" So you can't talk in your closing argument about any evidence that wasn't actually admitted at trial, whether it was excluded by a pretrial ruling or not. If it didn't come into evidence, don't talk about it. For example, Johnnie Cochran wasn't allowed to call some witnesses he might have liked to have as part of his case because he neglected to put them on the witness list or provide their witness statements to the prosecution during discovery. Since those witnesses didn't testify at trial, the things they knew weren't part of the evidence and Mr. Cochran wasn't allowed to talk about them during his closing argument.

It's not okay for a lawyer to state a personal opinion. A good rule of thumb for a lawyer is to cut out all references to himself and his thoughts altogether. It's not okay for a lawyer to say something like, "I believe this witness and you should, too," or "I promise you that my client is a good man," or "This is the worst miscarriage of justice I've ever seen." The lawyer is not a witness in the trial and should not be testifying. You'll sometimes hear a lawyer tell a story about himself to use as an analogy, and that can be permissible. Cochran's statement that he and the jury have been working together now a long time is okay, as is his description of his own struggles to make the prosecution's case fit together in his mind. But it wouldn't be okay for him to say something like, "I believe my client is innocent." This is prohibited by Model Rule of Professional Conduct 3.4, which says an attorney may not "assert personal knowledge of facts in issue except when testifying as a witness, or state a personal opinion as to the justness of a cause, the credibility of a witness, the culpability of a civil litigant or the guilt or innocence of an accused." While you do want to connect with the jury on an emotional level, you can't ask the jury to base its verdict on anything other than the evidence and the law. So an argument that appeals to prejudice or fear would be improper.

In a civil trial, the jury is typically responsible not only for rendering a verdict but for awarding damages if they are appropriate. There is a rule about how to argue damages in civil cases properly, known informally as the golden rule. That rule says that you're not allowed to ask the jury to imagine what it would be like to be the victim and to award damages accordingly. If the case doesn't involve punitive damages, it would also be improper to argue that the jury should return a verdict that would punish the defendant. The idea is that the law defines the proper amount for damages depending on the kind of case that it is, and that's what the jury should be using to determine what damages to award. The award shouldn't be based on the jury's gut feelings about these things when the law lays out a different way to calculate damages.

It is impermissible to encourage the jury not to follow the law, or to think about the consequences of a particular verdict when determining whether or not to render that verdict. If the prosecution in the O.J. Simpson trial had argued that the jury had to lock O.J. up out of fear that he might come hurt their families next, that would be improper. Similarly, if the defense were to argue that the jury shouldn't punish O.J. because if they did, there would be no one left to take care of his children, that also would be improper. A lawyer also may not misstate the law. The judge will instruct the jury about the law that governs the case, and it's okay to refer to what that law is so that the jury understands what questions they are supposed to answer. But you need to state the law correctly. For example, if the prosecution in the O.J. case had said that O.J. has to prove that he's innocent, that would have been a misstatement of the law and would have resulted in a mistrial.

Let's talk now about what the judge will tell the jury about the law. We talked about jury instructions briefly when we discussed pretrial motions. The judge gives the instructions to the jury toward the end of a trial. They typically come after the lawyer's closing arguments, though some jurisdictions flip this and have the jury instruction come before closings. These instructions will tell the jury what the law says and what they need to determine. For example, Judge Lance Ito's jury instructions in the O.J. Simpson case explained that the defendant was accused of the crime of murder, which the judge defined as "Unlawfully killing a human being with malice aforethought." He then explained what "malice aforethought" is, essentially, intending to kill someone and then doing it. He also explained other legal issues. For example, he defined circumstantial evidence as evidence that proves a fact from which the inference of another fact may be drawn. He told the jury that it can be given as much weight as direct evidence.

In many jurisdictions, a lot of the language in jury instructions is drawn from pattern jury instructions. These are published by the court system of a particular jurisdiction, and contain approved language for explaining the different pieces of the law. The lawyers in a case submit their requests for particular instructions to the judge, and he or she rules on which instructions to include. If your jurisdiction has pattern jury instructions, the judge will use that language because he knows it's been approved. Using it makes it less likely that the judge will be reversed on appeal for making a mistake in the instructions.

When the jury deliberates, it is given a verdict form that it uses to report the verdict. That form tracks the judge's instructions. Sometimes, a lawyer will use this form as a visual aid in closing argument, showing the jury which box he hopes it will check.

In the O.J. Simpson case, the verdict form asked the jury first to determine if O.J. was guilty of the murder of Nicole Brown Simpson, and second, if he was guilty of the murder of Ronald Lyle Goldman. The jury found O.J. to be not guilty on both counts. In a subsequent civil trial, the jury found that O.J. had killed both of these victims, and awarded the victims' families large sums in financial damages. But in the criminal trial, the jury found reasonable doubt of the guilt, very likely because of the problems with the blood evidence that Johnnie Cochran emphasized so skillfully in his closing argument.

UNDERSTANDING THE APPELLATE PROCESS

T he right to appeal is the right to question the outcome of the trial process. It's a check on the power of lower courts, and an acknowledgment, based on centuries of experience, that even the smartest minds and the best-run institutions sometimes make mistakes. This lecture examines the appeals process, with particular focus on the standards of review applied by appellate courts and the nuts and bolts of appellate advocacy.

THE APPEALS PROCESS

★ Most jurisdictions have two levels of appellate courts: courts of appeal, which review decisions made by trial courts, and an even higher level judicial tribunal—typically known as a supreme court—which reviews decisions made by the courts of appeal. Decisions of these higher courts, whether in the federal or state court systems, are generally issued in written opinions and have binding authority for the courts below them in the same jurisdiction.

★ Many trials don't generate appeals. Maybe the parties settle, thereby resolving the dispute, which happens a lot in civil cases. Maybe a defendant in a criminal case is found to be not guilty. Maybe there's no legal right to an appeal. You can't appeal simply because you don't like the verdict; you have to be able to point to a particular legal error.

* Even rarer is the case that makes it all the way to a supreme court—whether a state supreme court or the Supreme Court of the United States. While most jurisdictions give you the right to appeal certain errors to an intermediate appellate court, particularly in criminal cases, most jurisdictions do not guarantee such access to the supreme court.

* Most supreme courts don't have the time to hear every appeal that's brought to them. The workload would be overwhelming. Instead, they choose their cases, looking for those that have special significance or might clear up a particularly important area of law.

* Appeals typically take place after a trial is over, but they can be made during the trial. If an appeal is made mid-trial, it's called an interlocutory appeal. For example, a prosecutor might file an interlocutory appeal if the trial judge has suppressed evidence that the government feels should lawfully be admitted.

* The law typically frowns on interlocutory appeals. It's more efficient to save all issues on appeal for the close of the case, so they can be heard all at once. But if there's an issue that just can't wait—for example, if a party says the court doesn't have jurisdiction even to hear the suit in the first place—then the party may have to file an interlocutory appeal concerning that issue.

* To bring an interlocutory appeal, you have to show that waiting to appeal the issue until the trial is over would be particularly prejudicial to the rights of one of the parties. In some jurisdictions, an interlocutory appeal will stay the lower court proceeding, halting the trial until the appellate court decides the matter. In other jurisdictions, the lower court proceeding isn't stayed, which could make things complicated.

* An appeal is not a retrial of a case. Trial courts and appellate courts play very different roles in the judicial process. Everything gets decided at the trial level. The jury gets to resolve all issues of fact—unless the trial isn't a jury trial, in which case the judge becomes the finder of

fact. In either case, the judge is responsible for ruling on all issues of law that are raised during the trial. Together, judge and jury see the whole picture.

★ The appellate court, by contrast, doesn't get to start from the beginning to decide if every little thing at issue was decided correctly. Appellate courts don't usually get to evaluate new evidence or hear from witnesses. Instead, the appellate court is only allowed to look at the particular legal issue raised on appeal. Usually, this will be an issue of whether the trial procedure was correct, or whether the trial judge interpreted the law correctly.

STANDARDS OF REVIEW

★ Another difference between a trial court and an appellate court is the standard by which the decision is made. In civil cases, the trial court typically will determine liability based on the preponderance of the evidence. That is, findings of fact will be based on whether the evidence shows that it is more likely than not that events were as the plaintiff claims. In a criminal case, the trial court will use the more demanding standard requiring proof beyond a reasonable doubt. An appellate court, however, applies different standards of review, based on the type of ruling the court is being asked to reconsider.

★ An appellate court will only overturn a finding of fact if it is clearly erroneous. This means that the appellate court will defer to the factual determinations of the trial court, unless the appellate court has a definite and firm conviction that there's been a mistake.

★ Evidentiary hearings usually involve evaluating the credibility of witnesses and other evidence. The trial court judge or jury are in a better position to make that evaluation, because they see the witness testimony and other evidence firsthand. The appellate court usually must rely on the party's legal briefs and a transcript of what happened, and that's not the same thing as actually being present at the trial.

* If the issue on appeal is a question of whether the trial judge interpreted the law correctly, then the appellate court has more discretion. Legal issues are reviewed de novo. This means that the appellate court is free to substitute its own judgment for that of the trial court. Mixed questions of law and fact typically are also reviewed de novo.

* Sometimes an appeal involves matters that are left to the discretion of the trial judge—for example, the sentencing of a criminal defendant who is found guilty at trial. Appellate courts use a highly deferential standard in such instances, overturning the lower court only if the trial judge's ruling constituted an abuse of discretion.

APPELLATE BRIEFS

* The lawyer appealing a case will have to file an appellate brief. Depending on the circumstances, he may also have the opportunity to make an oral argument before the appellate court.

* In general, appellate courts make their decisions based primarily on written briefs filed by the parties. A brief will start with a statement of the facts of the case, a statement of the question the appellate court is being asked to decide, a summary of the case's procedural history, and a discussion of the applicable standard of review. The brief will then go on to lay out the party's arguments.

* Writing an effective brief is an art that every appellate lawyer has to master. An effective brief will be well written, and its arguments will be based on sound logic. Logical reasoning is absolutely critical.

* Basic legal argumentation usually follows the form of an Aristotelian syllogism: a major premise and a minor premise point the way to a conclusion (if A and B are true, then C must be true). In a legal brief, the major premise is the rule of law governing the case, the minor premise is the facts particular to the case, and the conclusion is the application of the law to the facts.

★ If your major premise is rooted in text, such as a statute, then you will need to interpret that statute for the court. The court will always want to start with the language of the statute itself, so that should be your starting point. Next, you may want to consider the legislative purpose—the reasons given by legislators for enacting the law in the first place.

★ You may also want to look at the statute's legislative history. For example, when Congress passes a statute, it creates reports that can be used to help interpret the language if the meaning is not totally plain, or to help explain the purpose of the statute. State legislatures have their own records that reveal legislative history. Sometimes the history shows that the legislative body considered a different version of the statute and rejected it. You can use that to argue that there are things the statute isn't meant to do.

* A lawyer interpreting a text should always read the entire text, because the court will want to understand the relevant portion of the text in context. The court will try to interpret the statute so that it is internally consistent. A court will also do everything it can to read a statute so that it is constitutional, because undoing the work of the legislature, a body elected by the people, is not something courts undertake lightly.

* Lawyers seeking to bolster their arguments about the proper interpretation of a text often make policy arguments, predicting the likely consequences of the text. Naturally, an interpretation of a statute that promises good public policy outcomes can be very persuasive. Lawyers arguing against a particular interpretation quite often invoke a "parade of horribles," describing all the terrible things that might result from the interpretation they oppose.

ORAL ARGUMENT

* Sometimes, an appellate court will decide a case based solely on the briefs written by the parties. In many cases, however, the court will also permit oral argument, giving the lawyers for each side an opportunity to make oral presentations about their case and answer questions from the appellate judges.

* Writing a brief and participating in oral argument involve very different skills, and an appellate lawyer needs to be able to do both well. In a brief, you can cover all the issues related to your appeal, including those issues that are less important, and you can include lots of footnotes to back up your points. In oral argument, however, you must be selective. You want to pick the one or two main issues that are really important to your case, and focus on those.

* Typically, an appellate court will have a panel of judges who hear the case. Each lawyer will have a limited amount of time to present, and the lawyer isn't the only one doing the talking. The lawyer might start the oral argument off with what she wants to say, but the judges will quickly jump in with questions.

✭ Good lawyers welcome questions from the appellate panel. If oral argument were simply a time for the lawyer to provide a short oral summary of what's in the brief, it wouldn't really add much. The judges' questions let you know what they really care about. The challenge of oral argument is to present your case confidently and professionally, while at the same time being careful not to sound too aggressive, even in the face of rough questioning.

Suggested Reading

◊ Davis, *The Argument of an Appeal.*

◊ Harlan, *What Part Does the Oral Argument Play in the Conduct of an Appeal?*

Questions to Consider

↗ Do you believe that a person who committed a crime should be able to be released on appeal because of a procedural error? Why is this our system?

↗ Do you think an appellate court should be able to review everything de novo, without deferring to the trial court's judgement? Why or why not?

UNDERSTANDING THE APPELLATE PROCESS

The United States has often been called an overly litigious society, and our system of appellate review is part of what some people criticize. It strikes them as unacceptable that a case should tie up our courts for years as the parties pursue their claims from appeal to appeal, sometimes all the way to the U.S. Supreme Court. There's no doubt that it can take quite a while for some cases to reach their final resolution in the courts. But if you have any doubts about the value of the appeals process, just think back to a case we considered previously—that of Clarence Earl Gideon.

Mr. Gideon, you may recall, was accused of breaking into a Florida pool hall in 1961 and stealing $55 and some drinks. He had only an eighth grade education and couldn't afford a lawyer, but state law barred the Florida trial court from appointing a lawyer for him. Mr. Gideon gamely tried to represent himself during his trial, protesting his innocence, but he lost and was sentenced to five years in prison. That would have been Mr. Gideon's fate, if it weren't for the right to appeal. But thanks to that right, he challenged the trial court's decision, arguing that a lawyer should have been appointed for him. He appealed to the Florida Supreme Court, which denied his petition. So he petitioned the U.S. Supreme Court, which consented to hear his case, ultimately agreeing with his argument and sending his case back to Florida to be tried again. And on his second try, this time with the help of a lawyer, Mr. Gideon won his case and his freedom. That's the power of the right to appeal: It's the right to question the outcome of the trial process and to demand that it be reviewed by a higher authority. It's a check on the power of lower courts and an acknowledgment, based on centuries of experience, that even the smartest minds and the best-run institutions sometimes make mistakes.

Some lawyers focus their careers on appellate advocacy. So let's talk about how the appeals process works. Most jurisdictions have two levels of appellate courts: a court of appeals, which might review a trial court's decision, and an even higher level judicial tribunal, typically known as a supreme court, which can review a decision by a court of appeals. Decisions of these higher courts, whether in the federal or state court systems, are generally issued in written decisions and have binding authority for the courts below them in the same jurisdiction. It's important to realize, though, in spite of the impression you might get from reading or hearing about important cases in the news, that many trials don't generate appeals. Maybe the parties settle, thereby resolving the dispute, which happens a lot in civil cases. Or maybe a defendant in a criminal case is found to be not guilty, which can't be appealed because of the prohibition in our Constitution against double jeopardy, which means trying a criminal defendant twice for the same crime. Maybe there's no legal right to an appeal. You can't just appeal because you don't like the verdict; you have to be able to point to a particular legal error in order to raise an appeal. Or maybe you can't appeal because the lawyer at trial didn't properly preserve the error by making an objection.

Even more rare is the case that makes it all the way to a supreme court, whether that be a state supreme court of the U.S. Supreme Court. While most jurisdictions give you the right to appeal certain errors to an intermediate appellate court—particularly in criminal cases—most jurisdictions do not guarantee that same access to the supreme court. Most supreme courts don't have the time to hear every appeal that's brought to them. The workload would be overwhelming. So they choose their cases, looking for those that have special significance or might clear up a particularly important area of law. So, inspiring as Clarence Gideon's vindication in the courts was, he was also very lucky. We'll talk in detail about the work of the U.S. Supreme Court separately.

Appeals typically take place after a trial is over, but they can be made during the trial. If an appeal is made mid-trial, that is called an interlocutory appeal. For example, a prosecutor might file an appeal mid-trial if the trial judge has suppressed evidence that the government feels should lawfully be admitted. The law typically frowns on interlocutory appeals. It is more efficient to save all issues on appeal for the close of the case, so they can be heard all at once. But if there's an issue that just can't wait—for example, if a party says the court doesn't have jurisdiction even to hear the suit in the first place—then you might be able to appeal on an interlocutory basis. To be able to bring an appeal mid-trial, you will have to show that waiting to bring an appeal after the trial is over would be particularly prejudicial to the rights of one of the parties. In some jurisdictions, an interlocutory appeal will stay the lower court proceeding, halting the trial until the appellate court decides the matter. In other jurisdictions, the lower court proceeding isn't stayed, which could make things complicated. But most appeals are raised after the trial is over. In a criminal case where the defendant is found guilty, you're likely going to see the defendant appealing the verdict.

It's important to understand that an appeal is not a retrial of a case. Trial courts and appellate courts play very different roles in the judicial process. Everything gets decided at the trial level. The jury gets to resolve all issues of fact, unless the trial isn't a jury trial, in which case the judge becomes the finder of fact. In either case, the judge is responsible for ruling on all issues of law that are raised during the trial. Together, judge and jury see the whole picture. In contrast, the appellate court doesn't get to start from the beginning to decide if every little thing at issue was decided correctly. Appellate courts don't usually get to evaluate new evidence or hear from witnesses. Instead, the appellate court is only allowed to look at the particular legal issue raised on appeal. Usually, this will be an issue of whether the trial procedure was correct, or whether the trial judge interpreted the law correctly.

Here's another difference between a trial court an appellate court: the standard by which the decision is made. The trial court typically will decide a civil case using a preponderance of the evidence standard. That is, findings of fact will be based on whether the evidence shows that it is more likely than not that events were as the plaintiff claims. For a criminal case, the trial court will use the more demanding "beyond a reasonable doubt" standard. But an appellate court has different standards of review, depending on what you're asking it to reconsider. An appellate court will only overturn a finding of fact if it is clearly erroneous. This means that the appellate court will defer to the factual determinations of the trial court, unless the appellate court has a definite and firm conviction that there's been a mistake. If there are two possible views of the evidence and the trial court's interpretation is plausible, then the appellate court has to go with the trial court's interpretation, even if the appellate court would have ruled differently if it had been overseeing the trial. That's because evidentiary hearings usually involve evaluating how credible witnesses and other evidence are, and the trial court judge or jury are in a better position to make that determination since they see the witness testimony and other evidence firsthand. The appellate court usually must rely on reading a transcript of what happened, and briefs about it, and that's not the same thing as actually being present at the trial. So if the issue is a factual one, the appellate court has to defer to the trial court. But if the issue on appeal is a question of whether the trial judge interpreted the law correctly, then the appellate court has more discretion. Legal issues are reviewed de novo, that is, "starting from the beginning." So when reviewing the trial court's interpretation of the law, the appellate court is free to substitute its own judgment for that of the trial court. A question of law could be something like whether a party has standing to bring a claim or whether a statute is unconstitutional.

What about when an issue on appeal is sort of a mix of law and facts? For example, a criminal defendant might say that he didn't waive his right to counsel after the police arrested him and read him his rights, but was questioned anyway, in violation of the Supreme Court's decision in *Miranda v. Arizona*. Violations of *Miranda* rights are a classic example of a mixed question of law and facts, where the rule of law is undisputed but the question is whether the facts of the case violate the rule. In these situations, the court can't rule on the law without revisiting the facts, so mixed questions of law and fact are also generally reviewed de novo.

Sometimes an appeal involves matters that are up to the discretion of the trial judge, which are reviewed under an abuse of discretion standard. You often see this in disputes about whether a defendant received the proper sentence. Sentences in federal courts are governed by sentencing guidelines, which give the court some discretion, but which can also seem unfair in certain cases. So sometimes a judge will depart from a sentencing guideline, and that might result in an appeal for abuse of discretion.

Those are the standards of review in most appellate cases, such as when a party in a state court appeals to the appellate court of that state. Some cases, however, can be appealed from state court to federal court, which is what happened in Clarence Gideon's case. There, the trial court's decision involved a constitutional issue that the U.S. Supreme Court chose to address. Here's how such an appeal can happen.

If a criminal case takes place in state court, the defendant can appeal to the state court of appeals and state supreme court. Once he's exhausted all his state appeals, he then can appeal to a federal district court through what's known as a habeas corpus petition. Habeas corpus, as you may know, is Latin for "you have the body," and it's shorthand for a legal procedure for objecting to the reasons or conditions of a person's confinement. The U.S. Constitution, Article 1, Section 9, says, "The privilege of the writ of Habeas Corpus shall not be suspended[.]" That essentially means that the government can't deprive people of their right to protest their imprisonment in court if they believe it to be unlawful. So the right shows up in the Constitution, but the particular parameters of what habeas corpus means are spelled out in federal law. The current version of habeas law, contained in the Antiterrorism and Effective Death Penalty Act, says that anyone convicted of a crime by a state court can bring a habeas petition in federal court, but you have to do it within a year of being convicted and exhausting your state post-conviction appeals. That statute also says that the federal judge can review what the state court did, but can't grant habeas relief unless the state court's decision is contrary to clearly established federal law as determined by the Supreme Court of the United States, or has resulted in a decision that was based on an "unreasonable determination of the facts." That's a pretty hard hurdle to surmount in most cases.

But it can happen. For example, we talked previously about the case of Brendan Dassey, who was made famous in a documentary called *Making a Murderer*. Brendan Dassey was 16 when he and his uncle, Steven Avery, were convicted of the rape and murder of a young woman named Teresa Halbach. The film called Dassey's conviction into question, highlighting Dassey's mental limitations and questioning whether he had been improperly interrogated by police, without a lawyer or parent present. Dassey was convicted in 2007 and appealed this conviction unsuccessfully to the Wisconsin Circuit Court and the Wisconsin Supreme Court. After exhausting his state court appeals in 2013, Dassey filed for a writ of habeas corpus in federal district court in Wisconsin in 2014. Dassey made two claims on appeal: that he was denied his Sixth Amendment right to effective assistance of counsel, and that his confession was obtained in violation of his Fifth Amendment right not to be compelled to testify against himself. The federal district court found that Dassey's Sixth Amendment rights weren't violated, but that his Fifth Amendment rights were. So his lawyer's decision to appeal from state to federal court proved to be a wise one.

Let's look first at the part of the decision involving Dassey's Sixth Amendment rights, because it will let you see how the power of an appellate court can be limited by its standard of review. In a scathing 91-page opinion, the federal magistrate judge outlined the incompetence of Dassey's first attorney. This lawyer, Leonard Kachinsky, was appointed to represent Dassey. Instead of protecting his client, Kachinsky gave media interviews in which he described his client as sad, remorseful, overwhelmed, and led "down the criminal path" by his uncle. He appeared on the *Nancy Grace* show, saying that, "there is, quite frankly, no defense" for his client. During the three weeks following his appointment, Kachinsky spent 10 hours speaking to the press, but only one hour speaking to his client. He allowed the 16-year-old mentally deficient Dassey to be interrogated by the police outside of his presence. He arranged for the meeting, but did not prepare Dassey for the interview or attend the interview to represent him. Shockingly, Kachinsky actually hired an investigator to help the prosecution's case—not the case for the defense, his client, but for the prosecution. The state public defender wrote a letter to the trial court calling Kachinsky's acts "indefensible," and the judge removed him as counsel.

In its opinion, you can feel the federal court's frustration with this attorney's conduct. Nevertheless, the court did not grant Brendan Dassey habeas relief on this ground. That's because Dassey's attorneys relied on the wrong case law precedent in making Dassey's appeal in the state courts. Dassey's attorneys raised the issue of inadequate legal representation as a claim under *Cuyler v. Sullivan*, a U.S. Supreme Court decision holding that a defendant has the right to be represented by an attorney whose actions are not impacted by a conflict of interest. They could have raised a claim under a different Supreme Court decision, *Strickland v. Washington*, which guarantees the right to effective assistance of counsel, and maybe that would have worked. It certainly would have made more sense. In fact, the trial court stated when removing Kachinsky from the case that Kachinsky's actions violated *Strickland*. But since the lawyers representing Dassey through his state appeals raised a *Sullivan* claim instead, his federal appellate attorneys—yet another set of lawyers—didn't have the option to make a *Strickland* claim, and the federal habeas court was limited to considering whether the lawyer had a conflict of interest under *Sullivan*. Kachinsky certainly did a great deal to help the prosecution, but he wasn't officially employed by the prosecution or compensated for his actions, so the court found no Sixth Amendment *Sullivan* violation. There was nothing more the court could do concerning Kachinsky. The court wrote, "Although it probably does not need to be stated, it will be: Kachinsky's conduct was inexcusable both tactically and ethically. It is one thing for an attorney to point out to a client how deep of a hole the client is in. But to assist the prosecution in digging that hole deeper is an affront to the principles of justice that underlie a defense attorney's vital role in the adversarial system. That said, Dassey's attempt to characterize Kachinsky's misconduct as a conflict of interest under *Sullivan* is misplaced...In the absence of any request from Dassey, the court finds it inappropriate to reconstrue his *Sullivan* claim as a *Strickland* claim. Such extraordinary action would be outside the permissible bounds of judicial action, especially given the policies that circumscribe the role of federal courts in reviewing state court convictions."

However, the court was able to help Dassey based on his second claim, that he was improperly interrogated under the Fifth Amendment. The court outlined how, as we discussed previously, the investigators supplied Dassey with details of the crime during their examination of him and made false promises to him, thereby contaminating his confession. The habeas court found that these actions violated Dassey's Fifth Amendment rights and overturned his conviction.

So we've talked about when a case might be appealed, and the way that appellate courts differ from trial courts because of the scope of their review. Now let's talk about appeals from the point of view of the lawyer bringing an appeal. The lawyer appealing a case will have to file an appellate brief, and may also have the opportunity to make an oral argument. We'll discuss both of those tasks.

Typically, appellate courts decide appeals based primarily on written briefs filed by the parties. A brief will start with a statement of the facts of the case and the question presented to the appellate court, a summary of the procedural history, and a paragraph telling the appellate court what standard of review it must apply. Then the brief will lay out the argument of the party. Writing an effective brief is an art that every appellate lawyer has to master. We've talked previously about how legal arguments work, the sort of logic that goes into thinking like a lawyer. This becomes very important in a legal brief. As we've discussed, basic legal argumentation usually follows the form of an Aristotelian syllogism: A major premise and a minor premise point the way to a conclusion, if A and B are true, then C must be true. In a legal proof, the major premise is the rule of law governing the case, the minor premise is the facts particular to your case, and the conclusion is the application of the law to the facts.

For example:

Anyone who maliciously sets fire to someone else's property has committed arson. Jack argued with Jeff, then threw a lit kerosene lamp through Jeff's window and burned Jeff's house down. Therefore, Jack committed arson. That's a legal proof. Here's how you turn it into an argument—the acronym is CRAC: conclusion, rule, application, conclusion.

Start with your conclusion: This court should rule that Jack has committed arson.

Rule, the major premise: Anyone who maliciously sets fire to someone else's property has committed arson.

Application, including dealing with bad facts and rebuttal, the minor premise: Jack argued with Jeff, then threw the lit kerosene lamp through Jeff's window and burned Jeff's house down. The fact that Jeff had stolen Jack's car doesn't matter. That's you handling bad facts.

Conclusion: Therefore, Jack has committed arson.

The major premise, that rule of law governing the case, usually comes from either a text like a statute or a regulation, or case law precedent. If your major premise is rooted in text, such as a statute, then you will need to interpret that statute for the court. The court will always want to start with the language of the statute itself, hoping to find plain meaning. So you begin your interpretation of the statute there. Second, consider the legislative purpose. The legislature that enacted the statute may have included a statement about the law's purpose. If so, you will want to consider that as well. Third, legislative history. When Congress passes a statute, it creates Congressional reports that can be used to help interpret the language if the meaning is not totally plain, or to help explain the purpose of the statute. State legislatures have their own records that reveal legislative history. Sometimes the history shows that the legislative body considered a different version of the statute and rejected it. You can use that to argue that there are things the statute isn't meant to do. Plain language, legislative purpose, and legislative history are important mechanisms of statutory interpretation.

A lawyer interpreting a text should always read the entire text—for example, the whole statute—because the court will want to understand any portion of that text in context. The court will try to interpret the statute so that it is internally consistent. For example, a word is presumed to have the same meaning throughout the statute, unless the statute explicitly says otherwise. Words are also presumed to have their normal meanings, unless the statute says otherwise. A court will also do everything it can to read a statute so that it is constitutional, because undoing the work of the legislature, a body elected by the people, is not something that courts undertake lightly.

Lawyers seeking to bolster their arguments about the proper interpretation of a text often make policy arguments, predicting the likely consequences of the text. Naturally, an interpretation of a statute that promises good public policy outcomes can be very persuasive. Lawyers arguing against a particular interpretation quite often invoke a "parade of horribles," describing all the terrible things that might result from the interpretation they oppose.

Let's say that the major premise of your argument before a court comes from precedent—that is, you are arguing that cases that have been decided in the past mandate that your side should win. In that situation, you will need to pay particular attention to the weight of the precedent. As we have discussed previously, courts are only bound by decisions in their own jurisdictions, and opinions by higher courts carry more weight than decisions by lower courts. The court will be very interested in whether there is binding precedent, and the weight of any binding precedent, that is, what kind of court issued the opinion you are relying on. Cases from other jurisdictions are not binding, though they can sometimes be helpful, especially if they address an issue that your court hasn't confronted before. Whatever case you cite, it's extremely important that you make sure that it's good law—that it hasn't been overruled by a subsequent decision. That process is called Shepardizing. It's named for a 19th century legal publisher named Frank Shepard, who developed a system of books that provide cross-references among decisions for just that purpose. This process is now done electronically through legal databases rather than through books, but it's still called Shepardizing, and it's an essential step before you try to build an argument on any previous judicial decision in court.

Just in case it occurred to you to do otherwise, please note: You cannot hide cases from the court. Rule 3.3(a)(2) of the Model Rules of Professional Conduct requires you to disclose the existence of a case that binds the court, even if it hurts your case and even opposing counsel hasn't cited it. So instead of trying to hide a case, disclose it, and then make your best argument about why it doesn't apply to the issue you are appealing. If you don't have a good argument, then maybe the underlying issue isn't a good one to raise on appeal.

So those are the things you would want to think about when writing an appellate brief. Sometimes, appellate courts decide cases based solely on the briefs, but some courts also permit oral argument, inviting the lawyers to make oral presentations about their case and answer questions from the appellate judges. Don't think you are ready for oral argument just because you've prepared a brief. The two activities involve very different skills, and an appellate lawyer needs to be able to do both well. In a brief, you can cover all the issues related to your appeal, including those issues that are less important, and you can include lots of footnotes to back up your points. But in oral argument, you should be selective. You will want to pick the one or two main issues that are really important to your case, and focus on those. Oral argument isn't about minutia, it is about the big picture. It's an opportunity to highlight the most important points for your side in the case. The court can figure out the less important or subordinate issues by reading the briefs.

Typically, an appellate court will have a panel of judges, often three judges, who hear the case. Each lawyer will usually have just 15 minutes to make an oral argument, and the lawyer doesn't get to talk that whole time. The lawyer might start the oral argument off with what he or she wants to say, but the judges will quickly jump in with questions. So those first few minutes are really important. That's the one time you know for sure you're going to be able to get out your most critical point, so you want to start with that.

And about those questions—good lawyers welcome them. If the oral argument were simply a time for the lawyer to provide a short oral summary of what's in the brief, then it wouldn't really add much. The questions let you know what the judges really care about. They're a valuable opportunity to address those concerns, and clear up any misunderstandings.

Chief Justice John Roberts, who argued before the U.S. Supreme Court many times before becoming chief justice, has talked about how important it is to answer questions when they are asked, and to be frank and forthcoming in your responses. His advice applies as much to arguing before lower appellate courts as to doing so in the Supreme Court itself. "When they ask you a question about a difficult case, it's better to sometimes say, 'Well I appreciate that that case doesn't support my side. I appreciate that that causes us some difficulty. Here's why I think you shouldn't rely so heavily on that case.' As opposed to, as soon as we ask it, saying 'No, that case doesn't hurt us at all, and here's why.' The justices like you to be part of the process that is helping them come to the right result."

A lawyer who receives a question from a judge or justice during oral argument should answer it right away. It's a bad idea to respond, "I will get to that in a minute." The judge who asked the question wants to hear the answer now and might be offended if you postpone answering. It's also a good idea to frontload your response with a quick answer: "Yes, and here's why" or "No, and here's why," because you may be interrupted if your answer is too long. After you answer, you can resume your argument in the time remaining.

Justice Roberts has said that he used to prepare for his appellate arguments by writing questions judges might ask on index cards, with answers on the other side. The process of writing answers out is a good one, it helps you figure out how to summarize important points into short, cogent sentences. Justice Roberts would also get colleagues to play the roles of the judges, so that he could practice answering their questions out loud. This process, called mooting an oral argument, is similar to the moot court exercise most law students must go through during their first year of law school. The law school moot court process includes both the writing of appellate briefs and participation in an oral argument simulation.

Justice Roberts has admitted that he was nervous every time he made an oral argument. This is perfectly natural—it's an important job, and that nervousness shows you are taking the job seriously. The challenge is to present your case confidently and professionally, while at the same time being careful not to sound too aggressive, even in the face of rough questioning. It can seem daunting, but at the most fundamental level, all you're really doing is what Clarence Gideon did on his own, without any training. You're asking the system to consider that it might be wrong, and demanding justice.

ARGUING BEFORE THE SUPREME COURT

E verything about the United States Supreme Court suggests an institution of great authority: the soaring Corinthian columns of its façade, the lofty height of the courtroom's ceiling, the elevated dais at which the justices sit in their robes. The nature of that authority, however, has changed over the years. In this lecture, you will examine the history of the Supreme Court, the role the Court plays in our government, and the importance of effective advocacy.

HISTORICAL BACKGROUND

☆ The Supreme Court was established by the U.S. Constitution. However, the details concerning the judicial branch—how the federal courts would be organized, for example—were left to Congress to decide. The modern Supreme Court and its relationship with the lower courts have thus been shaped by various acts of Congress and decisions by the court itself over the years.

☆ Figuring out how the courts were going to work was a high priority for the founding fathers. After America won the Revolutionary War, the very first bill introduced into the United States Senate became the Judiciary Act of 1789, the law establishing our first court system.

★ The Judiciary Act split the country into three judicial regions, called circuits—the Eastern, the Middle, and the Southern. Each circuit contained judicial districts, but each district contained only trial courts; no intermediate courts of appeals existed. In this beginning, the six justices of the Supreme Court were required to hold court not only in the nation's capital, but also in federal circuits across the country.

★ The jurisdiction of the Supreme Court is addressed in the Constitution, which says that federal judicial power extends to cases arising under the Constitution, federal laws, treaties, admiralty and maritime law, cases in which the United States is a party, controversies between states or between citizens of different states, and cases involving foreign countries or foreign subjects. Those are the only kinds of cases the Supreme Court and lower federal courts can hear. All other matters belong in state court.

★ In the 1803 case *Marbury v. Madison*, the Supreme Court ruled that Congress can't pass a statute giving the court more power than the Constitution permits the court to have. The Constitution trumps. So *Marbury v. Madison* stands for the proposition that the Constitution is the top of the heap, the paramount law.

    ★ *Marbury v. Madison* also stands for the proposition that it's the Supreme Court's job to say what the Constitution means, and to invalidate an act of Congress if it violates the Constitution. Chief Justice John Marshall wrote, "It is emphatically the province and duty of the judicial department to say what the law is."

★ By 1869, the number of Supreme Court justices had grown from six to nine, one for each of the judicial circuits in existence as of 1866. That's also how many justices there are on the Supreme Court today.

★ For most of its history, the Supreme Court was peopled by white, Protestant men. Its composition has changed over time, with changes in American society's attitudes and composition. The first Catholic on the court was Roger Taney, who was appointed in 1835. Louis Brandeis was the first Jewish man, appointed in 1916. The first African-American man on the court was Thurgood Marshall, appointed in 1967. But no women served on the court until 1981, when Sandra Day O'Connor was appointed by President Reagan.

★ There have been efforts over the years by the other branches of government to influence the Supreme Court through the appointment process. Probably the most famous of these was President Franklin D. Roosevelt's court-packing scheme. During the Great Depression, Roosevelt was at first given a great deal of power to enact legislation to help suffering people. In 1933, during the first 100 days of his presidency, he signed 15 major pieces of legislation, ushering in the New Deal era. But by 1936, the Supreme Court had invalidated some of Roosevelt's plans, holding that some of what he wanted to do exceeded his power.

★ Roosevelt responded by proposing judicial reforms. He said that the Supreme Court had an overwhelming caseload, and suggested that he be allowed to add up to five additional Supreme Court justices. The idea was that he would pick five people sympathetic to his reforms, who would back him up. Roosevelt couldn't get public support for the plan, however, and his court-packing scheme failed.

★ Ideally, the president who nominates you should not affect how you function as a Supreme Court justice. As the highest authority within a branch of government independent from the executive and legislative branches, the Court has an interest in maintaining its own legitimacy. If Supreme Court justices were mere puppets of the presidents who appointed them, then confidence in the Supreme Court as an institution would erode.

PROCEDURAL MATTERS

* The Supreme Court gets to decide which cases it wants to hear. This wasn't always the way it worked, however. During the 19th century, the Supreme Court had to hear all cases within its jurisdiction. Congress changed the law when it became clear that the workload was too great.

* Nowadays, parties file petitions for writs of certiorari, attempting to demonstrate to the Court that their cases are of sufficient general interest to warrant the Court's review. Other interested parties also sometimes weigh in on a petition by filing what are known as amicus briefs.

* A minimum of four justices must agree that a case merits the Court's time. In almost all cases, the Supreme Court denies the petition for certiorari and lets the lower court's decision stand without endorsing it—either because the case doesn't raise a significant enough issue, or because the court simply doesn't have the time.

* If the Court accepts the case, it will hear an oral argument about the matter. If the United States is a party to the case, one of those lawyers arguing will be from the office of the Solicitor General—the federal government's lawyer in the Supreme Court. Approximately two-thirds of the cases the Supreme Court hears involve the Solicitor General. People who work in the Solicitor General's office sometimes go on to serve on the Supreme Court itself.

* In a typical case, after receiving briefs and hearing oral argument, the justices of the Supreme Court will have a private conference to vote on how the case should be decided. The most senior justice in the majority decides who writes the majority opinion. If there is going to be a dissenting opinion, the most senior justice among the dissenters decides who will write it.

* Sometimes a justice might agree with the conclusion of the majority, or with the conclusion of a group of dissenting justices, but might disagree with their reasoning, or want to emphasize some aspect of the case that the other justices have not. In that situation, the justice might write his own concurring or dissenting opinion.

* Once the justices have written their drafts, they circulate them to the other justices. This process is especially noteworthy, because it can actually change minds. As the drafts go through different iterations, justices may change their votes, and a dissent could become the majority opinion.

IMPORTANT FUNCTIONS

* The cases heard by the Supreme Court are a great example of the power that litigation offers the private citizen. We clearly have the power to shape the law based on the representatives that we elect. But we also have the power to influence the law by having our day in court. And while financial resources can make a difference, that power is available to corporations and individuals alike.

✶ Our system is not fragile. It is robust, and litigation is one way that we keep it strong. In our democracy, rather than having rules handed down by a king, we, the people, make the rules. And we are constantly refining and improving them. The legislature passes laws; the executive branch approves and enforces them; the judiciary interprets them; and we, the people, test them—and sometimes even challenge and change them—through the courts.

✶ Obviously, the law isn't perfectly responsive to changes in our society. It is a system built on caution, on checking to make sure that things have come out properly. But over time, our system has achieved some amazing things: protections for civil rights, free speech, equal protection, due process, the right of each citizen to vote—innovations of which we can be proud, and which keep our social fabric strong.

Suggested Reading

♦ McCloskey, *The American Supreme Court.*

♦ Scalia and Garner, *Making Your Case.*

Questions to Consider

↗ Why is the Supreme Court so formal? Does the formality of language and dress serve a purpose?

↗ Do you believe that Supreme Court justices should decide cases according to their own political beliefs?

ARGUING BEFORE THE SUPREME COURT

E verything about the United States Supreme Court suggests an institution of great importance and durability: the soaring Corinthian columns of its façade, the lofty height of the courtroom's ceiling, the elevated dais at which the justices sit in their robes. When the marshal, dressed in formal attire, opens each proceeding by striking his gavel and calling "Oyez! Oyez! Oyez!", the sense of the court's authority is palpable. Yet the nature of that authority, and the way the court exercises it, have changed significantly over the years, and august as the institution is, the debates that take place within its walls can be messy and fierce. A lawyer stepping into the arena of the Supreme Court to argue a case faces the intimidating prospect of constant interruptions from the justices, whether they are challenging her assertions or just trying to understand them. She has the opportunity, by the force of her advocacy, to reshape the law of the land. But that's an opportunity, never a guarantee.

So it was for Elena Kagan when she argued before the Court on September 9, 2009. If you ever find yourself complaining about the stresses in your life, consider Kagan's probable state of mind on that day. At age 48, she had just been appointed by President Barack Obama as Solicitor General of the United States—the first woman ever to hold that job—and she was tasked with arguing the federal government's position in a rehearing of perhaps the most significant case affecting the American political system in a century, *Citizens United v. Federal Election Commission*. As if that wasn't enough pressure, it was her first argument before the Supreme Court. In fact, it was the first time she had ever argued a case in any court. Her first three sentences went quite smoothly. She began:

"Mr. Chief Justice, and may it please the Court, I have three very quick points to make about the government position. The first is that this issue has a long history. For over a hundred years Congress has made a judgment that corporations must be subject to special rules when they participate in elections, and this Court has never questioned that judgment. Number 2—"

That's when Justice Scalia interrupted with, "Wait, wait, wait, wait!" The rest of Kagan's argument was a bit like a game of Whack-a-Mole, with the Solicitor

General striving mightily to smack down each challenge to her points and return to her script while the Court's conservative justices kept raising new concerns. She has probably had more enjoyable days. But her experience was actually just a somewhat exaggerated version of what lawyers encounter at the Court on a regular basis.

In this lecture, we'll talk about practicing before the high court and the role that the Court plays in our system of government, using the *Citizens United* case as an example. But first, let's consider the history of the U.S. Supreme Court and how it functions. Article III, Section 1 of the U.S. Constitution says, "The judicial power of the United States shall be vested in one Supreme Court, and in such inferior courts as the Congress may from time to time ordain and establish." So the Constitution established the Supreme Court, but it left the details about the organization of the judicial branch to Congress. As a result, our modern-day Supreme Court and its relationship with the lower courts has been shaped by various acts of Congress and decisions by the court itself over the years.

Figuring out how the courts were going to work was a high priority for the founding fathers. After America won the Revolutionary War, the very first bill introduced into the United States Senate became the Judiciary Act of 1789, establishing our first court system. That law split the country into three judicial regions or circuits: the Eastern, the Middle, and the Southern. Each of those circuits had judicial districts, 13 in all, but each district contained only trial courts; no intermediate courts of appeals existed. Supreme Court justices were told to hold court in the nation's capital, but to hear appeals from trial court decisions, they were also charged with riding circuit—that is, travelling from place to place within a circuit to hold court. There were six justices at first, a Chief Justice and five Associate Justices, and they were required to hold court twice a year in each judicial district.

As you can imagine, that must have been completely exhausting given the challenges of travel in the early United States. The job of Chief Justice was such an enormous burden that the first to hold the position, John Jay, ultimately quit to become the governor of New York, and wouldn't come back even though President John Adams begged him to. John Marshall, the highly influential justice who was appointed by John Adams in 1801 and served as the Chief Justice until 1835, broke his collar bone riding circuit, when his carriage wheel broke and the carriage flipped over. Another justice, Stephen Johnson Field, who served during the presidency of Abraham Lincoln, had to hear cases in California, and would travel from Washington, D.C. by way of boat to Panama, cross Panama by burro, and then sail up the west coast to San Francisco. What a pain. Even so, the Supreme Court justices continued to ride circuit for over 100 years, until the Judiciary Act of 1891 established United States Courts of Appeals to handle intermediate appeals, so the justices could stay closer to home.

Here's another difference between the original Supreme Court and the court we know today. Back when the justices rode circuit, the lawyers on the circuit travelled with them. They shared meals, and sometimes even shared beds. Today, a justice would have to recuse himself if he had a conflict of interest, which a close relationship with the lawyer arguing a case might cause.

The jurisdiction of the Supreme Court is addressed in Article III, Section 2 of the Constitution. That section says that federal judicial power extends to cases arising under the Constitution, federal laws, treaties, admiralty and maritime law, cases in which the United States is a party, controversies between states or between citizens of different states, and cases involving foreign countries or foreign subjects. Those are the only kinds of cases the Supreme Court and the lower federal courts can hear. All other matters belong in state court. That part about cases "arising under the Constitution" has proved to be very important. Chief Justice Marshall, that one who broke his collar bone, wrote in the now famous 1803 decision of *Marbury v. Madison* that the Supreme Court gets the final say in interpreting the Constitution. If you like the musical *Hamilton*, you may be especially interested in this case, because you'll recognize some familiar characters. Here's what happened.

The second president of the United States, John Adams, was a Federalist. That was the party of Alexander Hamilton and other people from New York—you could think of it as the non-Southern party. Thomas Jefferson and his friend, James Madison, were Virginians, and they were Southern Democratic Republicans. There was great animosity between the Federalists and the Republicans. Just before leaving office, Adams appointed a bunch of new justices of the peace for the District of Columbia. Adams signed commissions for the justices of the peace, but they hadn't been properly delivered by the time he left office. Here's something funny, those commissions were also signed by John Adams' secretary of state, who was John Marshall himself, the very person who then became the Chief Justice writing this opinion. Nowadays, Marshall would probably have to be recused from the case, but not in those days.

Here's where the dispute arose: Jefferson, the president succeeding Adams, refused to honor those appointments. So the would-be justices of the peace, including William Marbury, the plaintiff, sued to compel Jefferson's Secretary of State, James Madison, the defendant, and later, the fourth President of the United States, to deliver their commissions. They did this by asking the Supreme Court to issue a "writ of mandamus," an order telling Madison to do his official duties—something the Judiciary Act said the Supreme Court could do. So you might think that Chief Justice Marshall would say, "Okay, I'm issuing that writ of mandamus. The Judiciary Act says I can. These are justices of the peace appointed by my buddy, John Adams, and I was the guy who signed the commissions in the first place, so I want to see them delivered so they can take effect! Madison, deliver those commissions!"

But that's not what he said. Instead, he looked at Article III of the Constitution, the part that describes when the federal courts have jurisdiction over cases. And Article III doesn't say that the Supreme Court has the power to issue a writ of mandamus or to hear cases against a federal officer. It was the Judiciary Act passed by Congress that granted that power, and the Act was inconsistent with Article III of the Constitution. Chief Justice Marshall said that Congress can't pass a statute giving the court more power than the Constitution permits it to have, because that statute would therefore be at odds with the Constitution. The Constitution trumps. So *Marbury v. Madison* stands for the proposition that the Constitution is the top of the heap, the paramount law. And it also stands for the proposition that it's the Supreme Court's job to say what the Constitution means and to invalidate an act of Congress if it violates the Constitution. Marshall wrote, "It is emphatically the province and duty of the judicial department to say what the law is."

Now, this is a good example of how the Supreme Court was able to define its own power. The Constitution doesn't actually say anywhere that the Supreme Court, and not Congress, gets the last word on what passes muster under the Constitution. It makes sense that the Supreme Court would get the last word—justices are appointed for life, not elected, so they're protected from the political pressure that members of Congress must manage. It's also easier for the Supreme Court to protect the rights of a political minority than it would be for Congress to do this, because members of Congress might be thinking about getting reelected and might therefore tend to side with the majority instead. Hamilton also wrote about this in the *Federalist Papers*. So at this point, it's pretty well established that the Supreme Court gets the final word in interpreting the Constitution. But notice that this result wasn't inevitable, when you look at the Constitution itself. It arose because of Marshall's opinion in *Marbury v. Madison*.

As I mentioned, the Supreme Court had six justices when it was first established. By 1869 that number had grown to nine, one for each of the judicial circuits in existence as of 1866, and that's how many justices there are on the Supreme Court today. For most of its history, the Supreme Court was peopled by white, Protestant men. Its composition has changed over time, with changes in American society's attitudes and composition. The first Catholic on the court was Roger Taney, who was appointed in 1835. Louis Brandeis was the first Jewish man appointed to the court in 1916. The first African-American man on the court was Thurgood Marshall, appointed in 1967. But no women served on the court until 1981, when Sandra Day O'Connor was nominated by President Reagan.

I just have to pause here to tell you Sandra Day O'Connor's story. She went to Stanford University both for college and for law school, and she graduated third in her law school class. Believe me, that's really hard to do. But even though she was obviously bright and talented, she couldn't get a job. She applied for law jobs in San Francisco and Los Angeles, but this was 1952, and women simply weren't lawyers. The only job she was offered was as a legal secretary, which is just ridiculous. So instead, she offered to work for the county attorney's office in San Mateo, California, for free—no salary, no office. And she excelled. She ended up opening her own law office, then was an assistant attorney general for the state of Arizona, and then became a state senator, a state judge, and finally the first woman to serve on the United States Supreme Court. I wonder if the folks who wouldn't give her a job when she graduated law school ever think about that.

There have been efforts over the years by the other branches of government to influence the Supreme Court through the appointment process. Probably the most famous of these was President Franklin Delano Roosevelt's court packing plan. During the Great Depression, Roosevelt was at first was given a great deal of power to enact legislation to help suffering people. In 1933, during the first 100 days of his presidency, he signed 15 major pieces of legislation, ushering in the New Deal era. But by 1936, the Supreme Court started invalidating some of Roosevelt's plans, saying that some of what he wanted to do exceeded his power. So Roosevelt responded by proposing judicial reforms. He said that the Supreme Court had an overwhelming caseload, and suggested that he be allowed to add up to five additional Supreme Court justices, one for every justice who did not retire by age 70 ½. The idea was that he would pick five people sympathetic to his reforms, who would back him. This plan didn't work. He couldn't get public support for it. Turns out he didn't need to do it anyway; by 1941, when Roosevelt still had most of another term to serve, four Supreme Court justices had retired, two more had died, and seven of the nine justices on the court were Roosevelt appointees.

Ideally, though, the president who nominates you should not affect how you function as a Supreme Court justice. As the highest authority within a branch of government independent from the executive and legislative branches, the Court has an interest in maintaining its own legitimacy. If Supreme Court justices were mere puppets of the presidents who appointed them, then confidence in the Supreme Court as an institution would erode. The best justices, like Justice Marshall in *Marbury v. Madison*, understand the importance of upholding the Constitution, even if the result is the opposite of what the president who appointed them would want.

The Supreme Court gets to decide which cases it wants to hear, but this wasn't always the way it worked. During the 19th century, the Supreme Court had to hear all cases within its jurisdiction, but Congress changed that because the workload was too great. Nowadays, parties file petitions for a writ of certioriari or "cert" to try to demonstrate to the Court that their cases are of sufficient general interest to warrant the Court's review. Typically, the federal circuits must have split or disagreed about how a federal law should be interpreted, or state supreme courts are disagreeing, or there's an important question of federal law raised that hasn't been settled by the court before, but should be. Other interested parties also sometimes weigh in on a petition by filing "friend of the court" or amicus briefs.

Once all the cert petitions have been filed, they go into the cert pool. This is a mechanism by which a law clerk in one of the Justices' chambers reads the petition and writes a memo to all the Justices about whether the Court should take the case. Supreme Court clerks, as you may know, are young lawyers who conduct legal research and help write the justices' opinions. This is one of the most prestigious jobs a recent law school graduate could hope to have, and many Supreme Court justices were themselves law clerks early in their careers.

A minimum of four justices must agree that a case merits the Court's time for it to be granted cert. About 99% of the time, the Supreme Court denies cert and lets the lower court's decision stand without endorsing it, either because the case doesn't raise a significant enough issue, or the court simply doesn't have the time. If the Court accepts the case, it will hear an oral argument about the matter. If the United States is a party to the case, then one of those lawyers arguing will be from the office of the Solicitor General, the federal government's lawyer in the Supreme Court. That's the position that Elena Kagan held when she argued *Citizens United* before the Court. About 2/3 of the cases that the Supreme Court hears involve the Solicitor General, which means he or she argues before the court a lot. People who work in the Solicitor General's office sometimes go on to serve on the Supreme Court itself, such as Justice Samuel Alito, and Chief Justice John Roberts—and Justice Kagan.

Given how selective the Supreme Court is in the cases it hears, each can fairly be said to be of great significance. But *Citizens United v. FEC* stood out even within that group, both for its impact and for the unusual way that the Court dealt with the case. It offers insights into how the court operates within the government, as well as how the political and ideological dynamics within the Court affect the cases that litigants bring before it. *Citizens United* focused on the campaign finance law known as the McCain-Feingold Act, which prohibited corporations from running political TV ads for or against Presidential candidates during the 60-day period before a general federal election, or the 30-day period before a primary. The idea was to regulate "big money" campaign contributions by getting rid of these ads. A nonprofit corporation called Citizens United had made a documentary called *Hillary: The Movie* that criticized then-presidential contender Hillary Clinton, and wanted to distribute it via video-on-demand during the 30-day period before the 2008 primary. The Federal Election Commission said it couldn't, under McCain-Feingold. Citizens United sued in federal district court, claiming violation of its First Amendment rights, but lost. The provisions of McCain-Feingold allowed Citizens United to appeal directly to the Supreme Court, so it did, and the Court granted cert.

That's a pretty interesting provenance already, but what really stands out about *Citizens United*'s procedural history is that the case was argued before the Supreme Court twice. The first time, the lawyer for Citizens United, Ted Olson, who himself had been the Solicitor General from 2001–2004, argued that the McCain-Feingold Act didn't apply to a movie like the one Citizens United had made. He said that the statute was aimed at commercials, not 90-minute documentaries, and argued that the court didn't need to declare any part of the law unconstitutional at all. He simply asked it to find that the statute didn't apply to the facts of the case, and therefore the documentary could be aired. In the course of his argument, though, Mr. Olson did assert that there was no constitutional difference between the distribution of *Hillary: The Movie* via video-on-demand and providing the same information through other media, such as DVDs or books.

The FEC was represented in this first hearing by Malcom Stewart, a Deputy Solicitor General. Oral arguments often don't affect the outcome of a case, but this time was an exception. Justice Alito asked Mr. Stewart whether the Constitution would permit the government to restrict the distribution of information via the other media that Mr. Olson mentioned. Mr. Stewart said it would. If Citizens United—which, again, was a nonprofit corporation—had written a book, he said, the government could place restrictions on its publication.

"That's pretty incredible," Alito responded. "The government's position is that the First Amendment allows the banning of a book if it's published by a corporation?" Mr. Stewart tried to point out that the question wasn't presented in the case, since Citizens United hadn't written a book, but Justice Kennedy interrupted.

"Well, suppose it were an advocacy organization that had a book. Your position is that, under the Constitution, the advertising for this book or the sale for the book itself could be prohibited within the sixty- and thirty-day periods?"

And Chief Justice Roberts joined in: "If it has one name, one use of the candidate's name, it would be covered, correct? …If it's a five-hundred-page book, and at the end it says, 'And so vote for X,' the government could ban that?" Stewart reluctantly agreed, although he sought to qualify the term "ban."

Notice how the justices' discussions of a case can range into areas that neither the plaintiffs nor the government intend. The Citizens United lawyer, Ted Olson, hadn't made an argument that the law violated the constitution. He was simply seeking an opinion that the law didn't apply to a video-on-demand documentary. The court could have written an opinion like that, and that could have been the end of things. But the Justices were concerned about the limits of the law that the FEC was trying to enforce, and they really didn't like the idea of the government banning books, even though there wasn't a book in this case.

In a typical case, after receiving briefs and hearing oral argument, the Justices will have a private conference to vote on how the case should be decided. The most senior justice in the majority decides who writes the majority opinion—so if the Chief Justice is voting with the majority, then he can choose who will write the opinion, or if the case is really significant, he might write the opinion himself to emphasize its importance. If there is going to be a dissenting opinion, then the most senior justice among the dissenters decides who will write it. Sometimes a Justice might agree with the conclusion of the majority or of the dissenters but might disagree with their reasoning, or might want to emphasize some aspect of the case that the other justices have not. In that situation, the Justice might write his own concurring or dissenting opinion. Once the Justices have written their drafts, they circulate them to the other Justices. This process is especially noteworthy, because it can actually change minds; as the drafts go through different iterations, Justices may change their votes, and a dissent could possibly become the majority opinion.

In fact, that's what happened in *Citizens United*. Justice Roberts first drafted a majority opinion in line with what Ted Olson had argued on behalf of Citizens United—that the law didn't apply to the organization's documentary. But Justice Kennedy wrote a concurring opinion that went further, calling the McCain-Feingold Act unconstitutional. The other conservative Justices were persuaded by Justice Kennedy's concurrence, so Justice Roberts agreed to let that concurrence become the majority opinion. But here was the problem: neither party's lawyers had raised or briefed that issue. And Justice Souter wrote a scathing dissent saying so. So instead of publishing the draft opinion and dissent, Justice Roberts decided the case needed to be re-argued. The Court therefore instructed the parties to file new briefs addressing whether the law was constitutional.

Enter Elena Kagan, for her very first courtroom argument. She probably knew, from the Justices' questions during the first hearing of the case, and from the issue they had asked the parties to brief for the second hearing, that things would not go her way. Still, she argued valiantly, trying to undo the damage done in the first hearing. At one point, Justice Ruth Bader Ginsburg asked her whether the government's answer was still that Congress could ban books under McCain Feingold. Kagan responded, "The government's answer has changed, Justice Ginsburg." That brought laughter from the audience in the courtroom.

The Court's decision in *Citizens United* was a 5–4 opinion, holding that McCain-Feingold did not apply to Citizens United's movie. More broadly, the Court found that First Amendment protections extend to corporations, thus freeing them to spend unlimited amounts of their money on political activities. Here is how the majority described the concern underlying its decision:

"The law before us is an outright ban, backed by criminal sanctions. Section 441b makes it a felony for all corporations—including nonprofit advocacy corporations—either to expressly advocate the election or defeat of candidates or to broadcast electioneering communications within 30 days of a primary election and 60 days of a general election. ...These prohibitions are classic examples of censorship."

The dissenters worried that organizations and corporations may have a bigger voice than a typical individual voter would because they have more money, but the majority rejected this concern. It wrote that "The rule that political speech cannot be limited based on a speaker's wealth is a necessary consequence of the premise that the First Amendment generally prohibits the suppression of political speech based on the speaker's identity." Even if corporations are richer than individuals, and therefore could exert more influence, that doesn't matter under the First Amendment, said the court.

Justice Stevens wrote a 90-page dissent. He thought the idea that a corporation is the same as a person was nonsense. Stevens wrote, "Unlike our colleagues, [the Framers] had little trouble distinguishing corporations from human beings, and when they constitutionalized the right to free speech in the First Amendment, it was the free speech of individual Americans that they had in mind." His conclusion: "While American democracy is imperfect, few outside the majority of this Court would have thought its flaws included a dearth of corporate money in politics." Justice Stevens' dissent is not the law, but his argument that democracy works best when no one's voice is drowned out continues to have persuasive influence on those who believe *Citizens United* was wrongly decided.

Whatever you think of the Court's decision, *Citizens United* illuminates how Supreme Court cases are argued and resolved, as well as how litigation shapes the law. Think about what this case was about. It was a dispute over a law passed by Congress, and a bipartisan law at that, the McCain-Feingold Act. That's the sort of activity Congress is supposed to engage in under Article I of the Constitution. The law was an effort to enact campaign finance reform, to make sure that federal elections, including Presidential elections, aren't unduly influenced by big money. As applied to Presidential elections, that is a check on the executive branch, established by Article II of the Constitution. But then there was a lawsuit. It went all the way to the Supreme Court. And the Supreme Court, established by Article III of the Constitution, said the law ran afoul of the First Amendment of the Constitution and struck that part of it down. *Citizens United* is a prime illustration of our great if untidy system of checks and balances at work. It's also a great example of the power that litigation offers the private citizen. We clearly have the power to shape the law based on the representatives that we elect, but we also have the power to influence the law by having our day in court. And while financial resources can make a difference, that power is available to corporations and individuals alike.

Our system is not fragile. It is robust, and litigation is a way that we keep it strong. In our democracy, rather than having rules handed down by a king, we, the people make the rules, and we constantly refine and question and improve them. The legislature passes laws; the executive branch approves and enforces them; the judiciary interprets them; and we, the people, test them and sometimes even challenge and change them through the courts. In that way, our law is a living thing, it evolves over time, in response to real people in our real society. Now, the law isn't perfect. In fact, it is a system built on caution, on checking to make sure that things have come out properly. Judge Learned Hand once said, "The spirit of liberty is the spirit which is not too sure that it is right." Sometimes a case may not come out exactly as you might like. But over time, our system has achieved some amazing things: protections for civil rights, free speech, equal protection, due process, the right of each citizen to vote, innovations of which we can be proud and which keep our social fabric strong. And each one of these social goods is the direct result of litigation. Sometimes the evolution of the law proceeds in fits and starts. But as Dr. Martin Luther King once remarked, "The arc of the moral universe is long, but it bends towards justice."

Criminal Law and Procedure

Joseph L. Hoffmann, J.D.

Joseph L. Hoffmann, J.D.

Harry Pratter
Professor of Law
Indiana University
Maurer School of Law

Joseph Hoffmann is the Harry Pratter Professor of Law at the Indiana University Maurer School of Law, where he has taught since 1986. He received a B.A. in Mathematics from Harvard College and a J.D. cum laude from the University of Washington School of Law. After law school, Professor Hoffmann clerked for the Honorable Phyllis A. Kravitch of the U.S. Court of Appeals for the Eleventh Circuit and for then–associate justice William H. Rehnquist of the U.S. Supreme Court. He was a Fulbright professor at the University of Tokyo in Japan and at Friedrich-Alexander University of Erlangen and Friedrich Schiller University of Jena in Germany.

Professor Hoffmann is a nationally recognized scholar in the fields of criminal law, criminal procedure, habeas corpus, and the death penalty. He also writes about Japanese law as well as law and psychology. Professor Hoffmann was a co-principal investigator for the Capital Jury Project, the largest empirical project ever to study jury decision making in capital cases. He served as co-reporter for the Massachusetts Governor's Council on Capital Punishment, testified before Congress on habeas corpus and death penalty issues, and has been involved in successful death penalty reform initiatives in Illinois and Indiana. Professor Hoffmann has been a consultant for both prosecutors and defense attorneys in criminal and death penalty cases before the U.S. Supreme Court and numerous federal and state appellate courts.

Professor Hoffmann is an award-winning teacher. At Indiana University, he has been recognized with the Outstanding Junior Faculty Award; the Leon H. Wallace Teaching Award; the Trustees' Teaching Award; the Teaching Excellence Recognition Award; and the Gavel Award, given by the law school's graduating class to the person who made the most significant contribution to their legal education. In addition to his regular law school courses, Professor Hoffmann teaches a popular course about law for honors undergraduates at Indiana University. He has served for more than 30 years on the faculty of The National Judicial College, teaching state, military, and tribal judges about death penalty law. Professor Hoffmann also teaches regularly at University Panthéon-Assas (Paris II) in France; Jagiellonian University in Kraków, Poland; and the University of Tokyo in Japan.

Professor Hoffmann is the coauthor of two of the leading casebooks used by law students across the United States: *Defining Crimes* (with the late William Stuntz) and *Comprehensive Criminal Procedure* (with Ronald Allen, Andrew Leipold, Debra Livingston, Tracey Meares, and William Stuntz). He also cowrote *Federal Criminal Law* (with Peter Low) and *Habeas for the Twenty-First Century: Uses, Abuses, and the Future of the Great Writ* (with Nancy King). In 2007, Professor Hoffmann appeared in the PBS series *The Supreme Court.* ▪

Criminal Law and Procedure

C riminal law and procedure involve the most basic of conflicts between the awesome power of the government and the fundamental rights of the individual. One of the most important responsibilities of any government is to protect its citizens from those who would transgress society's rules and norms, and thereby do harm to others. Criminal law is where we identify those rules and norms, and where we set the punishments for those transgressions.

No two cases are exactly alike, however, so the established rules of criminal law must always be tempered with the discretion to do justice in individual cases. Similarly, the government's power to investigate and prosecute crimes is one that can easily be misused or abused. Criminal procedure must therefore strike a delicate balance, allowing the police and prosecutors to seek justice and protect the public, while simultaneously protecting the right of the accused to a fundamentally fair process.

The first half of this course addresses some of the most important issues in contemporary criminal law. In this part of the course, you'll learn how crimes are defined, and why criminal law has become both more rigid and more punitive. You'll see how judges have managed to retain the discretion to spare defendants who don't deserve to be punished as criminals. You'll study the different kinds of homicide crimes, including murder and manslaughter, and learn all about the doctrine of self-defense. You'll examine the key differences between federal crimes and state crimes. You'll also take a close look at the Eighth Amendment, which regulates and limits the punishments that can be imposed for crimes.

The second half of the course concerns the fundamentals of modern criminal procedure—the rules that govern how criminal cases are handled by the police, prosecutors, and the courts. In this part of the course, you'll learn about the Due Process Clause of the Fourteenth Amendment, and how it became the basis for applying the Bill of Rights to state criminal cases. You'll study the Fourth Amendment's ban on unreasonable searches and seizures, and its role in preserving individual privacy—a role that's become increasingly important, and increasingly difficult, in the modern age of technology. You'll explore the Fifth Amendment's privilege against self-incrimination, discovering how it led to the famous *Miranda* warnings. You'll also learn about plea bargains and jury trials—two ways in which many criminal cases ultimately get resolved.

The primary goal of this course is to teach you about the key issues that shape modern criminal law and procedure. Along the way, you'll encounter some of the most famous cases in legal history. You'll explore death, taxes, and free will. You'll learn about the Constitution and the Supreme Court. In the end, however, the two questions that frame this course are deceptively simple: How can criminal law best achieve justice? And how can criminal procedure best ensure fairness? ▪

WHO DEFINES CRIMES, AND HOW?

This lecture examines the development of criminal law in America—in particular, the codification of criminal law by state and federal legislatures. It also considers the definitional roles of various institutional actors outside the legislature, including prosecutors, police, defense attorneys, judges, and juries.

CRIMINAL CODES

✶ The term "common law" refers to law made by judges through individual decisions rendered in individual cases. America inherited its legal system from England, and many areas of Anglo-American law—including criminal law, contract law, tort law, and property law—evolved over the centuries through the common law process.

✶ During the early 20th century, a reform initiative to codify criminal law swept America. The basic idea was that people should be able to look up the definition of a crime and learn exactly what kind of conduct is prohibited. As a result of this codification movement, in modern America all crimes are now defined by statutes. We no longer permit judges to create new, common-law crimes.

✶ In the modern criminal justice system, consideration of cases inevitably begins with the text of the relevant criminal statute. That statute will contain a definition setting forth the specific elements of the crime— the elements that the prosecution must prove beyond a reasonable doubt at trial in order to secure a conviction.

✶ Almost all crimes in America—more than 90 percent of them—are crimes prohibited by state law, not federal law. This is because our federal government is one of limited powers; it can only exercise those powers that have been granted to it by the Constitution. The Constitution doesn't give Congress the power to enact general crime statutes.

✶ During the common law era, criminal law was mostly a private matter. For most of English legal history, crimes were not prosecuted by a public official called a prosecutor. In fact, until the late 1700s, there was no such thing as a public prosecutor. That institution originated in the American colonies.

✸ In precolonial England, crimes were prosecuted by the victim, or by a member of the victim's family. The victim would hire a private lawyer and press criminal charges, similar to the way civil suits are filed today. In the American colonies, however, legal authority to file criminal charges gradually migrated from victims to a public prosecutor, an official acting on behalf of society as a whole.

INSTITUTIONAL ROLES

✸ In modern America, crimes are defined by the complex interaction of several different institutions. Chief among these is the legislature, which enacts the statute that provides the formal definition and that identifies the required elements of the crime.

✸ Next comes the prosecutor. Working closely with the police, the prosecutor oversees the criminal investigation process. It is the prosecutor who ultimately makes the decision whether, based on the evidence, a particular individual will be charged with a particular crime.

✸ Any person who's been formally charged with a crime has a constitutional right, under the Sixth Amendment, to be represented by an attorney. If the defendant can afford to hire a lawyer, he will usually do so. If he can't, he'll be represented by a lawyer appointed by the government—either a private defense lawyer willing to take the case, or, especially in larger cities, a public defender.

✸ Once the defendant has a lawyer, the prosecutor will begin to negotiate with the defense lawyer concerning a possible plea bargain. That's how the vast majority of criminal cases—almost 95 percent—get resolved. As a result, defense lawyers also play an indirect role in defining crimes.

✸ If the two sides can't agree on a plea bargain, the case will go to trial. In criminal cases where a defendant could be sentenced to more than six months in prison, the defendant has a constitutional right to a jury trial. Juries play a key role in defining crimes, because they possesses the absolute and legally unreviewable power to acquit, even in the face of overwhelming evidence of guilt, if the jury believes that the behavior of the police or prosecutor, or even the criminal law itself, is unjust.

* Last, but not least, there's the judiciary. Every criminal trial occurs under the supervision of a trial judge, who has the authority to dismiss the charges if she concludes that the evidence of guilt is legally insufficient to meet the prosecution's burden of proof beyond a reasonable doubt.

* Every guilty plea, including the terms of any plea bargain, must be approved by the judge. In trial courts and appellate courts, judges serve as the official interpreters of the law, including criminal statutes and any defenses or constitutional challenges that might be raised.

SHIFTING INTERPRETATIONS

✶ The shift in the institutional balance of power can be observed in many modern criminal law cases. One excellent example is the 1998 case *Brogan v. United States*. James Brogan was a union official suspected by the FBI of taking bribes to sell out the interests of the union. One evening, federal agents knocked on Brogan's door. When he answered, the agents identified themselves and told Brogan they were seeking his cooperation in a criminal investigation. The agents asked Brogan if he had taken bribes. Brogan replied, "No." The agents, already in possession of documents proving that Brogan had taken bribes, arrested him.

✶ Brogan was charged with bribery, but he was also charged with violating a federal statute that prohibits making "false statements" to the federal government. The statute, located in Section 1001 of Title 18 of the U.S. Code, provides:

> Whoever, in any matter within the jurisdiction of any department or agency of the United States, knowingly and willfully falsifies, conceals, or covers up … a material fact, or makes any false, fictitious, or fraudulent statements or representations … shall be fined not more than $10,000 or imprisoned not more than five years, or both.

✴ Brogan was convicted at trial, and he appealed all the way to the U.S. Supreme Court. Brogan's lawyer argued that the Court should create a special exception to the Section 1001 for someone who, like Brogan, utters a simple "No" in response to a question from a government agent about whether he committed a crime. This proposed exception—described as the "exculpatory no" exception—had previously been recognized by several lower federal courts.

✴ Brogan's lawyer argued that the "exculpatory no" exception was necessary to avoid putting people like Brogan in the position of being pressured by the government into admitting their own guilt—which would violate the spirit, if not the letter, of the Fifth Amendment privilege against compelled self-incrimination. Brogan's lawyer also pointed out that Brogan didn't actually mislead federal agents, because the agents already knew that Brogan had taken bribes.

✴ The Supreme Court upheld Brogan's conviction. According to the majority opinion, written by Justice Antonin Scalia:

By its terms, Section 1001 covers "any" false statement .... The word "no," in response to a question, assuredly makes a "statement" .... In fact, petitioner [Brogan] concedes that under a "literal reading" of the statute he loses.

Petitioner asks us, however, to depart from the literal text that Congress has enacted, and to approve the doctrine ... which excludes from the scope of Section 1001 the "exculpatory no."

[I]t is not, and cannot be, our practice to restrict the unqualified language of a statute ... . Courts may not create their own limitations on legislation, no matter how alluring the policy arguments for doing so ... . Because the plain language of Section 1001 admits of no exception for an "exculpatory no," we affirm the judgment.

★ This is the essence of modern textualist interpretation of criminal statutes. The U.S. Supreme Court—the highest court in the land—felt powerless to consider the argument that Congress wouldn't want Section 1001 to apply to someone who utters merely a simple, "exculpatory no." Instead, the Court found the plain language of the statute completely conclusive.

★ Textualism has had two primary effects on the criminal justice system. First, the system has become more punitive, in terms of both the breadth of the criminal law and the severity of criminal punishments. Politically speaking, legislatures always have a strong incentive to enact broader and tougher criminal statutes; no politician wants to be seen as "soft on crime." As a result, America's prison population has exploded.

★ Second, the power of prosecutors has been greatly increased. For someone like Brogan, the best shot at leniency—perhaps the only shot—is to cut a favorable plea bargain with the prosecutor. Prosecutors have learned how to use effectively the leverage they gained as a result of the shift in power from judges to legislatures. As a result, the rate at which defendants agree to plea bargains continues to climb.

★ Notwithstanding these trends in favor of legislatures and prosecutors, judges do still retain power over one key aspect of criminal law—namely, the requirement that all defendants must be proven to have acted with "evil intent," often referred to as mens rea.

★ Most crime statutes don't specify the mens rea requirement for any particular crime. Legislatures tend to focus their attention instead on defining the criminal act itself. As a result, judges have to fill in the gaps—just like they did in the days of common law.

✳ Judicial power to define and apply mens rea requirements—which extends to matters relating to self-defense, intoxication, and insanity—means that judges can still pursue the ends of justice in individual criminal cases. Even in a textualist era, judges can still find ways to reverse criminal convictions that seem unfair. And that's a good thing, because in the end, criminal law is all about justice—to the defendant, to the victim, and to society.

Suggested Reading

- Regina v. Dudley & Stephens.

- Brogan v. United States.

- Fuller, "The Case of the Speluncean Explorers.".

Questions to Consider

➚ What are the pros and cons of relying on judges, legislatures, and prosecutors to define criminal law?

➚ Do you agree that the necessity defense should never apply to the crime of murder—even in a case where it's clear that the killing actually saved lives?

Lecture 1 Transcript

WHO DEFINES CRIMES, AND HOW?

O
n May 5, 1884, four men set out in a small yacht called the *Mignonette*, planning to sail it from England, around the tip of South America, to Sydney, Australia, where they would deliver it to its new owner. The four sailors were Captain Tom Dudley, Mates Edwin Stephens and Edmund Brooks, and a 17-year-old cabin boy named Richard Parker. Two months later, on July 5, the *Mignonette* suddenly sank in a violent storm in the middle of the South Atlantic. The crew found themselves marooned in a tiny lifeboat, more than 1,600 miles from any land, with only two tins of turnips and no drinking water. They managed to catch a turtle, which sustained them for a few days. But their situation quickly grew dire. By the eighth day adrift, the men were reduced to drinking their own urine. A week later, Richard Parker began drinking seawater, and his condition rapidly deteriorated. As desperation set in, Captain Dudley, Stephens, and Brooks talked about drawing lots to decide which of the four men would be sacrificed so the others could eat his body and survive for a while longer. But they couldn't agree about the details, and Brooks opted out of the plan altogether. On July 24th, with no hope of rescue, and with Parker delirious and hovering near death, Dudley and Stephens made a fateful decision. And their decision ultimately led to one of the most important cases in the history of Anglo-American criminal law. The case of *Regina v. Dudley and Stephens* is the classic introduction to a first-year Criminal Law course. It's the very first criminal case most students read in law school.

In this course, we're going to learn all about criminal law: How crimes are defined, how the criminal law tries to ensure that only the truly deserving get convicted and punished, and how various institutions—including legislatures, prosecutors, defense attorneys, courts, and juries—work together to achieve society's goals and the ends of justice. We're also going to learn about criminal procedure—about the legal rules, mostly derived from the Constitution—that try to make the investigation, prosecution, and adjudication of a criminal case as fair as it can possibly be. I hope you're ready to join me on this fascinating journey.

Let's return now to that tiny lifeboat, and those desperate men stranded in the South Atlantic. And I apologize in advance, but this is going to get a little bit graphic. That's actually one of the challenges of teaching criminal law, because sometimes, you've got to talk about the terrible things that people do to one another. Anyway, here's how Captain Tom Dudley himself later described what happened next:

"No vessel appearing on the morning, I made signs to Stephens and Brooks that we had better do it, but they seemed to have no heart to do it, so I went to the boy, who was lying at the bottom of the boat with his arm over his face. I took out my knife—first offering a prayer to God to forgive us for what we were about to do and for the rash act, that our souls might be saved—and I said to the boy, 'Richard, your time is come.' The boy said, 'What, me, Sir?' I said, 'Yes, my boy.' I then put my knife [into the side of his neck.] The blood spurted out, and we caught it in the bailer and we drank the blood while it was warm. We then stripped the body, cut it open, and took out his liver and heart, and we ate the liver while it was still warm."

Five days later, having drifted for a total of 24 days, the three remaining survivors of the *Mignonette* were miraculously rescued by a passing German ship. When they returned to England, Tom Dudley and Edwin Stephens, but not Brooks, who'd opted out of the plan, were charged with murder. This was an unusual move. There were many shipwrecks in those days; the same year the *Mignonette* went down, almost 400 ships were lost at sea. Although cannibalism was rare, it wasn't unheard of when sailors were stranded at sea. And if those responsible survived, the law mostly looked the other way. But once the story of the *Mignonette* got around, the authorities decided it was time to put a stop to the practice of cannibalism, once and for all. The criminal case against Dudley and Stephens became the biggest public sensation of its day.

There was no doubt that Dudley and Stephens, acting together, intentionally caused the death of Richard Parker. Dudley did the deed by his own hand, and Stephens was an aider and abettor because he supported the idea, thus encouraging Dudley to go through with it. The two men fit squarely within the legal definition of the crime of murder unless they could offer up some kind of defense. At trial, Captain Dudley candidly told the whole story about what happened in that lifeboat. He did so because he assumed he wouldn't be convicted or punished, based on the well-established legal defense of "necessity." Namely, that the killing of Richard Parker was necessary to save the lives of the others, and therefore was not a crime.

The jury, after deliberating, surprised the court by handing down a so-called "special verdict." The jury concluded that all of the relevant events happened exactly as Tom Dudley described them, but declined to make a decision about guilt or innocence. The jury instead kicked the case back to the court, asking the judges to make a legal ruling about whether the "necessity" defense applies to the crime of murder. The five judges of the Queen's Bench soon issued their decision. Lord Coleridge wrote the unanimous opinion, finding Dudley and Stephens guilty of murder, and sentencing both men—as English law then required—to death by hanging. But why? What purpose would be served by hanging Tom Dudley and Edwin Stephens?

Criminal law is often thought to serve various purposes. One purpose is retribution, which means giving a convicted defendant the punishment he deserves, in light of the crime and the defendant's moral blameworthiness. But were Dudley and Stephens murderers in any normal sense of that word? Did they derive any pleasure, or moral satisfaction, from what they did? Did their acts reveal a truly heinous or evil character? Or were they simply two average human beings, driven by unspeakable conditions to commit an unspeakable act? Can we really be confident that, if we'd been trapped in that lifeboat literally starving to death, we would have done any better? In the court's opinion, Lord Coleridge wrote eloquently about the moral dimensions of the case:

"Though law and morality are not the same, and many things may be immoral which are not necessarily illegal, yet the absolute divorce of law from morality would be of fatal consequence...To preserve one's life is generally speaking a duty, but it may be the plainest and the highest duty to sacrifice it." Lord Coleridge acknowledged that the defendants "were subject to terrible temptation, to sufferings which might break down the bodily power of the strongest man and try the conscience of the best." But he also noted, "We are often compelled to set up standards we cannot reach ourselves, and to lay down rules which we could not ourselves satisfy." So maybe the idea of retribution does apply to Tom Dudley and Edwin Stephens. They may not have been any better, or any worse, than the rest of us, but that's not an excuse for what they did to Richard Parker. And, according to Lord Coleridge, that makes them deserving of criminal punishment.

What about incapacitation, another purpose behind the criminal law? Sometimes we put dangerous people in prison, or even execute them, just to make sure that they aren't free to commit more crimes. But it seems strange to apply that rationale to Dudley and Stephens. Because unless those two men somehow got shipwrecked again, and marooned at sea again, there's no reason to think they would ever kill again.

For the same reason, rehabilitation doesn't seem applicable to Dudley and Stephens. And in any event, the death penalty isn't really very much about rehabilitation, unless you're persuaded by the words of Samuel Johnson, who once observed, "When a man knows he is to be hanged in a fortnight, it concentrates his mind wonderfully." By the way, rehabilitation was once a major goal of the American criminal justice system, hence the use of terms like "reformatory" and "penitentiary" to describe prisons, but during the 1960's, Americans became cynical about the prospect of rehabilitation and largely gave up on the idea. That's not so in other parts of the world; for example, in modern Japan, pretty much the entire criminal justice system is designed to help convicted criminals realize the error of their ways, and prepare to reenter society as law-abiding citizens.

What about deterrence, yet another purpose of the criminal law? Was it necessary to hang Dudley and Stephens to deter others from doing the same thing under the same circumstances? Deterrence sounds plausible at first, but think about this: Could any threat of legal punishment, even the death penalty, ever manage to deter someone who's already staring death straight in the eye? But maybe that's not really the focus of the deterrence in this case. Maybe the goal isn't to deter someone else who actually ends up the same dire circumstances as Dudley and Stephens. Maybe that's not possible. But maybe the law still needs to lay down a clear rule, to deter others in the future from choosing to become judge, jury, and executioner of someone like poor Richard Parker, under circumstances that might not be quite as dire.

As Lord Coleridge explained: "Who is to be the judge of this sort of necessity? By what measure is the comparative value of lives to be measured? Is it to be strength, or intellect, or what? It is plain that the principle leaves to him who is to profit by it, to determine the necessity which will justify him in deliberately taking another's life to save his own...Such a principle, once admitted, might be made the legal cloak for unbridled passion and atrocious crime." In other words, even if Dudley and Stephens, and those in similar straits, couldn't possibly be deterred by the law, maybe we need to make an example of them anyway; because otherwise, the "necessity" defense could provide others with the opportunity to get away with murder.

In the end, Dudley and Stephens were sentenced by the court to hang. But Lord Coleridge also added, "If...the law appears to be too severe on individuals, [we] leave it to the [Queen] to exercise that prerogative of mercy which the Constitution has entrusted to the hands fittest to dispense it." And that's precisely what happened—the Queen commuted the sentences of Tom Dudley and Edwin Stephens to six months in prison.

Dudley and Stephens is a wonderfully rich case, with facts worthy of a Hollywood movie and a legal opinion that reads like a learned treatise in moral philosophy. And the holding in the case, that the "necessity" defense can't be used to avoid a charge of murder because no person is entitled to take another's innocent life, even to save his own, remains true in both English and American criminal law right up to the present day. Moreover, the idea that executive clemency sometimes should be used to mitigate the harshness of the criminal law, also remains totally valid today. State governors and, in the federal system, the President of the United States, still possess the very same power to commute sentences and to pardon convicted defendants that the Queen of England enjoyed in 1884. Nowadays, the executive rarely grants clemency, because most politicians don't want to be seen as "soft on crime." But there's another kind of executive discretion that's grown up to take its place. I'm talking here about the power of the prosecutor to offer a plea bargain that, in exchange for the defendant's guilty plea, drops some charges or reduces the sentence. Plea bargaining today accounts for almost 95% of all criminal convictions. Trials are a rare exception, not the rule.

In short, *Regina v. Dudley and Stephens* continues to be relevant to modern criminal law. That's why we still teach the case in law school. However, in a number of important respects, *Dudley and Stephens* is not at all representative of the real world of American criminal law today. For one thing, murder is an exceptionally unusual crime. In the United States, for every person arrested and charged with murder, nearly 1,000 people are arrested and charged with other, less serious crimes. The largest single category of crimes for which people get arrested is the possession, sale, and use of illegal drugs. Second on the list is larceny or theft, followed by driving under the influence, simple assault, public intoxication, and disorderly conduct. Most of the day-to-day practice of criminal law isn't about serious violence. Instead, it's mostly about low-level drug crimes, property crimes, and crimes against the public order.

Another key difference is that the *Dudley and Stephens* case arose during the era of "common law" crimes. As you may already know, the term "common law" refers to law as made by judges, through the individual decisions those judges render in individual cases. America inherited its legal system from England, and many areas of Anglo-American law, including contract law, tort law, and property law, evolved over the centuries through the common law process. And so, too, did criminal law. That's why the judges in *Dudley and Stephens* were required to define the crime of murder, and to decide whether or not the "necessity" defense could apply to that crime. There was no other place to look for the answer; it was completely up to the judges. But that's not the way criminal law works in America today. During the early 20th century, a reform initiative to codify the criminal law swept America. The basic idea was that people should be able to look up the definition of a crime, in a statute, and learn exactly what kind of conduct is prohibited. As a result of this codification movement, in modern America all crimes are defined by statutes enacted by legislatures. We no longer permit judges to define new, common-law crimes. So today in America, a case like *Dudley and Stephens* would inevitably start with the text of the relevant crime statute that defines the specific elements of the crime, the elements that must be proved by the prosecution, at trial, "beyond a reasonable doubt," to secure a conviction.

By the way, I should point out that almost all crimes in America—more than 90% of them—are defined as crimes under state law, not federal law. That's because our federal government is strictly limited to exercising only those powers granted to it by the Constitution, and the Constitution doesn't give Congress the power to enact general crime statutes.

During the common-law era, criminal law was mostly a private matter. For most of English legal history, crimes were not prosecuted by a public official called a "prosecutor." In fact, until the late 1700s, there was no such thing as a "public prosecutor." That institution originated in the American colonies. In pre-colonial England, crimes were prosecuted by the victim or by a member of the victim's family. The victim would hire a private lawyer and press criminal charges, sort of like filing a civil tort lawsuit. In the American colonies, the legal authority to file criminal charges gradually migrated from victims to the new "public prosecutor." And that remains the rule today; the American criminal justice system no longer allows for "private prosecutions." Criminal law has become the sole province of the government acting on behalf of society as a whole, rather than on behalf of crime victims.

In modern America, as a result of these gradual changes over time, we can say that crimes are defined by the complex interaction of several different institutions. First comes the legislature, which enacts the statute that provides the formal definition and identifies the required elements of the crime. Next comes the prosecutor, who, working closely with the police, oversees the criminal investigation and ultimately makes the decision that, based on the evidence, a particular individual should be charged with a particular crime.

Any person who's been formally charged with felony crime has a constitutional right under the Sixth Amendment to be represented by a defense lawyer. If the defendant can afford to hire a lawyer, he will usually do so. If he can't, then he'll be represented by a lawyer who's paid by the government, either a private defense lawyer willing to take the case, or, especially in larger cities, by a public defender who works for a government agency with the official responsibility to provide legal aid to indigent criminal defendants. Once the defendant has a defense lawyer, the prosecutor will begin to negotiate with the defense lawyer about a possible plea bargain. Remember, that's how the vast majority of criminal cases—almost 95%—get resolved. So defense lawyers also play an indirect role in defining crimes. If the two sides can't agree on a plea bargain, then the case will go to trial. In all criminal cases where a defendant could get more than six months in prison, the defendant has a constitutional right to a jury trial. Jury trials are rare, but the jury still plays a key role in defining crimes because the jury possesses the absolute and legally unreviewable power to acquit—even in the face of overwhelming evidence of guilt—if the jury believes that the behavior of the police or prosecutor or the criminal law itself is unjust. Last, but not least, there's the role of the judiciary. Every criminal trial occurs under the supervision of a trial judge, with the authority to dismiss the charges if the judge concludes that the evidence of guilt is insufficient to meet the prosecution's burden of "proof beyond a reasonable doubt." Every guilty plea, including the terms of any plea bargain, also must be approved by the judge. And judges, both at trial and even more so on appeal, serve as the official interpreters of the law, including both the crime statute, and any defenses or constitutional provisions that might come into play.

To summarize, then, defining crimes requires the involvement of legislatures, prosecutors and police, defense lawyers, juries, and judges. But because everything starts with the crime statute and because everything usually ends with a plea bargain, the legislature and the prosecutor have become the key players in defining crimes today. Meanwhile—and contrary to the way things are portrayed in courtroom dramas on TV and in the movies—the relative importance of juries and, especially, of judges has gradually diminished over time.

This shift in the institutional balance of power can be observed in many modern criminal law cases. One great example is the 1998 case of *Brogan v. United States*. James Brogan was a union official suspected by the FBI of taking bribes from the company to sell out the interests of the union. One evening, federal agents knocked on Brogan's door, and when he answered, the agents identified themselves and told Brogan they were seeking his cooperation in a criminal investigation. The agents asked Brogan if he had taken bribes. Brogan replied, "No." The agents, who already possessed documents proving that Brogan had, in fact, taken bribes, then arrested Brogan. He was charged with bribery, and also with violating a federal statute, 18 U.S. Code Section 1001, that prohibits making "false statements" to the federal government. The "false statement" crime statute provided: "Whoever, in any matter within the jurisdiction of any department or agency of the United States, knowingly and willfully falsifies, conceals, or covers up…a material fact, or makes any false, fictitious, or fraudulent statements or representations…shall be fined not more than $10,000 or imprisoned not more than five years, or both."

Brogan was convicted at trial, and he appealed all the way to the U.S. Supreme Court. Brogan's lawyer argued that the Court should create a special exception to the "false statement" crime for someone who, like Brogan, utters a simple "No" in response to a question from a government agent about whether he committed a crime. This proposed exception, described as the "exculpatory no" defense, had already been recognized by several lower federal courts, but had not yet been ruled upon by the Supreme Court. Brogan's lawyer argued that the "exculpatory no" exception was necessary to avoid putting people like Brogan in the position of being pressured by the government into admitting their own guilt, which would violate the spirit, if not the letter, of the Fifth Amendment privilege against compelled self-incrimination. And Brogan's lawyer also pointed out that Brogan didn't actually mislead those federal agents, because the agents already knew perfectly well that Brogan was guilty of taking bribes.

The Supreme Court, by a vote of 7–2, upheld Brogan's "false statement" conviction. According to the majority opinion, written by Justice Antonin Scalia: "By its terms, Section 1001 covers 'any' false statement…The word 'no,' in response to a question, assuredly makes a 'statement'…In fact, petitioner [Brogan] concedes that under a 'literal reading' of the statute he loses. Petitioner asks us, however, to depart from the literal text that Congress has enacted, and to approve the doctrine…which excludes from the scope of Section 1001 the 'exculpatory no…[I]t is not, and cannot be, our practice to restrict the unqualified language of a statute…Courts may not create their own limitations on legislation, no matter how alluring the policy arguments for doing so…

Because the plain language of Section 1001 admits of no exception for an 'exculpatory no,' we affirm the judgment."

This is the essence of modern textualist interpretation of crime statutes. The United States Supreme Court—the highest court in the land—felt powerless to consider the argument that Congress wouldn't want the "false statement" crime to apply to someone who merely utters a simple "exculpatory no." Instead, the Court found the plain language of the statute completely conclusive. Because the text of the statute makes no reference to an "exculpatory no" defense, the defense can't exist. End of story. This is clearly a far cry from the kind of free-wheeling, moral-philosophical discussion about the proper scope of the "necessity" defense that we saw in Lord Coleridge's majority opinion in *Dudley and Stephens*. If *Dudley and Stephens* represented judging in the bygone era of common-law crimes, *Brogan* represents judging in the modern era of textualism.

Textualism has had two primary, practical effects on the criminal justice system. One practical effect is that the system has become more punitive, in terms of both the breadth of the criminal law and the severity of criminal punishments. This occurred because legislators are politicians, and no politician ever got elected by being "soft on crime." Politically speaking, legislatures always have a strong incentive to enact ever-broader, and ever-tougher, crime statutes. And, for decades, our state and federal legislatures have done exactly that, which helps explain why America's prison population has exploded since the 1960's. Only when prison populations exceed prison capacities, forcing tax increases to build new prisons, do legislators start to think twice about being so tough on crime. Textualism also has had the practical effect of greatly increasing the power of prosecutors. If even the Supreme Court can't save a defendant like Brogan from the literal interpretation of a crime statute like the federal "false statement" statute, then who can? For someone like Brogan, the best shot at leniency—indeed, perhaps the only shot—is to cut a favorable plea bargain with the prosecutor. Prosecutors have learned how to use effectively the leverage they've gained as a result of the shift in power from judges to legislatures. That's why our plea bargain rates continue to climb: Because defendants know that, these days, the prosecutor is just about the only game in town.

Now, notwithstanding these modern trends in favor of legislatures and prosecutors, judges do still retain power over one key aspect of criminal law, namely, the traditional requirement that all defendants must be proven to have acted with "evil intent," sometimes described as an "evil mind," or, in Latin, mens rea. As a matter of general principle, we don't want to convict someone of a crime unless they deliberately did something truly wrong, truly immoral, truly evil. Indeed, this is often identified as one of the basic requirements for any valid crime. The defendant must commit a voluntary act or an omission with an "evil mind," that either causes, or creates a risk of causing, harm to a person, to property, or to some other tangible or intangible interest protected by the law. But most modern crime statutes don't address the specific mens rea requirements for a particular crime. Legislatures tend to focus their attention mostly on defining the criminal act, or actus reus, rather than on the mental aspect of the crime. Does the prosecutor need to prove that the defendant committed the prohibited act intentionally, or is it enough to commit the act recklessly, or negligently? These kinds of questions tend not to be answered by the text of most crime statutes. Which means that judges have to keep filling in the gaps, just like they did back in the days of common-law crimes. It's the one area where textualist statutory interpretation won't work, because the legislature usually doesn't provide any text. The judicial power to define and apply the mental, or mens rea, requirements of crimes—which includes the power to decide about such related matters as self-defense, intoxication, and the insanity defense—means that judges can still pursue the ends of justice in individual criminal cases.

So maybe the core of criminal law hasn't really changed all that much since the days of *Dudley and Stephens*. Because Lord Coleridge didn't have to deal with a rigid criminal statute, he was free to make whatever decision seemed right, in light of the facts of the case and the goals of the criminal law. Judicial discretion today is much more limited. Yet even in a textualist era, where statutes and plea bargains tend to dominate, judges can still find ways to reverse criminal convictions that seem unfair. And that's a good thing, because in the end, criminal law is all about justice—to the defendant, to the victim, and to society.

CRIME AND THE GUILTY MIND

This lecture explores the contours of mens rea, a fundamental component of criminal law. In this lecture, you will learn how criminal intent is traditionally defined, what happens when a criminal defendant claims to have been mistaken the facts or the law, and when a defendant can be convicted even without proof of criminal intent.

GENERAL INTENT

* The concept of mens rea, the "guilty mind," was developed centuries ago as part of the common law of crimes. By the 18th century, Sir William Blackstone, the famous English judge and legal commentator, was able to declare with certainty that no crime could be committed without a "vicious will." In 1922, the U.S. Supreme Court explained that "the general rule at common law was that the scienter was a necessary element in the indictment and proof of every crime."

* Traditionally, most crimes are defined in a manner that requires only what the criminal law calls general intent. General intent means that you intended to do the act that's defined as the crime. It wasn't done by accident, in other words; you meant to do it.

✶ Consider the crime of simple assault. This crime is typically defined as an actual or threatened touching of another person's body in a manner that's unwanted and either painful, harmful, or offensive. If you touch another person in this way, and if it wasn't an accident—if you meant to touch them—then you satisfy the requirement of general intent. It doesn't matter whether you intended to cause the victim any pain, harm, or offense. The law says that the act you committed speaks for itself, and your general intent to commit that act makes you a criminal.

✶ Many other crimes are defined in terms of general intent. One such crime is possession of illegal drugs. If illegal drugs somehow appeared your pocket, and you never even knew they were there, then your possession would be accidental, and you wouldn't be guilty. But if you meant to possess the drugs—if it wasn't an accident—then you satisfy the law's requirement of general intent, and you would be guilty.

★ General intent is the most common mens rea requirement for crimes. In fact, the criminal law presumes that all crimes are general intent crimes, unless there's a strong reason to conclude otherwise. That reason might be found in the text of the statute that defines the crime, or in the legislative intent behind the statute. In some cases, it can arise because a court decides that the statute—if construed as requiring only general intent—would create too great a risk of unfairly punishing innocent people.

★ In modern America, we no longer allow our courts to create or define common law crimes. All crimes must now be defined by statute, which means legislatures are primarily the ones who define crimes. But legislatures tend to focus their attention mostly on criminal acts. Often, they don't say anything at all in a crime statute—or say only vague and indeterminate things—about the mens rea of the crime. As a result, judges often have to fill in the gap and decide what the mens rea should be.

★ Whenever there's a significant risk that treating the crime as a general intent crime might end up unfairly punishing innocent behavior— behavior that doesn't speak for itself, in terms of establishing the defendant's criminality—the judge often has at least some discretion to do justice. The judge can use the authority to define or interpret the mens rea requirements of the crime, and can insist on proof of some additional amount of evil, or moral culpability, before convicting the defendant of the crime.

SPECIFIC INTENT

★ Consider the crime of intentional homicide, or murder. To be guilty of that particular crime, you have to intend not only the act that caused the victim's death—whatever that act may be—but also the result of the act. Specifically, you have to intend to take a living person and, by your act, turn them into a dead one. This is what the criminal law calls specific intent.

* Specific intent is the criminal law's other big category of mens rea. If a crime is based on specific intent, it means the defendant must be proven to have intended not only to commit the criminal act, but also to cause the specific harmful result, or consequence, of the act. Because general intent is the default rule, specific intent applies only when the crime statute—or the legislative intent behind the statute—specifically requires it.

* A classic example of a specific intent crime is theft. Traditionally, theft is defined as taking the property of another with the intent to permanently deprive of the property. It's not enough simply to take another person's property. You have to take it with the specific intent to change someone else's property into your property.

* Specific intent can be hard even for courts to understand. In the case of *Commonwealth v. Liebenow*, for example, the defendant was accused of theft for taking some steel pipes and metal plates from an active construction site. The site was marked as private property, and there were construction machines and work trailers parked all around. One morning, Liebenow simply drove up in a pickup truck and started taking stuff. When a worker asked what he was doing, Liebenow said he was picking up some junk.

* When he was later arrested by the police, Liebenow at first claimed not to know anything about the items in the back of his truck. Later, however, he admitted that he had taken them from the construction site. But Liebenow still denied any wrongdoing; he said he honestly believed that the items had all been abandoned.

* The Massachusetts Court of Appeals initially held that Liebenow's belief didn't matter one way or the other, and affirmed Liebenow's theft conviction. But the Massachusetts Supreme Court later reversed the conviction, holding that if Liebenow honestly believed that the property was abandoned, and that he was therefore free to take it, he couldn't be found guilty of theft.

★ For a general intent crime, a mistake of fact is no defense, unless the mistake is one that is both honest and reasonable. For specific intent crimes like theft, however, an honest belief—even if patently unreasonable—is a defense, if it negates the specific intent required for the crime. In the *Liebenow* case, an honest belief about whether the property was abandoned could have negated the specific intent required for the crime of theft.

★ In general, criminal law doesn't care at all whether you know that what you're doing is defined as a crime. You can't murder someone, for example, and then complain to the judge that you didn't know it's a crime to murder someone. Ignorance of the law would be no defense.

★ There are some cases, however, where a mistake about the law would be a valid defense. If you're accused of theft, for example, and your defense is that you honestly—but mistakenly—believed that the property in question legally belonged to you, that might be a defense. In that case, an honest mistake about the legal ownership of the property could very well have prevented you from possessing the specific intent required for a theft conviction.

★ A similar point can be made about intoxication. Intoxication is never a defense to a general intent crime. But for specific intent crimes, if you were too drunk to form any specific intent about the harmful consequences of your actions, then it's at least possible that your intoxication might give you a defense to the crime.

STRICT LIABILITY

★ Strict liability typically refers to liability without any mens rea requirement. It's sometimes described as liability without fault. If you commit the criminal act, then you're guilty, regardless of your state of mind.

★ The leading federal cases on strict liability arose during the first half of the 20th century, when the federal government started to become heavily involved in regulating certain risky businesses, like the food and drug industries, to protect public safety. The consumer protection statutes enacted during this period contained regulations designed to ensure that dangerous products wouldn't be sold or distributed to innocent consumers. To make sure the new rules would be obeyed, Congress often added criminal sanctions for anyone who violated them.

✭ The Supreme Court upheld strict liability as a basis for criminal conviction in these types of cases. As long as the legislature clearly states that a regulatory crime is based on strict liability, then—according to the Supreme Court—it's okay to dispense with the usual requirement of mens rea, because the goal is to place the duty on the business to avoid the danger to the public.

Suggested Reading

⬧ Morissette v. United States.

⬧ State v. Varszegi.

⬧ Commonwealth v. Liebenow.

⬧ United States v. Dotterweich.

Questions to Consider

↗ Do you agree that theft should be defined as a specific intent crime?

↗ In cases where mens rea becomes an issue, how can the law determine what was really going through the defendant's mind at the time of the crime?

Criminal Law and Procedure

CRIME AND THE GUILTY MIND

A man named Morissette went deer hunting with his brother-in-law on land that was part of the Oscoda Air Base in Michigan. The U.S. military leased the land from the State of Michigan, and had used it for many years as a practice bombing range. The land was clearly marked with signs that read, "Danger—Keep Out—Bombing Range," but deer hunters frequently hunted there anyway. Morissette, a World War II vet who worked as a fruit stand operator in summer and a scrap iron collector in winter, didn't get any deer. So he decided to pay for his hunting trip by loading up three tons of spent bomb casings into the back of his truck, driving away, and selling them. He made $84. Morissette was charged with violating a federal criminal statute that provides, "Whoever embezzles, steals, purloins, or knowingly converts" government property is subject to a fine and imprisonment. Morissette admitted taking the bomb casings, but argued that he hadn't done anything wrong—the bomb casings were just sitting there, rusting away, so he thought they'd been abandoned. Morissette was convicted, and was sentenced to either two months in prison or a $200 fine.

The U.S. Supreme Court reversed Morissette's conviction. The decision in *Morissette v. United States* is famous in the criminal law, mostly because of what the case says about the legal requirement of mens rea, sometimes known as scienter, or the "guilty mind." Here's what Justice Robert Jackson wrote, for a unanimous Court: "The contention that an injury can amount to a crime only when inflicted by intention is no provincial or transient notion. It is as universal and persistent in mature systems of law as belief in freedom of the human will and a consequent ability and duty...to choose between good and evil. A relation between some mental element and punishment for a harmful act is almost as instinctive as the child's familiar exculpatory 'But I didn't mean to'...Wrongdoing must be conscious to be criminal..."

In this lecture, we'll explore the contours of this fundamental requirement of mens rea, or the guilty mind, in criminal law. We'll see how criminal intent is traditionally defined. We'll learn about related terms like malice and motive. We'll discuss what happens when a defendant claims to lack mens rea or scienter, because of a mistake about the facts, or about the law. And we'll examine the concept of strict liability, or criminal liability without fault.

Mens rea is a concept that was developed centuries ago, as part of the common law of crimes. By the 18th century, Sir William Blackstone, the famous English judge and legal commentator, was able to declare with certainty that no crime could be committed without a "vicious will." And in 1922, the U.S. Supreme Court explained that "the general rule at common law was that the scienter was a necessary element in the indictment and proof of every crime." So what, exactly, is mens rea? What counts as criminal intent, or as a vicious will? Traditionally, most crimes are defined in a manner that requires only what the criminal law calls general intent. General intent means that you intended to do the act that's defined as the crime. It wasn't done by accident, you meant to do it.

Consider the crime of simple assault, or as some states choose to label it, assault and battery. This crime is defined as an actual or threatened touching of another person's body, in a manner that's unwanted and either painful, harmful, or offensive. If you touch another person in this way and if it wasn't an accident—if you meant to touch them—then you satisfy the requirement of general intent. It doesn't matter that you didn't intend to cause the victim any pain, or harm, or offense. That would be called your motive for acting the way you did, and motive usually doesn't matter in the criminal law. The law says that the act you committed speaks for itself, and your general intent to commit that act makes you a criminal.

Lots of crimes are defined in this way. Possession of illegal drugs, for example. If the drugs somehow fell out of the sky and into your pocket or backpack and you never even knew they were there, then your possession would be accidental and you wouldn't be guilty. But if you meant to possess the drugs, if it wasn't an accident, then you satisfy the law's requirement of general intent and you're guilty. Selling illegal drugs works the same way. If you somehow managed to sell some drugs accidentally—like they were hidden inside an antique chest that you sold to someone else, but you never actually meant to sell any drugs—then you would lack general intent and you wouldn't be guilty of selling drugs. But if you meant to sell the drugs, then it doesn't matter why you did it. Your act speaks for itself and you're guilty.

General intent is the most common mens rea requirement for crimes. In fact, the criminal law presumes that all crimes are general intent crimes, unless there's a strong reason to conclude otherwise. That reason might be found in the text of the statute that defines the crime or in the legislative intent behind the statute. Or it can arise because a court decides that the statute, if construed as a general intent statute, would create too great a risk of unfairly punishing innocent people.

In modern America, as we've already seen, we no longer allow our courts to create or define common law crimes. Today, all crimes must be defined by statute, which means that legislatures are the ones who primarily define crimes. But legislatures tend to focus their attention mostly on the criminal act and often don't say anything at all in the crime statute, or say only vague and indeterminate things, about the mens rea of the crime. And that means judges often have to fill in the gap, by deciding what the mens rea for the crime should be. So, whenever there's a significant risk that treating the crime as a general intent crime might end up unfairly punishing innocent behavior that doesn't truly speak for itself in terms of establishing the defendant's criminality, the judge often has at least some discretion, or wiggle room, to do justice. The judge can use the authority to define or interpret the mens rea requirements of the crime, and can insist upon proof of some additional amount of evil or moral culpability before convicting the defendant of the crime.

Let's look at a few examples. Sometimes the legislature actually does provide in the crime statute that a defendant can't be convicted of the crime unless they acted with malice. Malice is basically a plus factor—an additional level of moral culpability that's required in some situations where the general intent to commit the criminal act doesn't speak for itself and doesn't adequately justify imposing the criminal punishment. Arson statutes often contain such a malice requirement. In the case of *In re V.V.*, a juvenile with the initials V.V. and his buddy, J.H., threw a lit firecracker that landed on a brush-covered hillside in Pasadena, California. The firecracker caused a brush fire that burned five acres. V.V. and J.H. were charged with arson under a statute that provided, "A person is guilty of arson when he or she willfully and maliciously sets fire to, or burns, or causes to be burned…any structure, forest land, or property."

Why would this statute require that the act of setting the fire be done maliciously? Because there are lots of situations where people intentionally set fires, but they shouldn't be treated as arsonists or as criminals at all. Firefighters set controlled fires to get rid of the brush and prevent brush fires. They also do it to fight wildfires, once they've started. Farmers do it to get ready for the next crop season. Setting a fire should only be a crime if you do it wrongfully. And that's basically what malice means. It means that you did the prohibited act with some kind of wrongful state of mind. It doesn't matter that much what kind of wrongfulness, it could be an intent to scare or harass or annoy someone, or maybe an intent to cause some minor harm or even an extreme degree of carelessness. Just about any kind of wrongfulness will do, and can satisfy the plus factor requirement of malice.

So in the *V.V.* case, the California Supreme Court had to decide whether throwing a lit firecracker onto a brushy hillside qualified as malicious. And it was a close call. The majority concluded that there was malice based on the fact that, although the two juveniles never intended to burn the hillside, they were well aware of the substantial risk of a brush fire and they deliberately and intentionally decided to throw the firecrackers anyway. The dissent argued that these were just two kids playing with fireworks, shortly after the Fourth of July. Should we really be punishing them as arsonists?

The *V.V.* case illustrates quite well what the criminal law is all about. The arson statute defines an act that can be a serious crime. And it's a general intent crime, meaning you can't be convicted unless you intended to do the act—in *V.V.*'s case, the act of throwing the firecracker. But the statute also requires proof of a relatively vague concept called malice, which gives the courts just enough wiggle room to debate whether or not two kids throwing firecrackers really deserve to be treated as arsonists.

My law students sometimes get upset about the way that criminal law seems to have a lot of unpredictability and subjectivity and case-by-case variation, but not a lot of super-clear legal rules. So I have to explain to them that the criminal law is that way for a good reason. Because when the government's going to lock you up for something you've done, we need to be sure that you really deserve it. Property law, contract law, those subjects are mostly about having clear and predictable legal rules, so that people can structure their daily affairs based on the rules. Criminal law is mostly about justice, which means that we can't just rely on rigid legal rules to tell us who's a criminal and who's not. We need rules, but we also need discretion to look at the facts of the individual case because both rules and discretion are necessary to do justice.

Another example of a crime that often requires a plus factor in addition to general intent, is child abuse. The problem here is two-fold. First, there's the problem that some cases of child abuse are based on passive behavior by the defendant. The California child abuse statute, for example, says you can commit child abuse by permitting a child to be placed in a situation where the child's health is endangered. But permitting a child to be in such a situation is pretty passive and may not speak for itself in terms of making the defendant evil enough to be treated as a criminal. What if a mother deliberately leaves her child with a babysitter, not knowing that the babysitter is completely untrained and has all sorts of dangerous stuff lying around that might harm the child? Is the mother guilty of child abuse?

The California courts have said no. To be guilty of child abuse based on such passive behavior, you must act with criminal negligence. Criminal negligence is basically gross negligence. It's a gross or extreme deviation from the way normal, reasonable people behave. And the California courts decided to add it as a plus factor—even though the statute didn't say anything about it—to address cases of passive child abuse where general intent isn't enough. So if the mother was aware that the babysitter wasn't trained, and knew about the dangerous stuff lying around, and decided to leave her child anyway, that might be child abuse. But without criminal negligence, it's not a crime.

The second problem with child abuse laws is that some parents still use corporal punishment against their children. And in many states, the law hasn't completely prohibited that choice. So the child abuse laws, especially in those states, have to be interpreted so that it isn't a crime for a parent to physically discipline their child. That's where the plus factor of malice can be very useful, because it provides enough wiggle room for courts to decide when the use of corporal punishment is legal and when it goes too far and becomes the crime of child abuse. Statutes that criminalize animal abuse raise the same kind of issue and often are subject to the same malice requirement.

Now consider the crime of intentional homicide, or murder. For that particular crime, you have to intend not only the act that caused the victim's death—whatever that act may be—but also the result of the act. More specifically, you have to intend to take a living person and, by your act, turn them into a dead one. This is what the criminal law calls specific intent. Specific intent is the other big category of mens rea. If a crime is based on specific intent, it means the defendant must be proven to have intended not only to commit the criminal act, but also to cause the specific harmful result, or consequence, of the act.

Because general intent is the default rule, specific intent applies only when the crime statute, or the legislative intent behind the statute, specifically requires that kind of intent. A classic example of a specific intent crime is theft, including all of its many variations: robbery, larceny, embezzlement, fraud, and so on. The traditional definition of theft is taking the property of another, with the intent to permanently deprive them of the property. Can you see why that's a specific intent crime? It's not enough simply to take another person's property. You have to take it with the specific intent to change someone else's property into your property.

The fact that theft crimes traditionally require specific intent gives rise to classic law school hypotheticals, like the tale of the "absent-minded professor." A professor walks into a classroom to deliver a lecture. At the end of the lecture, the professor starts to leave the classroom, when he suddenly notices an umbrella propped up against the wall. He says to himself, "That's lucky, I almost forgot my umbrella!" He grabs the umbrella, and walks out. Unfortunately, the professor didn't bring his umbrella to class that day, and what he took was an umbrella belonging to one of his students. Is the professor guilty of theft? The answer, of course, is no. The professor may have committed the act of taking the umbrella, and he may even have had the general intent to commit that act in the sense that he meant to pick up the umbrella and walk away with it. But he lacks the specific intent to take the umbrella of another person and make it his own. Which means he's not guilty of theft.

Specific intent is also why there's a big difference in criminal law between joyriding and auto theft. If you take someone else's car without permission, intending to drive it around for a little while and then bring it back where you found it, that's joyriding. It's a crime, but not a very serious one. On the other hand, if you take someone else's car without permission, and you never intend to bring it back, that's auto theft, and that's a very serious crime. The legal difference between joyriding and auto theft is that joyriding requires only the general intent to take someone else's car without permission. It doesn't matter why you did it, nor whether you intended to keep it. As long as you meant to do the act, you're guilty of joyriding. But auto theft is a specific intent crime. The prosecution has to prove that you also intended to keep the car, or at least never to return it. And if you satisfy the specific intent requirement, you're guilty of a much worse crime than joyriding.

Specific intent can be hard even for courts to understand. In the case of *Commonwealth v. Liebenow*, the defendant was accused of theft for taking some steel pipes and metal plates from an active construction site. The site was posted "No Trespassing" and "Private Property," and there were construction machines and work trailers parked all around. One morning, Liebenow simply drove up in a pickup truck and started taking stuff. When a worker asked what

Criminal Law and Procedure

he was doing, Liebenow said he was picking up some junk. When he was later arrested by the police, Liebenow at first claimed not to know anything about the items in the back of his truck, but then he admitted that he took it from the construction site. Still, Liebenow denied any wrongdoing, because he said he honestly believed it had all been abandoned. The Massachusetts Court of Appeals initially held that Liebenow's belief didn't matter one way or the other, and they affirmed Liebenow's theft conviction. But the Massachusetts Supreme Court later reversed the conviction because, even if Liebenow seems like an idiot and a jerk, he simply can't be guilty of the crime of theft if he honestly believed that the property was abandoned, and that he was therefore free to take it. A mistake of fact can't be a defense to a general intent crime, unless the mistake was both honest and reasonable. But for specific intent crimes like theft, an honest belief—even if patently unreasonable—can be a defense, if it negates the specific intent required for the crime. And in the *Liebenow* case, an honest belief about whether the property was abandoned, no matter how unreasonable that belief may have been, negates the specific intent required for the crime of theft.

Note, by the way, that Liebenow could still be convicted of theft, but only if it was determined at trial that he really didn't honestly believe, in his own mind, that the property was abandoned. His criminal liability turns completely on whatever he honestly believed about the status of the property. That's how specific intent works.

And that's why the maxim "Ignorance of the law is no defense," is actually only partially true. In general, the criminal law doesn't care at all whether you know that what you're doing is defined as a crime. You can't murder someone and then complain to the judge that you didn't know it's a crime to murder someone. "Ignorance of the law is no defense." But if you're accused of theft, and your defense is that you honestly, but mistakenly, believed that the property in question legally belonged to you, that might be a defense. One famous case involved a landlord named Varszegi who believed, based on language in the lease agreement he'd signed with his deadbeat tenant, that he had the legal right to break into the apartment and seize the tenant's own computer and other personal property. A police officer actually told Varszegi that the lease provision was illegal, but Varszegi still believed that what he was doing was legal. And eventually, the Connecticut Court of Appeals reversed Varszegi's theft conviction because even if his belief was totally unreasonable, he still didn't have the specific intent to take someone else's property and make it his own. Instead, he believed he was taking property that already legally belonged to him under the terms of the lease. And it's in this sense that, for specific intent crimes, a mistake of law sometimes can be a defense. By the way, a similar point can be made about intoxication. Intoxication is never a defense to a general intent crime, but for specific intent crimes, if you were too drunk to form any specific intent about the harmful consequences of your actions, then it's at least possible that your intoxication might give you a defense to the crime.

At this point, you might be able to figure out why the U.S. Supreme Court reversed Morissette's conviction for taking those spent bomb casings. It's the same as in *Liebenow*, or in *Varszegi*. Morissette was charged with a specific intent crime, a federal version of the traditional crime of theft. So he can't be guilty, unless he specifically intended to take property that belonged to someone else and make it his own. But Morissette said he believed that the bomb casings had been abandoned by the government. Whether we call this a mistake of fact or a mistake of law, it really doesn't matter; as long as Morissette honestly believed it, then he can't be guilty of the crime of theft.

So far, we've defined general intent and specific intent. We've learned about motive and malice. And we've talked about mistakes, both of fact and of law. The last mens rea topic we need to discuss is strict liability.

Strict liability is generally defined as criminal liability without any mens rea or moral culpability. It's often described as criminal liability without fault. If you commit the criminal act, you're guilty, period, regardless of your state of mind. And the U.S. Supreme Court has held, despite the traditional requirement of the guilty mind, that crimes can sometimes be based on strict liability. The leading federal cases on this subject arose during the first half of the 20th century, when the federal government started to become heavily involved in regulating certain risky businesses, like the food and drug industries, to protect public safety. These new federal consumer protection statutes contained regulations designed to ensure that dangerous products wouldn't be sold or distributed to innocent consumers. And then, to make sure the regulations would be obeyed, Congress often added criminal sanctions for anyone who violated the regulations.

In cases like *United States v. Balint* and *United States v. Dotterweich*, the Supreme Court upheld these strict liability crimes against the challenge that they were unconstitutional, because they didn't require proof of any mens rea. For example, the regulatory statute in *Dotterweich* prohibited "the introduction or delivery…into interstate commerce of any…drug…that is adulterated or misbranded." The statute then added that "any person" violating this provision is guilty of a misdemeanor crime. *Dotterweich* was the president and general manager of a corporation that shipped some mislabeled drugs, and he was convicted of the crime. The Court explained that this new kind of statute was different from traditional common-law crimes, and therefore required a different approach to mens rea: "Congress has preferred to place it upon those who have at least the opportunity of informing themselves of the existence of conditions imposed for the protection of consumers before sharing in illicit commerce, rather than to throw the hazard on the innocent public who are wholly helpless."

As long as the legislature clearly states that a regulatory crime is based on strict liability, then, according to the Supreme Court, it's okay to dispense with the usual requirement of mens rea because the goal is to place the duty upon the business to avoid the danger to the public. We call these kinds of regulatory crimes *malum prohibitum*, meaning "just because the government said so," to distinguish them from traditional crimes that everyone should already know are wrong, and which we call *mala in se*.

But take a closer look at what the Court actually said in *Dotterweich*. The Court said that the crime is aimed at those "who have at least the opportunity of informing themselves" about the danger. So consider this: What if the prosecutor tried to charge the FedEx driver who picked up the crate of mislabeled drugs from the plant and delivered them to the pharmacy? Would the FedEx driver be guilty of the crime? After all, he did exactly what the statute prohibits, he "delivered" the mislabeled drug into commerce, where it could harm an innocent consumer. And yet, it seems wrong to charge the FedEx driver, because nobody would reasonably expect him to open the crate of drugs and check to see if they're labeled correctly. That's not his job.

Here's what the Court had to say about that in *Dotterweich*: "In the interest of the larger good, [the statute] puts the burden of acting at hazard upon a person otherwise innocent but standing in responsible relation to a public danger...It would be too treacherous to define, or even to indicate by way of illustration, the class of employees which stands in such a responsible relation...In such matters, the good sense of prosecutors, the wise guidance of trial judges, and the ultimate judgment of juries must be trusted."

In other words, although the FedEx driver might literally satisfy the terms of the statute, he shouldn't be convicted of the crime because he isn't responsible for the danger. It wouldn't be reasonable to make him open the crate and check the labels. It's not his duty to do that. It's the duty of the company president, and the chief operating officer, and the plant manager, and the person in charge of regulatory compliance. They are the ones responsible for designing and implementing a system to make sure that no drugs get shipped without the proper labels.

And that, my friends, is how strict liability really works. I sometimes refer to it as so-called strict liability, because it's not really criminal liability without fault. It's criminal liability where the prosecutor isn't initially required to prove the defendant's fault, but the defendant can still argue that he wasn't a responsible actor and it wasn't his duty to try to prevent the harm. Once again, we find that in the criminal law, even when we're talking about strict liability, it's really all about justice.

HOMICIDE AND MORAL CULPABILITY

This lecture examines the criminal law governing homicide crimes. In this lecture, you will learn about the different types of homicide, a category of crimes that includes first- and second-degree murder and voluntary and involuntary manslaughter. You will also learn how first-degree murder differs from other types of homicide.

ELEMENTS OF HOMICIDE

✴ Homicides are unique among crimes. There is no crime more foul, more heinous, more devastating in its impacts upon the victim and society. And there is no other crime that prompts in the rest of us such a strong desire to delve deeply into the mind—and the soul—of the criminal.

✴ Homicides are also unique in the criminal law. Almost all crimes are defined by reference to a particular criminal act, or an act committed under a particular set of circumstances. Take money or property from someone else, and you've committed theft. Take it by force, and you've committed robbery. Punch another person—or, indeed, touch them in any manner that's unwanted and offensive—and you've committed assault. None of these crimes require the defendant to cause any particular result, or any particular amount of harm to the victim.

✴ Homicide crimes are defined differently. The essential conduct element in the definition of all homicide crimes is exactly the same: causing the death of another human being. You can commit a homicide by shooting, by stabbing, by strangling, by running the victim over with a car, by or pushing them off a cliff. Any act will do, as long it results in the victim's death.

✴ In many cases, homicide doesn't even require an affirmative act. You can commit homicide by failing to do something you're legally required to do—failing to feed your infant child, for example. Homicide simply requires proof that the defendant's act or omission—whatever it may have been—caused the death of another human being.

✴ Homicide law is one of the few areas of criminal law where courts debate the meaning of causation. What, exactly, does it mean to say that a defendant's act or omission caused the victim's death? This may seem like a simple question. In some murder cases, however, this issue is anything but simple.

⋆ Causation for legal purposes is not a simple, scientific fact. The simple, scientific fact of causation does exist, of course; in the legal world, it is sometimes referred to as but-for causation. This refers to the concept that but for a certain event, a certain other event would not have happened. That's something we can treat as a scientific fact, something that's either true or false.

⋆ The problem is that but-for causation is woefully insufficient to establish legal causation. This is because there are an infinite number of but-for causes of any particular event. Without consciously thinking about it, however, we instinctively know how to limit the boundless universe of but-for causes of an event to a much smaller set of causes that we treat as relevant to issues of moral responsibility and blame.

✱ Whenever a tragic event occurs, we make an unconscious choice about which specific cause or causes we want to blame for the loss. It's important recognize that this is a choice—there's nothing true or false about it. To put it another way, the causal judgments we make are normative, not empirical. For moral purposes, we choose the cause that we think should be blamed for the tragic outcome.

✱ This is the kind of instinctive thought process that psychologists call heuristic thinking. We learn to do it from childhood. And it happens unconsciously—most of the time, at least, until a hard case forces us to bring our thought process out into the open.

✱ The law has a name for the cause that gets blamed for a particular harmful result: proximate cause. Proximate cause is a legal term without a scientific definition. The term simply refers to whatever cause the law decides to treat as responsible for the particular harm at issue.

✱ There's no magic formula to proximate causation. Our unconscious minds pay attention to many factors, which combine to produce the final judgment about causation. Some factors are obvious: As the term itself suggests, we tend to attribute proximate causation to causes that are more proximate—closer in time and space—to the result. We also tend to focus on causes that are foreseeably connected to the result, rather than those that almost nobody would have guessed might lead to that result.

✱ There are two special factors that greatly affect causal judgments. One factor is that, as human beings, we need to believe that we have free will. We don't want to think of ourselves as mere automatons reacting to external stimuli, because this would deprive our lives of all moral significance. The second factor is that we tend to base our causal judgments on morality. Whenever a bad result happens, we tend to blame whomever is seen as the worst actor in the situation.

CATEGORIES OF HOMICIDE

✶ Distinctions between various homicide crimes depend on what the defendant was thinking at the time of the act or omission that caused the victim's death. It's all about the defendant's moral culpability for the death, or what the criminal law calls mens rea. The law creates a hierarchy of homicide crimes, in which the seriousness of each crime depends on the defendant's level of moral culpability.

✶ The least serious homicide crime is involuntary manslaughter. The crime of involuntary manslaughter generally consists of causing another person's death with the culpable mens rea of recklessness, or perhaps criminal negligence. The punishment varies from state to state, generally ranging from 1 to 10 years in prison.

★ The next homicide crime in the hierarchy is second-degree murder, which can get you 20 years or more in prison. The legal definition of second-degree murder is a killing committed with malice. In criminal law, however, "malice" does not mean "anger" or "ill will." Rather, "malice" is a catch-all term that signifies a certain kind of evil.

★ There are a number of different ways that a murder defendant can exhibit the kind of evil that qualifies as malice. The paradigmatic case is an intentional killing. If you walk up to somebody, and you suddenly decide to shoot them in the head and kill them, that certainly qualifies as malice.

★ If you intend to cause grievous bodily injury to another person—even if you don't actually intend to kill them—and they die from the injury, that also qualifies as malice. Grievous bodily injury is the kind of injury that could easily turn out to be fatal, such as cutting off an arm or leg, or shooting someone in the chest rather than the foot.

★ If you commit a felony considered by the law to be inherently dangerous to human life, and someone dies as a result of your crime, that qualifies as malice, even if the death was unintended or accidental. This is called the felony murder rule, and it is the subject of much debate. Proponents of the rule say that someone who chooses to commit a dangerous crime deserves to be treated as a murderer when an innocent victim dies. Opponents argue that the rule unreasonably punishes individuals for a death they had no intent to cause.

★ If you do something so extremely reckless that the law considers it a manifestation of an abandoned and malignant heart, and someone dies as a result, that qualifies as malice. The "abandoned and malignant heart" language comes from the traditional legal terminology, which is why the crime is sometimes abbreviated as AMH murder. AMH murder involves a level of recklessness that's closer to depravity.

* The next homicide crime in the hierarchy is first-degree murder. Just like the paradigmatic example of second-degree murder, first-degree murder involves an intentional killing. The difference is that in first-degree murder, the victim's death must be premeditated.

* First-degree murder cases often involve a decision to kill made over an extended period of time. Nevertheless, courts often say that premeditation doesn't require any specific amount of time. The cases also often involve advance planning, but courts say that planning is not required.

* The best way to think about the legal concept of premeditation is that it expresses something about the quality of thought that went into the decision to kill—not the quantity. First-degree murder involves a rational, cold-blooded decision to kill, as opposed to the impulsive kind of decision that's the hallmark of second-degree murder. Rational decision-making can occur in an instant. Of course, the more time spent making the decision, the more likely it is that a court will find premeditation. Similarly, advance planning isn't required, but it can be strong evidence of rational thought.

* The punishment for first-degree murder is severe. A conviction for first-degree murder could mean life in prison, or even—if aggravating circumstances are present and the relevant state law so provides—the death penalty.

* The law also treats some felony murders as first-degree murders, if the felony the defendant was committing is one that the legislature has included on a statutory list. Most states list robbery, burglary, arson, kidnapping, and rape. If you commit any of these felonies, and someone dies as a result of your crime, you can be charged with first-degree murder—even if you never intended for anyone to die.

VOLUNTARY MANSLAUGHTER

✶ Voluntary manslaughter is a homicide crime that is defined as a special exception to the crime of second-degree murder. If the defendant qualifies, his punishment is typically reduced to half of what it would have been if he had been convicted of second-degree murder. Voluntary manslaughter thus operates as a kind of partial defense to a murder charge; you're still guilty of a homicide crime, but a much less serious one.

✶ The doctrine of voluntary manslaughter was developed by judges hundreds of years ago. The basic idea was to mitigate the punishment in certain homicide cases where the defendant's act was motivated by extreme anger, due to a provoking event that would make most people at least feel homicidal—even if most people wouldn't actually kill over it.

★ We often describe voluntary manslaughter as taking place in the heat of passion. If the provocation would be adequate to push even a reasonable person into the heat of passion, and if the killing occurs before sufficient time has passed for a reasonable person to cool off, then the crime becomes voluntary manslaughter instead of murder.

★ Two classic situations led to the creation of the voluntary manslaughter doctrine. The first was mutual combat: Two men get into a fight, the fight escalates, and one of them ends up dead. This can't be self-defense, because both men were responsible for the initial violence. But judges decided it shouldn't be murder, either, because the victim was just as responsible as the defendant for creating the situation that led to his death.

★ The second classic situation was spousal adultery: A man finds his wife in bed with another man, and kills his wife, the other man, or both. Once again, judges decided that this shouldn't be murder, because the killing was only partly the fault of the defendant; it was also the fault of the adulterous lovers who created the situation. In both scenarios, the crime was reduced to voluntary manslaughter, and the punishment was reduced by roughly half.

★ Notice how both of these classic situations reflect a testosterone-driven view of the world. The early common law judges who devised the doctrine were all men. And the decision to mitigate the crime and punishment in these cases reflected a male-centric perspective. It's like saying, "boys will be boys"—and sometimes boys will kill, if you get them mad enough.

★ It's proven much harder over the years for female defendants to benefit from the voluntary manslaughter doctrine. A battered wife who kills her abusive husband out of fear for her life, but does so while the husband is sleeping, can't qualify for self-defense because she's not in imminent danger. She also may not qualify for voluntary manslaughter, however, because very few women kill, even under circumstances of extreme emotion.

Suggested Reading

- Robertson v. Commonwealth.

- Commonwealth v. Welansky.

- Mayes v. People.

- Austin v. United States.

- Percy, Hoffmann, and Sherman, "Sticky Metaphors."

Questions to Consider

↗ Do you agree that a rational intentional killing should be defined by the criminal law as a more heinous crime than an impulsive intentional killing?

↗ Should the law provide a partial defense to people who kill others out of extreme, provoked anger?

HOMICIDE AND MORAL CULPABILITY

We begin this lecture with a case of "murder most foul." A small-town lawyer in the Upper Peninsula of Michigan gets a phone call from a woman named Laura Manion. Laura asks the lawyer to represent her husband, U.S. Army Lieutenant Frederick "Manny" Manion, who's been arrested and charged with first-degree murder in the shooting death of the bartender at a local inn. At the jail, Manny admits to the lawyer that he fired the fatal shot, but says he did it in a blind rage after the bartender beat up and raped Laura. The lawyer thinks he might be able to argue that it's a case of temporary insanity due to "irresistible impulse." The prosecutor, on the other hand, tells the lawyer that it really doesn't matter why it happened. Even if Laura was raped, Manny still went to the bar with a loaded gun and shot the bartender in cold blood, which makes it first-degree murder. And the lawyer gradually uncovers yet another disturbing possibility: It turns out that Laura's a notorious flirt, and she might well have had an affair with the bartender, leading a jealous Manny to kill out of revenge. Now, you may recognize this story as the plot of the famous Hollywood movie, *Anatomy of a Murder*. But it's also based, very loosely, on an actual Michigan murder case; in fact, the original novel was written under a pseudonym by John Voelker, who represented the real-life defendant, and who later became a Justice on the Michigan Supreme Court.

So, what's the criminal law governing such a case? What are the legal elements of first-degree murder, and how does murder differ from other homicide crimes, such as second-degree murder, voluntary manslaughter, and involuntary manslaughter?

Homicides are, of course, unique among crimes. There is no crime more foul, more heinous, more devastating in its impacts upon the victim and society. And also no crime that prompts in the rest of us such a strong desire to delve deeply into the mind and the soul of the criminal. That's why murder is the subject of so many books, plays, and movies: *Macbeth*, *Hamlet*, *Crime and Punishment*, *Compulsion*, *Dial M for Murder*, *Psycho*, *In Cold Blood*, *Silence of the Lambs*, *Midnight in the Garden of Good and Evil*, *Gone Girl*, *Memento*—the list goes on and on.

Homicides are also unique in the criminal law. Almost all crimes are defined by reference to a particular criminal act, or an act committed under a particular set of circumstances. Take money or property from someone else, and you've committed theft. Take it by force, and you've committed robbery. Punch another person, or indeed, touch them in any manner that's unwanted and offensive, and you've committed assault. None of these crimes require the defendant to cause any particular result, or any particular amount of harm to the victim. They require only that the defendant commit the act that's defined as the crime. Homicide crimes are defined differently. The essential conduct element in the definition of all homicide crimes is exactly the same: Causing the death of another human being. Notice that the definition doesn't say anything at all about what specific conduct must cause the death; you can commit a murder by shooting, by stabbing, by strangling, by running the victim over with a car, by pushing them off a cliff, or even by dropping a piano on their head like in the Saturday morning cartoon shows. Any act will do, as long as the act causes the victim's death. In fact, homicide doesn't even require an affirmative act. You can commit homicide by failing to do something you're legally required to do, such as failing to feed your infant child so that the child starves to death. Homicide isn't about a particular act at all. Instead, homicide simply requires proof that the defendant's act or omission—whatever it may have been—was the cause of a particular result, specifically the death of another human being. For this reason, homicide law is just about the only place in the criminal law where courts end up debating the meaning of causation. What exactly does it mean to say that a defendant's act or omission caused the victim's death? This may seem like a simple question. I can assure you, however, that in at least some murder cases, it is anything but simple.

Let's consider a couple of real-world examples. In *Robertson v. Commonwealth*, the defendant was about to be arrested for possessing marijuana. He broke free of the police officer's grasp, and took off running down the road toward a high bridge over the Ohio River. The officer radioed for help and began chasing Robertson on foot. When Robertson reached the bridge, he vaulted over a concrete barrier that separated the roadway from a parallel pedestrian walkway, and continued running down the walkway. A second officer, by the name of Michael Partin, drove his car onto the bridge, got out of the car, and tried to jump over the same concrete barrier to intercept Robertson. However, Officer Partin slipped through a gap between the road and the walkway, falling almost 100 feet to his death. Robertson was charged with the homicide crime of manslaughter, which we'll discuss shortly. But did Robertson cause the death of Officer Partin? Hmmm. Not a simple question, right?

Here's another example: Dr. Jack Kevorkian became known as "Doctor Death" during the 1990s because he championed the right of every human being to decide to end his or her own life. But Dr. Kevorkian wasn't just an advocate for assisted suicide. Instead, he actually designed and built a series of suicide machines that enabled people to kill themselves even if they were too ill or too weak to pick up a gun or throw themselves off a tall building. In several cases, Dr. Kevorkian was charged with homicide crimes. But did he cause the deaths of his patients? Or were they the cause of their own deaths?

It might seem strange, but legal "causation" is not a simple, scientific fact. Yes, it's true there is a simple scientific concept of causation. We call this scientific concept "but-for" causation. It means that, "but for" one event, the other event would not have happened. And that's something we can treat as a scientific fact, it's something that's either true or false. "But for" Robertson vaulting over that concrete barrier, Officer Partin wouldn't have died, at least not at that specific place and time. "But for" Dr. Kevorkian building his suicide machines, his patients wouldn't have died, at least not at that particular place and time. The problem is that "but-for" causation is woefully insufficient to establish legal causation. Here's why: There are an infinite number of scientific, "but-for" causes of any particular event. Imagine that Smith and Brown get into a fight at a bar. Smith pulls out a gun and shoots Brown to death. Who is the "but-for" cause of Brown's death? Surely Smith, the shooter, is a "but-for" cause. But so, too, is Brown, because if he hadn't been at the bar, he wouldn't be dead now. And so too is the taxi driver who brought Smith to the bar. What about the bouncer who could have prevented the shooting, but was outside having a smoke at the time? If only he'd been where he was supposed to be, Brown wouldn't have died. And what about the gun dealer who sold Smith the gun and bullets? And the owner of the bar? Aren't they all "but-for" causes of Brown's death, at least in terms of the specific time and manner in which that death occurred? Of course they are. But that's not all.

What about Smith's parents? Without them, there would be no Smith. And what about their parents? And their parents? As you can see, that's a line that goes all the way back to Adam and Eve. And what about Brown's parents? And their parents, and their parents? What about the parents of the taxi driver? And their parents, and their parents? What about the parents of the gun dealer? The bar owner? You get the point. There are an uncountable number of persons who would qualify as "but-for" causes of Brown's death in that bar on that night. You may be thinking, but wait a minute! Nobody would ever blame Brown's parents for their own son's untimely death. That's crazy talk. And indeed, it is crazy. But why? It seems crazy because, without consciously thinking about it, we instinctively know how to limit the boundless universe of "but-for" scientific causes of an event to a much smaller set of causes that we treat as relevant to issues of moral responsibility and blame. Whenever a tragic event occurs, we make an unconscious choice about which specific cause or causes we want to blame for the loss. But it's important to recognize that this is a choice—there's no "true" or "false" about it. To put it another way, the causal judgments we make are normative, not empirical. We choose the cause that we think should be blamed for the tragic outcome.

This is the kind of instinctive thought process that psychologists call heuristic thinking. We learn to do it from childhood. And it happens unconsciously, at least most of the time, until a hard case forces us to bring our thought process out into the open. The law has a specific term for the cause that gets blamed for a particular harmful result: it's called the proximate cause. Proximate cause is a legal term without a scientific definition. Instead, proximate cause simply means whatever cause the law decides to treat as responsible for the particular harm at issue.

So what goes into this process of causal judgment, leading up to a finding of proximate cause? There's no magic formula for it. Instead, our unconscious mind pays attention to many factors, which combine to produce the final judgment about causation. Some of these factors are obvious. As the term itself suggests, we tend to attribute proximate causation to causes that are more proximate, or closer in time and space, to the result. That's why we instinctively reject treating parents, grandparents, and other ancestors as proximate causes, even though they qualify as "but-for" causes. We also tend to focus on causes that are foreseeably connected to the result, rather than on those that almost nobody would have guessed might lead to that result. The gun dealer probably couldn't have foreseen that Smith would use the gun he was buying to kill someone. Now, on the other hand, if Smith had actually told the gun dealer exactly why he was buying the gun, that might be a different case, and we might actually think about treating the gun dealer as a proximate cause of the death.

There are two special factors that greatly affect causal judgments. One factor is that, as human beings, we need to believe that we have free will. We don't want to think of ourselves as mere automatons reacting to external stimuli, because this would deprive our lives of all moral significance. So, in cases like

Robertson or *Kevorkian*, we generally think that the last human actor had the free will to make a choice about what to do. Officer Partin could have chosen not to make that risky jump, and Kevorkian's patients had a choice whether or not to activate the suicide machine. Unless, of course, their free will was taken away, or compromised, by the earlier acts of someone else. And that's where the second special factor comes into play. We also tend to base our causal judgments on morality. Whenever a bad result happens, like a tragic and untimely death, we tend to blame whomever is seen as the worst actor in the situation. So, in the *Robertson* case, we might initially be tempted to say that Officer Partin acted out of free will and therefore was to blame for his own death. But because Officer Partin was the good guy in the situation, and because Robertson was the bad guy who put Officer Partin into that situation, we're more likely to blame Robertson for the death. And that's exactly what happened in the actual case—the court held that Robertson was the proximate cause of Officer Partin's death, and Robertson was convicted of manslaughter. As for Dr. Kevorkian, the outcome was never so clear, precisely because some people saw Kevorkian as a hero standing up for the rights of others, while others viewed him as a monster trying to make it easier to get rid of the sick and elderly. And that's basically why the courts kept disagreeing about Kevorkian, right up to the end of his own life. In some earlier cases, Kevorkian was held not to be the proximate cause of his patients' deaths. But the last time he was prosecuted, in 1999 for second-degree murder, Kevorkian was judged to be the proximate cause, and his murder conviction was upheld.

So, to summarize: All homicide crimes require the defendant to do, or not do, something that proximately causes the death of the victim. What's the difference, then, between murder and manslaughter? Or between first-degree and second-degree murder? These differences depend entirely on what the defendant was thinking at the time of the act or omission that caused the victim's death. It's all about the defendant's moral culpability for the death, or what the criminal law calls mens rea. The law creates a hierarchy, or a pyramid, of homicide crimes, depending on the mental state of the defendant.

Let's start at the bottom of the pyramid, with the least serious homicide crime, involuntary manslaughter. The crime of involuntary manslaughter generally consists of causing another person's death with the culpable mens rea of recklessness, or perhaps criminal negligence. The punishment varies from state to state, ranging from one to ten years in prison. One example was the terrible fire at the Cocoanut Grove nightclub in Boston in 1942, where almost 500 patrons died after they couldn't escape the flames. The club's owner, Barney Welansky, was charged with multiple counts of involuntary manslaughter, based on evidence that he ignored the fire code requirements to maintain safe exits. This was judged to be reckless behavior, and Welansky was convicted. Notice, by the way, that Welansky was nowhere near the club on the night of the fire, yet, as the culpable owner, he was still held to be a proximate cause of the deaths.

Moving up the pyramid of homicide crimes, we next encounter the crime of murder. More specifically, second-degree murder, a crime that can get you 20 years or more in prison. The legal definition of second-degree murder is a killing committed with "malice." What's malice? As we've seen previously, it's not what it sounds like. Malice in criminal law does not mean "anger," or "ill will." Instead, malice is a catch-all legal term that signifies a certain kind of evil, or wrongfulness. To understand what malice really means, in this particular context, we need to explore the different ways that a murder defendant can exhibit the kind of evil that qualifies as malice. The paradigmatic case of second-degree murder is an intentional killing. If you walk up to somebody, and suddenly decide to shoot them in the head and kill them, that certainly qualifies as malice. But there are other ways to satisfy the requirement of malice. If you intend to cause grievous bodily injury to another person—even if you don't actually intend to kill them—and they die from the injury, that's also malice. Grievous bodily injury means the kind of injury that could easily turn out to be fatal, such as cutting off an arm or leg, or shooting someone in the chest, as opposed to shooting them in the hand or foot. The law treats that kind of evil intent as the functional equivalent of intent to kill, so it's malice, and it's second-degree murder.

Now let's say you're committing a felony crime, meaning a crime punishable by more than a year in prison. Let's also say that the felony crime you're committing is considered by the law to be "inherently dangerous to human life," and that someone dies as a result of your crime, even though the death was unintended or accidental. That counts as malice, too. So, if you're selling heroin, which is considered an inherently dangerous felony, and you see a cop, and you jump into your car and speed away, but you accidentally run over and kill a pedestrian, that's second-degree murder. Law professors have railed against this so-called "felony murder rule" for years, claiming that it's unfair. But the rule persists because many people believe that one who chooses to commit a dangerous felony crime deserves to be treated as a murderer when an innocent victim dies.

All of these situations count as malice. And there's still one more that we need to discuss. It's when a person does something so extremely reckless that we say it manifests an "abandoned and malignant heart," and then someone dies as a result. "Abandoned and malignant heart" is actually the traditional legal terminology for this—it's why we sometimes refer to these cases as AMH murders. A classic case from the 19th century involved a man who got angry and threw a heavy beer stein at his wife while she was carrying a lit oil lamp. The stein shattered the lamp, and the wife burned to death. In another case, a man threw a heavy timber off a tall building, just to see what would happen. He wasn't trying to hit anybody below, but he did, and the victim died. In both cases, the defendants were convicted of second-degree murder. So what makes AMH murder cases different from reckless involuntary manslaughter? It's the sheer level of depravity. As reckless as Barney Welansky was for failing to maintain safe exits at the Cocoanut Grove nightclub, he was basically just a struggling businessman trying to cut costs and make an extra buck or two. In the AMH cases, however, the defendants had no plausible reason to do what they did. Why would you ever think about throwing a beer stein in anger at someone? Why would you ever throw something heavy off a tall building? These acts seem deliberately spiteful, and demonstrate a complete and utter lack of concern for the welfare of others. And the law treats that special kind of depravity as yet another form of malice.

We now move up to the crime of first-degree murder. Just like the paradigmatic example of second-degree murder, first-degree murder involves an intentional killing. The difference is that, in first-degree murder, the intent must be premeditated. What does that mean? First-degree murder cases often involve a decision to kill made over an extended period of time, but courts also say that premeditation doesn't require any specific amount of time. Many of the cases also often involve advance planning, but courts will say that planning is not required. So what, exactly, is premeditation?

The best way to think about the legal concept of premeditation is that it expresses something about the quality of thought that went into the decision to kill, not the quantity. The classic description of a premeditated killing is one committed "in cold blood." In other words, first-degree murder involves a rational, cold-blooded decision to kill, as opposed to the impulsive kind of decision that's the hallmark of second-degree murder. Rational decision-making can occur in an instant, although the more time spent making the decision, the more likely that a court will find premeditation. Similarly, advance planning isn't required, but it can be strong evidence of rational thought. In the end, what matters is whether the defendant made a rational, cold-blooded decision to kill. If so, it's first-degree murder, and the punishment could be life in prison, or even—if aggravating circumstances are present and the relevant state law so provides— the death penalty. The law also treats some felony-murder cases as first-degree murder, if the felony the defendant was committing appears on a statutory list of the most evil of all felonies. Most state statutes define these especially evil felonies as robbery, burglary, arson, kidnapping, and rape. If you commit any of these felonies, and someone dies as a result of your crime, it's first-degree murder, even if you never intended anyone to die.

Last, but not least on our pyramid of homicides, there's one remaining crime we haven't yet discussed. It's called voluntary manslaughter. And it's actually defined as a special exception to the crime of murder, which means that, if the defendant qualifies, the punishment gets reduced to about half of what it would normally be for second-degree murder. In other words, voluntary manslaughter operates as a kind of partial defense to a murder charge—you're still guilty of a homicide crime, but a much less serious one. The doctrine of voluntary manslaughter was developed by judges during the Dark Ages of the common law, hundreds of years ago. The basic idea was to mitigate the punishment in certain homicide cases where the defendant's act was motivated by extreme anger, due to a provoking event that would make most people at least feel homicidal, even if most people wouldn't actually kill over it. We often call this a "heat of passion" killing. If the provocation would be adequate to push even a reasonable person into the "heat of passion," and if the killing occurs before sufficient time has passed for the reasonable person to "cool off," then the crime becomes voluntary manslaughter instead of murder.

Two classic situations led to the creation of the voluntary manslaughter doctrine. The first was mutual combat: Two men get into a fight, and it escalates, and one of them ends up dead. This can't be self-defense, because both men were responsible for the initial violence. But judges decided it shouldn't be murder, either, because the situation led to the death, and the victim was just as responsible for creating that situation as the defendant. The second classic situation was spousal adultery: A man finds his wife in bed with another man, and kills her, or him, or both. Once again, judges decided that this shouldn't be murder, because the killing was only partly the fault of the defendant—it was also partly the fault of the adulterous lovers who created the situation. In both scenarios, the crime was reduced from murder to voluntary manslaughter, and the punishment reduced by roughly half. Notice how both of these classic situations reflect a testosterone-driven view of the world. The early common law judges who devised the doctrine were all men, and the decision to mitigate the crime and punishment in these cases reflected a male-centric perspective. It's like saying, "boys will be boys," and sometimes boys will kill, if you get them mad enough. It's actually proven much harder, over the years, for female defendants to benefit from the voluntary manslaughter doctrine. A battered wife who kills her abusive husband out of fear for her life, but does so while the husband is sleeping, can't qualify for self-defense because she's not in imminent danger. But she also may not qualify for voluntary manslaughter, because very few women kill, even under circumstances of extreme emotion. And the law also has trouble thinking of this as a "heat of passion" killing, because the motivation is fear rather than anger. As in many other areas of the law, the legal standard seems to be defined primarily in terms of the "reasonable man." Which has led some scholars to question whether the voluntary manslaughter doctrine should exist at all. Maybe we should start judging these kinds of cases by the standard of the "reasonable woman," instead of the "reasonable man."

In any event, the voluntary manslaughter doctrine still survives, and still provides a partial way out for defendants charged with murder in cases involving extreme emotion—especially anger—that's provoked, at least in part, by something the victim did. Like everything else we've discussed, this doctrine provides another way for the criminal law to fine tune its response to this most heinous of crimes.

Now that we've learned all about homicide crimes, let's apply what we've learned to *Anatomy of a Murder*. First, you should understand that there's actually no such thing in contemporary criminal law as "temporary insanity." Those rules have changed. Either you're legally insane—which is generally defined as having a mental disease or defect that prevents you from knowing right from wrong, or from controlling your actions—or you're not. And the burden of proof on insanity usually rests with the defendant. So let's assume, for sake of argument, that Manny Manion can't prove he was legally insane when he killed that bartender. Then what homicide crime did Manny commit? He might be guilty of second-degree murder, because he made an impulsive, irrational decision to kill. He might be guilty of first-degree murder if we conclude that he thought about the crime rationally, and the fact that he went to the bar with a loaded gun in his pocket might be enough to support a finding of premeditation. If, on the other hand, we decide that Manny was enraged by the discovery that the bartender raped his wife, and if he didn't have enough time to reasonably "cool down" before he fired the fatal shot, then maybe it's a case of voluntary manslaughter. Indeed, even if Laura Manion actually had an affair with the bartender, that still might qualify as legally adequate provocation, and Manny still might get his crime reduced to voluntary manslaughter.

In the end, it would be up to the jury to decide Manny's fate. And I wouldn't envy them having to make such a hard decision. Would you?

THE LAW OF SELF-DEFENSE

Criminal law tries to strike a balance between the rights of those who feel their lives may be threatened, and the rights of those who are—or who may be mistakenly perceived as—a threat. A key component of this difficult balancing act is the doctrine of self-defense. Related issues include battered spouse syndrome, the duty to retreat, and police use of deadly force.

SELF-DEFENSE BASICS

* Self-defense has a long history in Anglo-American law. As the doctrine is traditionally defined, a person is legally allowed to use force—including deadly force—when he reasonably believes that he, or another person, is in imminent danger of death or serious bodily injury from an assailant. The person claiming the right to self-defense must not be the initial aggressor, and the amount of force used must not be excessive.

* The doctrine of self-defense is usually based on what a person reasonably believes. This means that it's possible to act legally in self-defense even if you are mistaken about the threat, as long as your mistake is reasonable. If you kill another person because you honestly but unreasonably thought the person was trying to kill you, that's still criminal homicide, but your charge might be reduced from murder to manslaughter.

* The doctrine of self-defense can be used in defense not only of yourself, but also of others. The law has long taken the position that you're never allowed to take another person's life on the ground of necessity. This means that even if killing one person will save another person's life—or 10 lives, or 100 lives—you can't do it. But if one person is actually trying to kill another person, you can kill the first person to save the second person's life.

* The traditional definition of self-defense requires that the perceived threat be imminent. This meanss you can't act in self-defense prematurely, killing someone because you believe they're likely to attack you in the future. Nor can you act in self-defense belatedly, killing them after the attack is over and you're no longer in any immediate danger.

BATTERED SPOUSE SYNDROME

* Self-defense's imminence requirement is sometimes a point of controversy, particularly in cases where the person facing a lethal threat may be unable to defend themselves in the heat of the moment. In such cases, the victim may need to wait until a safer time and place to deal with the attacker. The classic example is someone trapped in a physically abusive relationship with a bigger stronger individual, a pattern known as battered spouse syndrome.

* Criminal law traditionally holds that a battered spouse can claim self-defense for killing her batterer only if she fights back when she's actually being attacked and when the threat to her life is imminent. In many cases, however, the battered spouse may be much more likely to be killed herself if she tries to fight back when her batterer is enraged.

And if the batterer is hitting her with his fists, the law might not allow her to use a gun to protect herself; that might be seen as an excessive use of force. As a result, the battered spouse may decide to wait until the attack is over before taking action.

★ Cases involving battered spouses have led many courts to reconsider the rules of self-defense. Some courts have loosened up the imminence requirement, interpreting it in light of how things would look to a battered spouse who can't plausibly fight back. Others have focused on the requirement that the perception of the threat be reasonable, concluding that reasonableness should be judged from the perspective of a reasonable person who's been battered.

★ Still other courts have turned to other legal doctrines, such as diminished mental capacity or acting in the heat of passion, to reduce charges brought against battered spouses from murder to manslaughter. Advocacy groups for battered spouses don't like these alternatives, however, because they still treat the battered woman as a criminal.

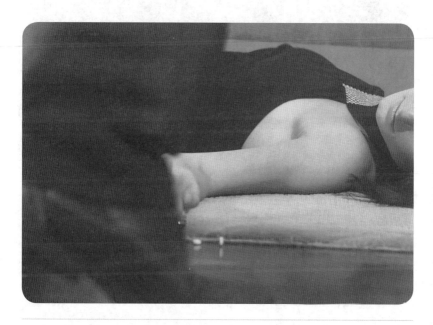

THE RETREAT DOCTRINE

⋆ The legal requirement of imminence and the prohibition against excessive force are both closely related to another important aspect of self-defense law. Some states require that a person must retreat—if it is possible for him to do so in safety—before using force in self-defense. This is known as the retreat doctrine.

⋆ Judicial decisions in the United States have long been split over the duty to retreat. Currently, less than half of the states require a person to retreat before using force in self-defense. These states tend to be located in the Northeast and Midwest. States that have rejected the retreat doctrine tend to be located in the South and West. Many of these adopted an entirely different standard known as the true man doctrine.

✴ The true man doctrine holds that a "true man" doesn't run away in the face of danger; he stands and fights. In states that have adopted the true man doctrine, even if a person who's about to be attacked can easily and safely escape the danger, he doesn't have to do so. He is legally authorized to stand and fight, using deadly force if necessary.

✴ The ongoing debate over the retreat doctrine and the true man doctrine seems to be a reflection of something deeply historical and cultural. In the South, there's always been a strong culture of personal honor. In the West, there is a tendency toward rugged individualism. In the Northeast and Midwest, by contrast, there's a greater sense of social interdependence, and thus a greater willingness to leave the use of deadly force to law enforcement.

THE CASTLE DOCTRINE

✴ Even in the minority of American states where the retreat doctrine still prevails, there's always been a special exception for attacks that occur inside the home. This is called the castle doctrine. The castle doctrine holds that you have no legal duty to retreat from an assailant if the attack happens inside your own home or place of residence. In such circumstances, if you reasonably fear for your life, you can stand and fight, using deadly force if necessary.

✴ There's an increasing tendency in many states to recognize, often by statute, broader versions of the castle doctrine. These broader versions often provide that, inside your own home, you can use deadly force not only in defense of your own life or the life of another, but also to stop an intruder from committing a felony or other serious crime, such as robbery, assault, rape, or kidnapping.

✴ Some states have broadened the castle doctrine even further, permitting the use of deadly force to prevent the commission of any crime by a trespasser inside your home. In some states, deadly force can be legally used to stop an unknown person from forcibly entering your home, even if you don't know why they're trying to get in. A few states even extend the castle doctrine to cover illegal entry into your vehicle.

★ These broader versions of the castle alter the traditional rule that you can only use force that's proportionate, and not excessive, relative to the specific threat you perceived. In fact, many of these laws create a legal presumption that the use of deadly force is permitted against any intruder, on the theory that you can reasonably assume anyone trying to break into your home intends to do you or your loved ones lethal harm.

★ The broadening of the castle doctrine in certain states doesn't mean you can accomplish the same thing by setting up a booby trap, a spring gun rigged to fire automatically, or some other such device. Many people have gone to prison for injuring or killing trespassing criminals in that manner—primarily because such devices are incapable of exercising any kind of reasonable judgment based on the facts of the particular situation.

★ Keep in mind that state laws vary widely and sometimes change rapidly. This course is not meant to be source of legal advice. The only person who can give you proper legal advice is a licensed attorney who is well versed in the laws of your particular state.

STAND-YOUR-GROUND LAWS

★ The longstanding debate between the retreat doctrine and the true man doctrine has been pushed aside in many states by the enactment of so-called stand-your-ground laws. The Florida stand-your-ground statute was one of the first to be enacted, and several other states used it as a model. The Florida statute provides:

> A person who is not engaged in an unlawful activity, and who is attacked in any place where he or she has a right to be, has no duty to retreat and has the right to stand his or her ground and meet force with force, including deadly force if he or she reasonably believes it is necessary to do so to prevent death or great bodily harm to himself or herself or another or to prevent the commission of a forcible felony.

* Notice that the statute eliminates any duty to retreat before using force in self-defense, and it allows the use of force—including deadly force—to stop or prevent any forcible felony, such as a robbery. In effect, the statute takes a broad version of the castle doctrine, a doctrine traditionally limited to defense of your home, and applies it to any place in the world you have a right to be.

* There are two huge, unanswered empirical questions about stand-your-ground laws. The first is whether such laws make the world a safer place by deterring illegal behavior, or a more dangerous place by encouraging people to rely on guns for protection from trouble.

* The second unanswered question is whether such laws have the unintended effect of making the world a more dangerous place for people who only seem to be threatening because of who they are and what they look like. In a society where young black men are often perceived as especially dangerous, stand-your-ground laws could make it especially dangerous to be a young black man.

POLICE USE OF DEADLY FORCE

* Police shootings of young black men erupted onto the American political scene in August 2014 with the death of Michael Brown in Ferguson, Missouri. The police officer who shot Brown was cleared of all criminal charges, but not without considerable controversy.

* The law governing police use of deadly force is surprisingly opaque. The Supreme Court has held that, under the Fourth Amendment, police officers can't use deadly force to stop fleeing criminals unless they present a significant risk of death or serious bodily injury to the officers or to others. Police officers charged with a crime can also avail themselves of the doctrine of self-defense, if applicable.

* Police officers have a special duty not to retreat from danger, even where others might have to. Given their special training and experience, they might also have a duty to be more prudent in their use of deadly force than civilians might be. So far, the courts haven't said much about how these considerations might affect the legality of police use of deadly force.

✻ In the end, the use of deadly force by police and by private citizens—whether to apprehend a fleeing criminal, to protect oneself or others from potential danger, or simply to stand up for law and order—is likely to remain highly contentious as we continue to debate how best to build a safe, fair, and just society.

Suggested Reading

⌕ People v. Goetz.

⌕ Mobley v. State.

Questions to Consider

↗ Do you agree with the verdict reached and the lenient punishment imposed in the *Goetz* case?

↗ How do you feel about modern stand-your-ground laws, like the one in Florida? Why do you feel that way?

Lecture 4 Transcript

THE LAW OF SELF-DEFENSE

Bernhard Goetz was a 37-year-old electrical engineer living in New York City in the mid-1980s. New York was a pretty dangerous place in those days, and Goetz had been mugged and beaten up once before. He'd also drawn his handgun—which he'd bought illegally, without a permit—on two other occasions to deter potential muggings. One Saturday afternoon, in late December 1984, Bernie Goetz boarded the southbound IRT express subway train at the 14th Street Station in lower Manhattan. In the same car were four young black men. One of them approached Goetz and said, "Give me five dollars." Goetz calmly drew his .38-caliber handgun and started shooting. He fired four times, hitting three of the youths but missing the fourth one, 19-year-old Darrell Cabey. Goetz walked up to Cabey and said, "I see you seem to be all right. Here's another." He then shot Cabey, severing his spinal cord. The train conductor heard the shots and made an emergency stop. As Goetz escaped into the tunnels, he told the conductor, "They tried to rip me off." All four of the youths survived, although Cabey suffered brain damage and was permanently paralyzed. Goetz remained on the loose for nine days, heading north toward Canada. Then he decided to turn himself in. Goetz was brought back to New York and charged with four counts of attempted murder, one count of reckless endangerment, four counts of assault, and four counts of illegal possession of a weapon. So began one of the most publicized and controversial criminal law cases of the 20th Century.

To some, Bernie Goetz was a hero. The tabloids dubbed him "The Subway Vigilante," and a *Daily News* poll showed that New Yorkers supported Goetz by a 49–31 margin. Some supporters were influenced by the fact that two of the youths turned out to be carrying screwdrivers they planned to use to break into video game machines, and three of them had prior criminal records—although, of course, Goetz knew none of that at the time of the shootings. Many New Yorkers simply felt that Goetz had acted out their own feelings of frustration that the government, and particularly the criminal justice system, just could not get a handle on New York City's crime problem. One commentator explained the local sentiment this way: "Last year, there were over 70,000 robberies…The outrage of New Yorkers about violence on the streets is very, very great."

To others, Bernie Goetz was a menace, taking the law into his own hands to exact some kind of warped sense of frontier justice. After all, even if those four young men were planning to take Goetz's money by force, there's no death penalty for robbery. As one local politician lamented, "It's now open season on black youths in New York City. If Goetz were a black man who shot four white youths on a subway train, there would be no doubt of the verdict. The media and the public would be screaming for the most stringent penalty possible." It's important to note that public opinion about Bernie Goetz did not split neatly along racial lines, partly because many in the black community felt just as frustrated, and just as angry, as Goetz about the prevalence of urban street crime. As a spokesman for the Congress on Racial Equality explained, "It's a question of who you want off the streets. I'll take Bernie Goetz any day. He does not go about mugging my sister, snatching my mother's pocketbook, or breaking into my apartment."

Goetz himself showed absolutely no remorse for his actions. In sworn statements to the police, he stated, "They wanted to play with me, you know, it's kind of like a cat plays with a mouse. It's horrible…When I saw what they intended for me, my intention was worse than shooting. My intention was to do anything I could do to hurt them…I know this sounds horrible, but my intention was to murder them, to hurt them, to make them suffer as much as possible." Goetz also said the only thing that eventually stopped him was a shortage of bullets: "If I had had more, I would have shot them again and again and again."

The Goetz case provides the ideal context for exploring the contours of the legal doctrine of self-defense. And that's just what we're going to do in this lecture. Along the way, we'll also discuss a number of closely related issues: The "retreat doctrine," the "battered spouse syndrome," the "castle doctrine," "stand your ground" laws, and the prevailing legal rules governing police use of deadly force. Our ultimate goal will be to achieve a better understanding of how the criminal law tries to strike a delicate balance between the rights of those who feel their lives may be threatened, and the rights of those who are—or who may be mistakenly perceived as—a threat. It's a balance that isn't so easy to achieve.

Self-defense has a long history in Anglo-American law. As the doctrine is traditionally and generally defined, a person is legally allowed to use force—including deadly force—when they reasonably believe that they, or another person, are in imminent danger of death or serious bodily injury from an assailant. The person claiming the right to self-defense must not be the initial aggressor, and the amount of force used must not be excessive in relation of the danger presented. New York's law of self-defense at the time of the Goetz case was pretty much the same, although the New York statute also provided that the person who's being attacked must retreat instead of using force in self-defense, if such a retreat can be accomplished with complete safety.

Let's try to break down the legal definition of self-defense. First, the doctrine is generally based on what a person "reasonably" believes. This means it's possible to act legally in self-defense, even if it turns out later that you were actually mistaken about the threat, as long as your mistake was reasonable. Some legal scholars argue that self-defense should be available any time a person honestly believes their own life is in danger, even if we later conclude that the mistake was unreasonable. But that's not the law. In most jurisdictions, if you kill another person because you honestly but unreasonably thought they were trying to kill you, that's still a criminal homicide, although the level of the homicide might get reduced from murder to manslaughter. We call this kind of case "imperfect self-defense."

Second, the doctrine of self-defense can be used in defense not only of yourself, but also of others. This rule is actually a little more complicated than it appears. The criminal law has long taken the position that you're never allowed to take another person's life on the ground of necessity. This means that even if killing one person will save another person's life, or ten lives, or a hundred lives, you can't do it. You may recall that this was the basis for the murder conviction of the shipwrecked sailors of the *Mignonette* after they sacrificed one of the group to save the others. But if one person is actually trying to kill another person, then you can kill the first person to save the second person's life. Killing an innocent person, even out of necessity, is prohibited. But killing someone who's trying to kill another is permitted, under the "defense of others" variation of self-defense, because in that case you're not taking an innocent life.

Third, traditional self-defense requires the perceived threat to be "imminent." This means you can't act in self-defense prematurely, because you believe you'll likely be attacked tomorrow, nor can you act in self-defense belatedly, after the attack is over and you're no longer in any immediate danger. Seems fair, right? Maybe you should just let the law, or the police, handle those situations. But the requirement of imminence can turn out to be controversial, because sometimes a person who's facing a lethal threat may be unable to defend themselves in the heat of the moment. Instead, they may need to wait until a safer time and place to deal with the attacker. The classic example of this is the sadly all-too-common situation of someone who's trapped in a physically abusive relationship with a bigger, stronger individual. Usually, though not always, it's a woman who's being beaten by her man. Sometimes the beatings become so violent that the woman reasonably fears for her life. What's she supposed to do? It's easy to say that she should just leave him, but in the real world, that's not always easy to do, for financial reasons, or psychological reasons, or simply due to the fear. She may feel trapped, with no escape. So what happens when she decides to fight back?

The criminal law traditionally holds that a battered woman can claim self-defense for killing her batterer only if she fights back when she's actually being attacked, and when the threat to her life is imminent. But if she tries to fight back when her man is enraged and beating on her, she's much more likely to be killed herself. And if he's hitting her with his fists, then the law might not allow her to use a gun to protect herself, because that might be seen as excessive or disproportionate force. So battered women sometimes decide to wait until the attack is over, and then act. In one infamous case in my home town of Bloomington, Indiana, a woman who'd been abused waited until her abuser was asleep. Then she took his 14-pound bowling ball, and dropped it repeatedly on his head, until he was dead. She was convicted of voluntary manslaughter and sentenced to eight years in prison.

How should the law treat such a case? As a general rule, it's not a valid case of self-defense, because the guy was sleeping and posed no immediate threat at the time he was killed. But I hope you can see how this can seem like an unfair application of the self-defense law, because it ignores the obvious physical differences between most men and most women. Because of these differences, a legal doctrine like self-defense, even if it's facially neutral, can turn out in practice to be highly unequal. These "battered spouse" cases have led many courts to reconsider the rules of self-defense. Some courts have loosened up the imminent threat requirement, interpreting imminence in light of how things would look to a battered woman who can't plausibly fight back against her attacker. Others have focused on the requirement that the perception of the threat must be reasonable, concluding that this should be judged from the perspective of a reasonable woman who's been battered. Still other courts have decided that self-defense just can't be stretched far enough to accommodate such cases. These courts have turned to other legal doctrines, such as diminished mental capacity, or the "heat of passion" defense, as alternative ways to reduce the criminal charges against the battered woman from murder to manslaughter. And that's basically what happened in the Bloomington case. Advocacy groups for battered women don't like these alternatives at all, because they still treat the battered woman as a criminal, just not as bad of a criminal. So the controversy persists.

The legal requirement of imminence, as well as the requirement to use only as much force as necessary to deal with the threat, are both closely related to another important aspect of self-defense law. As we've already seen, some states, like New York, require that a person must retreat, if this can be done safely, before resorting to the use of force in self-defense. This is known as the "retreat" doctrine.

In England, from whence our law came, the "retreat" doctrine has always been a standard part of self-defense law. But here in the states, it's not so standard. Judicial decisions in the U.S. have long been split over the duty to retreat. Nowadays, fewer than half of the states require a person to retreat before using force in self-defense. The minority of states that still require retreat tend to be located mostly in the Northeast and the Midwest. By contrast, courts in most of the Southern and Western states have rejected the "retreat" doctrine in favor of the so-called "true man" doctrine. The "true man" doctrine holds that a "true man" doesn't run away in the face of danger, he stands and fights. In "true man" states, even if a person who's about to be attacked can easily and safely escape the danger—say, by running into a nearby police station—they don't have to do so. They are legally authorized to stand and fight, including with lethal force if necessary. As the Missouri Supreme Court once put it in a 1902 decision: "It is true, human life is sacred, but so is human liberty. One is as dear in the eye of the law as the other, and neither is to give way and surrender."

The ongoing debate between the "retreat" doctrine and the "true man" doctrine seems to be a reflection of something deeply historical and cultural. In the South, there's always been a strong culture of personal honor, a culture that supported historical practices like dueling. In the West, it seems to be more about rugged individualism, and the reality that often you had to rely on yourself for protection, since the long arm of the law was probably too far away to help. In the Northeast and Midwest by contrast, there's more of a culture of social interdependence, and a generally greater willingness to turn the tough job of protecting the good guys from the bad guys over to the police. As is often true, the debate between the "retreat" doctrine and the "true man" doctrine is about more than the law itself. It's also about the very nature of our society.

Even in the minority of states where the "retreat" doctrine still prevails, there's always been a special exception for attacks that occur inside your own home. This is called the "castle" doctrine, based on the old maxim, which first appeared in an English case in 1604, that a man's home is his castle. The "castle" doctrine holds that there's no legal duty to retreat from an assailant, if the attack happens inside your own home or place of residence. In that situation, and if you reasonably fear for your life, you can stand and fight, and you can use deadly force if necessary. Nowadays, there's an increasing tendency in many states to recognize, often by statute, broader versions of the "castle" doctrine. These broader versions often provide that, inside your own home, you can use deadly force not only in defense of your own life or the life of another, but also to stop an intruder from committing a felony or other serious crime, including such crimes as robbery, assault, rape, or kidnapping. Some states allow the use of deadly force to prevent the commission of any crime by a trespasser inside your home. Moreover, some states allow the use of deadly force to stop an unknown person from forcibly entering your home, even if you don't know why they're trying to get in. You can shoot first and ask questions later. A few states even extend the "castle" doctrine to cover illegal entry into a vehicle.

The key to understanding these broader, modern versions of the traditional "castle" doctrine is that you don't necessarily have to show that you reasonably feared for your life, or that you knew the intruder was armed or dangerous. Basically, these laws alter the traditional rule that you can only use force that's proportionate and not excessive in relation to the specific threat you perceived. In fact, many of these laws create a legal presumption that the use of deadly force is permitted against any intruder, on the theory that you can reasonably assume anyone trying to break into your home intends to do you or your loved ones lethal harm. By the way, I should make clear that no matter what kind of force your state law may allow you to use in defense of yourself, your loved ones, or your home, that doesn't mean you can accomplish the same thing by setting up a booby trap or a spring gun that's been rigged to fire automatically or some other kind of automatic device. Plenty of people have gone to prison for injuring or killing trespassing criminals in that way, mostly because such devices are incapable of exercising any kind of reasonable judgment based on the facts of the particular situation.

Now, before someone goes out and gets themselves killed, or kills someone else, by drawing a gun on an intruder, please keep in mind that state laws vary widely and they can also change very rapidly. More importantly, I'm not giving you legal advice here, I'm just teaching a course about criminal law. The only person who can give you proper legal advice is a licensed lawyer who's well versed in the laws of your particular state.

Okay, now back to the lesson. The longstanding judicial debate in the United States between the "retreat" doctrine and the "true man" doctrine has been pushed aside in many states by the enactment of so-called "Stand Your Ground" statutes. One of the first of these statutes was passed in Florida, and the Florida statute still serves as the model for most of the others. In Florida, the "Stand Your Ground" statute provides: "A person who is not engaged in an unlawful activity, and who is attacked in any place where he or she has a right to be, has no duty to retreat and has the right to stand his or her ground and meet force with force, including deadly force if he or she reasonably believes it is necessary to do so to prevent death or great bodily harm to himself or herself or another or to prevent the commission of a forcible felony."

Notice exactly what this "Stand Your Ground" statute does: The statute eliminates any duty to retreat before using force in self-defense, and allows the use of force—including deadly force—to stop or prevent any forcible felony crime, such as a robbery. In other words, the statute essentially takes a very broad version of the "castle" doctrine, a doctrine traditionally limited to the defense of your own home, and makes the doctrine applicable everywhere in the world, as long as it's a place you have a right to be. That includes all public places, as well as all places of business that invite customers inside, such as restaurants, bars, and shops. If someone attacks you or tries to commit a forcible felony crime against you, anywhere that you're legally allowed to be, you have the right to "Stand Your Ground" and use force against them—including deadly force—if you reasonably believe it's necessary.

Consider the case of Gabriel Mobley. Mobley and a friend named Chico were eating dinner with several women friends at a Chili's restaurant in Miami. While Mobley and Chico stepped outside to have a smoke, two men they didn't know—Jason Gonzalez and Roly Carrazana—came over and started talking to the women. Chico, upon returning to the table, thought the women were being bothered, so he told the two men to leave. This led to an argument that gradually escalated, until the point when Jason and Roly finally left the restaurant. Mobley and Chico waited until it looked like the two men were gone, and then headed to their cars. Mobley went into his car, retrieved his loaded .45 Glock handgun from the glove compartment, and put it into a holster around his waist. Mobley and Chico then hung around in the parking lot, having another smoke. Suddenly Jason appeared and sucker-punched Chico hard in the face, drawing blood. Jason and Mobley then started to square off, like two boxers. Mobley noticed Roly running in his direction, and he later testified that he thought Roly was reaching under his baggy shirt, possibly for a weapon, although a surveillance video didn't seem to show any such move by Roly. Mobley drew his Glock and fired five shots. Roly was hit four times and Jason once, in the chest. Both men died. Neither man was armed.

Mobley was charged with two counts of second-degree murder. The Florida Court of Appeals, however, decided that Mobley should not have been convicted in light of Florida's "Stand Your Ground" law. Here's what the court had to say about the case: "It may have been more prudent for Mobley and Chico to skitter to their cars and hightail it out of there when they had the chance. However, Mobley and Chico had every right to be where they were, doing what they were doing, and they did nothing to precipitate this violent attack. The preponderance of the evidence demonstrates that…Mobley's use of deadly force was justified."

The court's colorful language clearly reflects how the "Stand Your Ground" issue is connected to our earlier discussion about history, culture, and the "true man" doctrine. But there are also two huge, unanswered empirical questions about "stand your ground" laws. The first question is whether such laws make the world a safer place by deterring illegal behavior, or a more dangerous place by encouraging people to rely on guns for protection from trouble, instead of trying harder to avoid trouble in the first place. Okay, Jason Gonzalez certainly shouldn't have sucker-punched Chico, and we'll never know exactly what Roly Carrazana had in mind as he ran toward the scene. But fistfights in restaurant parking lots usually don't end up with two people dead. And this particular fistfight probably wouldn't have happened at all, if Mobley and Chico had been, to use the court's words, "more prudent."

The second empirical question is whether "Stand Your Ground" laws have the unintended effect of making the world a more dangerous place for people who only seem to be threatening, because of who they are and what they look like. You may recall that, on February 26, 2012, Trayvon Martin, an unarmed black teenager, was shot to death inside a gated community in Sanford, Florida, by George Zimmerman, the head of the local neighborhood watch program, who'd accosted Martin on suspicion that he was up to some kind of trouble. Zimmerman was acquitted of the homicide based on self-defense. And the case technically wasn't a "Stand Your Ground" case at all; Zimmerman claimed he had no chance to retreat because he was on his back, being pummeled by Martin. But in general terms, "Stand Your Ground" laws reinforce the view that it's okay to draw your weapon, and to use it, whenever you feel threatened. In a society where young black men often are perceived as especially dangerous, that might make it especially dangerous to be a young black man like Trayvon Martin. The danger may arise not only from armed private citizens like George Zimmerman, but also from armed officers of the law. Police shootings of young black men erupted onto the American political scene in August 2014, with the shooting death of Michael Brown in Ferguson, Missouri. The police officer who shot Michael Brown was cleared of all criminal charges by a local grand jury and also by the U.S. Department of Justice, but not without significant controversy.

The law governing police use of deadly force is surprisingly opaque. The Supreme Court has held that, under the Fourth Amendment, police officers can't use deadly force to stop fleeing criminals unless they present a significant risk of death or serious bodily injury to the officers or to others. And if charged with a crime, police officers can use the same defenses we've already discussed, including self-defense, defense of others, the "castle" doctrine and—where applicable—"Stand Your Ground." But police officers also have a special duty not to retreat from danger, even where others might have to. And police officers might also have a duty, given their special training and experience, to be more prudent in their use of deadly force than others might be. So far, the courts haven't said very much about how any of that might affect the legality of police use of deadly force.

In the end, the use of deadly force by police and by private citizens—whether to apprehend a fleeing criminal, to protect oneself or others from potential danger, or simply to stand up for law and order—is likely to remain highly contentious, as we continue to debate how best to build a safe, fair, and just society.

On June 16, 1987, Bernhard Goetz was acquitted on all charges related to the subway shootings, except for the relatively minor crime of illegal weapons possession. He served eight months in jail. Was it a just result? Reasonable minds may differ.

Perhaps there's one more important lesson we can learn from the Goetz case. As Bernie Goetz told the police, shortly after his arrest, "People are looking for a hero or they're looking for a villain, and neither is the truth. What this is…and you won't understand—this is survival instinct." And, of course, Goetz is right. When one faces an existential threat, either real or perceived, one is not likely to think about whatever the governing legal rule may be, or what the law might say about balancing rights. Which means that the law probably can't do very much to influence how someone like Bernie Goetz is going to behave in the heat of the moment. This is an area where the practical limitations of the law are patently obvious. Maybe the most the law can ever hope to do is vindicate, after the fact, whatever society believes the proper balance to be.

Lecture 5

FEDERAL CRIMES AND FEDERAL POWER

There are important distinctions in scope, meaning, and effect between state criminal law and federal criminal law. In this lecture, you'll learn about the limits placed by the United States Constitution on the federal government's power to enact criminal laws. You'll also examine some of the ways that federal crimes differ from state crimes.

LIMITED AUTHORITY

✶ The United States federal government may be the most powerful government in the world, but its power to prohibit and punish crimes is relatively constrained. For example, even if Congress were to decide that murder had become a national crisis requiring a concerted response, it would be patently unconstitutional for Congress to pass a federal statute criminalizing all murders.

⋆ Shortly after the Revolutionary War ended, delegates from the 13 former colonies met in Philadelphia to draft a Constitution. The delegates knew they had to forge a strong union, but the last thing they wanted to was create a federal government that might become too strong. After all, they'd just fought a long and bloody war to gain their freedom from an overbearing central government—the British Crown.

⋆ James Madison, a delegate from Virginia, proposed a solution that was simple but brilliant: The newly independent states would agree to give up only a few of their sovereign powers to the new federation. Within those few areas of sovereignty specifically granted to the federal government by the text of the Constitution, the federal government would reign supreme. But all other sovereign powers of government would remain with the states—and in those areas, the federal government would have no authority at all, and the states would retain complete sovereignty.

⋆ This system of dual sovereignty has helped keep America both strong and free for more than 200 years. As Madison and the other framers of the Constitution recognized, individual liberty can be better protected by having two governments, because those two governments will constantly compete with each other for power, which will help keep both of them in check.

✸ In the Constitution, the framers listed a number of specific powers that would be transferred by the states to the new federal government. Among these enumerated powers were those necessary to raise and maintain a military, to engage in foreign affairs and diplomacy, to control immigration and customs, to create a national currency, to construct a national transportation system of post roads and waterways, to encourage invention and the creative arts through patents and copyrights, and to regulate interstate and foreign commerce.

✸ One very important power not given to the federal government was the general power to act in the best interests of the American people. This fundamental power of sovereign government— sometimes called the health, safety, and wellness power, or the police power—remains, to this day, with the states. And it is this power that allows the states to create generally applicable criminal laws. The federal government, by contrast, can create a criminal law only if it is within the scope of federal power under the Constitution.

★ Federal crimes fall into one of three broad categories. The first involves criminal statutes that are directly related to a power enumerated in the Constitution. For example, Congress can make counterfeiting a federal crime, based on its authority to create a national currency. Congress can also make it a federal crime to blow up a post office, or to enter the country illegally. According to the Constitution, these are federal matters.

★ Second, Congress can enact criminal laws to govern federal places, such as the District of Columbia, military bases, and other federal lands. The same principle applies to areas that lie outside the legal jurisdiction of any state, such as the offshore territorial waters of the United States, or the air and space above.

★ Third, Congress can enact federal criminal statutes to protect the federal government itself, its institutions, and its officers and employees. This is akin to the doctrine of self-defense for individuals, and it's an implied power that belongs inherently to all governments. It was this basis upon which Congress, following the Kennedy assassination, passed a law making it a federal crime to assassinate the President.

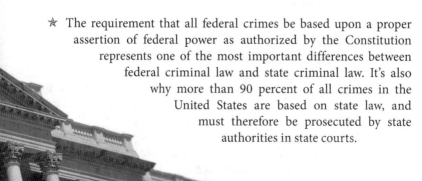

★ The requirement that all federal crimes be based upon a proper assertion of federal power as authorized by the Constitution represents one of the most important differences between federal criminal law and state criminal law. It's also why more than 90 percent of all crimes in the United States are based on state law, and must therefore be prosecuted by state authorities in state courts.

BROAD READINGS

★ Despite its limitations, the role of the federal government in defining, prosecuting, and punishing crimes has grown significantly over the years. In the earliest decades of American history, there were very few federal crimes. But over time, the scope of federal constitutional power has increased—and with it, the scope of federal criminal law.

★ Much of the expansion of federal criminal law has been based on the federal government's authority to regulate interstate and foreign commerce. When the framers drafted the Constitution, there wasn't much interstate or foreign commerce to speak of; most commerce was entirely local. That gradually changed over the course of the 19th and 20th centuries. Commerce that was originally local became regional, then national, and eventually global. This meant that the scope of Congress's power to regulate had also changed.

★ During the Great Depression of the 1930s, Americans turned to a new President—Franklin Delano Roosevelt—who promised to bring about a New Deal and solve the greatest economic crisis in our history. With the help of a willing Congress, Roosevelt immediately began to implement a series of bold new federal laws designed to regulate many aspects of the national economy, in the hopes of increasing employment and reducing poverty.

★ The new laws were initially struck down by the U.S. Supreme Court. The Court ruled that, under the Commerce Clause, the federal government could not regulate the economy in general—only economic activity that actually crossed state lines. Around 1937, however, the Court began to change its views about the Commerce Clause.

★ The expansion of the Commerce Clause reached its apogee in the 1942 case *Wickard v. Filburn*, in which the Court held that Congress can regulate even purely intrastate commercial activity as long as that activity has some effect on interstate commerce. Given the increasingly interconnected nature of the American economy, this meant that Congress could regulate almost anything.

* In the 1995 case *United States v. Lopez*, the Supreme Court demonstrated that Congress's power to legislate under the Commerce Clause was not truly unlimited. In *Lopez*, the Court held that the Gun Free School Zones Act, a federal statute making it a crime to carry a firearm within a school zone, exceeded Congress's power under the Commerce Clause. According to the Court, the Commerce Clause requires a substantial effect on interstate commerce, not one that is speculative and remote.

COMPLEX CASES

* Many federal crimes involve complicated subjects, from securities transactions to food safety. Sometimes these complex federal laws are aimed primarily at businesses and the people who run them. In such situations, the federal courts typically have little sympathy for claims by corporate defendants that they didn't know what the law required of them. If you're running a business in a heavily regulated industry, you have an obligation to find out what the relevant legal requirements are.

* Sometimes, however, complex federal laws affect average citizens. The Supreme Court has adopted two special rules to protect average citizens from unfair criminal liability due to overly complicated federal statutes. These rules are much more lenient to federal criminal defendants than most state laws would be.

* The first special rule is that a defendant must know the facts that make his conduct illegal. The second rule provides that in some cases—prosecutions based on complex portions of the federal tax code, for example—an honest mistake about what the law requires can be a defense.

* Perhaps the strangest aspect of the often confusing relationship between federal criminal law and state criminal law is the way that, over the years, federal and state statutes have inconsistently regulated the production, sale, and possession of marijuana. Despite recent changes in state law, marijuana is currently still designated by the U.S. Drug Enforcement Agency as a dangerous drug, and its production, sale, and possession remained strictly prohibited under federal law.

* This odd discrepancy between state and federal law has led to all sorts of practical problems. It can be very difficult, for example, to get a bank account or a loan for a marijuana business in states where marijuana has been legalized, because the activity in question remains a serious federal crime. Similarly, it can be difficult to find lawyers willing to give legal advice about matters relating to the marijuana industry, because such advice could be construed as telling someone how to commit a federal crime—which could get a lawyer disbarred, if not prosecuted.

★ The Constitution provides that, within the proper scope of the federal enumerated powers, federal law reigns supreme. This means that the states that have legalized marijuana are deliberately skating on thin ice, hoping that the federal government decides not to enforce federal law. This dynamic has created what amounts to a new frontier in the never-ending battle of federalism.

Suggested Reading

○ Wickard v. Filburn.

○ United States v. Lopez.

○ Staples v. United States.

○ Cheek v. United States.

○ Ratzlaf v. United States.

Questions to Consider

↗ Should the federal government have the power to enact general criminal laws?

↗ Do you agree with the Supreme Court's decision to let Cheek off the hook for tax evasion, given his (unreasonable) belief that he didn't have to pay taxes?

FEDERAL CRIMES AND FEDERAL POWER

At roughly 12:30 PM Central Standard Time on Friday, November 22, 1963, John F. Kennedy, the 35th President of the United States, was riding in the back of the Presidential limousine through Dealey Plaza in Dallas, Texas, when he was assassinated by shots fired from a high-powered rifle. Texas Governor John Connolly, sitting in front of the President, was seriously wounded, but survived. The assassination of President Kennedy shocked America and, indeed, the entire world. Most of us who were alive at the time can vividly recall exactly where we were when we first heard the news; I know I can, even though I was only six-years old. Witnesses in Dealey Plaza immediately described to police a man seen looking out the 6th floor window of the Texas School Book Depository, from where the shots came. An All-Points Bulletin was sent out, and about an hour later, a Dallas police officer named J.D. Tippit encountered a man who matched the description. When Tippit tried to question him, the man—Lee Harvey Oswald—shot and killed Officer Tippit. Oswald was arrested by Dallas Police a few minutes later. But Lee Harvey Oswald never made it to trial. On Sunday morning, November 24, Oswald was being transferred by the Texas Rangers from the Dallas City Jail to the county lockup when he was shot, on live television, by Dallas nightclub owner Jack Ruby. Oswald died a couple of hours later. Did you ever wonder why, at the time he was shot, Lee Harvey Oswald—who'd assassinated the President of the United States—was still in the custody of local Texas authorities? Why wasn't Oswald in federal custody? Where were the U.S. Marshals? Where was the FBI?

Yes, it's true that Oswald also shot and wounded the Governor of Texas. And yes, it's also true that Oswald murdered Dallas Police Officer Tippit. But that's not why he was being held by the Texas Rangers, instead of the Feds. The real answer, perhaps surprisingly, is that back in 1963, the federal government had no legal authority to arrest or to try Lee Harvey Oswald for killing President Kennedy. The only crime that Oswald could be charged with committing was the state-law crime of murder, just as if he'd killed any other person on that November day in Dallas. Now, to be sure, the federal government did possess the power to make it a federal crime to assassinate the President. And Congress eventually did just that. In August 1965, almost two years after President Kennedy's assassination, Congress finally enacted a federal statute prohibiting the murder, kidnapping, and assault of the President or Vice-President. It took the assassination of another Kennedy, Senator Robert F. Kennedy, in June 1968, on the night of the California presidential primary, to prompt Congress to extend the reach of federal criminal law to include the murder of a member of Congress.

The strange and curious fact that, at the time, there was no federal crime that could be charged against the killers of John F. Kennedy and Bobby Kennedy is revealing, in terms of the important distinctions in scope, meaning, and effect between state criminal law and federal criminal law. And that's the subject of this lecture. We'll discuss the limits placed by the United States Constitution on the federal government's power to enact criminal laws, and we'll also talk about some of the ways that federal crimes differ from state crimes.

The United States federal government may be the most powerful government in the world—perhaps even in the history of the world—but the federal government's power to prohibit and punish crimes is relatively constrained. For example, even if Congress were to decide that murder has become a major national crisis requiring a concerted national response, it would be patently unconstitutional for Congress to pass a federal statute criminalizing all murders. Same thing with a federal law prohibiting all robberies, or all rapes. Congress simply can't enact such laws. They would be flat-out, 100% unconstitutional.

The reason goes all the way back to America's founding. Shortly after the Revolutionary War ended, delegates from the 13 former colonies, which had now become 13 tiny, little nation-states, met in Philadelphia to draft a new Constitution that would create a new union, or federation, of the states. The vast majority of these delegates held two conflicting goals firmly in mind. On the one hand, they knew they had to forge a stronger union—certainly stronger than the old, weak Articles of Confederation—or it was nearly certain that England, or maybe France or Spain, would soon show up and turn the states back into colonies once again. On the other hand, the delegates also knew that the last thing they wanted to do was create a union that might become too strong. After all, they'd just fought a long and bloody war to gain their freedom from an overbearing central government—the government of England. And the delegates also shared a deep distrust of government in general. Indeed, that's why most of the colonists emigrated to America in the first place.

Keep in mind that, at the time of the Constitutional Convention, all of the sovereign powers of government—those inherent powers that derive from the social contract between the government and the governed—resided with those 13 independent nation-states. Each state had its own constitution, its own laws and courts, its own legislature, and its own chief executive. Each state was a tiny little nation unto itself. And most of the delegates were more or less okay with that, because if any government was necessary at all, much better to have it be a small government close by, than a big one far away. But how, then, could they create the kind of stronger union necessary for self-defense against the big European powers, yet not allow that stronger union to infringe upon the sovereignty of the states and the liberty of the people? How, in other words, could they manage to create a new federation that would be both strong and weak at the same time?

James Madison, a delegate from Virginia, deserves much of the credit for solving this dilemma. Madison advocated a solution that was simple but brilliant; indeed, it was perhaps the most brilliant innovation in the history of political philosophy. The states would all agree, in the new Constitution, to give up only a few of their sovereign powers to the new federation. Within those few areas of sovereignty specifically granted to the federal government, by the text of the Constitution, the federal government would reign supreme. But all other sovereign powers of government would remain with the states, and in those areas, the federal government would have no authority at all, and the states would retain complete sovereignty. This new system of government, designed by James Madison and his colleagues at the Constitutional Convention, is called "dual sovereignty," and it is America's unique political gift to the world. It's a system that's helped keep America both strong and free for more than 200 years. As Madison and the other Framers of the Constitution recognized, individual liberty can be better protected by having two governments than one, because those two governments will constantly compete with each other for power, which will help keep both of them in check.

In the Constitution, the framers listed a number of specific enumerated powers that would be transferred by the states to the new federal government. Among these were the power to raise and maintain a military, to engage in foreign affairs and diplomacy, to control borders and customs, to create a national currency, to construct a national transportation system of post roads and waterways, to encourage invention and the creative arts through patents and copyrights, and to regulate interstate and foreign commerce. These enumerated federal powers, and a few others, are listed in Article I Section 8 of the Constitution. But one very important power was not given to the federal government. That's the general power to act on behalf of whatever is in the best interests of the people. This fundamental power of sovereign government, which we call the "health, safety, and welfare" power, or, a bit strangely, the "police power," remains, to this day, with the states. And it is this general "health, safety, and welfare" power that includes the power to enact generally applicable criminal laws. In the Federalist Papers, a series of highly influential essays written to explain various aspects of the newly drafted Constitution, James Madison specifically identified the power to enact general criminal laws as a power that should belong to the states, not the federal government.

Now, that doesn't mean Congress can't create any federal crimes. Instead, it means Congress can create a federal crime only if it's within the scope of federal power under the Constitution. Federal crimes fall into one of three broad categories. The first involves criminal statutes directly related to one of the enumerated powers in Article I Section 8. So, for example, Congress can make counterfeiting a federal crime, based on the power to create a national currency. And Congress can make it a federal crime to blow up a post office, or to enter the country illegally. According to the Constitution, these are federal matters, so they can also be the basis for creating federal crimes. Second, Congress can also enact federal criminal laws to govern federal places, such as the District of Columbia, federal military bases, and other federal lands. Same thing for areas that lie outside the legal jurisdiction of any state, such as the offshore territorial waters of the U.S. or the air and space above. And lastly, Congress can enact federal criminal statutes to protect the federal government itself, its institutions, and its officers and employees. This is something like the law of self-defense for individuals, and it's an implied power that belongs inherently to all governments. That's the basis upon which Congress eventually made it a federal crime to assassinate the President.

The main point here is that any time Congress wants to enact a statute defining a new federal crime, there must be a specific legal basis, either expressly stated in the Constitution or implied in terms of federal places or federal self-defense, for Congress to do so. Otherwise, the federal statute is unconstitutional. End of story. This requirement, that all federal crimes must be based upon a proper assertion of federal enumerated power specifically authorized by the Constitution, represents one of the most important differences between federal criminal law and state criminal law. And it's the main reason why more than

90% of all crimes in the United States are defined as crimes by state law, and must be prosecuted by state authorities in the state courts. To be sure, the role of the federal government in defining, prosecuting, and punishing crimes has grown significantly over the years. In the earliest decades of American history, there were very few federal crimes. But over time, the scope of federal constitutional power has increased, and with it, the scope of federal criminal law.

Much of the expansion of federal criminal law has been based on the federal government's authority, under Article I Section 8, to regulate interstate and foreign commerce. At the time when the framers drafted the Constitution, there just wasn't that much interstate or foreign commerce. Most commerce was entirely local—farmers grew food and sold it to their neighbors, or to folks in nearby towns, and craftsmen made goods to sell to other local people. All that gradually changed during the course of the 19th and 20th centuries. Commerce that was originally local became regional, then national, and eventually global. Which meant that the scope of federal power under the Commerce Clause also changed. That change didn't become apparent right away. But during the Great Depression of the 1930s, Americans turned to a new President, Franklin Delano Roosevelt, who promised to bring about a New Deal and solve the greatest economic crisis in our history. With the help of a willing Congress, Roosevelt immediately began to implement a series of bold new federal laws designed to regulate many aspects of the national economy, in the hopes of increasing employment and reducing poverty.

At first, the U.S. Supreme Court consistently struck down these new laws as unconstitutional. The Court ruled that, under the Commerce Clause, the federal government could not regulate the economy in general but only economic activity that actually crossed state lines. Most of FDR's early New Deal legislation was therefore invalidated by the Court. Roosevelt, as you may recall, was so frustrated by these decisions that he had legislation introduced in Congress to authorize packing the Court with additional Justices, who presumably would favor his ideas. Although the "Court-packing" plan would have been legal— because there's actually nothing in the Constitution that says how many Justices there must be—the plan failed miserably in the court of public opinion, and FDR never got the chance to implement it. Nevertheless, whether by coincidence or not, the Court began to change its views about the Commerce Clause in 1937, the very same year that FDR proposed to pack the Court.

The expansion of the Commerce Clause reached its apogee in 1942, in the case of *Wickard v. Filburn*, where the Court held that Congress can regulate even purely intra-state or local commercial activity, so long as that activity has some effect on interstate commerce. The case involved a farmer, Roscoe Filburn, who grew wheat solely for himself and his neighbors, and who sued to challenge a federal law regulating how much wheat he was allowed to grow. The Court held that, even though Filburn's wheat never crossed state lines, he was nevertheless subject to federal regulation because his local wheat had an effect on interstate commerce. Because Filburn grew his own wheat, and fed that wheat to his animals, he didn't buy as much wheat from others, thus affecting the national market for wheat. The federal law was upheld.

Wickard v. Filburn, and other similar decisions made by the Court during the latter half of FDR's presidency, gave Congress much greater power to enact federal laws, including federal criminal laws, using the constitutional authority of the Commerce Clause. Almost anything could be regulated by Congress, as long as the subject matter of the regulation had some effect on interstate commerce. And given the increasingly interconnected nature of the American economy, that meant almost everything.

Or at least it seemed that way, until 1995. In that year, the Supreme Court took up the case of *United States v. Lopez*. The *Lopez* case involved the federal Gun Free School Zones Act. This statute made it a federal crime to carry a firearm within a school zone. This was already a crime under state law in more than 40 states, but not in Texas. Alfonso Lopez was a 12th grade student who carried a concealed but unloaded .38 caliber revolver into a high school in San Antonio, Texas, and was arrested, charged, and convicted for violating the federal law. But the Supreme Court reversed his conviction. The Court held that the Gun Free School Zones Act exceeded Congress's power under the Commerce Clause—the first time such a holding had been made by the Court in almost 60 years. The Court rejected the government's argument that guns in school zones affect interstate commerce by making students distracted and unable to learn, thus becoming less productive members of society. According to the Court, the Commerce Clause requires a substantial effect on interstate commerce, not one so speculative and remote. Moreover, the Court noted that the statute in question actually regulates simple possession, rather than economic activity such as selling, buying, or manufacturing of guns. Finally, at least some of the Justices were influenced by the fact that the case involved a federal criminal law, and under the Constitution, criminal law is supposed to be left primarily up to the states.

Since *Lopez*, the federal courts have become more careful in reviewing federal criminal cases involving statutes based on the Commerce Clause. One good example of such a statute is the Hobbs Act. The Hobbs Act, originally enacted in the 1930s, makes it a federal crime if any person "in any way or degree obstructs, delays, or affects" interstate commerce, or the movement of any item in commerce, "by robbery or extortion." The language of the Hobbs Act, quite differently from the language of the Gun Free School Zones Act, requires federal prosecutors to prove in every individual case, that the defendant's act of robbery or extortion had an effect on interstate commerce. But sometimes, this effect on commerce can turn out to be minor enough to raise a serious constitutional question, especially in light of the *Lopez* decision.

Consider the 2012 case of *United States v. Shavers*. Defendant Glorious Shavers and two codefendants were convicted under the Hobbs Act for robbing the patrons of an unlicensed speakeasy in North Philadelphia. The robbers got away with two cell phones, a wallet, and $121 in cash. Shavers argued on appeal that the crime did not have a sufficient effect on interstate commerce to qualify as a valid federal crime. The federal court of appeals admitted that the case "stands at the outer limit of Hobbs Act jurisdiction," but affirmed the conviction anyway, because the speakeasy was an established, profit-making business, the alcohol sold there came from outside the state of Pennsylvania, and the crime led the speakeasy's owner to close down the business three months later. This, the court said, was barely enough to meet the minimum requirements of the Commerce Clause.

Lopez stands for the general proposition that Congress's power under the Commerce Clause, while great, is not unlimited. As the Court said in *Lopez*, there must be some limit, or else the very principle of federalism is dead. At the same time, it's clear that even after *Lopez*, Congress can regulate pretty much anything that qualifies as economic activity. And this includes the power to completely prohibit all commerce in a particular product, such as dangerous drugs or certain kinds of weapons. Moreover, whenever Congress decides to prohibit all commerce in a particular product and enacts a comprehensive set of federal laws designed to implement the ban, those laws can include criminal prohibitions on simple possession even though simple possession is not itself an economic activity. That's how Congress manages to prohibit the simple possession of heroin and hand grenades.

Another important difference between federal criminal law and state criminal law is that many federal crimes tend to involve relatively complicated subject matters, such as financial dealings, securities transactions, federal income taxation, food and drug safety, and the like. Sometimes these complex federal laws are aimed primarily at profit-making businesses and the people who run them. In such situations, the federal courts typically have little sympathy for the claim by a defendant that he or she didn't know about the requirements of the law. After all, as every school child knows, "ignorance of the law is no defense." And if you're running a business in a heavily regulated industry like the pharmaceutical industry, you have an obligation to find out what the legal requirements are. Which is why the federal courts sometimes go so far as to interpret these kinds of laws to be based on "strict liability," meaning the defendant is automatically guilty any time the prohibited result occurs. And the prosecutor doesn't even have to prove that the defendant was negligent for failing to comply with the law.

But sometimes complicated federal crime statutes impact average citizens who may not be as aware of what the law requires them to do. For example, the federal Internal Revenue Code is hundreds of pages in length, and unless you're a really sophisticated tax lawyer, it's easy to get it wrong, even if you're trying your best to get it right. The Supreme Court has adopted two special rules to protect average citizens from unfair criminal liability due to overly complicated federal statutes. These rules are special because they are much more lenient to federal criminal defendants than would usually be the case under most state laws.

The first special federal rule is that "a defendant must know the facts that make his conduct illegal." This rule was implicated in a 1994 case called *Staples v. United States*. There, a man was convicted under federal law for illegally possessing a machine gun. He complained that he didn't know the gun had been modified in a manner that turned it into a machine gun, and the Court reversed his conviction. The fact that he might have been negligent for not noticing the modification didn't matter. If he didn't actually know the gun had been modified, then he couldn't be guilty of the crime.

The second, even more special federal rule arose in a 1991 case called *Cheek v. United States*. John Cheek was an airline pilot who went to some tax protestor seminars. At the seminars, bad lawyers told gullible people that they don't actually have to pay federal income taxes on their wages, because wages are paid in equal exchange for labor and therefore don't qualify as income. Cheek fell for this ridiculous line, and stopped paying his federal income taxes. He was convicted of willful failure to pay his taxes, and he appealed to the Supreme Court. Surprisingly, the Court ruled in his favor. According to the Court, failure to pay federal income taxes can't be described as willful if a defendant honestly believes that he's not legally required to pay taxes. And it doesn't matter how absurd or stupid that belief is, only that the defendant holds the belief sincerely. Even the fact that Cheek had previously attended trials where he watched some of his tax protestor friends go to jail didn't change the Court's view.

The Court reached a similar result in its 1994 decision in *Ratzlaf v. United States*. Waldemar Ratzlaf went to Vegas and won a lot of money at a casino. Under federal law, he was required to file a report about any bank deposit of more than $10,000. The casino suggested that Ratzlaf take his winnings in smaller portions and deposit them separately, so as to avoid the federal reporting requirement. And that's what Ratzlaf did. What Ratzlaf didn't know is that it's a federal crime to willfully evade the reporting requirement. Ratzlaf was convicted, but the Supreme Court reversed his conviction. The Court, citing the earlier *Cheek* case, held that Ratzlaf couldn't be found guilty unless he actually knew about both the reporting requirement and the federal law that prohibited evasion of the reporting requirement. Congress later amended the statute to eliminate the word "willfully," but it was too late to catch Ratzlaf.

The *Cheek* and *Ratzlaf* decisions, which allow at least some federal defendants to prevail based on a pure "mistake of law," represent a truly remarkable deviation from the general rule about "ignorance of the law" that prevails in most state criminal cases. The special federal rule seems to reflect the Supreme Court's perception that at least some federal statutes, like the Internal Revenue Code, have grown so complicated that it's become too easy for average citizens to get screwed up and make honest mistakes. Which might make them stupid, but should not make them a criminal.

Perhaps the strangest aspect of the often confusing relationship between federal criminal law and state criminal law is the way that, over the years, federal and state statutes have inconsistently regulated the production, sale, and possession of marijuana. Starting in the late 1990s, a few states began to legalize medical marijuana, or marijuana prescribed by a physician to treat certain medical conditions. That number quickly grew to include a majority of the states. And in 2012, Colorado became the first state to legalize recreational marijuana. A lucrative legal marijuana industry quickly sprang up in Colorado, and large amounts of tax revenue began to accrue to the state each year, prompting more and more states to jump on the legalization bandwagon. Despite these changes in state law, however, the production, sale, and possession of marijuana remained strictly prohibited under federal law. This odd discrepancy between state and federal law gave rise to all sorts of practical problems. For example, it was really hard to get a bank account, or a loan, for a marijuana business that was legal under Colorado law, because the activity in question remained a serious federal crime. It was also pretty hard to convince lawyers to give legal advice about matters relating to the marijuana industry in Colorado, because such advice could be construed as telling someone how to commit a federal crime, which could get the lawyer disbarred and perhaps even prosecuted.

Congress clearly has the constitutional power to regulate marijuana, including completely prohibiting its possession, because marijuana is clearly a matter of interstate commerce. And as long as state law was roughly consistent with federal law on the subject, this overlapping jurisdiction created no federalism concerns. But once the law in Colorado and other states began to diverge from the federal law, it created what lawyers call a "conflict of laws."

How do we deal with such a conflict? The Constitution provides that, within the proper scope of the federal enumerated powers, federal law reigns supreme. Which meant that Colorado was deliberately skating on thin ice, hoping the federal government would keep its powder dry and choose not to enforce the federal law, at least not within the boundaries of Colorado.

The disparate federal and state regulation of marijuana opened up a new frontier in the never-ending battle of federalism, and I can't predict how that conflict ultimately will be resolved. We've seen similar conflicts before over slavery, desegregation, immigration, and other controversial issues. In the end, as long as it's a matter within the federal government's enumerated power as determined by the U.S. Supreme Court, federal law will prevail. States have the ability to innovate, in criminal law and elsewhere, but those innovations are always subject to appropriate federal limits. That's the dynamic tension inherent in our federalism, and it's a huge part of what makes America great.

Lecture 6

CRUEL AND UNUSUAL PUNISHMENTS

The Eighth Amendment, which regulates the punishments that society can inflict upon those who are convicted of crimes, is a constitutional enigma. In this lecture, we'll explore the history and meaning of the Eighth Amendment—specifically, its ban on cruel and unusual punishments—to discover why it's been so problematic for courts to apply to real-world criminal cases.

LIFE WITHOUT PAROLE

★ Ronald Allen Harmelin was convicted in a Michigan court of simple possession of 672 grams of cocaine. For this crime, he was sentenced to a mandatory term of life imprisonment without possibility of parole—even though he had not been found to be a drug dealer, and even though he had no prior felony convictions. The trial judge had no choice, because the Michigan statute required imposition of the life-without-parole sentence.

★ Harmelin appealed to the U.S. Supreme Court, arguing that his life-without-parole sentence violated the Eighth Amendment's ban on cruel and unusual punishments because the sentence was wildly disproportionate to the seriousness of his crime. In *Harmelin v. Michigan*, decided in 1991, the Supreme Court rejected Harmelin's claim and upheld the sentence.

★ There was no single majority opinion in Harmelin. Instead, two separate opinions—one by Justice Antonin Scalia and the other by Justice Anthony Kennedy—had to be added together to produce the result. Justice Scalia's opinion rejected Harmelin's argument on the ground that the Eighth Amendment doesn't require any kind of proportionality between crime and punishment.

★ According to Scalia, the Eighth Amendment prohibits only "cruel methods of punishment that are not regularly or customarily employed." In other words, it precludes the legislature from enacting specific kinds of punishment, such as the medieval rack, that would be cruel and unusual as applied to any crime.

★ Justice Kennedy's concurring opinion articulated a somewhat broader view of the purpose and effect of the Eighth Amendment. According to Kennedy, the ban on cruel and unusual punishments prohibits both particular kinds of punishment that are always cruel and unusual, as well as punishments disproportionate to the particular crime.

★ Kennedy pointed out that the Supreme Court had recognized a proportionality principle within the Eighth Amendment for more than 80 years, and he was unwilling to overturn that precedent. At the same time, Kennedy tried to clarify the scope of this proportionality principle—and in so doing, essentially guaranteed that it would never be used to invalidate a prison sentence.

★ Under either Justice Scalia's narrow view of the Eighth Amendment or Justice Kennedy's slightly broader view, it would be nearly impossible to find any prison sentence—even one as severe as mandatory life imprisonment without possibility of parole—unconstitutional under the Eighth Amendment. And that's exactly how things have worked out in the years since *Harmelin* was decided.

THE DEATH PENALTY

* Christopher Simmons, a 17-year-old resident of Missouri, came up with a plan to murder a woman named Shirley Crook. He convinced two younger friends to help him. Simmons and one of the friends broke into Mrs. Crook's home, bound her hands, covered her eyes, then drove her to a nearby state park and threw her off a bridge. Simmons later confessed. He was convicted of first-degree murder and sentenced to death.

* Simmons appealed his sentence to the U.S. Supreme Court, claiming that it would violate the Eighth Amendment to execute a defendant whose crime was committed before the defendant turned 18. At the time, of the 38 states with valid death penalty statutes on their books, 18 prohibited imposing the death penalty on anyone under the age of 18. Missouri was not one of them.

* In *Roper v. Simmons*, a 5–4 majority of the Supreme Court found application of the death penalty to a juvenile under age 18 to be cruel and unusual punishment, and therefore unconstitutional under the Eighth Amendment. In a majority opinion written by Justice Kennedy, the Court held that Missouri was constitutionally barred from imposing the death penalty against a juvenile because most other states wouldn't allow such a punishment.

* Kennedy's opinion noted that 12 states had no death penalty at all, which—combined with the 18 states that limited the death penalty to defendants over the age of 18—added up to a majority of 30 states rejecting the juvenile death penalty. a few of those states had done so in the preceding few years, making it look like some kind of a trend was developing in the states.

* Justice Scalia, in dissent, rejected the majority's conclusion that this evidence represented an emerging "national consensus" against the juvenile death penalty, given that 20 states, including Missouri, still authorized such a punishment. Scalia also pointed out the strangeness of counting states that didn't have a death penalty at all, describing

this as comparable to "including old-order Amishmen in a consumer-preference poll on the electric car. Of course they don't like it," Scalia wrote, "but that sheds no light whatever on the point at issue."

★ Kennedy's majority opinion also included an extensive discussion of the psychology of juveniles, in an effort to show that juveniles are both less likely to be fully responsible for their actions, and more likely to change and possibly rehabilitate in the future. Kennedy added that abolishing the juvenile death penalty would bring America into alignment with other civilized nations around the world.

★ The contrast in approach between *Harmelin v. Michigan* and *Roper v. Simmons* could not be more striking. *Harmelin* is based on almost complete deference to the state legislature's judgment about criminal punishment. *Roper*, by contrast, reveals an interventionist Court looking to overturn the state legislature's decision. The best explanation for this disparity is that the Court has long viewed the death penalty as a special case under the Eighth Amendment.

THE COUNTER-MAJORITARIAN DILEMMA

★ The counter-majoritarian dilemma refers to the fact that the Supreme Court and the Constitution often operate by imposing limits on what the majority in society can do. Legislatures generally follow the will of the people, and so, too, does the executive. But every once in a while, the Supreme Court steps in to protect the rights of the minority.

★ The majority doesn't need the same kind of protection, because the majority can get what it wants through the political process. The minority can't. That's why the Constitution sets forth fundamental values and norms that are meant to transcend the ever-changing sentiments of the day and limit the potential harm to the minority.

★ The dilemma is that the Supreme Court is acutely aware that its own power is severely limited. The Court has no way to enforce its own decisions; it doesn't have a military, and its police force consists of a few officers tasked with protecting the Supreme Court building. So whenever the Court makes a decision, it has to turn to the political branches of government, state and federal, to enforce that decision.

★ Whenever the Supreme Court is about to make a decision that's going to be unpopular with a majority of the American people, or even the people within a particular state, the Court always has to think— and swallow—hard. Yes, the Court sometimes has to stand up to the majority. But the Court can't do it too often, or go too far, without risking a loss of respect and public legitimacy. That's the counter-majoritarian dilemma.

★ The counter-majoritarian dilemma doesn't mean that the Court does whatever it thinks the majority wants. Rather, it's that the Court always keeps a close eye on what the majority wants, so that the Court can protect its own legitimacy in the eyes of the public. This is a subtle but absolutely crucial aspect of how the Court functions.

✷ The Eighth Amendment, with its plain and simple text, highlights the counter-majoritarian dilemma. When the Court decides to invalidate a democratically approved punishment under the Eighth Amendment, the Court must declare—publicly—that the legislature that authorized the punishment, the jury of citizens that voted to convict the defendant, and the judge who imposed the sentence all behaved in a manner that's "cruel."

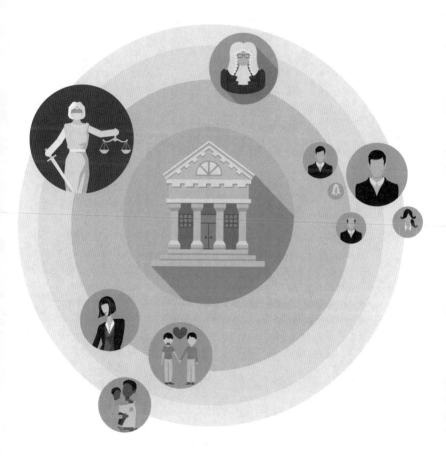

⭐ This is why the Court has traditionally viewed the Eighth Amendment in terms of the "evolving standards of decency" of a "maturing society," and has looked for the clearest possible evidence of a national consensus before striking down a punishment as cruel and unusual. It's also why very few punishments—outside the unique context of the death penalty—have ever been struck down by the Court.

Suggested Reading

- Harmelin v. Michigan.

- Roper v. Simmons.

- Furman v. Georgia.

- Gregg v. Georgia.

- Trop v. Dulles.

Questions to Consider

↗ Does the U.S. Supreme Court—as an unelected branch of the federal government—play too large a role in resolving major social issues and controversies in America?

↗ How do you feel about the death penalty, and why?

CRUEL AND UNUSUAL PUNISHMENTS

T he Eighth Amendment, which regulates the punishments that society can inflict upon those who are convicted of crimes, is a constitutional enigma. The text of the Amendment is quite simple and straightforward: "Excessive bail shall not be required, nor excessive fines imposed, nor cruel and unusual punishments inflicted." But in practice, this seemingly plain language has frequently presented the Supreme Court with a serious quandary. In this lecture, we'll explore the history and meaning of the Eighth Amendment—more specifically, the "cruel and unusual punishments" clause—to see why the Court has had so much trouble figuring out how to apply this provision to real-world criminal cases.

Let's start with two examples: Ronald Allen Harmelin was convicted in a Michigan court of simple possession of 672 grams of cocaine. For this crime, Harmelin was sentenced to a mandatory term of life imprisonment without possibility of parole, even though he had not been found to be a drug dealer and even though he had no prior felony convictions. The trial judge had no choice, because the Michigan statute required imposition of the life-without-parole sentence. Harmelin appealed to the U.S. Supreme Court, arguing that his life-without-parole sentence violated the Eighth Amendment's ban on cruel and unusual punishments because the sentence was wildly disproportionate to the seriousness of his crime. In the case of *Harmelin v. Michigan*, decided in 1991, the Supreme Court, by a vote of five to four, rejected Harmelin's claim and upheld the sentence.

There was no single majority opinion in *Harmelin*. Instead, two separate opinions, one by Justice Antonin Scalia and the other by Justice Anthony Kennedy, had to be added together to produce the result. Justice Scalia's opinion rejected Harmelin's argument on the ground that the Eighth Amendment's "cruel and unusual punishments" clause doesn't require any kind of proportionality between crime and punishment. Indeed, at the time the Eighth Amendment was adopted as part of the Bill of Rights, many state constitutions contained both a "cruel and unusual punishments" clause and a separate clause barring disproportionate punishments, indicating that the former didn't necessarily include the latter. According to Scalia, the "cruel and unusual punishments" clause prohibits only "cruel methods of punishment that are not regularly or customarily employed." In other words, the Eighth Amendment precludes the legislature from enacting specific kinds of punishment, such as the medieval rack or some other form of brutal torture, that would be "cruel and unusual" as applied to any crime.

Justice Kennedy's concurring opinion articulated a somewhat broader view of the purpose and effect of the "cruel and unusual punishments" clause. According to Kennedy, the clause does prohibit both particular kinds of punishment that are always "cruel and unusual," and also punishments that are disproportionate to the particular crime. Kennedy pointed out that the Court had recognized a proportionality principle within the Eighth Amendment for more than 80 years, and he was unwilling to overturn that precedent. At the same time, Kennedy tried to clarify the scope of this proportionality principle, and in doing so, he pretty much ensured that it would never be used to invalidate any prison sentence.

First, Kennedy made it clear that legislatures are in charge of defining crimes and sentences, and that courts should grant broad deference to the legislature's judgment. Second, he noted that there are many legitimate purposes of criminal punishment, which makes it even more important for courts to defer to legislatures on the subject. Third, our federal system of government is partly based on the idea that experimentation by the states is a good thing, which means that some states will always have harsher punishments than others, even for the same crimes. Fourth, courts must use objective factors whenever they review punishments for possible disproportionality, and the most important objective factor is the type of punishment. It's a lot easier for courts to compare two different types or kinds of punishment, such as imprisonment and the rack, than it is to compare two different prison sentences that differ only by degree. Last, but not least, Kennedy identified a fifth principle that emerged directly from the other four. He wrote, "The Eighth Amendment does not require strict proportionality between crime and sentence. Rather, it forbids only extreme sentences that are 'grossly disproportionate' to the crime."

Applying these five principles to the *Harmelin* case, Justice Kennedy had little trouble concluding that Michigan's mandatory-life-without-parole sentence complied with the Eighth Amendment. Yes, the punishment was extremely severe, but so was the crime of possessing a large amount of cocaine, which Kennedy described as posing "grave harm to society." Given the seriousness of the crime, Kennedy wasn't even willing to look at the sentences for other crimes in Michigan, or at the sentences for the same crime in other states. According to Kennedy's approach, such comparisons are necessary only "to validate an initial judgment that a sentence is grossly disproportionate to a crime." Here, Kennedy couldn't perceive a "gross disproportionality," so there was no need to do any further comparisons.

By the way, the Michigan Supreme Court, just one year after the *Harmelin* decision, struck down the state's mandatory-life-without-parole sentencing statute under the state constitution, which included the phrase "cruel or unusual punishment" instead of "cruel and unusual punishment." That shows you what a difference a single word can make.

In any event, the bottom line of *Harmelin* was clear. When you add up the votes for Justice Scalia's narrow view of the Eighth Amendment, and those for Justice Kennedy's ever-so-slightly-broader view, you get to the end result that it's almost impossible to find any prison sentence—even one as severe as mandatory life imprisonment without possibility of parole—unconstitutional under the Eighth Amendment. And that's exactly how things have worked out in the years since *Harmelin*.

For example, in the 2003 case of *Ewing v. California*, the Court affirmed a mandatory prison sentence of 25 years to life, under California's "Three Strikes" law, for a repeat offender who walked out of a golf course pro shop with three golf clubs concealed in his pants leg. The Court, using Justice Kennedy's approach, found Ewing's sentence to be "justified by the state's public-safety interest in incapacitating and deterring recidivist felons." No gross disproportionality, hence no problem under the Eighth Amendment. At least with respect to prison sentences, it's almost as if the "cruel and unusual punishments" clause doesn't exist.

Now consider another famous case. In *Roper v. Simmons*, the Supreme Court had to decide whether the Eighth Amendment allowed the State of Missouri to impose the death penalty for a crime committed by a person under the age of 18. Christopher Simmons, age 17, came up with a plan to murder a woman named Shirley Crook, and he convinced two younger friends to help him. Simmons and one of the friends broke into Mrs. Crook's home, bound her hands and covered her eyes, then drove her to a nearby state park and threw her off a bridge. Simmons later confessed, and he was charged with premeditated murder. Simmons was convicted and sentenced to death. Simmons appealed his sentence to the U.S. Supreme Court, claiming that it's a violation of the Eighth Amendment to execute a defendant whose crime was committed before age 18. At the time, of the 38 states with valid death penalty statutes on their books, 18 of them prohibited giving the death penalty to anyone under 18. The other 20 death-penalty states, like Missouri, authorized the punishment, even for juveniles under age 18.

Based on what happened in *Harmelin*, and the method of analysis used there by both Justice Scalia and Justice Kennedy, what do you think happened in *Roper v. Simmons*? Surprise, the Supreme Court, by five to four, found Missouri's application of the death penalty to a juvenile under age 18 to be unconstitutionally "cruel and unusual" punishment. Now, remember that in *Harmelin*, Michigan's punishment of mandatory life-without-parole for simple possession of 672 grams of cocaine was, by far, the most severe punishment in the country for that particular crime. No other state came close. Indeed, in many states, the typical punishment for premeditated murder wasn't as severe as mandatory life-without-parole. And yet the U.S. Supreme Court affirmed the Michigan statute. After all, some state will always have the most severe punishment for any particular crime. It's inevitable.

But in *Roper v. Simmons*—in a majority opinion written by Justice Kennedy, the very same Justice who devised the Harmelin proportionality test—the Court held that Missouri was constitutionally barred from imposing the death penalty against a juvenile, because most of the other states wouldn't allow such a punishment. Kennedy's opinion noted that 12 states had no death penalty at all, which, combined with the 18 states that limited the death penalty to defendants over the age of 18, added up to a majority of 30 states rejecting the juvenile death penalty. Moreover, at least a few of those states had done so just in the preceding few years, making it look like some kind of a trend was developing in the states. Justice Scalia, in dissent, rejected the majority's conclusion that this evidence represented an emerging national consensus against the juvenile death penalty, given that 20 states, including Missouri, still authorized such a punishment. Scalia also pointed out the strangeness of counting states that didn't have a death penalty at all, describing this as comparable to "including old-order Amishmen in a consumer-preference poll on the electric car. Of course they don't like it," Scalia wrote, "but that sheds no light whatever on the point at issue."

Justice Kennedy's majority opinion in *Roper v. Simmons* also included an extensive discussion of the psychology of juveniles, in an effort to show that juveniles are both less likely to be fully responsible for their actions, and more likely to change and possibly rehabilitate in the future. And Kennedy added, in a section of the opinion that really ticked off Justice Scalia, that abolishing the juvenile death penalty would bring America into alignment with other civilized nations around the world. Kennedy wrote, "It is proper that we acknowledge the overwhelming weight of international opinion against the juvenile death penalty." To which Scalia retorted, "I do not believe that the meaning of the Eighth Amendment...should be determined by the subjective views of five members of this Court and like-minded foreigners."

The contrast in approach between *Harmelin* on the one hand, and *Roper v. Simmons* on the other, could not be more striking. *Harmelin* is based on almost complete deference to a state legislature's judgment about criminal punishment, even if that state stands completely alone, compared to the punishments in other states. *Roper v. Simmons* reflects an interventionist Court, looking for some kind of justification to overturn the state legislature's decision. What's up with that? The best explanation for the stark difference between *Harmelin* and *Roper v. Simmons* is that the Court has long viewed the death penalty itself as a special case under the Eighth Amendment. The death penalty has long been a hugely controversial issue in America. The controversy exploded in the Supreme Court in 1972, when the Court decided *Furman v. Georgia*, holding that capital punishment, as it was then administered in the United States, violated the Eighth Amendment.

At the time of *Furman*, in almost all death penalty states, the penalty was left up to the largely unfettered discretion of the jury. After the jury reached a verdict of guilt on the capital crime, they were sent back to the jury room to deliberate about the punishment. And the court typically gave the jurors no legal guidance on how to make that fateful decision. The jurors were simply told to consider everything they'd seen and heard during the trial and sentencing hearing, and then to decide if the defendant should live or die. That's the system the Court reviewed in *Furman*.

Furman was a fascinating decision on many levels. For one thing, each of the nine Justices wrote a separate, individual opinion, making it one of the longest cases in terms of total page length in the history of the Supreme Court. For another, each of the Justices in *Furman* took a different approach to deciding whether or not the death penalty was constitutional. The overall vote was five to four. Three of the Justices in the majority felt that the main problem wasn't the death penalty itself, but how the decision to impose the death penalty was being made. One said the jury decisions were "arbitrary and freakish," like being struck by lightning. Another said that giving juries such broad discretion allowed them to discriminate on the basis of race and class. And a third said the death penalty wasn't being imposed often enough, which deprived the penalty of any deterrent effect and made it pointless. Only two Justices, Brennan and Marshall, felt that the death penalty itself was always, no matter how it was administered, "cruel and unusual" punishment. But they faced a major challenge to explain why, given that a narrow majority of Americans at the time still supported capital punishment. The Eighth Amendment had long been interpreted by the Court to be based on the "evolving standards of decency of a maturing society." So if most Americans still believed in capital punishment, how could it be cruel?

Justice Brennan based his *Furman* opinion on the trend lines. Public support for capital punishment had been declining for years, and was getting close to 50–50. Brennan argued that the Court didn't have to wait for the moment when most Americans would finally oppose capital punishment; rather, the Court could anticipate that moment, and invalidate the punishment based on the fact that it would soon be rejected by a majority of American society. Unfortunately for Brennan, he turned out to be wrong in his prediction about the future. The public opinion polls began turning around right about the same time as the *Furman* decision, and they've remained more supportive of capital punishment ever since.

Justice Marshall took a different tack. Marshall wrote that the only reason most Americans still supported capital punishment was because they didn't know how it really worked. If they did, they would reject it. And that was good enough, according to Marshall, for the Court to act.

Furman held the death penalty unconstitutional, but not for long. The states that wanted to keep the death penalty realized they could reinstate the punishment if they enacted new statutes to solve, at least in theory, the administrative problems that led three of the Justices to vote against the death penalty. Five of these new statutes were reviewed by the Supreme Court in 1976, in the combined case of *Gregg v. Georgia*.

By a seven to two majority, the Court in *Gregg* upheld three of the five new death penalty statutes. North Carolina and Louisiana tried to fix the problems with their pre-*Furman* statutes by making the death penalty mandatory for certain crimes. Those statutes were struck down again by the Court in *Gregg*, because they gave no discretion to the sentencer. But the other new statutes from Georgia, Florida, and Texas, were upheld. Their new statutes were based on the concept of "guided discretion," meaning that the jury is given some guidance about how to make the death penalty decision, while still retaining some discretion to make the decision based on the facts of the individual case. According to the *Gregg* majority, this guided discretion approach was sufficient to make the death penalty constitutional again. Justices Brennan and Marshall of course didn't agree, and they continued to oppose the death penalty right up until their departures from the Court in 1990 and 1991, respectively.

The concept of guided discretion remains a constitutional requirement for capital punishment today. The way it generally works is that the jury is given a list of aggravating circumstances, which point toward imposing death, and must also consider all possible mitigating circumstances, which point toward life. The ultimate jury decision is based on balancing the aggravating and mitigating circumstances against each other.

Although the decision in *Gregg* restored the death penalty's constitutionality, it left a host of unanswered procedural questions. So, starting with *Gregg*, the Supreme Court waded deeply into the troubled waters of trying to figure out how best to administer a capital punishment system. And as of this taping, the Court still hasn't managed to find its footing and wade back out. Year after year, the Court reviews numerous death penalty cases under the Eighth Amendment, constantly trying to tweak the system in the hope that it can be made to work in a fair and equitable manner. This constant judicial oversight of capital punishment in the states consumes a significant amount of the Court's time and attention, and often causes major consternation among state government officials charged with the responsibility to carry out the death penalty.

Given the Court's aggressive use of the Eighth Amendment to review the administration of capital punishment, why doesn't the Court take a similar hands-on approach to non-capital criminal punishments? Why such extreme deference to the legislature when it comes to prison sentences, as in the *Harmelin* case? It's true that the Court has relied upon the Eighth Amendment to strike down one particular kind of prison sentence, namely the sentence of life imprisonment without parole for a juvenile offender. But that's probably more indicative of the Court's evolving view of juveniles as seen in *Roper v. Simmons*, than it is about the Court's willingness to review prison sentences more generally. The Court has shown absolutely no indication that it wants to go back and revisit *Harmelin*. Moreover, even such extreme practices as solitary confinement or prolonged incarceration on Death Row, both of which have been proven to cause severe psychological harm to inmates, have not prompted the Court to want to invoke the Eighth Amendment's "cruel and unusual punishments" clause. To date, the Court's been willing to rest on its 1891 decision in *McElvaine v. Brush*, which upheld New York's practice of holding condemned prisoners in solitary confinement while awaiting execution.

So why is the Court still so reluctant to engage in serious review of prison sentences under the "cruel and unusual punishments" clause? The answer to this question requires us to delve more deeply into the history of the Eighth Amendment. For more than 175 years after the ratification of the Eighth Amendment, the "cruel and unusual punishments" clause was used only a few times by the Court to invalidate non-capital criminal punishments. And the leading cases where the Eighth Amendment was invoked illustrate something important about the Amendment.

In 1910, in the case of *Weems v. United States*, the Court reviewed a strange punishment called *cadena temporal*, a historical Spanish punishment that involved forcing a prisoner to wear a heavy chain and engage in hard labor for at least 12 years and a day. *Cadena temporal* didn't exist anywhere in the United States until we annexed the Philippines in 1898, following the Spanish-American War. The Court held in *Weems* that *cadena temporal* was a cruel and unusual punishment that violated the Eighth Amendment.

The other leading Eighth Amendment case is *Trop v. Dulles*, decided in 1958. Albert Trop was a U.S. citizen who deserted his Army post in Morocco for one day during the Second World War. For this he was court-martialed, and his sentence, under the Nationality Act of 1940, included a loss of U.S. citizenship. Trop learned about this only in 1952, when his application for a passport was denied. He appealed, and the Supreme Court eventually held that loss of citizenship is a punishment barred by the Eighth Amendment. Although denationalization had been common in times past, the Court in *Trop v. Dulles* found it to be "a form of punishment more primitive than torture," because it inflicts the "total destruction of the individual's status in organized society." No doubt the Court's new thinking about the horror of becoming stateless was strongly influenced by the shocking events of the war years, and especially the fact that Jews in Germany and elsewhere were stripped of their citizenship during the Holocaust.

What's the common thread between these two rare Eighth Amendment decisions? It's the fact that both of the cases involved punishments—*cadena temporal* and, at least after the tragedy of the Holocaust, loss of citizenship—that no American legislature plausibly would vote to impose. These punishments existed as historical oddities, in one case because we suddenly acquired a new territory, and in the other case because world events suddenly shocked us into recognizing the horror of what we'd done before. And that made it okay for the Court to invoke the Eighth Amendment to strike down these odd punishments as cruel and unusual.

But in the more typical situation, where a punishment authorized by a statute enacted by a democratically-elected legislature, and imposed by a local judge after a trial before a local jury, gets challenged by a defendant on Eighth Amendment grounds, the Court faces a serious problem. And it's a problem that strikes at the very core of what's often called the "counter-majoritarian dilemma." The counter-majoritarian dilemma refers to the fact that the Supreme Court and the Constitution often operate by imposing limits on what the majority in society can do. Legislatures generally follow the will of the people, and so, too, does the executive. But every once in a while, the Supreme Court has to step in and say to the majority, "Sorry, you can't do what you want to do, because it would infringe the rights of a minority." The majority doesn't need that kind of judicial protection, because the majority can get what it wants through the political process. The minority, almost by definition, can't, and that's why the Constitution sets forth fundamental values and norms that are meant to transcend the ever-changing sentiments of the day, and limit the harm that the majority can do to a minority. The dilemma is that the Supreme Court is acutely aware that its own power is severely limited. The Court has no way to enforce its own decisions, it doesn't have a military, and its police force consists of a few officers tasked with protecting the Supreme Court building. So whenever the Court makes a decision, it has to turn to the political branches of government, state and federal, to enforce that decision. The Court basically relies on respect and public legitimacy to ensure that its rulings will be followed. That's a key aspect of what we call the "Rule of Law." And the Rule of Law is something that must be preserved, and protected, at all costs, lest we descend into a situation where the law becomes powerless, and brute force seizes the day. Which means that, whenever the Supreme Court is about to make a decision that's going to be unpopular with a majority of the American people, or the people within a particular state, the Court always has to think, and swallow, hard. Yes, the Court sometimes has to stand up to the majority. But the Court can't do it too often, or go too far, without risking a loss of respect and public legitimacy. That's the counter-majoritarian dilemma.

As a famous cartoon character once said, "No matter whether the Constitution follows the flag or not, the Supreme Court follows the election returns!" It's not that the Court does whatever it thinks the majority wants, that's certainly not true. Rather, it's that the Court always keeps a close eye on what the majority wants, so that the Court can protect its own legitimacy in the eyes of the public. This is a subtle but absolutely crucial aspect of how the Court functions, and the Justices have proven extremely adept at it, over the more than 200 years of the Court's existence.

The Eighth Amendment, with its plain and simple text, highlights the counter-majoritarian dilemma. Many provisions in the Constitution are written in lawyer's language. What does "due process" mean, anyway? What's "probable cause?" When the Court makes a decision based on those kinds of constitutional provisions, the public often doesn't understand the details, it just looks like a decision based on the law, and therefore legitimate. Other provisions in the Constitution speak in vague terms like "reasonable," or "equal." When the Court makes a decision based on that kind of vague language, it frequently devises some kind of balancing approach that weighs factors on both sides. Once again, that makes it relatively easy for the Court to protect its legitimacy, by situating the essential value judgments within the legalistic language of a multi-factor balancing test.

The Eighth Amendment's text allows no such easy way out for the Court. When the Court decides to invalidate a democratically approved punishment under the Eighth Amendment, the Court must declare publicly that the legislature that authorized the punishment, the jury of citizens that voted to convict the defendant, and the judges who imposed and affirmed the sentence, all behaved in a manner that's cruel. Which raises the obvious question: Why should such a decision be left up to nine unelected Supreme Court Justices—or even five—rather than to the collective will and sound judgment of the people? That's why the Court has traditionally viewed the Eighth Amendment in terms of the "evolving standards of decency of a maturing society," and has looked for the clearest possible evidence of a national consensus, before striking down a punishment as cruel and unusual. That's why very few punishments, outside the unique context of the death penalty, have ever been struck down by the Court. That's why the Eighth Amendment is a constitutional enigma.

Justice Joseph Story once wrote that the Eighth Amendment "would seem wholly unnecessary in a free government, since it is scarcely possible, that any department of such a government should authorize, or justify, such atrocious conduct." But the Eighth Amendment's "cruel and unusual punishments" clause is not a complete nullity. As we've seen, it's become the primary legal battleground for our national debate over the death penalty. And the Eighth Amendment remains always vigilant, ready to be invoked whenever we encounter a strange and cruel new punishment, or suddenly realize that we just weren't thinking clearly about a punishment we previously approved. In most contexts, however, the Eighth Amendment is likely to remain dormant, because it's so hard and potentially so dangerous for the Supreme Court to tell a majority of the people that they're being cruel.

DUE PROCESS AND THE RIGHT TO COUNSEL

I n the modern era of criminal procedure, due process and effective legal assistance are considered fundamental rights, guaranteed by the U.S. Constitution to defendants in all criminal proceedings, state and federal. But this wasn't always the case. This lecture examines the development of the law in this area, including the shift in constitutional interpretation that allowed the U.S. Supreme Court to change the way states handle criminal scases.

INDIVIDUAL RIGHTS

* Adopted in 1791, the first 10 amendments to the U.S. Constitution were the result of a political compromise. Some framers wanted to emphasize that the new federal government should not interfere with the most important rights of individual citizens. Others thought this was obvious, and feared that listing particular rights might suggest that others were not protected. Eventually, the two sides agreed to draft a set of 10 amendments—what became known as the Bill of Rights—to be adopted shortly after ratification.

* The Bill of Rights was designed only to protect individual rights against the new federal government. The various state governments were already in existence, and they had constitutions of their own—including their own provisions concerning individual rights.

★ Many of the guarantees written into the Bill of Rights involved the rights of people accused of crimes. This makes sense, because one of the most important powers of government is the power to lock someone up—or even execute them—as punishment for committing a crime.

★ One of the abiding lessons of the Civil War was that states can't always be trusted to protect the rights of their own citizens. The states that had joined the Confederacy continued to persecute freed slaves, even after the war was over. To address this issue, the Constitution was amended. One of the so-called Civil War Amendments was the Fourteenth Amendment, which provides:

> All persons born or naturalized in the United States, and subject to the jurisdiction thereof, are citizens of the United States, and of the State wherein they reside. No State shall make or enforce any law which shall abridge the privileges or immunities of citizens of the United States; nor shall any State deprive any person of life, liberty, or property, without due process of law; nor deny to any person within its jurisdiction the equal protection of the laws.

★ The Fourteenth Amendment emphasizes the concept of national citizenship. Prior to the Civil War, most Americans considered themselves citizens only of their particular state. But the Fourteenth Amendment says otherwise: "All persons born or naturalized in the United States, and subject to the jurisdiction thereof, are citizens of the United States, and of the State wherein they reside."

★ As part of this new concept of national citizenship, the Fourteenth Amendment provides that the states can't take away a person's life, liberty, or property without due process of law. And the federal government will enforce this new constitutional right of due process— as well as the right to equal protection of the laws—against any possible infringement by the states.

★ The Civil War Amendments represented a turning point in American constitutional law. They were the first amendments to the Constitution to directly address, and directly limit, the power of the states to act in ways that might harm their own citizens. This was a huge shift in the balance of American federalism.

DUE PROCESS

★ With the ratification of the Fourteenth Amendment in 1868, the U.S. Supreme Court became responsible for ensuring that state officials wouldn't deprive people of life, liberty, or property, without "due process of law." This was very important for criminal justice, as the vast majority of criminal cases were and are prosecuted by state governments. And in criminal cases, the life, liberty, or property of the defendant is always on the line.

★ The word "process," defined literally, means "procedure." The Due Process Clause of the Fourteenth Amendment thus has something to do with the specific procedures a state must follow if it wants to take away your life, liberty, or property.

* The Supreme Court had to figure out how to give sensible meaning to this vague constitutional language. In the late 19th century, the Court took a conservative approach. Basically, the Court held that the procedures to which the Due Process Clause entitles you are whatever procedures the state has written into its validly enacted statutes and rules. Once a state enacts a law that guarantees you a particular form of process, the state must follow that law.

* By the early 20th century, the Court became concerned that this approach wasn't protective enough. At the time, all a state had to do to deny someone a right was enact a new law stating that people no longer have that particular right.

* In the landmark case *Powell v. Alabama*, the Supreme Court held that the procedures to which the defendants had been subjected violated the Fourteenth Amendment's Due Process Clause. More specifically, the Court held that the defendants were denied a fair trial by virtue of the fact that they were essentially forced to go to trial without the assistance of counsel.

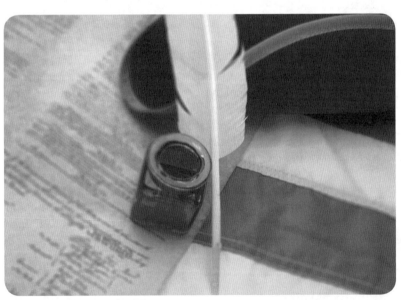

✳ The Court in *Powell* adopted a more rigorous analysis for potential Due Process violations, examining whether the state's established criminal procedures—or the application of those procedures in the case at hand—provided the defendant with a "fundamentally fair" trial. If not, the procedures were held to be a violation of the Due Process Clause.

✳ In practice, analyzing the fundamental fairness of criminal procedures often required judges to rely purely on their own intuition. In one case, decided in 1952, California forcibly pumped the stomach of a criminal suspect to make him disgorge illegal drugs he'd swallowed. The Supreme Court held that this procedure violated the Due Process Clause because it "shock[ed] the conscience."

✳ Much later, in 1993, Justices Blackmun and Scalia got into a spat over the procedures used in a Texas death penalty case. On behalf of several dissenting justices, Blackmun wrote that the state's procedures had indeed shocked the conscience—to which Scalia replied, "perhaps they should doubt the calibration of their consciences, or better still, the usefulness of 'conscience shocking' as a legal test."

✳ Fundamental fairness is a vague standard, and was therefore dependent entirely on the subjective views of nine unelected Supreme Court justices. To address this problem, the Court began trying to tie the concept of fundamental fairness to something a little more concrete. Specifically, they began to consider whether the procedures at issue were fundamental in light of the country's Anglo-American history and tradition.

✳ This new approach enabled the Court to look to respected historical sources—the Magna Carta, for example, or the Declaration of Independence—to decide whether a particular procedure violated the Due Process Clause. Many sources proved to be too vague, however, so the Court turned to the Bill of Rights.

✯ The incorporation of the Bill of Rights into the Fourteenth Amendment's Due Process Clause played a central role in the criminal procedure revolution of the 1960s. The Supreme Court, led by Chief Justice Earl Warren, applied the federal constitutional provisions found in the Bill of Rights against the states, forcing states to provide better treatment for all criminal defendants.

✯ By the end of the 1960s, every criminal procedure guaranteed by the Bill of Rights with respect to federal cases had been incorporated, and was thus applicable to state criminal cases as well—with the singular exception of the Fifth Amendment's right to grand jury review of criminal charges, which was never incorporated.

✯ Procedures that were incorporated include the prohibition of unreasonable searches and seizures, the requirement that warrants be based on probable cause, the freedom not to testify against yourself, and the right to a jury trial. States must now provide these procedures, along with all others incorporated by the Supreme Court, to each and every criminal defendant.

THE RIGHT TO COUNSEL

✯ The Supreme Court's most famous incorporation case was *Gideon v. Wainwright*. On March 18, 1963, the Court ruled unanimously that, by refusing to provide an indigent named Clarence Earl Gideon with a defense lawyer for his felony criminal trial, Florida had denied Gideon his constitutional right to the assistance of counsel as guaranteed by the Sixth Amendment—and as applied to Florida by means of the Fourteenth Amendment's Due Process Clause.

✯ Today, the right to counsel applies not only to felonies, but also to any misdemeanor case where the defendant receives any actual imprisonment. The right to counsel is no panacea, but it's still the most important procedural right that criminal defendants have.

* Unfortunately, the criminal justice system still works unequally. Rich criminal defendants hire the best lawyers money can buy. Poor defendants are assigned public defenders, many of whom are juggling massive caseloads that would crush most lawyers. Public defenders also don't have access to expensive investigators and jury consultants.

* In the 1984 case *Strickland v. Washington*, the Court held that the Sixth Amendment guarantees a criminal defendant not just any lawyer, but a reasonably effective lawyer. The standard used by the Court in *Strickland* to evaluate the defendant's representation is one that still governs claims based on ineffective assistance of counsel.

* In *Strickland*, the Court held that, in order to get a conviction or sentence overturned based on ineffective assistance of counsel, the defendant must show two things: (1) The defense lawyer's performance fell below an objectively reasonable standard, given prevailing professional norms in the area; and (2) The lawyer's subpar performance was prejudicial to the defendant, in the sense that the outcome might reasonably have been different had adequate representation been provided.

* The *Strickland* test is very difficult to satisfy. Most criminal defendants have lots of evidence against them, which means that even the best defense lawyer likely couldn't get them acquitted. As a result, most defendants wouldn't be able to satisfy the prejudice prong of the *Strickland* test.

* In essence, the *Strickland* test allows the courts to overturn convictions or sentences only in the most extreme cases, where the defense lawyer did an especially bad job and the defendant would have had a fighting chance to win with a better lawyer. Otherwise, the defendant has to accept the outcome of the trial.

Suggested Reading

○ Powell v. Alabama.

○ Gideon v. Wainwright.

○ Strickland v. Washington.

Questions to Consider

↗ Has the Supreme Court gone too far in providing criminal defendants with constitutional rights and procedural protections?

↗ How can we do a better job of providing equal justice under the law?

DUE PROCESS AND THE RIGHT TO COUNSEL

The year was 1931, in the midst of the Great Depression. Nine black youths, transient and illiterate, were traveling through the South together, riding the rails. They were on a freight train in Northern Alabama, bound for Memphis, when they encountered a group of poor white youths who'd hopped the same train. A fight broke out, and most of the white boys were tossed off the train. They went straight to the authorities, who stopped the train near the town of Scottsboro, Alabama. Two white girls on the train, possibly prostitutes trying to cover their tracks, told the sheriff they'd been raped by the black youths. The nine blacks, who were between 12 and 20 years old, were arrested and charged with rape—a capital crime. An angry white mob formed outside the Jackson County Courthouse and Jail, where the defendants were held, and the Alabama National Guard had to be called in to prevent a lynching.

Thus began one of the most important cases in the history of American criminal procedure law, *Powell v. Alabama*, better known as the Scottsboro case. It's the case that launched the modern era of criminal procedure, an era during which the U.S. Supreme Court took upon itself the responsibility to compel the wholesale reform of state criminal justice systems, by requiring the states to provide all criminal defendants—black and white, rich and poor—with certain fundamental rights. *Powell v. Alabama* was one of the first links in a chain of decisions that eventually led, by the 1960s, to such landmark Warren Court rulings as *Gideon v. Wainwright*, *Mapp v. Ohio*, and *Miranda v. Arizona*. But without *Powell v. Alabama*, some three decades earlier, the Criminal Procedure Revolution of the 1960s might never have occurred. How did all of this happen? Where did the Supreme Court find the legal authority to force the states to change the way they handle criminal cases? That's what this lecture is all about.

Our story begins with the Bill of Rights, those first ten amendments to the United States Constitution, adopted in 1791, just a few years after ratification of the original Constitution. The Bill of Rights was a political compromise. Some of the framers wanted to emphasize that the creation of the new federal government should never interfere with the most important rights of individual citizens. Others thought it was already obvious, from the text and structure of the Constitution, that the federal government lacked the power to do so, and they feared that mentioning some individual rights in the Constitution it might suggest that others aren't protected. Both sides eventually agreed not to add a list of individual rights to the original document, but instead to put those rights into a separate set of Amendments that could be added to the Constitution after ratification. And that's what happened.

Did you know, by the way, that the original proposal for the Bill of Rights actually contained 12 Amendments? I learned this when I visited the National Archives during Constitution Week, and saw an original draft of the Bill of Rights. I was shocked to see that what we now know as the grand and glorious First Amendment, with its guarantees of freedom of religion, and speech, and the press, was originally proposed as the grand and glorious third Amendment. Doesn't have quite the same ring, does it? But the original First Amendment, which laid out a complicated system for apportioning federal representatives based on population, was never ratified. And the original Second Amendment, which barred Senators and Representatives from raising their own pay during their time in office, wasn't ratified until 1992. So that's how the proposed third Amendment became the first Amendment.

Anyway, back to our story. It's important to recognize that, at the time, the Bill of Rights was designed only to protect individual rights against the new federal government the framers had just created. The framers didn't think there was any reason to put a lot of stuff in the federal Constitution to limit the power of the states, because the states existed before the new federal government, and already had, in their own state constitutions, all kinds of protections for individual rights. The concern of the framers was about the new federal government, and how it might someday become too big and powerful, trampling on the rights and liberties of the people. That's the last thing the framers wanted, especially after they'd just fought a long and bloody war to get rid of another big and powerful government.

So that's what the Bill of Rights was about: Providing guarantees of individual rights, so the people wouldn't have to worry about those rights ever being infringed by the new federal government. Many of the guarantees written into the Bill of Rights involved the rights of people accused of crimes, which makes sense because one of the most important, and most terrifying, powers of government is the power to lock someone up or even execute them, as punishment for committing a crime. But once again, keep in mind that these criminal procedure rights originally applied only to federal criminal cases. And that's the way things remained for a very long time. The Bill of Rights applied only to the federal government, not to the states. The Supreme Court even explicitly held this to be so, in the 1833 case of *Barron v. Baltimore.*

After the Civil War, for the very first time in our history, Americans began to think that maybe the federal Constitution should contain language to protect individuals against the infringement of their rights by their own states. The states that joined the Confederacy not only fought a catastrophic war to try to preserve the evil institution of slavery, they continued to persecute the freed slaves even after the war ended. One of the abiding lessons of the Civil War and its aftermath was that you can't always trust a state to protect the rights of its own citizens. And so, the federal Constitution was amended. And one of these so-called "Civil War Amendments" was the Fourteenth Amendment, which provides: "All persons born or naturalized in the United States, and subject to the jurisdiction thereof, are citizens of the United States, and of the State wherein they reside. No State shall make or enforce any law which shall abridge the privileges or immunities of citizens of the United States; nor shall any State deprive any person of life, liberty, or property, without due process of law; nor deny to any person within its jurisdiction the equal protection of the laws."

Now that's some powerful language. The Fourteenth Amendment was intended to emphasize a whole new kind of citizenship in America, national, or federal, citizenship. Before the Civil War, most Americans would have considered themselves, for the most part, to be citizens of their particular state. But the Fourteenth Amendment says otherwise: "All persons born or naturalized in the United States, and subject to the jurisdiction thereof, are citizens of the United States, and of the State wherein they reside." As part of this new concept of national citizenship, the Fourteenth Amendment provides that the states can't take away a person's life, liberty, or property without due process of law. And the federal government will enforce this new constitutional right of due process, as well as the right to equal protection of the laws, against any possible infringement by the states.

The Fourteenth Amendment represented a turning point in American constitutional law. The original Constitution and the Bill of Rights, contained many provisions to protect individual rights, including a separate Due Process Clause, in the Fifth Amendment. But as we've seen, at least in the beginning, those provisions applied only to the federal government. The Civil War Amendments to the Constitution were the first ones to directly address, and directly limit, the power of the states to act in ways that might harm their own citizens. Through the Civil War Amendments, the federal government, for the first time, acquired the constitutional authority to act in defense of individuals, and to protect them as national citizens from mistreatment by their own states. This was a huge shift in the balance of American federalism.

So, when the Fourteenth Amendment was ratified in 1868, the U.S. Supreme Court became responsible for ensuring that state officials wouldn't deprive people of life, liberty, or property, without "due process of law." And of course, this was very important for criminal justice, because the vast majority of criminal cases are prosecuted by state governments. And every criminal case is about the government trying to take away a defendant's life, liberty, or property.

But what exactly does the term "due process" mean? Literally speaking, "process" means "procedure." So the Due Process Clause has something to do with the specific procedures a state must follow, if it wants to take away your life, liberty, or property. But what does it mean to say that a particular procedure is "due"? Well, we use the word "due" in lots of ways: We say that your rent is "due." That a library book is "due." That you have to pay your "dues." The common meaning in all of these expressions is that something is "due" when you have an obligation to provide it. When it's owed to someone. When they're entitled to it. When they deserve it. So, "due process" literally means, "the procedures that are owed to you, or that you deserve," before the state tries to take away your life, liberty, or property. Great. How does THAT help us to define the meaning of due process? It doesn't. The language of the Due Process Clause is completely circular. It says that the state must give you whatever procedures you deserve. What are those procedures? Whatever you deserve!

The Supreme Court had to figure out how to give sensible meaning to this vague constitutional language. In late 1800s, the Court took a conservative approach. Basically, the Court held that the procedures you're entitled to, under the Due Process Clause, are whatever procedures the state has written into its validly enacted statutes and rules. Once the state enacts a law that guarantees you some particular procedure, then they have to follow that law and provide you with that procedure. So, for example, if a particular state's law says you're entitled to have a grand jury to review criminal charges against you before you actually go to trial, then the state has to follow its own rules and provide you with a grand jury. But if the state law doesn't grant you that right, then you aren't entitled to it. Which means the Due Process Clause is really nothing more than the Rule of Law.

Criminal Law and Procedure

By the early 1900s, the Court became concerned that this Rule of Law approach wasn't protective enough, because all a state had to do, in order to deny someone a right, was enact a new law stating that people no longer have that particular right. Could a state get away with enacting a new law placing the burden of proof in a criminal case on the defendant instead of the prosecutor? Or denying criminal defendants a trial altogether? Surely the Fourteenth Amendment's Due Process Clause must mean something more than that. Moreover, what if the state has a statute that actually does guarantee a specific procedural right to criminal defendants, but then applies that law in a manner that effectively denies the right to a particular defendant in a particular case?

That's basically what happened in *Powell v. Alabama*. The Scottsboro defendants were charged with a capital offense, and they were too poor to hire a lawyer. Under Alabama law, that meant the trial judge was required to appoint a defense lawyer to represent them. So the judge proceeded to appoint every lawyer in Scottsboro, all seven of them, to serve as defense counsel. But in rural Alabama, during the heyday of Jim Crow, not one of those lawyers was actually willing to step up and represent a black man accused of raping a white woman. So those local lawyers did nothing to prepare for the impending capital trial.

The trial was scheduled to begin only 12 days after the defendants were arrested. On the morning of the trial, a lawyer from Chattanooga, Tennessee, named Stephen Roddy, who'd been asked to go to Scottsboro by the families of some of the defendants, hesitantly offered to take the case. But Roddy was a real estate lawyer, and knew nothing about Alabama court procedures. So he asked for some help from the judge, who then convinced an elderly, semi-retired local attorney to advise Roddy. Neither of these lawyers had any time to investigate the facts, or even to talk to the defendants. But the judge insisted on proceeding anyway. The trial was split up into three parts, each involving three of the defendants. Over the course of three days, all nine defendants were convicted of rape. Eight of the defendants were sentenced to death—only the youngest was spared. The Alabama Supreme Court overturned one of the convictions, but affirmed all the others.

The seven condemned defendants took their case to the U.S. Supreme Court, where they became known as the "Scottsboro Seven." And in *Powell v. Alabama*, the Court held that what happened to the Scottsboro Seven violated the Fourteenth Amendment's Due Process Clause because the defendants were denied a fair trial by virtue of the fact that they were essentially forced to go to trial without the assistance of counsel. Here's what the Court said:

"In a capital case, where the defendant is unable to employ counsel and is incapable of making his own defense adequately because of ignorance, feeble mindedness, illiteracy, or the like, it is the duty of the court, whether requested or not, to assign counsel for him as a necessary requisite of due process of law, and that duty is not discharged by an assignment at such a time or under such circumstances as to preclude the giving of effective aid in the preparation and trial of the case."

The Scottsboro Seven case is a prime example of how the Court gradually began to think about the Due Process Clause in much broader terms than merely obeying the Rule of Law. The Court began to ask a tougher question: Did the state, by its established criminal procedures or by the way those procedures were applied to the facts of the particular case, provide the defendant with a fundamentally fair trial? If not, then that's a violation of Due Process.

But what, exactly, is "fundamental fairness?" That's really hard to say. It sounds like a judge's intuition, or a gut feeling, and that's just about exactly how it worked. In one case decided in 1952, the State of California forcibly pumped the stomach of a criminal suspect to make him disgorge the illegal drugs he'd swallowed. The Supreme Court held this violated Due Process, because what the state did "shock[ed] the conscience." Much later in 1993, Justice Blackmun and Justice Scalia got into a spat over the procedures used in a Texas death penalty case. Blackmun wrote, on behalf of several dissenting Justices, that what happened in the Texas case shocked the conscience, to which Scalia replied, "Perhaps they should doubt the calibration of their consciences, or better still, the usefulness of 'conscience shocking' as a legal test."

And that's the big problem with the fundamental fairness approach to due process, including the related "shock the conscience" test; it's just too vague to avoid the rap that it depends entirely on the subjective views of nine unelected Supreme Court Justices. So the Court began trying to tie the concept of fundamental fairness to something a little more concrete, by asking an additional question: Is the requested procedure fundamental, in light of our Anglo-American legal history and tradition? This enabled the Court to look to respected historical sources, like the Magna Carta and the Declaration of Independence, to help decide if a particular procedure is guaranteed by Due Process. But even these historical sources didn't provide specific enough guidance. So by the 1960s, the Court turned to the Bill of Rights. After all, what better expression could there be, of the specific criminal procedures that are seen as fundamental in our legal history and tradition, than the ones the framers chose to guarantee for federal criminal cases by putting them into the Bill of Rights?

We refer to this process as "Incorporation" of the Bill of Rights into the Fourteenth Amendment's Due Process Clause. Did the people who wrote the Fourteenth Amendment way back in the 1860s think that's what they were doing? The historical evidence is far from clear, but it's how the Supreme Court eventually decided to settle the meaning of "Due Process."

Due Process Incorporation of the Bill of Rights played a central role in the "Criminal Procedure Revolution" of the 1960s, as the Supreme Court, led by Chief Justice Earl Warren, applied these federal constitutional provisions to force the states to start treating all criminal defendants better, no matter what their race or class. By the end of the 1960s, every criminal procedure right written into the Bill of Rights for federal criminal cases was incorporated into the Due Process Clause of the Fourteenth Amendment, and thereby made applicable to state criminal cases as well, with the singular exception of the Fifth Amendment's right to grand jury review of criminal charges. That right was never incorporated, and it still isn't considered part of due process, which means that the states are still free to make their own choices about whether or not to use grand juries.

All of the other criminal procedure rights in the Bill of Rights—including the right to be free from unreasonable searches and seizures, to have warrants be based on probable cause, to be free from double jeopardy, to not be compelled to be a witness against yourself, to have a speedy and public trial, to have a trial by jury, to confront the witnesses against you, to use compulsory process to gather evidence, and to be free from cruel and unusual punishments—have now been incorporated, by decisions of the Supreme Court, into the Fourteenth Amendment's Due Process Clause, which means the states must provide these rights to all criminal defendants.

Powell v. Alabama was a huge step along the way to Due Process Incorporation. The *Powell* case eventually led to the most famous of all the Court's Due Process Incorporation cases: *Gideon v. Wainwright*. On March 18, 1963, the Court ruled unanimously that by refusing to provide an indigent named Clarence Earl Gideon with a defense lawyer for his felony criminal trial, the State of Florida denied Gideon his constitutional right to the assistance of counsel as guaranteed by the Sixth Amendment and as applied to Florida by means of the Fourteenth Amendment's Due Process Clause.

Most other states had already recognized a right to appointed counsel, under state law, for indigents charged with felony crimes, meaning crimes with a possible punishment of more than a year in prison. Indeed, as far back as 1854, the Indiana Supreme Court had declared: "It is not to be thought of in a civilized community for a moment that any citizen put in jeopardy of life or liberty should be debarred of counsel because he was too poor to employ such aid." But Florida was one of about a dozen states where only capital defendants enjoyed a legal right to appointed counsel. In the *Gideon* decision, the U.S. Supreme Court ruled that the appointment of defense counsel for indigent defendants is a fundamental constitutional right, mandatory in every state. Clarence Gideon was granted a new trial, at which he was represented by counsel, and he was acquitted of the crime. And today, the right to counsel under *Gideon* applies not only to felonies, but also to any misdemeanor case where the defendant receives any actual imprisonment.

The right to counsel is no panacea. But it's still the most important procedural right that criminal defendants have. The right to counsel under *Gideon* is basically a promise, a promise that America will at least try to provide "equal justice under law." Just like those famous words carved on the marble façade of the Supreme Court Building in Washington, DC. As the Court once said, in the 1956 case of *Griffin v. Illinois*, "There can be no equal justice when the kind of trial a man gets depends on the amount of money he has." But, you might be thinking, doesn't the criminal justice system still work unequally? Rich criminal defendants hire the best lawyers money can buy. Poor defendants get some public defender, or maybe a local volunteer lawyer, to represent them. Don't get me wrong here, most public defenders are great, dedicated lawyers— in fact, I think they're practically saints, given how hard it is to do their job. But public defenders tend to have massive caseloads that would crush most lawyers. And public defenders also don't have high-powered investigators and jury consultants to help them. So is criminal justice really "equal?"

The Supreme Court's been trying to figure out how to deal with that problem ever since the day *Gideon* was decided. In the 1984 case of *Strickland v. Washington*, the Court held that the Sixth Amendment guarantees a criminal defendant not just any lawyer, but a reasonably effective lawyer. After all, the text of the Sixth Amendment says that a defendant is entitled to the "assistance of counsel for his defense." If your defense lawyer is drunk, or sleeping, or incompetent, or so overworked that they can't pay attention to your case, then that lawyer isn't really giving you very much assistance, are they?

The *Strickland* case established the test that still governs claims of "ineffective assistance of counsel." In *Strickland*, the Court held that, in order to get a conviction or sentence overturned based on ineffective assistance of counsel, the defendant must show two things. Number one: the defense lawyer's performance fell below an objectively reasonable standard, given prevailing professional norms in the area, and number two: the defendant was prejudiced, in the sense that there's a reasonable probability the outcome would have been different, had the defense lawyer performed adequately. The Strickland test is really hard to satisfy, especially because most criminal defendants have lots of evidence against them, which means that even the best defense lawyer couldn't get them acquitted, which means they can't meet the prejudice prong of the Strickland test. Why would the Supreme Court make the test so hard? It's probably because the Court knows that being a criminal defense lawyer is already a tough job, and the Court doesn't want to make it even tougher by encouraging convicted defendants to spend all their time in prison writing up petitions accusing their lawyers of constitutional malpractice. In essence, the Strickland test allows the courts to overturn convictions or sentences only in the most extreme cases, where the defense lawyer did an especially bad job and the defendant would have had a fighting chance to win with a better lawyer. Otherwise, the defendant has to accept the outcome of the trial.

But that means we really haven't achieved equal justice in criminal cases, have we? Not when public defenders often have to handle so many cases that they can't give most of them the time of day. In Miami, Florida, in 2013, each public defender handled an average of more than 400 cases per year. Some public defenders had 50 felony criminal trials scheduled within a week. So the Miami public defender's office started refusing to take any more cases, despite a state statute requiring them to accept the cases. The Florida Supreme Court eventually ruled that the public defender had a legal right to refuse, because "excessive caseloads caused by underfunding meant the office could not carry out its legal and ethical obligations to the defendants." The court also concluded that waiting for judges to review individual claims of ineffective assistance of counsel, as *Strickland* generally requires, would be "tantamount to applying a band aid to an open head wound."

Funding for public defender services has never been adequate, and doesn't even come close to the amount society provides to prosecutor's offices. And this disparity isn't ever likely to change, because who really wants to pay more taxes to help accused criminals get better legal representation, which means they might go free? Better to give the money to those who are trying to get the bad guys off the streets, and keep the rest of us safe.

In short, *Gideon's* Promise of "equal justice under law" remains unfulfilled, more than 50 years after the *Gideon* case was decided. How much longer will it take? That's a question nobody can answer. Would the Scottsboro case have turned out differently if the defendants had been given qualified defense lawyers, with enough preparation time to be reasonably effective? In Alabama during the 1930s, probably not. After all, even Atticus Finch in *To Kill a Mockingbird* couldn't persuade the jury to see the truth about accused rapist Tom Robinson.

In the real-world Scottsboro case, after the decision in *Powell v. Alabama*, each defendant was retried, this time with appointed counsel, and they were all reconvicted and resentenced to death, despite the fact that one of the alleged victims completely recanted her testimony. The U.S. Supreme Court reversed those convictions, too, this time because the jury selection process was blatantly discriminatory, excluding almost all blacks from the jury. That led to still another round of trials, at which most of the defendants were once again convicted. In the end, the Scottsboro defendants avoided the gallows. But they ended up serving between five and 20 years in prison, for a crime they probably did not commit. Which illustrates how even the best of legal procedures, and the best of defense lawyers, can't always make up for the worst in human nature.

GOVERNMENT SEARCHES AND PRIVACY RIGHTS

I n this lecture, you'll explore the fascinating history behind the Fourth Amendment. You'll also look closely at the amendment's scope, examining in particular the terms "search" and "seizure." These terms define the nature and extent of the Fourth Amendment's privacy protections, and greatly influence how the police investigate crimes.

HISTORY AND PURPOSE

★ The Fourth Amendment to the U.S. Constitution provides:

> The right of the people to be secure in their persons, houses, papers, and effects, against unreasonable searches and seizures, shall not be violated. And no Warrants shall issue, but upon probable cause, supported by oath or affirmation, and particularly describing the place to be searched, and the persons or things to be seized.

★ The Fourth Amendment was one of the most important provisions written into the Bill of Rights. Indeed, the American Revolution was motivated in significant measure by the resentment the colonists felt about the fact that British soldiers—armed only with a "general warrant," based on some vague claim that someone was an enemy of the Crown—could barge into that person's home, perhaps even in the middle of the night, and ransack it, looking for seditious papers or other evidence of disloyalty.

* The Fourth Amendment was designed to accomplish two different but related goals. The second half of the amendment, with its list of requirements for a warrant, was designed to eliminate the hated general warrant. In America, warrants would have to describe specifically what the authorities were looking for, as well as where they could go looking for it. Warrants would also have to be based on sworn statements indicating that evidence of a crime would be found, and could be issued only if they were based on probable cause.

* The first half of the amendment, by contrast, is written in more general terms. It was designed to prohibit all searches and seizures that are "unreasonable," whether or not those searches or seizures involved a warrant. But the grand language of the amendment leaves one key question unanswered: What qualifies as a "search" or a "seizure"?

* Defining "search" and "seizure" is important, because these terms let us know when the protections of the Fourth Amendment apply. If a particular activity isn't considered a search or a seizure, the amendment doesn't regulate it. This means that the government can act that way to anyone, for any reason, as often as it wants.

EXPECTATIONS OF PRIVACY

✴ In the early years of the Fourth Amendment, there was a pretty clear consensus about what was a "search." The framers believed in the sanctity of private property rights almost as much as they believed in privacy. So a "search" basically meant any action that infringes on your private property, for the purpose of a government investigation.

✴ During the 18th and 19th centuries, Fourth Amendment notions of privacy and property were inextricably linked: Your privacy was protected because your property was protected. For a nation whose very concept of citizenship—including the right to vote—was often based on the ownership of land, this property-based approach to the Fourth Amendment made some sense.

✴ The Fourth Amendment's protection is no longer limited to cases where property rights are infringed. Over the years, the U.S. Supreme Court has been forced to adopt a more expansive interpretation. These days, a reasonable expectation of privacy is all that's required for the Fourth Amendment to apply.

✴ The Court's privacy-based approach ran into trouble almost as soon as it was adopted. In *United States v. White*, the defendant, James A. White, was suspected of involvement in illegal narcotics. The government convinced one of White's friends to wear a concealed radio transmitter and talk to him about the crimes. No warrant was obtained. White said incriminating things, and the tapes were used to convict him. The Court held that this was not a "search" within the meaning of the Fourth Amendment, and thus that which no warrant was required.

✴ In *White*, the Court noted that any time a person shares a secret with another person, it's no longer really a secret. If you choose to confide your crimes to a trusted friend, you must realize that he or she might go to the police and report what you said. In White's case, the recording by police simply ensured the accuracy of his friend's report. Any subjective expectation of privacy White may have had was, at least according to the Court, unreasonable.

★ The legal implications of sharing information with a third party have returned with a vengeance in the modern era of cellular phones, e-mail, and social media. But before we get there, let's look at a few other cases where the Supreme Court applied an empirical view of privacy and reasonable expectations to reach a problematic result.

★ In *Oliver v. United States*, police officers—without a warrant—drove onto Oliver's property and past his house. They exited their car, walked past a gate marked "No Trespassing," and continued walking for over a mile across open fields until they found Oliver's marijuana plants. The Court held that this was not a "search" under the Fourth Amendment, because everybody knows that stuff you do in open fields might not remain private. For one thing, airplanes might fly overhead and see your stuff. Similarly, hikers might come onto your land and see your stuff, despite your "No Trespassing" signs. Oliver lost.

★ In *Florida v. Riley*, the defendant's marijuana plants were in an enclosed greenhouse, right up against the side of his home. The police, without a warrant, hovered 400 feet above Riley's house in a helicopter until they were able to see the marijuana. The Court held that this was not a "search," because everybody knows that airplanes and helicopters fly overhead all the time. The fact that this particular helicopter flew so low didn't matter, because the low-altitude flight was permitted by FAA regulations. Riley lost.

★ In *California v. Greenwood*, the question was whether it's a "search" if the police, without a warrant, look through your garbage once it's left out on the curb—in a closed, opaque plastic bag—for trash pickup. The Court held that this is was not a "search," because everybody knows that sometimes raccoons tear open garbage bags, exposing their contents to public view. Children, scavengers, and snoops might do so, too. Plus, the trash collector can be considered a third party with whom the defendant voluntarily shared his trash. Who knows whether, or when, the trash collector might decide to go through the garbage to find something of value? Greenwood lost.

★ Using the Supreme Court's empirical approach, the only relevant issue is how likely the particular privacy intrusion might be. a normative approach, by contrast, might generate a different and perhaps more appropriate inquiry: Instead of assessing how likely it is that raccoons will go through your garbage, you might ask yourself whether you want to live in the kind of society where the police can go through your garbage—without a warrant—every single day, for whatever reason they want, for the rest of your life.

TECHNOLOGY AND PRIVACY

★ In today's tech-driven world, almost every aspect of our lives gets shared, one way or another, with third parties. Sometimes we share voluntarily—like posting things for your friends to see on Facebook. Sometimes, it's done in a manner that's technically voluntary, but almost impossible to resist—like swiping your loyalty card at the grocery store, which is necessary to get discounts, but also shares your purchase history with the store and, eventually, other companies too.

★ In some cases, we share things about us without even thinking consciously about it—like when you do a search on Google, or when you agree to certain privacy policies as you sign up for a news or entertainment website. Other times, the sharing of information is mandatory—like when the government makes you provide financial information to the IRS, or to your bank or employer.

★ Every e-mail you write and text message you send is "shared" with the companies that provides you with that service, if only so they can transmit them to the intended recipient. Of course, you're also sharing those messages with the intended recipient, which looks a lot like the third-party sharing that took place in the *White* case. Does the government have a free pass to read your messages because you willingly shared them with someone else?

★ Other types of information about you get collected by the government or by private companies without your knowledge or consent. Think about the now-ubiquitous security and traffic cameras. These cameras generally record things that happen in public places, or in businesses that are open to the public. They capture information about your life—whom you're with, where you're going, what you're doing—that you share without thinking every time you go out in public.

✴ One solution might be to ask our legislatures to enact statutes to provide us with greater protection than we'd get from the Fourth Amendment. This has actually been done a few times already. For example, there's a federal statute that provides some extra protection for stored communications, which are copies of messages stored by Internet Service Providers and wireless carriers.

✴ In 2015, terrorists in San Bernardino, California, killed 14 people and wounded 22 more. The FBI wanted to get into an encrypted iPhone belonging to one of the terrorists. They first tried to force Apple to get around the encryption. When Apple refused, the FBI paid a hacker more than $1 million to do the job. If that hadn't worked, it's very likely that we would have seen legislation requiring cell phone companies to provide backdoor access to the government, at least under certain circumstances.

★ In many cases, it falls to the judiciary—the branch of government that's supposed to make sure we stay true to our Constitution and our core values—to regulate the government's access to information in the age of technology. If the Supreme Court continues to apply an empirical standard, the result may be a society where the government—without a warrant—can get inside our cell phones, our computers, and our social media accounts, anytime, anywhere, for any reason, as often as it wants.

Suggested Reading

- Boyd v. United States.

- Katz v. United States.

- United States v. White.

- Florida v. Riley.

Questions to Consider

⊅ Should the government be granted access to the contents of a cell phone, without a warrant or probable cause, if the owner is suspected of being involved in terrorism or another criminal activity?

⊅ How do you feel about the presence of surveillance cameras in public places? Do they enhance our security, or do they invade our privacy?

GOVERNMENT SEARCHES AND PRIVACY RIGHTS

The Fourth Amendment to the United States Constitution provides "The right of the people to be secure in their persons, houses, papers, and effects, against unreasonable searches and seizures, shall not be violated. And no Warrants shall issue, but upon probable cause, supported by oath or affirmation, and particularly describing the place to be searched, and the persons or things to be seized." In this lecture, the first of a two-part lesson on the Fourth Amendment, we'll explore the fascinating history behind this provision. We'll also look closely at the scope of the Fourth Amendment. What, exactly, is a search? What is a seizure? These are fundamental questions of criminal procedure whose answers determine the nature and extent of the privacy protection the framers tried so hard to enshrine in the language of the Fourth Amendment. And the answers to these questions also greatly influence how the police investigate crimes.

The Fourth Amendment was one of the most important provisions written into the Bill of Rights, which was proposed just one year after the ratification of the original Constitution. Indeed, the American Revolution was motivated in significant measure by the resentment that the colonists felt about the fact that British soldiers, armed only with a "general warrant" based on some vague claim that you were an enemy of the crown, could barge into a person's home, perhaps even in the middle of the night, and ransack it looking for seditious papers and other possible evidence of disloyalty.

The Fourth Amendment was actually designed to accomplish two different but related goals. The second half of the Amendment, with its list of requirements for a warrant, was designed to get rid of the hated "general warrant." Instead, in America, all warrants would have to describe specifically what the authorities were looking for, and where they could go looking for it. The warrant would have to be based on someone's sworn statement indicating that evidence of a crime would be found there. And the warrant could be issued only if there was probable cause to believe that you were indeed guilty of a crime.

The first half of the Amendment, by contrast, is written in more general terms. It was designed to prohibit all searches, and all seizures, that are "unreasonable," whether or not those searches and seizures involved a warrant. This is great stuff, and it speaks to the framers' strong desire to build a nation of citizens who could live their lives in peace, without the fear of government agents banging on their door in the night. But the grand language of the Fourth Amendment leaves one key question unanswered: What, exactly, qualifies as a search, or a seizure, of evidence within the meaning of the Fourth Amendment? In other words, how do we know when these wonderful protections of the Fourth Amendment apply, and when they don't? Because if a particular governmental behavior doesn't count as a search, or a seizure, then the Fourth Amendment doesn't regulate that behavior at all. Which means that the government can do that behavior anytime, anywhere, to anyone, for any reason, as often as it wants.

Let's focus our attention on the term search. In the early years of the Fourth Amendment, there was a pretty clear consensus about what was a search. The framers believed in the sanctity of private property rights almost as much as they believed in privacy. So a search basically meant any action that infringes on your private property, for the purpose of a government investigation. If a government agent comes onto your land without permission to try to find some information or evidence, that's a trespass—and a search. If the agent comes to your place of business to take a look at some of your papers, that's a search, because those papers belong to you, and the agent has no right to touch them, or even to look at them. And if the agent tries to take those papers away, that becomes a seizure as well.

You could say that, during the 18th and 19th centuries, Fourth Amendment notions of privacy and property were inextricably linked: Your privacy was protected because your property was protected. For a nation whose very concept of citizenship—including the right to vote—often was based on the ownership of land, this property-based approach to the Fourth Amendment made some sense. But what if the government doesn't need to come onto your land, or mess with your stuff, to get the information they want? What if they just order you to turn it over to them? Is that still a search, or a seizure?

One of the most important cases in the early history of the Fourth Amendment was the 1886 case of *Boyd v. United States*. Boyd was a New York City importer of plate glass who was suspected of failing to pay the required customs duties. The federal prosecutor ordered 35 cases of plate glass to be seized on the ground that the glass was forfeitable to the government for non-payments of duties, and

Boyd went to court to try to stop the seizure. At the trial, a key piece of evidence was an invoice for 29 cases of plate glass that Boyd had imported previously. The invoice had been obtained by the prosecutor, not by means of a warrant and a search, but instead through a court order requiring Boyd to turn it over. The U.S. Supreme Court held that the federal statute authorizing the judge to issue the order that required Boyd to turn over the invoice was unconstitutional. The problem for the Court was explaining why. The Court acknowledged that the prosecutor never searched for the invoice, nor did he technically seize it, because Boyd gave it to him, pursuant to the court order. Another possibility was that the order might violate the Fifth Amendment's provision that says you can't be compelled in a criminal case to become a witness against yourself, but this wasn't a criminal case, it was a civil forfeiture proceeding. So, at least in terms of the literal meaning of the Fourth and Fifth Amendments, the court order to turn over the invoice didn't technically violate either provision. But the Supreme Court then decided to take the analysis one step farther. According to the Court, the entire history of the Fourth and Fifth Amendments reveals that their purpose—especially when considered together—was to create a zone of privacy that's protected against governmental intrusion.

Here's what the Court said in *Boyd*: "The principles laid down in this opinion affect the very essence of constitutional liberty and security. They apply to all invasions on the part of the government and its employees of the sanctity of a man's home and the privacies of life. Breaking into a house and opening boxes and drawers are circumstances of aggravation. But any forcible and compulsory extortion of a man's own testimony or of his private papers to be used as evidence to convict him of crime or to forfeit his goods, is within the condemnation of the judgment. In this regard, the Fourth and Fifth Amendments run almost into each other."

According to *Boyd*, the Fourth and Fifth Amendments actually were designed to work together to protect our privacy and our property from the government. Which makes the court order in the Boyd case unconstitutional, just the same as if the police had pushed their way into Boyd's home to search for that invoice, and just the same as if the prosecutor had placed Boyd on the witness stand at trial and forced him to admit that he never paid those customs duties. It's not the technical form of the violation that matters, it's the substance. And notice that it doesn't even matter whether or not the government gets a warrant to search for the invoice. Under the *Boyd* decision, the government simply can't get hold of that invoice, no matter what. And the Court later extended *Boyd* to cover all items of evidence in which a person retains a valid property right. The government simply can't come looking for such mere evidence, even with a warrant.

If you're thinking this all sounds very different from the way search warrants work today, you're right. The broad 19th Century view of the Fourth and Fifth Amendments—that they "run almost into each other," and work together to provide an inviolable zone of protection for privacy and property rights— didn't survive into the 20th Century. Instead, as the need for government regulations grew in modern industrialized society, and as the concomitant need for government access to information to enforce those regulations also grew, the Court began to back away from the bold statements in *Boyd*. This backing away happened first in the context of business-related information, the same context that was involved in *Boyd* itself. But the change later spread to personal information as well. And it happened in several stages.

First, in 1906, the Court held that corporations do not have Fifth Amendment rights to refuse to answer incriminating questions. So the government can get information from a corporation, just by addressing its request to the corporation itself. Second, in 1927, the Court held that any item used in the commission of a crime became an "instrumentality" of the crime, and is no longer protected as personal property. So the government can come looking for that item, as long as they get a warrant. Third, in 1948, the Court held that any records the government requires you to make and keep do not belong to you in the same way that private papers do, which means they can be subject to search and seizure, as long as the government gets a warrant.

The end for *Boyd* came in the 1960s, when the Court decided three cases that essentially decoupled the Fourth and Fifth Amendments once and for all. In *Schmerber v. California*, the Court upheld the forced taking of a blood sample from a person suspected of drunk driving, because the government had a warrant for the blood sample and it wasn't an unreasonable search. The Court also said this didn't violate the Fifth Amendment, because the blood sample wasn't really the same thing as being a witness against yourself. In *Warden v. Hayden*, the Court reversed its earlier position on mere evidence, holding that a valid warrant allows the government to search for, and seize such evidence, despite the claim of an individual property right in the item. And in *Berger v. New York*, the Court struck down a New York statute allowing wiretaps on the basis of broad, open-ended warrants issued by a state judge. But the Court made clear that New York could do exactly what it wanted by the simple expedient of requiring its wiretap warrants to be more specific and less like a general warrant. That's what Congress did when it enacted the federal wiretap statute, which is now the model for most state wiretap laws.

Meanwhile, in 1967, the Court made another decision with far-reaching implications for privacy and the scope of the Fourth Amendment: *Katz v. United States*. Katz was suspected of involvement in illegal gambling. The FBI, without a warrant, attached an electronic listening device to the outer wall of a public telephone booth. You remember telephone booths, right? Those glass contraptions with folding doors, that used to hold pay telephones? Nowadays I have to show my law students photos of phone booths, so they'll know what I'm talking about! Anyway, the FBI agents used the listening device to hear and record phone calls made by Katz about gambling. Katz argued at his criminal trial that this was an unconstitutional search. The prosecution, however, claimed that there was no search at all, because the FBI agents never physically intruded into the phone booth, and therefore violated no property rights of Katz. The Supreme Court held that the use of the listening device was a search, and moreover an unconstitutional one because it was conducted without a warrant. According to the Court, it was high time to get rid of the trespass view of the Fourth Amendment, the view that linked privacy rights with property rights. Instead, as the Court put it: "The Fourth Amendment protects people, not places. What a person knowingly exposes to the public, even in his own home, is not a subject of Fourth Amendment protection. But what he seeks to preserve as private, even in an area accessible to the public, may be constitutionally protected. One who occupies a phone booth, shuts the door behind him, and pays the toll that permits him to place a call is surely entitled to assume that the words he utters into the mouthpiece will not be broadcast to the world. To read the Constitution more narrowly is to ignore the vital role that the public telephone has come to play in private communication."

Justice John Harlan wrote an important concurring opinion in *Katz*, which contained the words that were later adopted by the Court as the new test for what counts as a search under the Fourth Amendment. Here's Harlan's two-part Katz test: "First, that a person have exhibited an actual subjective expectation of privacy, and second, that the expectation be one that society is prepared to recognize as 'reasonable.'"

After Katz, It's no longer necessary to limit the Fourth Amendment's protection to cases where property rights are infringed. A "reasonable expectation of privacy" is all that's required for the Fourth Amendment to apply. So far, so good. But the new privacy-based Katz test almost immediately ran into trouble.

Just four years later, in *United States v. White*, James A. White was suspected of involvement in illegal narcotics. The government convinced one of White's friends, Harvey Jackson, to wear a concealed radio transmitter—a "wire"—and talk to White about the crimes. No warrant was obtained. White said incriminating things, and the tapes were used to convict him.

The Supreme Court held that this was not a search within the meaning of the Fourth Amendment, which meant that no warrant was required. The Court noted that any time a person shares a secret with another person, it's no longer really a secret. If you choose to confide your crimes to a trusted friend, you must realize that your so-called friend might go to the police and report what you said. The tape recording simply ensured the accuracy of the friend's report. According to the Court, what the police did can't be a search, because it fails the second part of the Katz test. White may have had a subjective expectation of privacy in his conversations with Jackson, but given the ever-present risk that a trusted friend will turn into a rat, White's expectation of privacy was unreasonable.

Justice Harlan, the author of the Katz test, dissented. Harlan apparently realized, only too late, that his language in *Katz* contained a latent ambiguity. What does it mean to say that a subjective expectation of privacy is reasonable? We commonly use the word reasonable in two very different ways. We say things like, "It's reasonable to believe it will rain tomorrow." Or it's not. Either way, the word reasonable says something about the empirical likelihood of rain. Similarly, we say things like, "It's reasonable to think the White Sox will win the World Series this year." Once again, it's a statement about empirical probabilities, about the likelihood of a future event. And that's precisely how the Court majority, in the White case, interpreted the word reasonable. It wasn't reasonable for White to think his conversation with Jackson would remain private, because he knew, or should have known, that there was a very real possibility that it wouldn't. But now think about the word reasonable another way. We also say things like, "It's reasonable to vote for the Democrats." Or the Republicans. That's not a statement about empirical reality, or a prediction of the future. There's no true or false in the statement, either. Instead, it's a statement about what we think should happen in the future. About what we think ought to happen. About what we want to happen. In other words, it's a normative statement, not an empirical one.

Justice Harlan realized, too late, that the Court was misinterpreting what he wrote in *Katz*. In his dissenting opinion in White, Harlan took the majority to task for placing too much emphasis on risk analysis, and not enough on the normative values of society. Here's what he said: "The analysis must, in my view, transcend the search for assumptions of risk. Our expectations, and the risks we assume, are in large part reflections of laws that translate, into rules, the customs and values of the past and present. We should not, as judges, merely recite the expectations and risks without examining the desirability of saddling them upon society. The critical question, therefore, is whether under our system of government, we should impose on our citizens the risks of the electronic listener or observer, without at least the protection of a warrant requirement." In other words, the real question, according to Harlan, isn't whether we know that talking to a trusted friend presents a risk of losing one's privacy. Instead, it's whether we want to live in the kind of society where the government can freely listen in on that conversation, anytime, anywhere, involving anyone, for any reason, as often as it wants. Because that's exactly what it means to say that it's not a search within the meaning of the Fourth Amendment.

The legal implications of sharing information with a third party have returned with a vengeance in the modern, high-tech era of cellular phones, e-mail, and social media. But before we get there, let's look at a few other cases where the Court applied the empirical view of the Katz test to reach a problematic result. In *Oliver v. United States*, police officers, without a warrant, drove onto Oliver's property and past his house. They exited their car and walked past a gate marked "No Trespassing" for over a mile across some fields, to find Oliver's marijuana plants. The Court held that this was not a search under the Fourth Amendment, because everybody knows that stuff you do in open fields might not remain private. For one thing, airplanes might fly overhead and see your stuff. And hikers might come onto your land and see your stuff, despite your "No Trespassing" signs. Oliver lost.

In *Florida v. Riley*, the defendant's marijuana plants were in an enclosed greenhouse, right up against the side of the defendant's home. The police, without a warrant, hovered 400 feet over the home in a helicopter until they saw the marijuana. The Court held that this was not a search, because everybody knows that airplanes and helicopters fly overhead all the time. The fact that this particular helicopter flew so low didn't matter, because the low-altitude flight was permitted by local FAA regulations. Riley lost.

Justice O'Connor and Justice Brennan, in separate opinions in *Riley*, got into a silly argument about just how likely such low-altitude flights really are. O'Connor surmised that there's probably "considerable public use" of the airspace at 400 feet and above. Brennan retorted that, although legal, such flights must be exceedingly rare. Seriously? C'mon guys, is that really how we should be deciding the proper scope of the Fourth Amendment?

One more example. In *California v. Greenwood*, the question was whether it's a search for the police, without a warrant, to look through your garbage once it's left out at the curb in a closed, opaque plastic bag for trash pickup. The Court held that this is not a search because everybody knows that sometimes raccoons tear open garbage bags, exposing their contents to public view. Children, scavengers, and snoops might do it too. And the trash collector is also a third party, with whom the defendant voluntarily shared his trash; who knows whether, or when, the trash collector might decide to go through the garbage to find something of value? Greenwood lost.

Greenwood is a perfect example of why it matters whether we use the empirical version, or the normative version, of the Katz test. Under the empirical version, the only relevant issue is how likely the particular privacy intrusion might be. That's why O'Connor and Brennan got into that silly argument about the frequency of low-altitude flights in *Riley*. But under the normative version of Harlan's test, we should be asking an entirely different kind of question. Instead of asking how likely it is that raccoons will go through your garbage, we should ask, "Do we want to live in the kind of society where the police can go through your garbage, without a warrant, every single day, for whatever reason they want, for the rest of your life?" If we decide we don't want to live that way, that doesn't mean the police can never search your garbage, it only means they'll need to get a warrant, based on probable cause, before they do.

Okay, so what about modern technology? How does it affect the scope of the Fourth Amendment? Here's the big problem: In today's tech-driven world, almost every aspect of our lives gets shared, one way or another, with third parties. Sometimes we share voluntarily, like posting things for our friends to see on Facebook. Sometimes, it's done in a manner that's technically voluntary, but almost impossible to resist, like swiping your loyalty card at the grocery store, which is necessary to get discounts, but also shares your purchase history with the store and other companies, too. Sometimes, it's done without you even thinking consciously about it, like when you do a search on Google, or when you agree to certain privacy policies as you sign up for a news or entertainment website. Who really reads all that small print anyway, right? Sometimes, the sharing of information is mandatory, like when the government makes you provide financial information to the IRS, or to your bank or employer. The point is, almost everything we do in the modern world is shared with someone else, one way or another. And that makes it subject to the Fourth Amendment's third-party sharing doctrine, dating all the way back to the 1971 *White* case. Which means that all your allegedly "private" information may be completely unprotected by the Fourth Amendment.

And it gets worse. Every e-mail you write, and every text message you send, gets shared with the company that provides you with that service, if only so they can transmit the message to the intended recipient. Not to mention the fact that you're sharing those messages with the intended recipient, which makes it look a lot like the *White* case. Does the government have a free pass to read your messages just because you willingly shared them with someone else? Moreover, a lot of information about you gets collected by the government itself, and by private companies as well, without you ever knowing, or consenting to it. Think about the now-ubiquitous security and traffic cameras. These cameras generally record only things that happen in public places, or in businesses that are open to the public, which means that, technically, you're always voluntarily sharing your information—about whom you're with, where you're going, what you're doing—with the cameras and with those who operate them. Once again, that information might not be protected by the Fourth Amendment.

Now, you may be thinking, can't we solve this problem through legislation? Is the Fourth Amendment the only way to protect our privacy from the government? Yes, it's true that we can ask our legislatures to enact statutes to provide us with greater protection than we'd get from the Fourth Amendment. And it's actually been done a few times; for example, there's a federal statute that provides some extra protection for stored communications, meaning copies of messages stored on computers at an Internet Service Provider or cell phone company. But ask yourself this question: If the government really wants to obtain your private information, do you really think that same government is going to enact a statute that protects the information from being obtained? And if such a statute does get enacted, do you think the government won't amend the statute, as soon as there's a compelling enough need to obtain the information? In 2015, a terrorist attack on an office holiday party in San Bernardino, California, killed 14 people and wounded 22 more. The FBI wanted to get into the encrypted iPhone belonging to one of the terrorists. First they tried to force Apple to beat the encryption. Then the FBI paid over $1 million to a hacker to do the job. If that hadn't worked, don't you think we'd now have a federal law requiring cell phone companies to provide back-door access to the government, at least under certain circumstances? You bet we would.

And that means we're probably back to the courts, the branch of government that's supposed to make sure we stay true to our Constitution and our core values, to regulate the government's access to information in the age of technology. And that means someday, we're probably going to have to get rid of the empirical version of the Katz test, and start asking the normative question that Justice Harlan posed: Do we really want to live in a society where the government, without a warrant, can get inside our cell phones, and our computers, and our social media accounts, anytime, anywhere, for any reason, as often as it wants? Because that's what's at stake, as we continue to try to balance.

THE SHRINKING WARRANT REQUIREMENT

This lecture considers the circumstances under which the police are permitted to enter and search private property without first obtaining a warrant. It also examines the warrant process, the particulars of probable cause, and judicial enforcement of the Fourth Amendment's protections against unreasonable searches and seizures.

AVAILABLE REMEDIES

✭ The first half of the Fourth Amendment states that all searches and seizures must be reasonable. The second half of the amendment sets forth the constitutional requirements for a valid warrant. What the amendment doesn't address is whether all searches—or even most—require a warrant. Was this simply an oversight by the framers? Probably not.

✭ The language of the Fourth Amendment reflects the reality of the period in which it was written. At the time, most government searches were based on warrants. There were no professional police forces in the late 18th century, and the courts hadn't yet developed the doctrine of qualified immunity, which protects police against most civil lawsuits. Law enforcement officers typically obtained a warrant to protect themselves against lawsuits for trespassing on the private property being searched.

✭ This history helps to explain another oddity of the Fourth Amendment: Nowhere in the text does it say what the remedy should be for a violation of the rights the amendment guarantees. The framers probably figured that the remedy would be a civil lawsuit for damages, because that was the only remedy they knew.

✭ Over time, however, civil remedies for such violations became more or less obsolete. Today, the likelihood of a person successfully suing a police officer for violating their Fourth Amendment rights is pretty close to zero. The only outliers are lawsuits challenging police use of excessive force, which have grown significantly in both number and dollar amounts in modern times.

★ Today, the primary legal remedy for Fourth Amendment violations is the exclusionary rule, which prohibits improperly obtained evidence from being used to prosecute the person whose rights were violated. The theory behind the exclusionary rule is that suppressing the evidence deprives the police of any benefit from an illegal search or seizure, thus deterring violations in the first place.

★ There are some important exceptions to the exclusionary rule, such as the exception for certain "good faith" violations by the police. Another notable exception concerns evidence that would inevitably have been found in the absence of any Fourth Amendment violation.

★ As a practical matter, the only direct beneficiaries of the exclusionary rule are criminals; if the police don't find evidence of a crime, there's nothing to exclude. And if the police don't actually care about obtaining a criminal conviction—if, for example, they want to seize a supply of drugs and simply move the drug dealers along—the exclusionary rule doesn't act as a deterrent. The rule isn't an ideal remedy, but it's what we've got.

PROBABLE CAUSE

✴ Not all searches and seizures require a valid warrant. If a warrant is necessary, however, there are several constitutional requirements that must be met. For example:

- The officer who presents the warrant application to the judge or magistrate must swear, by oath or affirmation, that the facts stated in the application are true.

- The facts stated in the application must provide enough information for the judge or magistrate to make an independent decision about the warrant's validity; he can't just rely on the officer's judgment.

- The magistrate must be neutral and detached. This means, for example, that local governments can't pay magistrates based on how many warrants they issue. Nor can warrants be issued directly by prosecutors.

- The warrant describe in detail the evidence to be searched for, as well as the location where the search will take place. In practice, this requirement is not particularly stringent. It's fine, for example, for the warrant to contain catchalls such as "any other evidence of the crime under investigation."

✴ There are also rules for the proper execution of a warrant—most notably, that police must knock and announce their presence before trying to enter a home or other premises. The Supreme Court has held that entering without knocking and announcing first is allowed only under special circumstances, such as when the police reasonably suspect that it would be dangerous or futile to do so, or that evidence is being destroyed inside.

★ The most important requirement for warrants to be valid under the Fourth Amendment is the requirement of probable cause. The phrase "probable cause" is a term of art, and a fairly vague one at that. In *Illinois v. Gates*, the leading case on probable cause, the Supreme Court described it as follows:

> Probable cause is a fluid concept—turning on the assessment of probabilities in particular factual contexts—not readily, or even usefully, reduced to a neat set of legal rules … . The task of the issuing magistrate is simply to make a practical, common-sense decision whether, given all the circumstances set forth in the affidavit before him, … there is a fair probability that contraband or evidence of a crime will be found.

> In a footnote, the Court added: "Probable cause requires only a probability or substantial chance of criminal activity, not an actual showing of such activity."

★ Given this low standard, judges and magistrates approve most warrant applications—as many as 95 percent of them. But this doesn't mean that the standard is useless. A police officer must still go through the hassle of writing up the warrant application and appearing in front of the judge or magistrate. This incentivizes the officer to be diligent in preparing his application; if it's rejected, his efforts will have been wasted.

NOTABLE EXCEPTIONS

★ There are several exceptions to the warrant requirement. For example, police don't need to get a warrant when the circumstances are such that it would be crazy to make them stop and go get one. The classic example involves an officer chasing someone who just robbed a bank. If the robber darts into a home, should the police officer have to abandon the chase and get a warrant before entering the home? Of course not. That would be crazy.

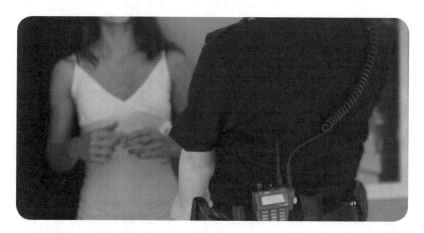

⋆ In criminal procedure, the exception illustrated by this example is known as the exception for exigent circumstances. When a situation like this arises, police must still have probable cause to justify their search, but they don't need to wait for a warrant before doing so.

⋆ The other classic example of exigency is when the police knock on someone's door and identify themselves as the police, only to hear excited voices inside saying, "Oh no! It's the cops, flush the drugs!" Perhaps they hear the sound of a toilet flushing. In that kind of situation, it's equally crazy to make the police wait for a warrant. By that time, all evidence of criminal activity would likely be destroyed.

⋆ Another exception to the warrant requirement is when the police see evidence in plain view. When this happens, they can seize the evidence from any place they're legally allowed to be. For example, if you invite a police officer into your home, and the officer sees illegal drugs on your kitchen table, he doesn't need a warrant to seize the drugs.

⋆ In the same example, if the officer is walking down the street and sees your drugs through an open window, he must obtain a warrant before entering the house and seizing the drugs. Of course, if he sees you grab the drugs and start flushing them down the toilet, he won't need a warrant; that's an exigent circumstance.

★ Cars are a big exception to the warrant requirement, for two reasons: First, cars are mobile, so they create their own "exigency." Second, people have a lower expectation of privacy in their cars than they do in their homes. After all, cars have glass windows and people can see inside them easily. Cars can also get into accidents, which means that your privacy might disappear without warning.

★ The only thing the police need to search a car is probable cause to believe there's criminal evidence somewhere inside the car. If they have it, they can search the entire car without a warrant—including the glove compartment, the trunk, and any containers in the car, such as backpacks or suitcases.

★ The only limit to the automobile exception is that police can't search places within the car where probable cause would be lacking. For example, if the police have probable cause to believe that you have a stolen big-screen TV in your car, that doesn't mean that they can rifle through the glove compartment.

★ Even if the police don't have probable cause, they can still search your car in the event that the car gets towed and impounded. In such cases, police can perform what's called an inventory search to make sure that all your stuff is properly accounted for and doesn't get stolen. If the police happen to find evidence of a crime during said inventory search, you're out of luck.

★ Another notable exception to the warrant requirement is for searches incident to arrest. Whenever the police arrest someone, they're allowed to search that person automatically, without a warrant, to make sure that the person doesn't have a weapon. Any evidence of criminal activity they find can then be seized.

If the arrest occurs in a building, the police can also search any area within reach of the person being arrested, to make sure that the person can't grab a weapon. They can also look into nearby rooms and closets to check for others who might attack them.

★ If a person happens to be in a car when they're arrested, that provides the police with two new reasons to search the car: First, they can search the car for a weapon—but only while the arrestee is still within reach of the car. Second, even after the arrestee's in custody, the police can search the car if there's reason to think that evidence of the crime might be found there.

* In an ever-growing number of situations, warrants are no longer presumptively required. Instead, police can search without a warrant—and even without probable cause—as long as they behave "reasonably." In fact, the exceptions to the warrant requirement have become so numerous that it wouldn't be much of a stretch to say that, today, the last bastion of the warrant requirement is the home. Almost everywhere else, the exceptions have swallowed the rule.

* The biggest change occurred the 1968 Supreme Court case *Terry v. Ohio*. This is the decision that gave police the authority to stop a person on the street and ask them questions, as long as the police have reasonable suspicion that the person is engaged in criminal activity. Police can also frisk the person, if the frisk is based on their reasonable suspicion that the person might be armed and dangerous. No probable cause is required, let alone a warrant.

* The *Terry* decision changed the rules of the Fourth Amendment in the interest of public safety. But at what cost? Maybe the most significant cost is that *Terry* disproportionately affects certain subsets of the population: racial and ethnic minorities, the poor, the young, and all those who look different and "scary." It authorizes police action based on little more than a hunch that a person might be up to no good. That kind of police discretion almost inevitably leads to snap judgments based on appearances, rather than hard evidence.

* A search can also be based solely on reasonableness when it serves a special governmental need, one that's different from catching criminals. For example, searches of school lockers can be based on reasonable suspicion, rather than probable cause, because they're done in the interest of school discipline. The same reasoning allows the desks of government employees to be searched (to promote an effective workplace), and pilots and train engineers to be tested for drugs (to protect public safety). Drunk-driving roadblocks and border searches fall into the same category.

★ Finally, searches are always legal if the police obtain consent for the search—as long as that consent is voluntary and not coerced. You'd be surprised how many people with illegal drugs in the trunk of their car consent to letting the police search the trunk. Consent searches happen all the time, and police find evidence all the time.

Suggested Reading

◊ Brigham City v. Stuart.

◊ Illinois v. Gates.

◊ Terry v. Ohio.

Questions to Consider

↗ Do you agree with the Supreme Court that people generally have a much lower expectation of privacy in their cars?

↗ Should the ability of police to stop and frisk be expanded, or should it be limited?

THE SHRINKING WARRANT REQUIREMENT

I n the early morning hours of July 23, 2000, police were called to a home in Brigham City, Utah, by neighbors who reported a loud and raucous party. As the officers approached the rear of the home, they heard shouting and saw two juveniles drinking beer in the back yard. They also saw, through a screen door and windows, an altercation inside. Four adults were trying to restrain a juvenile, who eventually broke free, swung a fist, and hit one of the adults in the face. The man who was hit spit blood into a sink. The other adults tried to gain control, pushing the juvenile up against a refrigerator so hard that it moved across the floor. At that point, one of the police officers opened the screen door and announced his presence. Nobody could hear him, so although he didn't have a warrant, he stepped inside the kitchen and tried again. As people gradually realized the police were there, the fighting stopped. Several people inside the home were arrested and charged with various crimes, including intoxication and disorderly conduct. Lawyers for the arrestees filed motions to suppress all of the evidence seized inside the home, arguing that the warrantless police entry was an unconstitutional search, in violation of the Fourth Amendment. The constitutionality of the police behavior that night in Brigham City went all the way up to the U.S. Supreme Court. So what do you think? Was it unconstitutional for the police to enter that home without a warrant?

In this second half of our two-part Fourth Amendment lesson, we'll learn the answer to this question. We'll also learn what it takes to get a search warrant, when the police can act with probable cause but without a warrant, and what kinds of searches can be conducted even without probable cause as long as they're reasonable. Before we do those things, however, let's first talk a little bit about how the Fourth Amendment gets enforced.

Recall the text of the Fourth Amendment: "The right of the people to be secure in their persons, houses, papers, and effects, against unreasonable searches and seizures, shall not be violated. And no Warrants shall issue, but upon probable cause, supported by oath or affirmation, and particularly describing the place to be searched, and the persons or things to be seized." The first half of the Amendment, which states that all searches and seizures must be reasonable, is called the "reasonableness clause." The second half, known as the "warrant clause," sets out several requirements for a valid warrant. But the Fourth Amendment doesn't actually say that all searches—or even most—require a warrant. It's almost as if the two parts of the Amendment are unrelated to each other. Was that an oversight by the framers?

Probably not. The language the framers wrote into the Fourth Amendment reflected their reality. At the time the Amendment was written, most government searches were based on warrants. There were no professional police forces in the late 1700s. London created the first police department in 1829, and the idea spread to the United States over the next few decades. And the courts hadn't yet developed the doctrine of "qualified immunity," which today protects police against most civil lawsuits unless they act with gross negligence, or worse. So at the time of the framing, law enforcement officers, such as local sheriffs, usually would get a warrant just to protect themselves from a lawsuit for trespassing on the property of the person searched. The warrant was important because it provided a defense to such lawsuits, ensuring that the sheriff wouldn't get stuck paying damages. That's probably the main reason why the Fourth Amendment doesn't say that warrants are required, because the framers thought that almost all searches would be based on warrants anyway. This same history also helps to explain another oddity of the Fourth Amendment: Nowhere in the text does it say what the remedy should be for a violation, of either the reasonableness clause or the warrant clause. The Framers probably figured that the remedy would be a civil lawsuit for damages, because that was the only remedy they knew. Over time, however, with the gradual rise of professional police forces, and also the creation of qualified immunity for police officers, the damages remedy gradually became more or less obsolete. Today, the likelihood of a person successfully suing a police officer for violating their Fourth Amendment rights is pretty close to zero. The only exception would be lawsuits challenging police use of excessive force, which have grown significantly in both number and dollar amounts in modern times.

If civil lawsuits can no longer be relied upon to enforce the Fourth Amendment, what other remedies might be available? One alternative might be injunctions: Court orders mandating the police to change their behavior and comply with the Constitution. This approach has proven successful in a few rare instances where violations were based on official policies. But courts generally don't like to issue injunctions against the police, because injunctions require long-term oversight and are politically unpopular. Another option might be criminal prosecution of the offending police officer. There are specific federal crimes for violating a person's Constitutional rights, and some state-law crimes might also apply. Once again, however, outside the special context of unlawful police use of force—such as the police beating of black motorist Rodney King in Los Angeles in 1991, which was caught on video and eventually led to the federal criminal convictions of several police officers—prosecutions are rare. And even when charges are filed, they're rarely successful, because, as you can imagine, juries tend to support police officers more often than the bad guys they're trying to catch.

One of the most promising ways to enforce the Fourth Amendment is through administrative review and internal police agency discipline. This remedy, at least in theory, should go hand in hand with the rise of modern professional police departments. But as anyone who watches cop shows on TV knows, there can be big problems with the police policing themselves. Independent police review boards can help, and most problems can be resolved if the political will exists. Nevertheless, internal remedies will probably always be a second-best option.

For all these reasons, the primary legal remedy for Fourth Amendment violations today—and for the past 100 years or so—is the exclusionary rule. The exclusionary rule provides that evidence searched for, or seized, in violation of the Fourth Amendment must be excluded from all criminal prosecutions against the person whose rights were violated. The theory behind the rule is that suppressing the evidence deprives the police of any benefit from the illegal search or seizure, and thus deters them from committing it in the first place. The rule was established for federal criminal cases by the Supreme Court in the 1914 decision of *Weeks v. United States*, and was extended to state criminal cases by the 1961 decision in *Mapp v. Ohio*. The rule has important exceptions, such as for some good faith violations by the police, or when the evidence inevitably would've been found anyway. But as a general matter, we can say that whenever the police violate the Fourth Amendment, and find evidence of a crime, that evidence can't be used to convict the person whose Fourth Amendment rights were infringed.

So that's how the Fourth Amendment mostly gets enforced. The police conduct a search, either with or without a warrant. They find evidence of a crime. Someone gets arrested and charged with the crime. Then the defendant's lawyer claims the search was unconstitutional. And if the courts agree, the evidence gets kicked out. As Judge Cardozo once put it, "The criminal is to go free because the constable has blundered." Notice, by the way, that the only people who ever benefit directly from the exclusionary rule are criminals, because if the police don't find any evidence of a crime, then there's nothing to exclude. Moreover, if the police don't really care about obtaining a criminal conviction—if, for example, the police only want to seize the drugs and get the drug dealers to move along—then the exclusionary rule is no deterrent to an illegal search or seizure. This makes the exclusionary rule seem like something less than an ideal remedy. But it's the best remedy we've got, and hopefully it serves the interests of all of us, by encouraging the police to be more careful about the Fourth Amendment.

So what, exactly, does the Fourth Amendment require? For most of the 20th Century, the Supreme Court consistently expressed the view that, subject only to a few narrow exceptions, all searches conducted without a warrant issued in advance by a judge or magistrate, are presumed to be unreasonable, and hence violate the Fourth Amendment. As Justice Robert Jackson once explained: "The point of the Fourth Amendment, which often is not grasped by zealous officers, is not that it denies law enforcement the support of the usual inferences which reasonable men may draw from evidence. Its protection consists in requiring that those inferences be drawn by a neutral and detached magistrate instead of being judged by the officer engaged in the often competitive enterprise of ferreting out crime."

Assuming that a warrant is required in order for a search to be constitutional—as the Court used to say the Fourth Amendment presumed—then what are the requirements for a valid warrant? There are several. First, the officer who presents the warrant application to the judge or magistrate must swear, by oath or affirmation, the truth of whatever facts are stated in the application. Second, those facts must provide enough information for the magistrate to make an independent decision about whether or not to issue the warrant—the magistrate can't just rely on the officer's judgment. Third, the magistrate must be "neutral and detached," which means, for example, that local governments can't pay magistrates based on how many warrants they issue. Nor can warrants be issued directly by prosecutors; in many other countries, that's the norm, but in America, it would violate the neutrality principle. Fourth, the warrant itself must be drafted to specifically describe what's to be searched for, and where the search will occur, although these requirements aren't as rigid as they seem. For example, it's fine for the warrant to contain catch-all terms like "any other evidence of the crime under investigation." And the Supreme Court has even upheld future warrants, meaning warrants based on the belief that evidence will be at a particular place in the future, although it's not there at the time of the warrant application.

There are also rules for the proper execution of a warrant, most notably, that police must "knock and announce" their presence before trying to enter a home or other premises. The Supreme Court has held that entering without knocking and announcing is allowed only under special circumstances, such as when the police "reasonably suspect" it would be dangerous or futile to do so, or that evidence is being destroyed inside. Also, the USA Patriot Act, enacted after the 9/11 attacks, authorizes special "sneak and peek" warrants, meaning the police can search while you're away from home and tell you about it later.

Probably the most important requirement for a warrant to comply with the Fourth Amendment is that it must be based on "probable cause." What's probable cause? Well, to be honest, it's a pretty vague standard.

In the leading case of *Illinois v. Gates*, the Supreme Court tried to define probable cause. Here's what happened. Police in Bloomingdale, a suburb of Chicago, got an anonymous letter reporting that a local couple, Sue and Lance Gates, were drug dealers. The letter said Sue drives their car down to Florida alone, drops it off there to have the trunk loaded up with drugs, and flies back home. Then Lance flies to Florida, picks up the car, and drives it back to Chicago. The letter also said the Gates currently had more than $100,000 worth of drugs in their home. The police did a little research, and found that Lance Gates had reserved a flight to West Palm Beach. When he arrived there, he took a cab to a hotel, where he checked into a room that had already been rented by a "Susan Gates." The next morning, Lance Gates and a woman—presumably Susan—left together in a car with Illinois plates, heading north. The license plate number belonged to the Gates'. Armed with this information, the police went to a local magistrate and got a search warrant for the Gates's car and home. The police waited until the Gates arrived home, then searched the car, where they found 350 pounds of marijuana. The home also contained more marijuana, plus weapons and other evidence.

Was the search legal under the Fourth Amendment? Did the police have probable cause to get the warrant? The Supreme Court said yes. The big problem in *Gates* was that the letter was anonymous. If the letter had been signed by a bishop or even by any known, law-abiding citizen, the case would be easy, because the police would have grounds to believe that the letter was telling the truth. But an anonymous letter is different. Who knows if the author has accurate information? Or if they're just trying to get someone they don't like in trouble with the cops?

In *Gates*, the police didn't just rely on the letter. They also checked out some of the details in the letter, to see if they could be verified. True, there's nothing criminal about taking separate trips to Florida, then driving back to Chicago the very next day. Also, the Gates's trip to Florida didn't happen exactly the way the letter said it would. Nevertheless, the Court found probable cause to be satisfied. Here's what they said: "Probable cause is a fluid concept—turning on the assessment of probabilities in particular factual contexts—not readily, or even usefully, reduced to a neat set of legal rules...The task of the issuing magistrate is simply to make a practical, common-sense decision whether, given all the circumstances set forth in the affidavit before him, ...there is a fair probability that contraband or evidence of a crime will be found..." Later, in a footnote, the Court added: "Probable cause requires only a probability or substantial chance of criminal activity, not an actual showing of such activity."

So there it is. Probable cause doesn't actually mean that a crime is probable. It means there's a "fair probability," or a "substantial chance," of a crime. As you can probably guess, given that low standard, magistrates approve most warrant applications—perhaps as many as 90 or 95% of them. Does that mean the magistrate's just a rubber stamp? Well, yes, but that doesn't mean the requirement is useless. Police must go through the hassle of writing up the warrant application and then appearing, either in person or these days, electronically—in front of the magistrate. And they're not going to want to do all that extra work unless they're pretty sure they've got enough information to meet the probable cause standard. In short, even if police almost always make it over the hurdle of the warrant application, the mere presence of that hurdle probably does some good.

Now, we've already seen that, historically, warrants were generally presumed to be required before police can conduct a search or seizure. So when are warrants not necessary? What are the exceptions to the warrant requirement?

One exception is pretty obvious. Police don't need to get a warrant when the circumstances are such that it would be crazy to make them stop and go get one. The classic example is this: A police officer sees someone rob a bank. The cop starts chasing the robber, in what we call "hot pursuit." Then the robber darts into a home. Should the police officer have to give up the chase, and go try to get a warrant, before entering the home? Of course not. That would be crazy. We call this kind of situation exigent circumstances. The police must have probable cause to justify the search or seizure, but they don't need to wait for a warrant. The other classic example of exigency is when the police knock on someone's door, and identify themselves as the police, only to hear excited voices inside saying, "Oh no! It's the cops, flush the drugs!" And perhaps the sound of a toilet flushing. In that kind of situation, it's equally crazy to make the police wait for a warrant. They can bust right in, to preserve the evidence that's being destroyed. And, by the way, whenever the police have the legal right to rush into a home without waiting, either for a warrant or for the person inside to answer the door, they can do so with force, including enough force to break the door down, if necessary.

Another exception to the warrant requirement is when the police see evidence in "plain view," and also can seize the evidence from a place they're legally allowed to be. If you invite a police officer into your home, and the officer sees illegal drugs on your kitchen table, they don't need a warrant to seize the drugs. If the officer's walking down the street and sees your illegal drugs through an open window, that's not a Fourth Amendment violation, but then the police still need to get a warrant if they want to enter the house and seize the drugs. Of course, if they see you grab the drugs and start flushing them down the toilet, then they don't need a warrant to rush into the house because that would be exigent circumstances.

Cars are a big exception to the warrant requirement. So big that my first piece of legal advice to a drug dealer would be, never keep the drugs in your car. The Court has recognized the "automobile exception" for two different reasons. First, cars are mobile, so they create their own exigency. Second, people have a lower expectation of privacy in their cars than in their homes and most other places. After all, cars have glass windows and people can see inside them easily, at least if they're not super-tinted—which by the way is illegal in many states. And cars also get into accidents, which means your privacy might disappear without warning. Under the automobile exception, all the police need to search a car is probable cause to believe there's criminal evidence somewhere inside the car. Then they can search the entire car without a warrant, including the glove compartment, the trunk, and even any containers in the car, such as backpacks or suitcases. The only limit is they can't search places within the car where probable cause would be lacking. So, for example, if the police have probable cause that you're carrying a stolen big-screen TV in your car, they can't look in the glove compartment, unless your car has a really big glove compartment.

By the way, even if the police don't have probable cause, they still might be able to search your car if the car needs to be towed and impounded for any reason, including because it broke down in an unsafe spot along the side of the road. Then the police can do an "inventory search," to make sure that all your stuff is properly accounted for and doesn't get stolen. And if the police happen to find your drugs during such an inventory search, you're out of luck.

One last exception to the warrant requirement is the "search incident to arrest." Whenever the police arrest someone, based on probable cause that the person committed a crime, the police can search that person automatically, without a warrant, to make sure they don't have a weapon. And the police can seize any other evidence they find during the search. If the arrest occurs in a building, police also get to search all places within reach of the person, so they can't grab a weapon. And police can look into nearby rooms and closets, to check for other people who might try to attack them. Finally, if a person happens to be in a car when they're arrested, that provides the police with two new reasons to search the car. First, they can search the car for a weapon, but only while the arrestee is still within reach of the car. Second, even after the arrestee's been put in the back of the police car, the police can go back and search the car if there's reason to think evidence of the crime of arrest might be found there. All of these searches flow naturally from the fact of the arrest.

So far, we've talked about searches based on warrants, and searches based on probable cause but without a warrant. But there's one more important subject we still need to discuss, and that's searches without either probable cause or a warrant. Remember that back in the 1960s, the Supreme Court often said there's a presumption that searches without a warrant are unreasonable. But this gradually changed, especially as the Court recognized more and more exceptions to the warrant requirement. Nowadays, the Court is much more likely to say that the true touchstone of the Fourth Amendment is reasonableness.

In an ever-growing number of situations, warrants are no longer presumptively required. Instead, police can search without a warrant and even without probable cause, as long as they behave reasonably. In fact, the exceptions to the warrant requirement have become so numerous that it wouldn't be much of a stretch to say that, today, the last bastion of the warrant requirement is the home. Except for exigent circumstances, there still aren't too many ways for police to get inside a home without a warrant. Almost everywhere else, however, the exceptions have swallowed the rule.

The biggest change occurred in 1968, when the Supreme Court decided *Terry v. Ohio*. *Terry* is the case that gave police the authority to stop a person on the street and ask them questions, based on reasonable suspicion of criminal activity, and also to frisk the person based on reasonable suspicion that they might be armed and dangerous. No probable cause required, let alone a warrant. Stop-and-frisk was specifically designed to help police intervene before a crime is actually committed. It's a big part of what I call "proactive policing."

Terry changed the rules of the Fourth Amendment in the interest of public safety. And *Terry* probably did make us safer. But at what cost? Maybe the most significant cost is that *Terry*'s burden falls disproportionately on certain subsets of the population: racial and ethnic minorities, the poor, the young, and all those who look different and scary. That's because *Terry* authorizes police action on barely more than a hunch about whether a person might be up to no good. And that kind of police discretion almost inevitably leads to snap judgments based on appearances rather than hard evidence. Studies have shown that police, both white and African-American, stop-and-frisk blacks much more often than whites. On the highways, this has become so common that it's often referred to, derisively, as the crime of "driving while black." All of this can lead to resentment and an unwillingness to trust the police in many communities of color.

A search can also be based solely on reasonableness when it serves a special governmental need that's different from catching criminals. So, for example, searches of school lockers can be based on reasonable suspicion rather than probable cause, because it's for the purpose of school discipline. Same thing for searching the desks of government employees, based on the need for an effective workplace, and drug testing of pilots and train engineers, based on public safety. Drunk-driving roadblocks and border searches fall into the same category.

Finally, searches are always legal if the police obtain consent for the search, as long as that consent is voluntary and not coerced. You'd be amazed how many people with illegal drugs in the trunk of their car consent to letting the police search the trunk. Do they really think that if they say yes, the police will say, "Okay, in that case I trust you, and I don't need to see inside the trunk?" Or that if they say no, the police will beat them up and then search the trunk anyway? I have no idea. But consent searches happen all the time, and police find evidence all the time.

Well, we're almost out of time, and I bet you're wondering what did the Supreme Court decide about that wild night in Brigham City, Utah? Here's the answer: The Court held that the police properly entered the home without a warrant, because they weren't doing it to catch criminals, they were trying to help someone who'd just been injured in a fight. And this was reasonable. The Court said it's basically like firefighters rushing into a burning home. They don't need a warrant either, because it's an emergency. The case of *Brigham City v. Stuart* was the first time the Court upheld a police entry into a home based solely on reasonableness, without a warrant or probable cause of a crime. It's true that the juvenile did throw a punch, which probably was a crime, but the Court never mentioned that in its opinion. The Court simply held that the situation justified reasonable police intervention to protect public safety.

Is this the beginning of the end for the last bastion of the warrant requirement? If police can enter a home without a warrant to help someone who's just been injured, can they also rush in to arrest someone who's about to commit a violent crime, because that crime will probably injure someone? That's a really good question, and only time can tell us the answer.

THE FIFTH AMENDMENT PRIVILEGE

The Fifth Amendment provides, in relevant part: "No person … shall be compelled to be a witness against himself." This is known as the privilege against compelled self-incrimination, and it's a core aspect of the Bill of Rights. This lecture explores the history behind the privilege against compelled self-incrimination, the meaning of the constitutional text, and the various kinds of legal protection the privilege provides.

HISTORY AND PURPOSE

✶ The privilege against compelled self-incrimination was written into the Fifth Amendment in direct response to the history of English criminal prosecutions for sedition and for heresy. In the late 16th and early 17th centuries, suspected heretics were forced to swear an oath to answer truthfully, and then asked about their religious beliefs and the identities of their fellow believers. Later, political dissidents faced the same kind of treatment.

✶ The Fifth Amendment privilege was designed to end these kinds of abuses at the hands of government officials. As a Puritan leader once put it, forcing a man to testify against himself is like putting "the conscience upon the rack." But exactly how far does the privilege go? What's the scope of the constitutional right to remain silent in the face of a criminal accusation? That's a much harder question to answer.

✶ In 1807, the Supreme Court presided over a criminal case against Aaron Burr, the former vice president and noted duelist, for conspiracy and treason. Allegedly, Burr was part of a conspiracy to take over part of the American West. During a grand jury hearing, a witness was called to testify about copying a document on Burr's orders. The witness refused to testify, stating that he might incriminate himself. Chief Justice Marshall, who was presiding over the Burr case, ruled in favor of the witness.

✶ According to Marshall, whenever a witness refuses to answer a question, the presiding judge must decide whether it's possible that the answer might be incriminating. If so, it's up to the witness to decide whether or not to answer. And that right extends even to facts that, on their own, might not be incriminating, but might instead provide a link in a chain of evidence that could become incriminating.

✶ Congress and many state legislatures soon passed new statutes authorizing government officials to grant immunity from prosecution to witnesses who asserted their Fifth Amendment privilege in response to official questioning. These statutes were designed to eliminate the Fifth Amendment problem, and allow officials to obtain the testimony of the reluctant witness, by making it impossible for the witness to be incriminated by his own testimony.

LEGAL REQUIREMENTS

✶ There are four requirements that must be satisfied in order for the Fifth Amendment privilege to apply. First, the person must be under compulsion to provide the information to the government. The paradigmatic case of Fifth Amendment compulsion is when a person is called to testify, under oath, as a witness in court. The compulsion comes from the fact that, if the witness refuses, they will be held in contempt of court, and will go to jail.

✶ Another example of compulsion occurs when a suspect gets arrested for a crime, and the police try to question the suspect. The Supreme Court held, in the famous *Miranda* case, that custodial police interrogation is so inherently coercive that the Fifth Amendment requires police to provide the now-familiar *Miranda* warnings to relieve the pressure.

✶ The Court has also recognized that compulsion may be present in situations where a person's choice to assert the Fifth Amendment privilege can itself get them in big trouble. The classic example is the 1965 case *Griffin v. California*. The defendant chose not to testify, which led the prosecutor to argue during closing arguments that the defendant's decision not to testify was evidence of his guilt. The Supreme Court held that this was a violation of the Fifth Amendment, because the prosecutor imposed an impermissible penalty against Griffin for exercising his Fifth Amendment privilege.

⭐ The second requirement for application of the Fifth Amendment privilege is that the information requested by the government be incriminating. Refusal to answer can be punished only if a court can conclude, with certainty, that the information couldn't possibly be incriminating. Otherwise, the person who's being asked gets to decide.

⭐ Sometimes the refusal to answer is based on fear not of criminal prosecution, but of some other kind of legal trouble. But the Supreme Court has held that there's a constitutional distinction between criminal punishment and civil penalties. For the most part, it's up to the legislature to define whether a particular sanction is criminal or civil. The courts can exercise oversight, however, in situations where a purportedly civil statute looks more like a criminal one.

⭐ The third requirement for application of the Fifth Amendment privilege is that the person must be giving testimony; that's what it means to be a witness against yourself. In *Schmerber v. California*, the Supreme Court held that a blood sample taken from the defendant was not "testimony" for Fifth Amendment purposes. Rather, it was more like a photograph of the defendant's face, or his fingerprints.

★ The fourth requirement for application of the Fifth Amendment privilege is that it the privilege must be asserted. This requirement can best be illustrated by considering the facts of three Supreme Court cases. Rather than lying, telling the truth, or even remaining silent, a suspect or defendant must affirmatively state that he is electing not to answer the question. He must make it clear that he's asserting his rights under the Fifth Amendment.

A DELICATE BALANCE

★ What happens if the government has a compelling need for information, but the only source for that information is a person who's properly asserted his Fifth Amendment privilege? That's a big problem, and it continues to grow as the role of government in our daily lives keeps expanding—from protecting the safety of our air, water, and food, to protecting us from identity theft and terrorist attacks. The Supreme Court has addressed this problem by attempting to strike a delicate balance between the rights of the individual and the needs of society.

★ Long ago, the Supreme Court has long held that corporations can't assert the Fifth Amendment privilege in order to hide information from the government. Corporations may enjoy the right to freedom of speech under the First Amendment, but they don't have Fifth Amendment protections against compelled self-incrimination. And both companies and individuals must turn over any records the government requires them to keep and maintain on a regular basis—tax and other financial records, for example.

★ When push comes to shove, courts sometimes seem to ignore the Fifth Amendment altogether. In 1988, child welfare officials in Baltimore obtained a court order requiring an abusive mother to either produce, or reveal the location of, her young son. The officials feared that the son, who'd been missing for months, was in danger—and that the mother, who had serious psychological and drug problems, might even have killed him. The mother refused to comply, and she was jailed for contempt of court.

✴ The sanction against the mother was upheld by the Supreme Court, which ruled that the Fifth Amendment privilege cannot be invoked to avoid compliance with legal obligations that serve an important public purpose unrelated to crime control. Even though the mother would surely be charged with a crime if her son turned up dead, that outcome was secondary to the law's primary goal of protecting the child's welfare.

Suggested Reading

○ Salinas v. Texas.

○ Griffin v. California.

○ Brogan v. United States.

○ Minnesota v. Murphy.

Questions to Consider

↗ Do you agree that a person should forfeit their Fifth Amendment privilege if they don't properly assert the privilege in response to government questioning?

↗ Should corporations have the same Fifth Amendment rights as individuals to refuse to provide potentially incriminating information to the government?

THE FIFTH AMENDMENT PRIVILEGE

On a December morning in Houston, Texas, two brothers were killed by shotgun blasts inside their own house. Police recovered six shell casings at the scene. Genovevo Salinas, who'd been a guest at a party hosted by the victims the night before, was suspected of committing the murders. Police visited Salinas at his home, and he agreed to turn over his shotgun for ballistics testing. Salinas also agreed to go down to the police station for questioning. Salinas was not placed under arrest, so he didn't have to receive the *Miranda* warnings, that famous recitation of rights you probably remember from the police dramas on TV. The police interview lasted one hour, and Salinas answered most of the questions. But then the interviewer asked Salinas if his shotgun "would match the shells recovered at the scene of the murder." Salinas didn't answer. Instead, he just tensed up, looked down at the floor, shuffled his feet, and bit his lip. Salinas was later arrested and charged with two counts of murder. At trial, Salinas chose not to testify. The prosecution introduced, as evidence of Salinas's guilt, his anxious silence in response to the question about the shotgun shells. Salinas was convicted.

The Fifth Amendment to the United States Constitution provides, in relevant part: "No person…shall be compelled to be a witness against himself." We call this the "privilege against compelled self-incrimination," and it's a core aspect of the Bill of Rights. Did the prosecutor's use of Genovevo Salinas's silence and obvious discomfort during that police interview as evidence to convict Salinas of murder, violate his Fifth Amendment privilege?

In this lecture, we'll explore this question. We'll learn about the history behind the Fifth Amendment privilege against compelled self-incrimination, the meaning of the constitutional text, and the various kinds of legal protection the privilege provides. We'll see how the Fifth Amendment privilege actually works, both in and out of court. And we'll discuss how, over time, the privilege has become subject to significant compromises that allow government investigators to obtain the information they need.

The privilege against compelled self-incrimination was written into the Fifth Amendment in direct response to the history of English criminal prosecutions for sedition and for heresy. In the late 16th and early 17th centuries, the ecclesiastical Court of High Commission in England ordered suspected heretics to swear an oath to answer truthfully, then asked them about their religious beliefs and the identities of their fellow believers. Later, political dissidents faced the same kind of treatment. These two kinds of cases obviously held special meaning for the American colonists, many of whom came here for either religious or political reasons. The Fifth Amendment privilege was designed to end these kinds of abuses at the hands of government officials. As a Puritan leader once put it, forcing a man to testify against himself is like putting "the conscience upon the rack." But exactly how far does the privilege go? What's the scope of the constitutional right to remain silent in the face of a criminal accusation? That's a much harder question to answer.

In 1807, Chief Justice John Marshall wrote an opinion in the conspiracy and treason case against Aaron Burr. Yes, the same Aaron Burr who served as Thomas Jefferson's Vice President, and who, during his last year in office, killed Alexander Hamilton in a duel. The criminal case against Aaron Burr wasn't about that, however; he was never tried for Hamilton's death. Instead, it was about an alleged conspiracy to take over part of the western lands of the United States for himself and a few of his buddies. During a grand jury hearing, a witness was called to testify about copying a document on Burr's orders. The witness refused to testify because the answer might incriminate himself.

Chief Justice Marshall, who was presiding over the Burr case, due to its enormous national significance, ruled in favor of the witness. According to Marshall, whenever a witness refuses to answer a question, the court must decide whether it's possible that the answer might be incriminating. If that's even a possibility, then it's up to the witness alone whether or not to answer. And that right extends even to facts that, on their own, might not be incriminating but that might provide a link in a chain of evidence that could become incriminating.

By the way, Aaron Burr eventually was acquitted of the conspiracy and treason charges. And Thomas Jefferson, who by that time had become Burr's sworn enemy, tried to get Chief Justice Marshall impeached over it. I guess politics has always been a contact sport.

After the Burr case, Congress and many state legislatures passed new statutes authorizing government officials to grant immunity from prosecution to witnesses who asserted their Fifth Amendment privilege in response to official questioning. These immunity statutes were designed to eliminate the Fifth Amendment problem, and allow officials to obtain the testimony of the reluctant witness, by making it impossible for the witness to be incriminated by their own testimony.

In the 1892 case of *Counselman v. Hitchcock*, the Supreme Court reviewed one of these immunity statutes and found it unconstitutional. The statute provided that no evidence given by a witness in a judicial proceeding could be used against him in a later criminal case. The Court found this kind of immunity insufficient to vindicate the Fifth Amendment privilege, because even if the evidence couldn't be used against the witness directly, it could still lead the government to other evidence that could be used. According to the Court, a valid immunity statute "must afford absolute immunity against future prosecution for the offense to which the question relates." In other words, immunity that covers only the use of specific evidence provided by a witness isn't good enough. It has to be immunity that covers the entire act or transaction that's the subject of the witness's testimony.

Congress almost immediately amended most of the federal immunity statutes to provide this broader kind of transactional immunity. And the Court upheld these new statutes. In *Brown v. Walker*, decided in 1896, the Court explained that extending Counselman's rule to invalidate such transactional immunity statutes would go too far: "Every good citizen is bound to aid in the enforcement of the law, and has no right to permit himself, under the pretext of shielding his own good name, to be made the tool of others, who are desirous of seeking shelter behind his privilege."

So there you have it: In the space of four short years, the Court issued two decisions, *Counselman v. Hitchcock* and *Brown v. Walker*, that still frame the debate over the scope of the privilege. The Fifth Amendment sets up a direct conflict between the rights of the individual and the interests of society. Especially in light of our history, and our deep commitment to individual liberty, we don't want to let the government force someone to reveal their private secrets and thereby become the instrument of their own downfall. But at the same time, we recognize that the government often has a legitimate, even compelling need for information, so that laws can be enforced and society can be protected from harm. The Fifth Amendment privilege requires us to balance these two fundamental but competing goals against each another. And that means Fifth Amendment law can get pretty messy.

The specific balance struck by the *Counselman* and *Brown v. Walker* cases, incidentally, was later altered by the 1972 decision in *Kastigar v. United States*.

There, the federal statute under review provided immunity against both direct and indirect, or derivative, use of a witness's testimony. The witnesses in question, who were asked about fraudulent medical deferments to avoid the Vietnam-era military draft, refused to answer, arguing that they should receive full transactional immunity against any criminal prosecution for violating the selective service laws. The Supreme Court disagreed. According to the Court, there's no reason to bar the government from prosecuting the witnesses altogether. For example, what if the government found independent evidence against them, that had no connection at all with their own testimony? Why should they get a blanket amnesty from prosecution? That's not what the Fifth Amendment privilege requires.

So, what does the Fifth Amendment privilege require? There are four requirements that must be satisfied, in order for the privilege to apply. First, the person must be under compulsion to provide the information to the government. The paradigmatic case of Fifth Amendment compulsion is when a person is called to testify, under oath, as a witness in court. The compulsion comes from the fact that, if the witness refuses, they will be held in contempt of court and will go to jail. Same thing for legislative or administrative hearings, where similar legal sanctions for noncooperation can apply. Another example of compulsion occurs when a suspect gets arrested for a crime, and the police try to question the suspect. The Supreme Court held, in the famous *Miranda* case, that custodial police interrogation is so inherently coercive that the Fifth Amendment requires the police to provide the now-familiar *Miranda* warnings to relieve the pressure. We'll discuss *Miranda*, and the law governing police interrogations in general, in greater detail in the future.

The Court has also recognized that compulsion may be present in situations where a person's choice to assert the Fifth Amendment privilege can itself get them in big trouble. The classic example is the 1965 case of *Griffin v. California*. Griffin was on trial for a crime, and chose not to testify on his own behalf. The prosecutor then told the jury during the closing arguments, that the defendant's failure to testify was evidence of his guilt. Otherwise, he would have taken the stand to explain what happened. The Supreme Court held this was a violation of the Fifth Amendment, because the prosecutor imposed an impermissible penalty against Griffin for exercising his Fifth Amendment privilege not to testify. For the same reason, a prosecutor can't even call the defendant to the witness stand in a criminal case and make him assert his Fifth Amendment privilege in open court, because the jury will inevitably hold that assertion against him. And in all criminal cases, the defendant is legally entitled to have the judge instruct the jury that his silence is not supposed to be used as evidence of his guilt. But it's really a bad idea for a defense lawyer to ask the judge to give such an instruction, because the practical effect would be to focus the jury's attention on the fact that the defendant didn't testify. It's called the "Pink Elephant" effect: If you tell someone not to think about pink elephants, that's exactly what they'll do!

The second requirement for the Fifth Amendment privilege is that the information requested by the government must be incriminating. Now, as we've already seen, to a certain extent, this is up to the person who's being asked for the information. The refusal to answer can be punished only if a court can conclude, with certainty, that the requested information couldn't possibly be incriminating. Otherwise, the person who's being asked gets to make that call.

Sometimes the refusal to answer is based not on a fear of being prosecuted, but instead on a fear of getting into some other kind of legal trouble. What kind of legal trouble counts as incrimination under the Fifth Amendment? The Supreme Court has held that there's a constitutional distinction between criminal punishment and civil penalties. And, for the most part, it's up to the legislature to define whether a particular legal sanction is criminal or civil. The courts can exercise some oversight, in situations where a supposedly civil penalty becomes too severe, or where the purpose of the statute seems too closely aligned with the traditional purposes of criminal punishment. But in general, if the legislature says it's a civil sanction, then it's a civil sanction. Which means that the Fifth Amendment privilege doesn't apply, and the person being questioned must give up the information, even if doing so might subject them to a serious civil penalty. Moreover, it's also not enough to invoke the Fifth Amendment that a person fears losing their job, or being excluded from a club or organization, or becoming ineligible for a passport, or suffering severe social stigma—none of these count as incrimination under the Fifth Amendment.

How big does the risk of incrimination need to be, in order for the Fifth Amendment's protection to kick in? Here, the Supreme Court has waffled a bit over the years. In *Brown v. Walker*, the Court said that "the danger...must be real and appreciable...not a danger of an imaginary and unsubstantial character." In 1951, in *Hoffman v. United States*, the Court seemingly took a more lenient view: "To sustain the privilege, it need only be evident from the implications of the question, in the setting in which it is asked, that a responsive answer to the question or an explanation of why it cannot be answered might be dangerous because injurious disclosure could result." And in 2004, in the *Hiibel* case, the Court quoted from both *Brown v. Walker* and *Hoffman v. United States*, leaving the rule about as clear as mud.

Hiibel was an interesting case on the facts. A sheriff's deputy in Humboldt County, Nevada, received a report that a man in a red-and-silver GMC pickup truck had assaulted a woman inside the truck. The deputy found such a truck parked on the side of the road, with a woman sitting inside and a man standing alongside, smoking a cigarette. The deputy also noticed skid marks, indicating the truck had come to a sudden stop. The deputy asked the man if he had any identification. The request was based on a Nevada statute requiring a person to identify himself to the police whenever there's reasonable suspicion that the person has committed, or is committing, or is about to commit a crime. Hiibel refused to give his name or provide any ID, and he was convicted of obstruction of justice. On appeal, Hiibel claimed that the Nevada identification statute violated the Fifth Amendment. But the Supreme Court disagreed, and affirmed the conviction. According to the Court, Hiibel couldn't possibly incriminate himself simply by providing his name to the sheriff, although the Court acknowledged that the answer might be different in some future case where a person's name might provide the police with a "link in the chain of evidence needed to convict the individual of a separate offense."

The third requirement for application of the Fifth Amendment privilege is that the person must be giving testimony. That's what it means to be a witness against yourself. So, in the famous 1966 case of *Schmerber v. California*, a person was suspected of drunk driving, and the police got a court order to take a sample of the suspect's blood, without the suspect's consent, to check the blood-alcohol content. The Court in *Schmerber* held this was not the same thing as testimony. Rather, it was more like taking a photograph of your face, or taking your fingerprints, so the Fifth Amendment wasn't implicated.

The line between physical characteristics like your face, fingerprints, or even blood, and testimonial evidence is not always so clear. What if the government orders you to provide your signature, which is necessary to get a foreign bank to turn over your account records, which in turn will be used to convict you of a crime? Is that a Fifth Amendment violation? In *Doe v. United States*, decided in 1988, the Supreme Court said no, because signing a form is not the same thing as disclosing incriminating information. Justice Stevens dissented, arguing that forcing someone to sign a form is still requiring them to use their mind, which makes it different from taking their fingerprints or their blood. Stevens also said the case was different from forcing a suspect to provide the government with the keys to a safe, which doesn't reveal the contents of the suspect's mind. But his view did not prevail.

The majority's decision in the *Doe* case, that the suspect can be forced to sign a form, also reflects the Court's current view of the theory behind the Fifth Amendment privilege. Namely, that the privilege was designed to break the so-called cruel trilemma. The cruel trilemma, meaning a dilemma with three parts instead of two, refers to the kind of situation that prevailed in the days of the High Commission. A witness gets put on the stand, takes an oath, and then is asked, essentially, "Did you commit the crime?" If he answers yes, then he's guilty. If he answers no, then he's told a lie under oath and he's guilty of perjury. If he refuses to answer, then he's held in contempt of court. No matter which way he chooses to respond, he's guilty of a crime. The Fifth Amendment privilege is supposed to provide a safe way out of the cruel trilemma.

But in *Doe*, there's no cruel trilemma, because there's no way for the suspect to lie. He either provides his signature, or he doesn't. Same thing with the blood sample in *Schmerber*. These just aren't cruel trilemma cases. And, under the prevailing view, that means they can't be violations of the Fifth Amendment, either. But wait a minute, couldn't the suspect in *Doe* have signed a false name? Isn't that basically the same thing as telling a lie? Hmm.

Okay, so what about this case: A suspect by the name of Muniz gets arrested for drunk driving. At the police station, Muniz is asked a series of questions: name, address, height, weight, eye color, date of birth, current age, and the date of his sixth birthday. Why would the police ask that question? Of course, they asked it to see if Muniz could mentally calculate the date, which would help prove whether or not he was drunk. Muniz responded that he couldn't remember the date of his sixth birthday, thus failing the idiot test, and his response, along with his slurred speech, was used as evidence at his criminal trial.

What do you think? Was the Fifth Amendment violated in *Muniz*? By five to four, the Supreme Court said yes. There was no single majority opinion, but the general view seemed to be that answering the sixth birthday question required Muniz to use his mind, which made his answer testimonial. On the other hand, most of the Justices in the majority agreed that it was fine for the prosecutor to use the suspect's slurred speech as evidence of his guilt, because that was a mere physical characteristic, same as a fingerprint or a blood sample. The dissenters pointed out that police make suspected drunk drivers do all kinds of idiot tests that require use of the mind, like walking a straight line, or balancing on one leg. Why isn't that a violation of the Fifth Amendment? The majority didn't even try to answer that question.

The fourth and final requirement for the Fifth Amendment privilege is that it must be asserted. This requirement can best be illustrated by considering the facts of three Supreme Court cases.

Case number one: In *Minnesota v. Murphy*, a convicted probationer was required by state law to participate in a sex-offender treatment program, to meet regularly with his probation officer, and to be completely truthful with the probation officer. Murphy revealed in confidence to his treatment counselor that he'd committed a previous rape and murder, and the counselor tipped off the probation officer. The probation officer subsequently asked Murphy about the prior crimes, and Murphy again admitted his guilt. The admission to the probation officer was used as evidence to convict Murphy of those crimes. Murphy argued that this violated the Fifth Amendment, because he was compelled to meet with the probation officer and to answer his questions truthfully. But the Supreme Court disagreed, stating, "A witness confronted with questions that the government should reasonably expect to elicit incriminating evidence ordinarily must assert the privilege, rather than answer, if he desires not to incriminate himself." In other words, when the probation officer asked Murphy about his past crimes, Murphy made the wrong choice. Instead of telling the truth, Murphy should have said, "Sorry, sir, but I choose not to answer that question."

Case number two: In *Brogan v. United States*, a union official was suspected of taking bribes from the company to sell out the union. Federal agents came to Brogan's house and asked him if he took bribes. Brogan said, "No." He was later arrested and charged with both the bribery crime, and also the separate crime of making a false statement to a government official. Brogan argued this was a violation of the Fifth Amendment, because the federal agents were trying to force him to admit his guilt. But the Supreme Court disagreed, stating: "Neither the text nor the spirit of the Fifth Amendment confers a privilege to lie. Proper invocation of the Fifth Amendment privilege…allows a witness to remain silent, but not to swear falsely." In other words, when the federal agents asked Brogan about the bribes, Brogan made the wrong choice. Instead of lying, Brogan should have said, "Sorry sir, but I choose not to answer that question."

Case number three: *Salinas v. Texas*. As we discussed at the beginning of this lesson, Salinas was asked by the police whether there was physical evidence linking him to a double murder. Salinas remained silent, although his body language indicated he was uncomfortable with the question. He was later arrested, and his silence and discomfort were used as evidence to convict him of the murders. Salinas argued that this was a violation of the Fifth Amendment, because he reacted the way he did only because the police were trying to make him admit his guilt. What do you think the Supreme Court said? By now, you may have figured out the answer. The Court rejected Salinas's Fifth Amendment claim, stating: "Petitioner's Fifth Amendment claim fails because he did not expressly invoke the privilege against self-incrimination in response to the officer's question. Although no ritualistic formula is necessary in order to invoke the privilege, a witness does not do so by simply standing mute." In other words, Salinas must lose because, like Murphy and Brogan, he made the wrong choice. Instead of just sitting there, silently squirming in his chair, Salinas should have said, "Sorry sir, but I choose not to answer that question."

Does this seem fair? Do you think Murphy, or Brogan, or Salinas really understood what they were supposed to do, when faced with a government official asking them if they'd committed a serious crime? Unlike a witness who testifies in court, or in front of a Congressional committee, these guys didn't have lawyers nearby to them legal advice. According to the Supreme Court, however, that doesn't matter. In Brogan, for example, the Court described as implausible the contention that people generally don't know they have a Fifth Amendment privilege they can assert. In any event, that's the governing rule, when it comes to the Fifth Amendment privilege: Assert the privilege, or it's gone. Don't tell the damning truth, as in Murphy, don't tell a damned lie, as in Brogan, and don't just sit there mute, as in Salinas. Speak up, and tell the inquiring government official that you don't want to answer the question. Make it clear that it's because you're asserting your rights under the Fifth Amendment. Otherwise, you will lose.

So what if the government really, really needs someone's information, and the person knows how to properly assert the Fifth Amendment privilege, and the assertion makes it impossible for the government to get the needed information? That's a big problem. And it's becoming ever bigger, as the role of government in our daily lives keeps expanding from protecting the safety of our air and our water and our food, to protecting us from identity theft and cybercrimes, to protecting us from terrorist attacks. And that's why the Supreme Court wants to maintain a delicate balance between the Fifth Amendment rights of the individual and the needs of society.

That's the reason why, long ago, the Supreme Court held that corporations don't get to assert the Fifth Amendment privilege to hide information from the government. Corporations may enjoy the right to freedom of speech under the First Amendment, but corporations don't have Fifth Amendment rights to be free from compelled self-incrimination. Moreover, both companies and individuals have to turn over to the government any records the government requires them to keep and maintain on a regular basis, such as tax and other financial records.

And that's also why, when push really comes to shove, courts sometimes seem to ignore the Fifth Amendment altogether. In April 1988, child welfare officials in Baltimore obtained a court order requiring an abusive mother to either produce, or reveal the location of, her young son. The officials feared that the son, who'd been missing for months, was in danger, and that the mother, who had serious psychological and drug problems, might even have killed him. The mother refused to comply, and she was jailed for contempt of court. The Supreme Court upheld the sanction, holding that the Fifth Amendment can't be invoked to avoid compliance with legal obligations that serve an important public purpose unrelated to crime control. Even though the mother would surely be charged with a crime if her son turned up dead, that was secondary to the law's primary goal of protecting the child's welfare.

Sadly, the missing child was never found. But the case stands, nevertheless, for the proposition that Fifth Amendment rights can be balanced away by the courts whenever the government's need for information becomes great enough. And when a young child's life is on the line, that's probably a good thing.

MIRANDA AND POLICE INTERROGATIONS

T he *Miranda* warnings are perhaps the most famous words in the history of American criminal justice. In this lecture, you'll learn about the historical and legal background of the Supreme Court's decision in the *Miranda* case. You'll also consider what the *Miranda* warnings mean, what purposes they serve, and how we as a society should feel about relying on police interrogations and confessions to solve serious crimes.

EVALUATING VOLUNTARINESS

⭐ To understand the historical and legal significance of *Miranda*, let's look back almost 20 years earlier to another famous case. On the afternoon of November 12, 1947, in Indianapolis, Indiana, police arrested Robert Watts, a 25-year-old black man, for assault. Shortly after the arrest, the police began to suspect that Watts was also responsible for the murder of a white woman whose body had just been discovered nearby.

⭐ For the rest of that day and for the next five days, Watts was held in solitary confinement at the county jail, with no place to sit or sleep except the floor. Each night, Watts was taken to police headquarters, where he was interrogated for hours on end. He was then returned to his barren jail cell, only to await the next round of interrogation. He was never told that he had a right to remain silent. He wasn't allowed to see his family or friends. And he had no lawyer to represent him.

✴ In the early morning hours of the sixth day in police custody, Watts finally broke down and signed a written confession. In a letter to the local chapter of the NAACP, however, Watts later said that he'd been framed, and that he'd signed the confession only because he "couldn't take it any longer" and the police "forced" him to sign it.

✴ When Watts's appeal came before the Supreme Court—where Watts was represented by Thurgood Marshall, himself a future Supreme Court justice—the Court agreed that Watt's confession had been "involuntary," and that it therefore should not have been used as evidence against him. The decision was based primarily on the Due Process Clause of the Fourteenth Amendment. Watt's conviction was reversed.

✴ The voluntariness rule recognized in Watts gave the Supreme Court the legal authority to go after the worst kinds of police abuses during pretrial interrogations. But it was never going to be a perfect solution. The Court simply couldn't keep up with the massive volume of criminal cases coming up from the lower courts, not to mention the more sophisticated psychological techniques developed by police.

A NEW APPROACH

☆ The Court had to find a new way to control police interrogation tactics before they got out of hand. Their efforts soon led them to the case of Ernesto Miranda, who had been convicted in Arizona of the brutal kidnapping and rape of an 18-year-old girl. Miranda was poor, had only an eighth-grade education, and had a history of schizophrenia and other psychological issues.

☆ After the victim picked Miranda out of a lineup, the police arrested him and subjected him to two hours of strenuous custodial interrogation. During this time, Miranda was never told he had a right to a lawyer, nor was he advised that he had a right to remain silent. He was convicted, and he took his case all the way to the Supreme Court.

☆ In *Miranda*, the Court adopted the Fifth Amendment privilege against compelled self-incrimination as the primary basis for regulating police interrogations. The key analytical move was the Court's conclusion that any suspect who is placed under arrest—and thus is in police custody—faces inherent pressure to confess. This meant that custodial police interrogations would always violate the Fifth Amendment—unless, the Court held, the police first give the suspect appropriate legal warnings, and the suspect waives his rights.

☆ The *Miranda* warnings are essentially a special form of advance protection—a prophylactic measure—designed to ensure that custodial police interrogations don't reach the point of violating the Fifth Amendment privilege against compelled self-incrimination. The warnings tell the suspect that he always remains in control. By saying the magic words "I'd like to stop now," the suspect can make the questioning stop at any time. Or, if he wishes, he can ask for the help of a lawyer, in which case the questioning also must stop. It's completely up to him.

⭐ Although *Miranda* warnings often state that the suspect the right to an attorney, that doesn't mean that he'll instantly be provided one upon request. Instead, the rule is simply that the police have to stop questioning the suspect as soon as he asks for a lawyer. In most instances, the suspect won't actually receive a lawyer until much later.

VOLUNTARINESS REVISITED

* If police officers physically assault or beat a man in order to make him confess, almost everyone would agree that that's an involuntary confession. These are the easy cases. Even in the modern context of mass terrorism, where some have argued that torture can be morally justified to save thousands of lives, no good attorneys believe that the resulting confession should be used as evidence in a court of law.

* One way of looking at voluntariness is that everything we choose to do, or not to do, is the product of a myriad of influences all around us—our genes, our family, our friends, our enemies, our education, the laws of science. From this perspective, nothing we do is ever truly voluntary.

* Now consider the opposite perspective. Even if someone puts a gun to your head and orders you to do something, you still have a choice. It's a difficult choice, of course; if you disobey the order, you take the bullet. But it's not an impossible choice, and people do make it on occasion. From this perspective, you always have a choice.

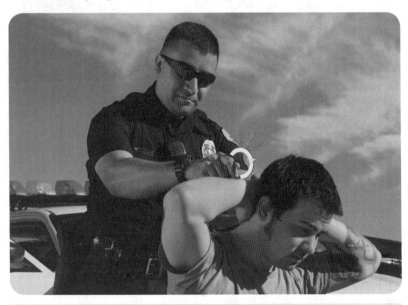

★ As these examples demonstrate, voluntariness can't be defined simply as the ability to choose, or as an exercise of free will. That's far too simplistic. Every human action involves some aspects of compulsion and some of free will. This contradiction—free will versus determinism—has been the subject of philosophical debate for millennia. It's the fundamental antinomy of the human condition.

★ From a legal perspective, we have to think about voluntariness in a different way. In *Miranda*, the Supreme Court didn't try to regulate all the strategies and psychological tricks used by the police—strategies that will surely evolve endlessly into the future. Instead, the Court established a clearer and simpler rule for police to follow.

★ If you're a police officer, all you have do is read the *Miranda* warnings and get the suspect's waiver, and then you can pretty much do whatever you want—as long as you don't cross the line into physical force or abuse. You can still lie to the suspect about the evidence against him. You can still tell him that his associates are turning on him, and that he should hurry up and spill the beans first. You can still tell him that you're his friend, and that you'll help him get more lenient treatment if he confesses.

★ How does *Miranda* protect the suspect against these kinds of psychological tactics by the police? The answer is that it doesn't—at least not directly. At any time, if the psychological pressure gets to be too much, the suspect can always say the magic words, and the police will have to leave him alone. But it's entirely up to the suspect. After he agrees to talk, and before he actually chooses to invoke his *Miranda* rights, he's fair game for the police.

★ The best empirical evidence suggests that roughly 80 percent of all suspects waive their *Miranda* rights and agree to talk to the police. This one of the main reasons why police rarely oppose *Miranda* these days. The case created a safe harbor for them. They know that if they follow the rules, they'll get their chance to persuade the suspect to confess, at least in most instances.

✳ Coercive interrogation techniques can lead to particularly unfortunate results when suspects are young, mentally ill, or simply naïve and suggestible. False confessions have shaken the criminal justice system to its core. We used to feel confident in the assumption that people who confess their own guilt are actually guilty. Now, we can't be so sure.

Suggested Reading

◌ Watts v Indiana.

◌ Miranda v. Arizona.

◌ Colorado v. Connelly.

◌ Berghuis v. Thompkins.

Questions to Consider

↗ Does *Miranda* help arrested suspects, by providing them with knowledge of their rights, or does it hurt them, by providing police with a greater opportunity to use psychological tactics to obtain confessions?

↗ Should the government be allowed to force arrested suspects—those suspected of terrorism, for example—to answer incriminating questions, if the answers would potentially save lives?

MIRANDA AND POLICE INTERROGATIONS

We begin today with perhaps the most famous words in the history of American criminal justice, words that have become an instantly recognizable part of our culture: "You have the right to remain silent. If you choose to give up this right and speak, anything you say can and will be used against you in a court of law. You have the right to an attorney, and to have an attorney present during any questioning. If you cannot afford an attorney, one will be appointed for you by the court." These, of course, are the famous *Miranda* warnings that police officers must give to any person unfortunate enough to be arrested for a crime.

The Supreme Court's controversial *Miranda* decision, handed down by the Court in June 1966, was designed to ensure that the Fifth Amendment rights of suspects in police custody, after an arrest, would always be honored and respected. In this lecture, we'll examine the historical and the legal background of the *Miranda* decision. Where did the original idea for the *Miranda* warnings come from? Why did the Supreme Court decide to require the warnings, and what gave the Court the legal authority to require them? What do the *Miranda* warnings really mean, and what purpose does *Miranda* really serve? Along the way, we'll focus on two key questions: First, how as a society should we feel about relying on police interrogations and confessions to solve serious crimes? Second, what exactly does the Supreme Court mean when it says that no confession should be used as evidence in court unless that confession was made voluntarily? These two questions were at the very heart of *Miranda*, and they remain just as difficult to answer today as they were back in 1966.

To understand the historical and legal significance of *Miranda*, let's look back almost twenty years earlier to another famous case. On the afternoon of November 12, 1947, in Indianapolis, Indiana, police arrested Robert Watts, a 25-year-old black man, for assault. Shortly after the arrest, the police began to suspect that Watts was also responsible for the murder of a white woman whose body had just been discovered nearby. For the rest of that day and for the next five days, Watts was held in solitary confinement at the county jail, with no place to sit or sleep except the floor. Each night, Watts was taken to police headquarters, where he was interrogated for hours on end, usually starting around 6 PM, and continuing until 2 or 3 in the morning. Then he was returned to his barren jail cell, only to await the next round of interrogation. Watts was never told that he had a right to remain silent, he wasn't allowed to see his family or friends, and he had no lawyer to represent him. In the early morning hours of the sixth day in police custody, Watts finally broke down and signed a confession to the murder. But he later wrote a letter to the local chapter of the NAACP in which he said he'd been framed, and signed the confession only because he "couldn't take it any longer" and the police "forced" him to sign it.

Watts was represented on appeal in the Supreme Court by the great Thurgood Marshall, the most renowned civil rights lawyer of his time, who later became the first African-American to serve on the Court. In the case of *Watts v. Indiana*, Thurgood Marshall argued that the confession should not have been used as evidence against Robert Watts, because it was an involuntary confession. A majority of the Supreme Court agreed with Marshall's argument. The Court's decision was based primarily on the Fourteenth Amendment to the United States Constitution, and more specifically on the Due Process Clause, which provides that no state may "deprive any person of life, liberty, or property, without due process of law." Although, as we've seen previously, the precise meaning of the term due process can sometimes be hard to determine, a majority of the Court had little trouble deciding that the intense, six-day police interrogation of Robert Watts violated due process, and produced an involuntary confession that could not be used as evidence against Watts. Watts' conviction was therefore reversed, by a vote of six to three.

Supreme Court Justice Robert H. Jackson strongly disagreed with some of what his fellow Justices wrote in the *Watts* case about due process and police interrogations, and he wrote his own separate opinion to explain why. And it is Justice Jackson's opinion that's best remembered to this day, because of the powerful arguments he made in defense of society's need to solve and prosecute heinous crimes, a societal need that sometimes requires allowing the police to press hard to obtain a confession.

Justice Jackson had spent much of his career as a prosecutor and federal government lawyer. He served as the U.S. Solicitor General and U.S. Attorney General before being confirmed to the Supreme Court in 1941—the only person in American history to hold all three posts. He also served as the Chief U.S. Prosecutor at the Nuremberg Trials following World War II. And, believe it or not, Justice Jackson didn't even graduate from law school. He acquired much of his legal education on his own, by reading law books and serving as an apprentice in a law firm. By the way, in a few states, it's still possible to qualify for the bar exam that way today.

Anyway, here's what Justice Jackson wrote in the 1947 Watts case: "The suspect neither had nor was advised of his right to get counsel. This presents a real dilemma in a free society. To subject one without counsel to questioning which may, and is intended to, convict him, is a real peril to individual freedom. To bring in a lawyer means a real peril to solution of the crime, because…any lawyer worth his salt will tell the suspect in no uncertain terms to make no statement to police under any circumstances." Justice Jackson went on to say that if the Constitution does ban custodial police interrogations, "The people of this country must discipline themselves to seeing their police stand by helplessly while those suspected of murder prowl about unmolested. Is [this] a necessary price to pay for the fairness which we know as 'due process of law'?"

As Justice Jackson explained so well in his Watts opinion, the Supreme Court was really stuck on the horns of a nasty dilemma. Nobody really wants to let a man suspected of committing a brutal murder walk away free. But on the other hand, the Justices have a sworn duty to uphold the Constitution, and to ensure that no one is convicted and punished for a crime in violation of the right to due process of law. That's the American way.

The voluntariness rule recognized in *Watts* gave the Supreme Court the legal authority to go after the worst kinds of police abuses during pre-trial interrogations like rubber hoses, or the prolonged deprivation of food and water, or the kind of harsh treatment suffered by Robert Watts. But it was never going to be a perfect solution, mostly because the Court just couldn't keep up with the massive volume of criminal cases coming up from the lower courts. Moreover, police gradually adapted to the voluntariness rule by becoming more sophisticated in their use of psychology. Today, these psychological interrogation tactics, such as the "good cop, bad cop" routine, are old hat. Everybody's seen that kind of stuff on TV. But by the 1950s and '60s, the Supreme Court was growing increasingly concerned that such tactics were turning into the modern-day equivalent of the rubber hose.

So the Court set out to find a new way to control police interrogation tactics before they got out of hand. In the 1964 cases of *Massiah v. United States* and *Escobedo v. Illinois*, the Court briefly toyed with the idea of requiring all suspects—even before the official filing of criminal charges—to have the protection of a defense lawyer by their side, pursuant to the Sixth Amendment's guarantee of the assistance of counsel. But the presence of a defense lawyer during all police interrogations would have basically eliminated confessions altogether, which was not really where the Court wanted to go.

So, shortly after deciding *Massiah* and *Escobedo*, the Court agreed to review four more police interrogation cases, in an effort to try to come up with a better solution. One of these cases involved Ernesto Miranda. Miranda was convicted of the brutal kidnapping and rape of an 18-year-old girl in Phoenix. Miranda was poor, had only an eighth-grade education, and had a history of schizophrenia and other mental-health issues. After the victim picked Miranda out of a lineup, the police arrested him and subjected him to two hours of strenuous custodial interrogation. During this time, Miranda was never told he had a right to a lawyer, nor was he ever advised he had a right to remain silent. Miranda was convicted, and he took his case all the way to the Supreme Court.

The Court decided all four of the 1966 confession cases together, but since Ernesto Miranda was the first case in the line, the Court's ruling became known forever as the *Miranda* decision. Too bad for the other defendants Vignera, Westover, and Stewart, because they didn't get to see their names in all the law books. But all four of the defendants got their convictions reversed by the Supreme Court, and I guess that's a pretty good consolation prize.

The *Miranda* decision was announced on June 13, 1966. In the decision, the Supreme Court completely backed away from the earlier idea that all suspects should be represented by defense lawyers during police interrogations, and turned in an entirely different direction. It's probably fair to conclude that sometime between 1964 and 1966, the Court had serious second thoughts about making it impossible for police to obtain confessions by providing all suspects with defense lawyers. So in *Miranda*, the Court decided instead to use the Fifth Amendment's privilege against compelled self-incrimination, rather than the Sixth Amendment right to counsel, as the primary basis for regulating police interrogations.

As we've already seen, the Fifth Amendment provides that "No person...shall be compelled in any criminal case to be a witness against himself." But how does this Fifth Amendment privilege lead to the requirement of the now-famous *Miranda* warnings? The key analytical move made by the Court in Miranda was to conclude that any suspect who is placed under arrest and who's now in the custody of the police faces inherent pressure to confess. In the words of the *Miranda* Court: "We have concluded that, without proper safeguards, the process of in-custody interrogation of persons suspected or accused of crime contains inherently compelling pressures which work to undermine the individual's will to resist, and to compel him to speak where he would not otherwise do so freely. In order to combat these pressures and to permit a full opportunity to exercise the privilege against self-incrimination, the accused must be adequately and effectively apprised of his rights, and the exercise of those rights must be fully honored."

Did you catch it? The analytical move made by the Court right there? The sleight-of-hand? The Court says that all custodial police interrogations are inherently compelling. That means custodial police interrogations will always violate the Fifth Amendment privilege against compelled self-incrimination, unless the police first give the suspect proper legal warnings and obtain a proper waiver of rights before starting the interrogation. Then the compulsion will be removed, and everything can proceed as usual.

The *Miranda* warnings are essentially a special form of advance protection, a prophylactic device, designed to ensure that custodial police interrogations don't reach the point of violating the Fifth Amendment privilege against compelled self-incrimination. The warnings tell the suspect that he always remains in control. By saying the magic words "I'd like to stop now," the suspect can make the questioning stop at any time. Or, if he wishes, he can ask for the help of a lawyer, in which case the questioning also must stop. It's completely up to him.

Notice, by the way, that the *Miranda* warnings clearly state, "you have the right to an attorney." But that's not actually true. If a suspect gets arrested and gets read the *Miranda* warnings and then says to the police, "Yes, sir, that sounds wonderful, I would like to have a lawyer, please," that does not necessarily mean that the suspect will immediately be given a lawyer. In fact, in most situations, there simply are no defense lawyers hanging around the police station waiting to talk to arrested suspects. Instead, the actual rule of *Miranda* is simply that the police have to stop questioning the suspect as soon as he asks for a lawyer. In most instances, the suspect won't actually receive a lawyer until much later, when the suspect stands before the trial judge at his arraignment, at which point the Sixth Amendment right to counsel will kick in and the judge will appoint him a defense lawyer. The *Miranda* warnings, in short, contain just a little bit of misinformation.

There's a much more fundamental problem, however, with *Miranda*, and with all confession cases, before and after *Miranda*. The bigger problem is this: What, exactly, makes a particular confession voluntary?

Let's start with some easy cases. If police officers physically assault or beat a man in order to make him confess, almost everyone would agree that that's an involuntary confession. Torture, the rack, the screw, electric shocks, waterboarding, the Spanish Inquisition, Jack Bauer on the TV show *24* shooting a suspect in the leg to get him to talk—these are the easy cases. Even in the modern context of mass terrorism, where some have argued that torture can be morally justified to save thousands of lives, no good lawyer seriously believes that the resulting confession should be used as evidence in a court of law.

But as soon as we move past these easy cases, things don't look so clear. I often ask my law students, "Did you come to class voluntarily today?" Hmm...On the one hand, nobody put a gun to their head and said, "Go to class!" On the other hand, they all know exactly what will happen to them if they don't show up for class: I will give them a failing grade, they won't graduate from law school, and they won't become a lawyer. They won't make enough money to pay off their student loan debts, and they'll end up poor and miserable. Okay, so maybe that's a bit of an exaggeration, but I think you see my point. Isn't it true that everything we choose to do, or not to do, is the product of all of the myriad influences all around us? Our genes, our parents, our schooling, our friends, our enemies, even natural forces? Looked at in a certain way, is there anything we do that's truly voluntary? But now think about it the opposite way: Even if I put a gun to your head, and order you to do something, you still have a choice, don't you? You can disobey my order and choose to take the bullet. Yes, I know, it's really hard to make that kind of choice, but it's not impossible, and people occasionally do it. There is always a choice.

The bottom line is that voluntariness can't be defined simply as the ability to choose or as an exercise of free will. That's way too simplistic. Every human action involves some aspects of compulsion and some aspects of free will. That's exactly why philosophers still can't resolve the age-old conundrum of free will versus determinism. And guess what? They never will. Because as human beings, we must believe that we have free will. That's essential to our identity as human beings. And yet, we also know perfectly well that we live in a deterministic world governed by cause and effect. We live with both of these contradictory ideas, because we must. It's the fundamental antinomy of the human condition.

So let's return to the confession problem. How do we decide if a confession is voluntary enough to be used as evidence in court? Don't all suspects, all the time, confess only when they feel compelled to do so, by the threat of more severe punishment, or by the fear of being ratted out by an accomplice, or by the simple desire to get it off their chest and clear their conscience? The voluntariness of a confession can't really be about the suspect's free will, because that takes us right back into the black hole of free will and determinism, from which there's no escape. Which means we need to think differently about voluntariness.

Consider the following remarkable case: On August 18, 1983, Francis Connelly walked up to Denver Police Officer Patrick Anderson and said that he'd committed a murder, and wanted to confess. Officer Anderson immediately read Connelly the *Miranda* warnings, but Connelly insisted on confessing, assuring the incredulous officer that he hadn't been drinking or using drugs, although he had been treated for mental illness. Connelly later explained that he confessed because he heard the "voice of God" ordering him to do so. The Supreme Court held, by a seven to two vote, that there was nothing unconstitutional about using Connelly's confession to convict him of the murder. Seriously? C'mon now, did Francis Connelly really confess voluntarily? What could possibly be more compelling than hearing the "voice of God" order you to confess to a crime? Surely that's much more likely to overcome a suspect's free will than even the most severe police beating.

It seems obvious that free will can't really be the issue here. So what is the real difference between the easy cases and the hard ones? Here's a thought: Maybe it's not about philosophical discussions of free will. Maybe it's more about judging how the police behaved. Whenever the police use physical force or psychological abuse or torture to obtain a confession, maybe we should say that the confession isn't voluntary so that we can exclude the evidence of the confession and punish the police for their bad behavior. To quote Justice Benjamin Cardozo again, "The criminal is to go free because the constable has blundered."

But in Francis Connelly's case, the police did absolutely nothing wrong. There was no reason to punish them because Connelly confessed all by himself. It's the same thing whenever a suspect confesses simply because he's racked with guilt. Is that compulsion? In a sense, maybe, but that doesn't matter once we understand that the legal doctrine of voluntariness is really about policing the behavior of the police.

Now we can look at *Miranda* in a whole new light. The Court chose in *Miranda* to escape from the difficulty of deciding on a case-by-case basis exactly which police interrogation tactics are okay and which are not. Instead of trying to regulate all the strategies and psychological tricks used by the police, which would surely continue to evolve endlessly into the future, the Court bailed and adopted an entirely different approach. And *Miranda* also created a much clearer and simpler rule for the police than the old voluntariness approach. *Miranda* means that, as a police officer, all you've got to do is read those warnings and get the suspect's waiver, and then you can pretty much do whatever you want as long as you don't cross the line into physical force or abuse. You can still lie to the suspect about the evidence against him. You can still tell him that his co-defendant buddies are turning on him, and that he should hurry up and spill the beans first. You can still tell him you're his friend, and if he confesses you'll help him get more lenient treatment.

How does *Miranda* protect the suspect against these kinds of psychological tactics by the police? It doesn't. At least not directly. Instead, the suspect is basically given a "get out of jail free" card, metaphorically speaking. At any time, if the psychological pressure gets to be too much, the suspect can always say the magic words, and the police will have to leave him alone. But it's entirely up to the suspect. After he agrees to talk, and before he actually chooses to invoke his *Miranda* rights, he's fair game for the police.

That's the grand compromise of *Miranda*. The Supreme Court wanted to regulate police interrogations, and control the worst of the abuses, but without eliminating the ability of the police to obtain confessions. As Justice Scalia once explained, voluntary confessions are actually a good thing, not only because they're good for the soul, but also because they're a prerequisite for serious rehabilitation. And *Miranda* didn't eliminate confessions at all. The best empirical evidence suggests that roughly 80% of all suspects waive their *Miranda* rights and agree to talk to the police.

By the way, that's one of the main reasons why police, for the most part, no longer oppose *Miranda* these days. *Miranda* has created a "safe harbor" for the police; they know that if they follow the rules, they'll get their chance to persuade the suspect to confess, at least in most instances.

Why do so many criminal suspects waive their *Miranda* rights? Who knows? If I wanted to get rich giving lectures to criminals about how to avoid getting in trouble, I'd start each lecture by saying, "Do not, under any circumstances, agree to talk to the police. Don't do it. Oh, and by the way, don't ever consent to let the police search the trunk of your car, where you keep your illegal drugs, either."

Surely a big part of the reason why so many suspects waive their *Miranda* rights is that the suspects are influenced to do so by the very same pressures, internal and external, that lead so many suspects to confess. To put it another way, if all custodial confessions are inherently compelled, then aren't all custodial *Miranda* waivers also inherently compelled? Of course they are. But that just goes to prove the main point, which is that *Miranda* never really was about the extent of free will exercised by the suspect. *Miranda* was about setting up clear ground rules for the police that could help to prevent the worst kinds of abuse during custodial interrogations while still allowing the police to exert some pressure and thereby obtain confessions. And in that sense, *Miranda* turned out to be a nearly complete success.

If *Miranda* represented a carefully drawn balance between the rights of arrested suspects and the need for police to be able to obtain confessions, that balance was substantially altered in favor of the police by the 2010 decision in *Berghuis v. Thompkins*. A murder suspect named Van Chester Thompkins was arrested and read the *Miranda* warnings. Thompkins declined to sign a form stating that he understood his rights, but he verbally indicated that he did. The police then began their interrogation. For more than two and a half hours, Thompkins said basically nothing in response to the police questioning; his only comments during the entire time were that he didn't want a peppermint, and that the chair he was sitting in was hard. Then, the interrogator asked Thompkins, "Do you believe in God?" Thompkins looked up and said, "Yes." The interrogator asked, "Do you pray to God?", and Thompkins again said, "Yes." The interrogator asked, "Do you pray to God to forgive you for shooting that boy down?" Thompkins said, "Yes." Thus ended the interrogation. The answers to these questions were introduced as evidence at trial, and Thompkins was convicted of murder.

In *Miranda*, the Court stated that "a heavy burden rests on the government to demonstrate that the defendant knowingly and intelligently waived his privilege against self-incrimination and his right to retained or appointed counsel." The *Miranda* Court added that "a valid waiver will not be presumed simply from the silence of the accused after warnings are given, or simply from the fact that a confession was in fact eventually obtained."

In *Thompkins*, the police never obtained a clear waiver of *Miranda* rights before starting the interrogation. And Thompkins remained almost completely silent throughout virtually the entire interrogation. But the Supreme Court upheld the conviction all the same. According to the Court, Thompkins's silence, during more than two and a half hours of police questioning, did not constitute an assertion of his right to silence under *Miranda*. Perversely, in order to properly assert his right to silence, Thompkins had to speak up. And when Thompkins finally answered those three questions about God, he was implicitly waiving his *Miranda* rights. This basically flips all of the central presumptions of *Miranda* on their heads. What happened to the heavy burden on the government to show waiver? What about not presuming waiver from a suspect's silence? In a world where we know that police often feel immense pressure to solve heinous crimes, and where we also know that psychologically susceptible suspects occasionally confess to crimes they did not actually commit, does it really seem like a good idea to water down whatever limited amount of protection *Miranda* once provided?

This problem, of course, is made even worse when suspects are young or mentally ill or simply weak-willed and prone to suggestion. False confessions have shaken the criminal justice system to its core, because we used to feel 100% confident in assuming that people who confess their own guilt really are guilty. Now, we can't be so sure. Which means that the ground rules of police interrogation as set forth in *Miranda* and as modified by *Berghuis v. Thompkins* are important, and likely to become even more so in the future.

PLEA BARGAINS, JURY TRIALS, AND JUSTICE

This lecture examines two major features of the American system of criminal justice: plea bargaining and trial by jury. In this lecture, you'll learn how plea bargains came to dominate criminal prosecutions, and what that means for the administration of justice. You'll also learn about the jury system, including the scope of the constitutional right to trial by jury, the requirements for selecting a jury, and the controversial principle of jury nullification.

PLEA BARGAINING

⭑ There is no evidence of plea bargaining in early American history. The practice appears to have begun during the 1800s. Over time, our legal system gradually abandoned the super-efficient summary trials common during the colonial period. Trial procedures were modernized, the rights of defendants came to the forefront, and legal representation of criminal defendants became more common.

⭑ The consequence of this trend toward modernization was that trials became much lengthier and costlier. Today, however, 19 out of every 20 criminal cases are resolved through plea bargaining. Instead of having a jury evaluate guilt or innocence, the defendant enters a plea of guilty at a pretrial hearing, almost always in exchange for a plea bargain that drops some of the charges, reduces the sentence, or both.

* Lawyers and judges truly love plea bargaining. It's incredibly efficient. In addition, most lawyers and judges—including most prosecutors—think that many of the criminal punishments enacted by legislatures are too harsh. Indeed, there's plenty of evidence to suggest that legislatures sometimes deliberately enact overly harsh punishments, knowing full well that prosecutors and judges will exercise their discretion and reach more reasonable outcomes through plea bargaining.

* Public opinion, on the other hand, is strongly against plea bargaining. Many people see the process as a way of "going easy" on the defendant, and they don't like it.

* Negotiating plea bargains and advising defendants when to accept them are central to the role of the modern criminal defense attorney. But these aren't skills that are often taught in law school. Law schools still spends most of their resources teaching lawyers how to litigate. Plea bargaining is quite different—and most lawyers have to learn how to do it through experience.

* An unfortunate side effect of plea bargaining is that almost all criminal defense lawyers eventually come to believe that almost all of their clients are guilty—simply because, in the end, almost all of them plead guilty. Even when a defendant tells his defense lawyer in the most passionate terms that he's innocent of the crime, the defense lawyer probably isn't going to believe it. And the lawyer also isn't likely to rush out and investigate the innocence claim.

* Instead, the lawyer will probably assume that his client's claim of innocence is just an opening gambit, a calculated move to get a better plea bargain. And every time the plea bargain gets offered and the defendant takes it, this perception gets reinforced. This can make life really difficult for the rare defendant who actually is innocent, as he might not be able to get his own lawyer to take his claim seriously.

CONSTITUTIONAL QUESTIONS

* By the mid-1900s, trial judges, prosecutors, defense lawyers, and defendants were all actively engaged in the practice of plea bargaining. They were doing it mostly under the table, however, because there were serious concerns about whether plea bargaining might be unconstitutional. Was plea bargaining consistent with the requirements of the Due Process Clause? Was it permissible for a prosecutor to essentially threaten the defendant with harsher punishment if he didn't agree to waive his right to a jury trial? Or was this too coercive?

* These questions were taken up by the Supreme Court in two cases: *Brady v. United States* and *Bordenkircher v. Hayes*. The defendant in *Brady* was charged with a capital crime, and pled guilty to a lesser charge to avoid the death penalty. Much later, Brady learned that the statute authorizing the death penalty for his crime was unconstitutional—which meant he didn't really have anything to fear in the first place. Brady challenged his guilty plea, arguing that it had been obtained involuntarily by the threat of an unconstitutional death sentence.

* The Supreme Court disagreed. According to the Court, the information upon which Brady based his decision was accurate at the time. As for Brady's claim that fear of the death penalty constituted coercion, thus making his plea involuntary, the Court pointed out that plea bargaining provides a "mutuality of advantage" that benefits both prosecution and defense. The Court did note, however, that guilty pleas must be voluntary, and that pleas induced by improper means might be involuntary in some cases.

* *Bordenkircher v. Hayes* addressed the other side of the coin. The defendant, Hayes, had been charged with forgery, and the prosecutor offered him a tough deal: "Plead guilty, and I'll recommend a sentence of five years in prison. If you don't plead guilty, I'll charge you as a repeat offender, and you'll face life in prison." Hayes refused to plead guilty, and went to trial. He was convicted and sentenced to

life. Hayes challenged the charge and the sentence as a violation of due process, arguing that he had been punished for exercising his constitutional rights.

★ The Supreme Court disagreed. According to the Court, "To punish a person because he has done what the law plainly allows him to do is a due process violation of the most basic sort. But in the 'give and take' of plea bargaining, there is no such element of punishment or retaliation, so long as the accused is free to accept or reject the prosecution's offer."

JURY TRIALS

★ With so many criminal cases resolved via plea bargaining, jury trials have become much less common. Trials still matter, however, because they are the benchmark against which plea bargains are measured. If you don't know what might happen at trial, you can't know what kind of plea bargain you should make.

★ The Sixth Amendment sets forth a constitutional right to trial by jury, one that now applies to both state and federal prosecutions. That right does not extend to all criminal prosecutions, however. The Supreme Court has held that the right to a jury trial doesn't apply to petty crimes—that is, misdemeanor cases where the defendant faces a potential sentence of less than six months in jail.

⋆ A defendant can waive the right to have a jury hear his case, if he so chooses. He can request a bench trial—that is, a trial before a judge, without a jury—and in most cases, the prosecution will agree. About 30 percent of all criminal trials are bench trials. But the jury trial is still the gold standard.

⋆ There are three important constitutional requirements for selecting a jury. The first is that juries must be impartial. This means that every person who serves on a jury must be able to perform the legal duties of a juror—to consider the evidence fairly, and to reserve final judgment until all the evidence has been introduced and all the arguments concluded. It doesn't mean that a juror must be a tabula rasa, knowing nothing at all about the case. It simply means that the juror must be able to set everything they know aside, and decide the case fairly.

⋆ The second constitutional requirement for jury selection is that the jurors must be selected from a fair cross-section of the community. Prior to the 1960s, jurors often were limited to the most upstanding members of the community. As the Supreme Court held, however, juries are supposed to represent the entire community. Any jury selection process that substantially excludes distinctive, identifiable groups within the community is a violation of the Sixth Amendment.

⋆ The third requirement for jury selection comes from the Equal Protection Clause of the Fourteenth Amendment, and concerns the discriminatory use of peremptory challenges. After prospective jurors have been screened for impartiality and other legal barriers to jury service, each side receives a small number of peremptory challenges, which they can use to strike potential jurors for almost any reason. According to the Supreme Court, however, peremptory challenges may not be used to exclude prospective jurors based on race or gender.

⋆ An important but lesser-known issue concerning jury trials is the concept of jury nullification. This is the implicit power of a jury to nullify an unjust criminal law by acquitting an obviously guilty defendant. There is a long history of jury nullification in America, it's one of the greatest protections we have against government overreach.

✶ Jury nullification is a power available to every jury. It's a strange power, one that courts don't inform jurors about. But it's very real. Whenever a jury finds a defendant not guilty, the jurors can't be asked, officially, why they did it, and their decision to acquit can't be appealed on any grounds.

Suggested Reading

◊ Brady v. United States.

◊ Bordenkircher v. Hayes.

◊ Alford v. North Carolina.

◊ Batson v. Kentucky.

Questions to Consider

↗ How do you feel about plea bargaining, and why?

↗ Do you agree with the power of juries to nullify criminal laws by acquitting clearly guilty defendants?

PLEA BARGAINS, JURY TRIALS, AND JUSTICE

W hen all is said and done, after a crime's been defined by law, after a victim's been harmed, after the police have gathered up all the evidence, and after a suspect's been arrested and officially charged with the crime, we finally get to the main event: the criminal trial. The realm of the jury, the pinnacle of our criminal justice system, the stuff of books and movies, the public drama that determines, once and for all time, the defendant's guilt or innocence. Except for one big problem: That's not how 95% of all criminal cases end. In 19 out of every 20 criminal cases, the defendant's guilt or innocence isn't determined by a trial. Instead, the defendant enters a plea of guilty at a low-key hearing before a judge, almost always in exchange for a plea bargain that drops some of the charges, reduces the sentence, or both. As the Supreme Court wrote in the 2012 case of *Missouri v. Frye*, quoting from an article written by my dear, late friend Professor Bill Stuntz and his colleague Bob Scott: "To a large extent...horse trading [between prosecutor and defense counsel] determines who goes to jail and for how long. That is what plea bargaining is. It is not some adjunct to the criminal justice system; it is the criminal justice system."

In this lecture, we'll take a closer look at both plea bargains and criminal trials. We'll learn how and why plea bargains came to dominate the criminal justice system, and what that means for the administration of justice. We'll also learn about the jury system, including the scope of the constitutional right to a jury trial, the requirements for selecting a jury, and the historical and cultural reasons why we still allow juries to exercise the power to nullify the law. And we'll see how these two parallel methods of adjudication, plea bargains and jury trials, actually complement each other, thereby serving the larger interests of justice.

In early American history, there was no plea bargaining, at least as far as we know. The practice seems to have started during the 1800s, probably due to several factors. One factor was that criminal trials gradually became more costly and time-consuming. The early common law trial was a summary proceeding, with hardly any legal rights for the parties to invoke. John Langbein, a legal historian, has documented that during the bygone days of Old Bailey, the chaotic 18th century criminal court in London that Charles Dickens wrote about in *A Tale of Two Cities*, judges handled between 12 and 20 felony jury trials a day; hard to believe, given that a modern criminal trial often takes several days, and sometimes much longer.

What changed? Mostly, it was the fact that these early criminal trials didn't involve lawyers. Under English common law the defendant couldn't bring a lawyer to court, and the prosecution of the crime, which was handled mostly by the victim, usually didn't involve a lawyer either. Moreover, there wasn't much evidence law back in those days. Most evidence was treated as admissible before the jury, and the trial judge managed the situation by telling the jury his own opinion about whether the evidence was believable or not. Today, we don't allow that kind of judicial commentary about the evidence. It's been replaced by complicated legal rules about the admissibility of evidence, rules that were unheard of in the 1700s.

One more important variable that's changed is that, during 18th century English trials, the criminal defendant himself often spoke up during the trial. This contributed to the efficiency of trials because the defendant can provide lots of useful evidence about what happened, usually, evidence that works against him. In modern America, however, the defendant can't be forced to testify against himself, because of the Fifth Amendment privilege against compelled self-incrimination. That has also made modern criminal trials much less efficient.

Was it a good thing that, in America, the legal system evolved from the super-efficient summary trials of Old Bailey to modern criminal trials that provide defendants with many legal rights and with a defense lawyer to vindicate those rights? Of course. But there's a downside as well, and the downside is that we may not want or may not even be able to afford to give every defendant such a lengthy and expensive trial.

So how did plea bargaining emerge as the preferred solution to this problem? That's a story most helpfully told by Professor George Fisher. Fisher studied the rise of plea bargaining in Middlesex County, Massachusetts, during the 1800s. Here's what he found: The rise of plea bargaining was inextricably linked with the rise of prosecutorial discretion. More specifically, with the power of prosecutors to control the sentences that defendants received for certain crimes, by the simple expedient of deciding which crime to charge. This power first emerged in the context of liquor laws, where the Massachusetts legislature took away the trial judge's traditional sentencing discretion by enacting mandatory punishments for various liquor-related crimes. Because the judge no longer had any control over the sentencing for these liquor crimes, the prosecutor became the most powerful figure in the case, the only one who could provide any leniency to the defendant by agreeing to reduce the original charge to a different one with a lower mandatory sentence.

Once the Massachusetts legislature found out that local prosecutors were using this new power to encourage plea bargains in liquor cases, the legislature changed the liquor laws, which almost snuffed out plea bargaining in its infancy. But by then, the prosecutors realized that a similar situation still prevailed in homicide cases. Homicide was another kind of crime that carried a range of mandatory sentences, which meant that once again prosecutors, rather than judges, had primary control over the defendant's fate.

Just as the prosecutors gradually became more and more enamored of plea bargaining, so too the trial judges also came to grudgingly accept it, mostly because during the latter half of the 19th century, the judges suddenly were swamped with cases on the civil side of their docket and needed to find a way to reduce the workload on the criminal side. The explosion of civil litigation was a byproduct of the Industrial Revolution and the proliferation of modern technologies like railroads and streetcars, both of which generated a huge number of personal injury lawsuits. Overwhelmed trial judges responded by using their discretionary sentencing powers, in criminal cases that didn't involve homicide, to give criminal defendants an incentive to settle and plead guilty. By the end of the 1800s, according to Fisher, plea bargaining had achieved its ultimate triumph, and we've never looked back.

Lawyers and judges truly do love plea bargaining. There's no other way to put it. But the public pretty much hates it, because it's seen as "going easy" on the defendant. So why the discrepancy? Professor Milton Heumann did a wonderful sociological study of plea bargaining in New Haven, Connecticut, during the 1970s. Heumann found that plea bargaining is somewhat related to caseload pressure, but that's not the whole story. Even in places like North Dakota, where there are relatively few crimes and plenty of courts to handle them, plea bargaining rates are almost the same as they are in the ultra-crowded courts of New York City. Why? Because lawyers and judges tend to see criminal trials as a waste of resources, and that's true even if you have plenty of resources to waste. After all, even rich people don't want to just burn their money, right? In the view of most lawyers and judges who handle criminal cases, there's just no need for a trial in most cases. The defendant knows he's guilty, the defense lawyer knows it, the prosecutor knows it, and the judge knows it. So why not just settle and save everybody the time and hassle of a trial?

In addition, most lawyers and judges, including even most prosecutors, think that many of the criminal punishments enacted by legislatures are too harsh. That's because legislators always want to look "tough on crime," and they don't have any real incentive to be lenient. Lock 'em up and throw away the key—that's how you get re-elected. Indeed, there's plenty of evidence suggesting that legislatures sometimes deliberately enact overly harsh punishments, knowing full well that prosecutors and judges will exercise their discretion to limit those punishments and reach more reasonable outcomes through plea bargaining. It's a dirty little secret, one that almost everybody within the criminal justice system understands.

That's why, as plea bargaining gradually developed during the 1800s, lawyers and judges gradually grew to love it. And it's now become central to the role of a criminal defense lawyer to negotiate about plea bargains and to advise the defendant about when it's time to take the deal. But it's not something that's often taught in law school. Law school still spends most of the time teaching lawyers how to litigate. Plea bargaining is quite different, and most lawyers have to learn how to do it through experience. Milton Heumann quoted one criminal defense lawyer's apt description of the process of learning how to plea bargain: "There are no courses given on it...I guess you could analogize it to making love. You know, it's something you can't teach; you can't put it [into] a book; you can't give a lecture on it. But, like making love, you do it enough times, you learn to like it, and you'll get good at it."

By the way, one unfortunate side effect of plea bargaining is that almost all criminal defense lawyers eventually come to believe that almost all of their clients are guilty, simply because in the end, almost all of them plead guilty. So even when a defendant tells his defense lawyer in the most passionate terms that he's innocent of the crime charged, the defense lawyer probably isn't going to believe it. And that lawyer also isn't likely to rush out and investigate the innocence claim. Instead, the lawyer will probably figure it's just an opening gambit to get a better plea bargain. And every time the plea bargain gets offered, and the defendant takes it, this perception gets reinforced. Which can make life really difficult for the rare defendant who really is innocent but who can't get his own lawyer to take his claim seriously.

There's still one more important piece to the historical story of plea bargaining that we need to discuss. By the mid-1900s, trial judges, prosecutors, defense lawyers, and defendants all were actively engaged in the practice of plea bargaining, but they were doing it mostly under the table. Why? Because there were serious concerns on all sides about whether plea bargaining might be unconstitutional. Was plea bargaining consistent with "due process of law?" Was it permissible for a prosecutor, or a trial judge, to essentially threaten the defendant with worse punishment if he didn't agree to give up his constitutional right to a jury trial? Or was this, instead, a kind of coercion?

These questions were finally taken up by the U.S. Supreme Court in two cases: *Brady v. United States*, in 1970, and *Bordenkircher v. Hayes*, in 1978. Brady dealt with one side of the coin. Brady was charged with a capital crime and he pled guilty to a lesser charge to avoid the death penalty. Much later, Brady learned that the statute authorizing the death penalty for his crime was unconstitutional, which meant he didn't really have anything to fear in the first place. So he challenged his guilty plea as involuntary, because it was induced by the threat of an unconstitutional death sentence. But the Supreme Court saw it otherwise. According to the Court, the information Brady had before him when he entered his guilty plea was accurate at the time. It wasn't until later, after all, that the death penalty statute was held unconstitutional. As for Brady's claim that fear of the death penalty constituted coercion, making his plea involuntary, the Court pointed out that plea bargaining provides a mutuality of advantage that benefits both prosecution and defense. The Court elaborated: "We cannot hold that it is unconstitutional for the state to extend a benefit to a defendant who in turn extends a substantial benefit to the state, and who demonstrates by his plea that he is ready and willing to admit his crime." The Court agreed that guilty pleas must be voluntary, and that pleas induced by improper threats or promises might be involuntary. But even so, the Court held, "a plea of guilty is not invalid merely because entered to avoid the possibility of a death penalty."

Bordenkircher v. Hayes, eight years later, dealt with the other side of the coin. Hayes was charged with a forgery crime, and the prosecutor offered a tough deal: "Plead guilty, and I'll recommend a sentence of five years in prison. If you don't plead guilty, I'll charge you as a repeat offender, and you'll face life in prison." Hayes refused to plead guilty, and went to trial. He was convicted, and he got life. Hayes then challenged the recidivist charge and life sentence as a violation of due process, because he was punished for exercising his constitutional rights. The Supreme Court disagreed. According to the Court, "To punish a person because he has done what the law plainly allows him to do is a due process violation of the most basic sort. But in the 'give and take' of plea bargaining, there is no such element of punishment or retaliation, so long as the accused is free to accept or reject the prosecution's offer." The Court added, "Acceptance of the basic legitimacy of plea bargaining necessarily implies rejection of any notion that a guilty plea is involuntary in a constitutional sense simply because it is the end result of the bargaining process."

After *Brady* and *Bordenkircher v. Hayes*, plea bargaining finally emerged into the light of day, where it remains. And that has allowed the courts to finally establish the legal rules that govern plea bargaining, legal rules that treat plea bargains as a special kind of contract, similar to but also different from, everyday commercial contracts. Plea bargaining involves a special kind of contract mostly because the defendant cannot be contractually bound, in advance, to plead guilty to a crime—that would be unconstitutional. He can always insist on his constitutional right to a trial. So until the moment the defendant actually stands before the trial judge and pleads guilty, he can always back out. On the other hand, a prosecutor who makes a promise of leniency or who promises to drop or reduce some of the charges, can be legally bound to fulfill those promises if the defendant accepts the deal, and if the defendant also gives up anything, such as information about accomplices, in reliance on the prosecutor's promise.

Some plea bargains can be hard to interpret. For example, when a prosecutor agrees to ask the judge for leniency at sentencing, just how persuasively must she do so? Is it good enough if she merely says the words, or does she have to say them like she really means them? In that kind of ambiguous situation, the courts will ultimately determine the meaning of the contract, which is why the lawyers have to pay close attention and make sure that the terms of the deal are clearly expressed.

One final observation about plea bargaining: The Supreme Court has held, in the case of *North Carolina v. Alford*, that it's constitutional for a state to allow a defendant to plead guilty to a crime, even if the defendant denies that he actually committed the crime. We call this unusual kind of guilty plea an *Alford* plea. And it seems like a particularly bad idea, because it basically deprives the entire criminal justice process of its moral significance. The defendant can choose to treat the guilty plea like a purely economic transaction: "You give me something, and I'll give you something in return, but I didn't do it!" Defendants who enter an *Alford* plea would seem to be particularly poor candidates for reform or rehabilitation. No parent would ever let their child get away with such a thing, so why did the Supreme Court decide to allow this kind of guilty plea?

It's because in America, we place a high value on personal autonomy, and the Court believed a criminal defendant who thinks it's in his best interests should have the right to plead guilty, even if he can't or won't acknowledge his factual guilt.

Time now to turn the page on plea bargaining, and talk about what happens if the defendant chooses not to plead guilty, and instead goes to trial. It doesn't happen very often, but criminal trials matter all the same because they are the benchmark against which plea bargains are measured. If you don't know what might happen at a trial, you can't know what kind of plea bargain you should make.

The Sixth Amendment provides: "In all criminal prosecutions, the accused shall enjoy the right to a speedy and public trial, by an impartial jury of the state and district wherein the crime shall have been committed." So there's a constitutional right to a trial by jury. But despite the clear text of the Sixth Amendment, that right does not extend to all criminal prosecutions. Just like the Sixth Amendment's right to counsel, the Supreme Court has held that the right to jury trial doesn't apply to petty crimes, meaning there's no right to a jury trial in misdemeanor cases where the defendant faces a potential sentence of less than six months in jail. But for felony cases involving more than a year of possible imprisonment, and also for more serious misdemeanors, jury trial is the norm. The defendant can ask for a bench trial, that is, a trial before a judge, without a jury, and in most cases, the prosecution will agree. About 30% of all criminal trials are bench trials. But the gold standard is still the jury trial.

Notice that the Sixth Amendment provides that juries must be impartial. That's actually just one of three important constitutional requirements for selecting a jury. The impartiality requirement means that every person who serves on a jury must be able to perform the legal duties of a juror, to consider the evidence fairly and to reserve final judgment until all of the evidence has been introduced and all the arguments have been concluded. It doesn't mean that a juror must be tabula rasa, knowing nothing at all about the case. It simply means that the juror must be able to set everything they know aside, and decide the case fairly.

The second constitutional requirement for jury selection is that the jurors must be selected from a fair cross-section of the community. Before the 1960s, jurors often were limited to the most upstanding members of the community. Many courts used a key man system, where a trusted civic leader would be asked to suggest names of other trustworthy people to serve on a jury. That kind of system was later struck down by the Supreme Court, because it restricted jury service to a small number of elites. According to the Court, juries are supposed to represent the entire community, so any jury selection process that substantially excludes distinctive identifiable groups within the community is a violation of the Sixth Amendment because that's just not what we mean by a jury.

The third requirement for jury selection comes from the Equal Protection Clause of the Fourteenth Amendment, and it's the requirement that neither side can use their peremptory challenges to exclude prospective jurors based on race or gender. After the prospective jurors have already been screened for impartiality and for other potential legal barriers to jury service, such as non-citizenship, a felony criminal record, or the inability to understand English, the two sides are each provided with a small number of peremptory challenges which they can use to exclude prospective jurors they think might be likely to favor the other side. Peremptory challenges were created to help ensure that the jury doesn't lean too far one way or the other. And peremptory challenges are, by their very nature, supposed to be challenges for which the lawyers don't have to give any reason. That's why we call them peremptory. But in 1986, in *Batson v. Kentucky*, the Supreme Court held that prosecutors can't use their peremptory challenges to eliminate prospective jurors based on their race. The Batson rule was later extended to defense-side peremptory challenges as well, because it's the prospective juror's right to serve that's being violated. And the Court also extended the rule to prohibit peremptory challenges based on gender. So peremptory challenges still exist, but they're just not as peremptory as they used to be before the Batson decision.

The framers included the right to jury trial in the Constitution because they believed in the jury system as the bulwark of liberty. Thomas Jefferson once wrote, "I consider [trial by jury] as the only anchor ever yet imagined by man, by which a government can be held to the principles of its constitution." In fact, the right to jury trial actually appears twice in the Constitution, not only in the Sixth Amendment but also in Article III, Section 2. That's how much it mattered to the framers. And that's because the framers had witnessed how a jury can help reign in an oppressive government. Two famous jury trials—one in England, and the other in the colonies—helped prove this point. The first trial occurred in 1670, and involved Quaker leaders William Penn and William Mead. Penn and Mead were charged with disturbing the peace by holding an unlawful assembly. The jury acquitted them, and the jurors were then arrested and imprisoned for perjuring themselves by rendering a false verdict. This was the English government's way of trying to control the jury—by prosecuting the jurors when the verdict didn't go the government's way. One of the jurors, Edward Bushell, appealed his imprisonment. In Bushell's case, the Court of Common Pleas ordered Bushell's release, holding that no one has the right to question, let alone punish, a jury's verdict. The decision in Bushell's case became a big part of American law after the Revolution, as we'll soon see.

The second trial, even more famous, was held in New York City in 1735. John Peter Zenger, a publisher, was charged with seditious libel based on an allegation that he published newspaper stories critical of the royal governor. The allegation was true, Zenger did publish the stories and he didn't really deny it. But Zenger's defense lawyer, Andrew Hamilton—no relation to the more famous Alexander Hamilton—made an argument to the colonial jury that the libel law itself was unjust, and that Zenger should therefore be acquitted despite the law. Hamilton's argument is now considered a classic:

"The question before the Court and you, gentlemen of the jury, is not of small or private concern. It is not the cause of one poor printer, nor of New York alone, which you are now trying. No! It may in its consequences affect every free man that lives under a British government on the main of America. It is the best cause; it is the cause of liberty. And I make no doubt but your upright conduct, this day, will not only entitle you to the love and esteem of your fellow citizens, but every man who prefers freedom to…slavery will bless and honor you as men who have baffled the attempt of tyranny, and by an impartial and uncorrupt verdict have laid a noble foundation for securing to ourselves, our posterity, and our neighbors, that to which nature and the laws of our country have given us a right—the liberty—of both exposing and opposing arbitrary power…by speaking and writing the truth."

Powerful stuff, right? Zenger was acquitted, and the case became an important part of the run-up to the American Revolution. That's why the framers believed so strongly in the jury system.

This implicit power of a jury to nullify an unjust criminal law, and to acquit an obviously guilty defendant without having to provide any explanation remains just as true today as it was in the days of William Penn and John Peter Zenger. But it's a very strange power. We don't tell juries they possess this power. In fact, trial judges routinely instruct juries that they must follow the legal instructions they receive from the court. And defense lawyers today are generally barred from arguing directly to the jurors that they should nullify the law, although good lawyers can still manage to get the point across in more subtle ways, as Johnnie Cochran famously did during the closing arguments in the O.J. Simpson trial, when he implored the jury to "Do the right thing."

Nevertheless, jury nullification is very real. And whenever a jury finds a defendant not guilty, the jurors can't even be asked officially why they did it. Their decision can't be challenged or appealed on any ground. That's the legacy of Bushell's case, and the *Zenger* case. And it's still one of the greatest protections we have against an overreaching government.

In a way, the story of jury nullification is a reflection of everything we've learned in this course. Government power is at its absolute maximum when a person is arrested and charged with a crime, and when the government tries to take away that person's property, their liberty, or even their life. It's an awesome power, one that must always remain subject to the rule of law. That's why we've constructed such a complicated system of constitutional criminal procedure rights, to help ensure that criminal investigations and criminal adjudications are fundamentally fair. And that's also why our criminal law provides so many opportunities for different actors—the prosecutor, the defense lawyer, the courts, and, as we've now seen, the jury—to "Do the right thing," and thereby fulfill the ends of justice.

BIBLIOGRAPHY

Litigation and Legal Practice

Cohen, George M. *The State of Lawyer Knowledge under the Model Rules of Professional Conduct.* 3 Am. U. Bus. L. Rev. 115 (2014). In this article, Professor Cohen considers the question of whether it is permissible, under the Model Rules of Professional Conduct, for an attorney to remain willfully blind to wrongdoing by his client. He recommends changes to the Model Rules, including clarifying when an attorney should be under a duty to investigate wrongdoing.

Constitution of the United States, http://www.law.cornell.edu/constitution/overview. To understand the American system of laws, one must start by reading the Constitution. Pay particular attention to the three branches of federal government (the legislative, executive, and judicial branches, established by Articles I, II, and III, respectively), as well as the powers reserved by the states (articulated in Article IV). The Bill of Rights and the Thirteenth, Fourteenth, Fifteenth, and Nineteenth Amendments are also particularly significant.

Davis, John W. *The Argument of an Appeal.* 3 J. App. Prac. & Process (2001). This is a reprint of a speech Judge Davis delivered to the Association of the Bar of the City of New York on October 22, 1940. In it, he offers 10 wise rules for successful appellate advocacy.

De Tocqueville, Alexis. *Democracy in America.* Translated by Harvey C. Mansfield and Delba Winthrop. Chicago: University of Chicago Press, 2000. This is a translation of an 1831 text by Alexis de Tocqueville about his visit to America and his observations about American democracy. It is a seminal and frequently quoted work about American culture and government.

Federal Rules of Evidence 401, 403, 404, 608, 801, 802 (2015), http://www.law.cornell.edu/rules/fre. This is a selection of some of the rules governing the use of evidence in federal trials. The advisory committee notes provide helpful explanations of each rule.

Garrett, Brandon. *Convicting the Innocent*. Cambridge, MA: Harvard University Press, 2012. This book examines the first 250 cases of wrongfully convicted people who were later exonerated by DNA evidence. It analyzes what went wrong in those prosecutions, tackling questions such as why innocent people might confess to crimes they did not commit and why eyewitness testimony can be fallible.

Harlan, John M. *What Part Does the Oral Argument Play in the Conduct of an Appeal?* 41 Cornell L. Rev. 6 (1955). Justice Harlan delivered these remarks at a judicial conference on June 24, 1955. He analyzes the significance of appellate oral argument, offering attorneys insight into how to persuade an appellate judge.

Harr, Johnathan. *A Civil Action*. New York: Random House, 1995. This nonfiction book tells the story of a lawyer, Jan Schlichtmann, who sues two large corporations for dumping carcinogenic chemicals into the water of Woburn, Massachusetts. The actions taken by the two corporations resulted the deaths of at least six children from leukemia. One of the fascinating aspects of this story is the relationship between the clients and their attorney, who becomes so committed to their cause that he ends up bankrupting himself in the process.

Hart, H. L. A. *The Concept of Law*. 3rd ed. Oxford: Oxford University Press, 2012. This is a classic book of legal philosophy. In it, Hart explores the nature of law, drawing a distinction between the core of a rule and the debatable edges of it, which he called the penumbra. His famous example involves imagining a rule prohibiting vehicles in a public park, and then asking whether that rule would extend to bicycles or roller skates.

Mauet, Thomas A. *Pretrial*. New York: Wolters Kluwer Law & Business, 2012. This text guides lawyers through pretrial preparation, including engaging in discovery, filing pretrial motions, and preparing witnesses. It is the classic pretrial preparation guide relied on by many practicing attorneys.

——. *Trial Techniques and Trials.* 9th ed. New York: Wolters Kluwer Law & Business, 2013. This is the standard handbook relied on by attorneys preparing for trial. It examines each stage of trial, including opening statements, direct examination, cross-examination, and closing arguments.

McCloskey, Robert G. *The American Supreme Court.* 6th ed. Chicago: University of Chicago Press, 2016. This book offers a comprehensive history of the U.S. Supreme Court. It considers the nature of judicial power as it traces the Court through different eras of American history.

Model Rules of Professional Conduct Rules 1.3, 1.2, 1.6 (2017). http://www.americanbar.org/groups/professional_ responsibility/publications/model_rules_of_professional_conduct.html. These are the ethical rules adopted by most jurisdictions in the United States to govern attorney conduct. The rules that regulate an attorney's obligation toward his client include helpful commentary that highlights the challenges of the attorney-client relationship.

Sacks, Michael J. and Barbara A. Spellman. *The Psychological Foundations of Evidence Law.* New York: NYU Press, 2016. This book explores the rules of evidence through the lens of psychology, asking whether the rules accomplish their objectives. It also suggests amendments to the rules of evidence to strengthen their efficacy.

Sayler, Robert N. and Molly Bishop Shadel. *Tongue-Tied America: Reviving the Art of Verbal Persuasion.* New York: Wolters Kluwer Law & Business, 2014. This text, coauthored by Professor Shadel, explores how to speak persuasively both in and out of the courtroom.

Scalia, Antonin and Bryan A. Garner. *Making Your Case: The Art of Persuading Judges.* St. Paul: Thomson/West, 2008. This book, coauthored by Justice Scalia, analyzes how advocates persuade judges. It also offers a view of the Supreme Court through the eyes of a controversial but influential justice.

Schauer, Frederick. *Thinking Like a Lawyer: A New Introduction to Legal Reasoning.* Cambridge, MA: Harvard University Press, 2009. In this text, Professor Schauer examines how lawyers and judges think, reason, and argue. It is an accessible, engaging articulation of the kind of reasoning that characterizes legal decision-making.

Shadel, Molly Bishop. *Finding Your Voice in Law School: Mastering Classroom Cold-Calls, Job Interviews, and Other Verbal Challenges.* Durham, NC: Carolina Academic Press (2013). This book, coauthored by Professor Shadel, examines the verbal challenges of law school, including trial exercises such as direct examinations and cross-examinations.

Sullivan, William, et al. *Educating Lawyers: Preparation for the Profession of Law.* Stanford: The Carnegie Foundation for the Advancement of Teaching, 2007. This book is the result of an extensive examination of American law schools by the Carnegie Foundation. It examines what law schools are teaching law students, including shortcomings in legal education. It is a critical examination of what it means to think like a lawyer.

Younger, Irving. *The Irving Younger Collection: Wisdom and Wit from the Master of Trial Advocacy.* Edited by Stephen D. Easton. New York: American Bar Association, 2010. Irving Younger was a lawyer and professor who was renowned for his lectures about trial advocacy. His "Ten Commandments of Cross Examination" is oft-repeated advice for trial lawyers. This book collects some of his most famous writings about trial advocacy.

Criminal Law and Procedure

Cases

Alford v. North Carolina, 400 U.S. 25 (1970). http://supreme.justia.com/cases/federal/us/400/25/case.html. Defendant can plead guilty to a crime even if he denies actually committing the crime.

Austin v. United States, 382 F.2d 129 (D.C. Cir. 1967). http://scholar.google.com/scholar_case?case=4535353936244583379&hl=en&as_sdt=6&as_vis=1&oi=scholarr. Detailed explanation of the meaning of premeditation in homicide law.

Batson v. Kentucky, 476 U.S. 79 (1986). http://supreme.justia.com/cases/federal/us/476/79/case.html. Peremptory challenges cannot be used to exclude prospective jurors based on their race.

Brady v. United States, 397 U.S. 742 (1970). http://supreme.justia.com/cases/federal/us/397/742/case.html. Defendant can be given an incentive to plead guilty through plea bargaining.

Brogan v. United States, 522 U.S. 398 (1998). http://supreme.justia.com/cases/federal/us/522/398/case.html. Example of modern textual interpretation of a criminal statute; also, defendant's lie in response to incriminating questions can be used as evidence against him, because Fifth Amendment privilege must be asserted.

Boyd v. United States, 116 U.S. 616 (1886). http://supreme.justia.com/cases/federal/us/116/616/case.html. Fourth and Fifth Amendments work together to protect a zone of privacy against the government.

Cheek v. United States, 498 U.S. 192 (1991). http://supreme.justia.com/cases/federal/us/498/192/case.html. Defendant can't be found guilty of willful violation of federal income tax law if he honestly believed that the law did not apply to him.

Colorado v. Connelly, 479 U.S. 157 (1986). http://supreme.justia.com/cases/federal/us/479/157/case.html. Suspect's confession is voluntary even though induced by the "voice of God," because police didn't do anything wrong.

United States v. Dotterweich, 320 U.S. 277 (1943). http://supreme.justia.com/cases/federal/us/320/277/case.html. Strict liability is permitted in a criminal case, if the relevant crime statute so provides.

Regina v. Dudley & Stephens, 14 Q.B.D. 273 (1884). http://cyber. harvard.edu/eon/ei/elabs/majesty/stephens.htmlk. Famous English case involving cannibalism on the high seas; court holds that the necessity defense does not apply to the crime of murder.

Furman v. Georgia, 408 U.S. 238 (1972). http://supreme.justia.com/ cases/federal/us/408/238/case.html. U.S. Supreme Court invalidates the death penalty under the Eighth Amendment.

Illinois v. Gates, 462 U.S. 213 (1983). http://supreme.justia.com/ cases/federal/us/462/213/case.html. Definition of probable cause in Fourth Amendment law.

Gideon v. Wainwright, 372 U.S. 335 (1963). http://supreme.justia. com/cases/federal/us/372/335/case.html. Famous U.S. Supreme Court case holding that indigent criminal defendants have a constitutional right to receive defense counsel at state expense.

People v. Goetz, 68 N.Y.2d 96 (1986). http://scholar.google.com/ scholar_case?case=8047552572288725205&hl=en&as_sdt=6&as_ vis=1&oi=scholarr. Famous NYC "Subway Vigilante" case involving shooting of black teenagers who asked defendant for money.

Gregg v. Georgia, 428 U.S. 153 (1976). http://supreme.justia. com/cases/federal/us/428/153/. U.S. Supreme Court restores constitutional validity of the death penalty.

Griffin v. California, 380 U.S. 609 (1965). http://supreme.justia. com/cases/federal/us/380/609/case.html. Prosecutor cannot suggest to the jury that the defendant's decision not to take the stand as a witness in his criminal case is evidence of guilt.

Harmelin v. Michigan, 501 U.S. 957 (1991). http://supreme.justia. com/cases/federal/us/501/957/. Mandatory sentence of life without parole for a first offense of possessing 672 grams of cocaine does not violate the Eighth Amendment.

Bordenkircher v. Hayes, 434 U.S. 357 (1978). http://supreme.justia. com/cases/federal/us/434/357/case.html. Defendant who declines to enter a guilty plea in the context of plea bargaining can be given a harsher sentence after being convicted at trial.

Katz v. United States, 389 U.S. 347 (1967). http://supreme.justia.com/cases/federal/us/389/347/case.html. Scope of the Fourth Amendment is based on privacy, not property rights; Justice Harlan's concurring opinion establishes the "reasonable expectation of privacy" test for Fourth Amendment searches.

Commonwealth v. Liebenow, 470 Mass. 151 (2014). http://scholar.google.com/scholar_case?case=2828790002348072830&hl=en&as_sdt=6&as_vis=1&oi=scholarr. Defendant cannot be convicted of theft of construction materials if he honestly believed that the materials were abandoned.

United States v. Lopez, 514 U.S. 549 (1995). http://supreme.justia.com/cases/federal/us/514/549/case.html. Federal Gun Free School Zones Act exceeds congressional power under the Commerce Clause.

Mayes v. People, 106 Ill. 306 (1883). http://h2o.law.harvard.edu/cases/1773. Example of "abandoned and malignant heart" second-degree murder.

Miranda v. Arizona, 384 U.S. 436 (1966). http://supreme.justia.com/cases/federal/us/384/436/. Famous U.S. Supreme Court case requiring warnings to be given by police to arrested suspects.

Mobley v. State, 132 So. 3d 1160 (2014). http://www.3dca.flcourts.org/Opinions/3D13-1566.op.pdf. Florida case where defendant is found not guilty of homicide crime due to stand-your-ground law.

Morissette v. United States, 342 U.S. 246 (1952). http://supreme.justia.com/cases/federal/us/342/246/case.html. U.S. Supreme Court case discussing mens rea in criminal cases; defendant cannot be convicted of theft of federal government property if he honestly believed that the property was abandoned.

Minnesota v. Murphy, 465 U.S. 420 (1984). http://supreme.justia.com/cases/federal/us/465/420/case.html. Defendant's truthful answers to incriminating questions can be used as evidence against him, because Fifth Amendment privilege must be asserted.

Powell v. Alabama, 287 U.S. 45 (1932). http://supreme.justia.com/cases/federal/us/287/45/case.html. Famous "Scottsboro Seven" case; the state's failure to appoint defense counsel for capital defendants was, under the circumstances, a denial of due process.

Ratzlaf v. United States, 510 U.S. 135 (1994). http://supreme.justia.com/cases/federal/us/510/135/. Defendant can't be found guilty of violating federal bank reporting law if he was unaware that the law applied to him.

Florida v. Riley, 488 U.S. 445 (1989). http://supreme.justia.com/cases/federal/us/488/445/case.html. U.S. Supreme Court holds that flying over a home to look for illegal drugs is not a "search" within the meaning of the Fourth Amendment.

Robertson v. Commonwealth, 82 S.W.3d 832 (2002). http://www.leagle.com/decision/200291482SW3d832_1911/ROBERTSON%20v.%20COM. Defendant whose behavior led a police officer to fall to his death from a high bridge was the cause of the officer's death, and therefore guilty of a homicide crime.

Salinas v. Texas, 133 S. Ct. 2174 (2013). http://supreme.justia.com/cases/federal/us/570/12-246/. Defendant's silence in response to incriminating questions can be used as evidence against him, because Fifth Amendment privilege must be asserted.

Roper v. Simmons, 543 U.S. 551 (2005). http://supreme.justia.com/cases/federal/us/543/551/. Death penalty is unconstitutional, under the Eighth Amendment, as applied to crimes committed by juveniles.

Staples v. United States, 511 U.S. 600 (1994). http://supreme.justia.com/cases/federal/us/511/600/case.html. In federal criminal cases, defendant must be aware of the facts that make his conduct a crime.

Brigham City v. Stuart, 547 U.S. 398 (2006). http://supreme.justia.com/cases/federal/us/547/398/. Police can enter a home, even without a warrant or probable cause of a crime, if they reasonably believe that entry is necessary to protect a person from bodily injury.

Terry v. Ohio, 392 U.S. 1 (1968). http://supreme.justia.com/cases/federal/us/392/1/case.html. Police can stop persons whom the police reasonably suspect is committing, or about to commit, a crime; police can also frisk if there is reasonable suspicion of a weapon.

Berghuis v. Thompkins, 560 U.S. 370 (2010). http://supreme.justia.com/cases/federal/us/560/08-1470/. U.S. Supreme Court case that changes the application of *Miranda* by holding that an arrested suspect's silence is not an assertion of *Miranda* rights, and that the suspect's answer to an interrogator's question can be an implied waiver of *Miranda* rights.

Trop v. Dulles, 356 U.S. 86 (1958). http://supreme.justia.com/cases/federal/us/356/86/case.html#93. Loss of U.S. citizenship is a punishment that violates the Eighth Amendment.

In re V.V., 51 Cal. 4th 1020 (2011). http://scocal.stanford.edu/opinion/re-vv-33976. Two juveniles are held to be guilty of arson for throwing firecrackers that cause a brush fire; detailed explanation of malice in criminal law.

State v. Varszegi, 33 Conn. App. 368 (1993). http://scholar.google.com/scholar_case?case=11607783415353985696&hl=en&as_sdt=6&as_vis=1&oi=scholarr. Defendant landlord cannot be convicted of theft of deadbeat tenant's property if he honestly believed that the property legally belonged to him.

Strickland v. Washington, 466 U.S. 668 (1984). http://supreme.justia.com/cases/federal/us/466/668/case.html. U.S. Supreme Court case defining the meaning of "effective assistance of counsel" as guaranteed by the Sixth Amendment.

Watts v Indiana, 338 U.S. 49 (1949). http://supreme.justia.com/cases/federal/us/338/49/case.html. Defendant's confession was involuntary because it was produced by prolonged interrogation under harsh conditions; Justice Jackson's separate opinion discussed the tension between due process and the protection of society from crime.

Commonwealth v. Welansky, 316 Mass. 383 (1944). http://masscases. com/cases/sjc/316/316mass383.html. Example of involuntary manslaughter.

United States v. White, 401 U.S. 745 (1971). http://supreme. justia.com/cases/federal/us/401/745/case.html. Defendant lacks a reasonable expectation of privacy that his trusted friend won't be cooperating with the police by wearing a wire; Justice Harlan's dissenting opinion explains that reasonableness should be viewed normatively, not empirically.

Wickard v. Filburn, 317 U.S. 111 (1942). http://supreme.justia. com/cases/federal/us/317/111/case.html. U.S. Supreme Court holds that the Commerce Clause authorizes Congress to regulate intrastate commercial activity, as long as it has an effect on interstate commerce.

Other Materials

Abramson, Jeffrey. *We, the Jury: The Jury System and the Ideal of Democracy.* Cambridge, Massachusetts: Harvard University Press, 2000. A defense of the American jury system as a manifestation of democracy, with proposals for reform that include elimination of the peremptory challenge and honest use of jury nullification.

Allen, Ronald J. "The Misguided Defenses of Miranda v. Arizona." 5 *Ohio State Journal of Criminal Law* 205 (2007). http://moritzlaw. osu.edu/students/groups/osjcl/files/2012/05/Allen-PDF.pdf. A legal and philosophical critique of the U.S. Supreme Court's famous *Miranda* decision, written in response to Professor Kamisar's defense of *Miranda* in the same volume.

Bedau, Hugo Adam. *Debating the Death Penalty: Should America Have Capital Punishment?* Oxford: Oxford University Press, 2005. Edited book containing a balanced presentation by seven leading experts of the legal, moral, and practical arguments for and against capital punishment.

Bodenhamer, David J., and James W. Ely, Jr. *The Bill of Rights in Modern America*. Bloomington, Indiana: Indiana University Press, 2008. Edited book contains scholarly chapters on the rights of criminal suspects (Chapter 7, by David J. Bodenhamer); police practices (Chapter 8, by Laurence A. Benner and Michal R. Belknap); the Eighth Amendment's "cruel and unusual punishments" clause (Chapter 9, by Joseph L. Hoffmann); and the right to privacy (Chapter 11, by Ken I. Kersch).

Bradley, Craig M. "Two Models of the Fourth Amendment." 83 Michigan Law Review 1468 (1985). http://www.repository.law.indiana.edu/cgi/viewcontent.cgi?article=1860&context=facpub. An influential article analyzing the U.S. Supreme Court's modern jurisprudence of the Fourth Amendment, with an emphasis on the distinction between bright-line rules based on the warrant clause and the "no lines" approach based on the reasonableness clause.

Bradley, Craig M., and Joseph L. Hoffmann. "Public Perception, Justice, and the 'Search for Truth' in Criminal Cases." 69 *Southern California Law Review* 1267 (1996). http://www.repository.law.indiana.edu/cgi/viewcontent.cgi?article=1509&context=facpub. An analysis of the various ways that due process and the "search for truth" conflict in criminal cases.

Fisher, George. *Plea Bargaining's Triumph: A History of Plea Bargaining in America*. Palo Alto: Stanford University Press, 2004. A historical study of how plea bargaining gradually came to dominate the American criminal justice system.

Fletcher, George P. *A Crime of Self-Defense*. Chicago: University of Chicago Press, 1988. Book describing and analyzing the Bernhard Goetz case, from the perspective of a law professor who sat with the defense team during the trial.

Friedman, Lawrence M. *Crime and Punishment in American History*. New York: Basic Books, 1994. A panoramic history of the American criminal justice system, entertainingly written by a Stanford law professor for a general audience.

Fuller, Lon L. "The Case of the Speluncean Explorers." 62 *Harvard Law Review* 616 (1949). http://fs2.american.edu/dfagel/www/ Class%20Readings/Fuller/TheCaseOfTheSpelunceanExplorers. pdf. Hypothetical court case involving cannibalism; in the various case opinions, Professor Fuller summarizes the arguments for and against broad judicial discretion to interpret the meaning of criminal statutes.

Goodman, James. *Stories of Scottsboro.* New York: Vintage Books, 1995. A rich historical account by a Harvard historian of the Scottsboro, Alabama, capital rape case, which led to the U.S. Supreme Court's 1932 decision in *Powell v. Alabama.*

Hamilton, Alexander, James Madison, and John Jay. *The Federalist Papers.* New York: Bantam Classics, 1982. The "Bible" of American federalism; a series of essays written by Hamilton, Madison, and Jay in support of ratification of the United States Constitution.

Heumann, Milton. *Plea Bargaining: The Experiences of Prosecutors, Judges, and Defense Attorneys.* Chicago: University of Chicago Press, 1978. The best empirical study of plea bargaining—how it works, how lawyers learn to do it, and why lawyers and judges love it (even though society hates it)—based on interviews conducted in New Haven, Connecticut.

Hoffmann, Joseph L. "On the Perils of Line-Drawing: Juveniles and the Death Penalty." 40 *Hastings Law Journal* 229 (1989). http://www. repository.law.indiana.edu/cgi/viewcontent.cgi?article=1900&conte xt=facpub. Article explaining the philosophical arguments for and against using bright-line rules to determine eligibility for the death penalty based on age.

Kamisar, Yale. "On the Fortieth Anniversary of the Miranda Case: Why We Needed It, How We Got It—and What Happened to It." 5 *Ohio State Journal of Criminal Law* 163 (2007). http://repository. law.umich.edu/cgi/viewcontent.cgi?article=1259&context=articles. A defense of the U.S. Supreme Court's *Miranda* decision, by a law professor who's often called the "father of *Miranda*" because of his influential scholarship on the subject.

Kelman, Mark. "Interpretive Construction in the Substantive Criminal Law." 33 *Stanford Law Review* 591 (1981). http://www.law.upenn.edu/institutes/cerl/conferences/actiolibera/reading/Interpretive%20Construction%20(Kelman).pdf. An extremely innovative article explaining how criminal law depends on certain interpretive choices—on such fundamental matters as causation and free will—that often are made unconsciously or subconsciously by judges, but that effectively determine the outcome of individual criminal cases.

King, Nancy J., and Joseph L. Hoffmann. *Habeas for the Twenty-First Century.* Chicago: University of Chicago Press, 2011. A historical and legal analysis of the writ of habeas corpus, which has been used by judges since the days of Magna Carta to free those wrongfully imprisoned and restore the proper balance of governmental powers.

Lewis, Anthony. *Gideon's Trumpet.* New York: Vintage Books, 1989. The famous book, later turned into a movie, recounting the story of Clarence Gideon and his fight to establish the federal constitutional right to appointed counsel for indigent criminal defendants in state criminal cases.

Percy, Elise J., Joseph L. Hoffmann, and Steven J. Sherman. "'Sticky Metaphors' and the Persistence of the Traditional Voluntary Manslaughter Doctrine." 44 *University of Michigan Journal of Law Reform* 383 (2011). http://repository.law.umich.edu/cgi/viewcontent.cgi?article=1096&context=mjlr. Article discussing the complicated reasons why the criminal law continues to provide some defendants with a partial defense to murder when they kill in the "heat of passion," but refuses to extend the defense to other similarly situated defendants.

Simpson, A.W. Brian. *Cannibalism and the Common Law.* Chicago: University of Chicago Press, 1984. A complete and fascinating historical account of the 1884 sinking of the *Mignonette* and the famous murder case, *Regina v. Dudley & Stephens*, to which it gave rise.

Stuntz, William J. *The Collapse of American Criminal Justice.* Cambridge, Massachusetts: Belknap Press, 2011. A sweeping historical and critical analysis of the American criminal justice system, written for a general audience by one of the most insightful modern scholars of criminal law and criminal procedure.

IMAGE CREDITS

Image Credits

NOTES

NOTES